AF352730

MODERN AND RADICAL

JEWS IN EASTERN EUROPE
*Jeffrey Veidlinger, Mikhail Krutikov, and
Geneviève Zubrzycki, Editors*

MODERN AND RADICAL

Politics, Culture, and Socialization of Jewish Youth in Interwar Poland

KAMIL KIJEK
TRANSLATED BY JAROSŁAW GARLIŃSKI

INDIANA UNIVERSITY PRESS

This book is a publication of

Indiana University Press
Herman B Wells Library
1320 East 10th Street
Bloomington, Indiana 47405 USA

https://iupress.org

Published in Polish as *Dzieci modernizmu: Świadomość, kultura i socjalizacja polityczna młodzieży żydowskiej w II Rzeczypospolitej* by University of Wrocław Press © 2017
© 2026 by Indiana University Press

All rights reserved
No part of this book may be reproduced or utilized in any form or by any means, electronic or mechanical, including photocopying and recording, or by any information storage and retrieval system, without permission in writing from the publisher.

For customers in the European Union with safety or GPSR concerns, please contact Mare Nostrum Group B.V., Mauritskade 21D, 1091 GC Amsterdam, The Netherlands. Email: gpsr@mare-nostrum.co.uk

First printing 2026

Cataloging information is available from the Library of Congress.

ISBN 978-0-253-07492-8 (hdbk.)
ISBN 978-0-253-07493-5 (pbk.)
ISBN 978-0-253-07495-9 (ebook)

In memory of my grandparents,
Yaakov Kodniy and Raisa Lerner

CONTENTS

ACKNOWLEDGMENTS

THIS BOOK WOULD NOT HAVE appeared without the help and advice of a great many people. From the very beginning, while still a sociology student, I became interested in the history of the Jews, and Professor Marcin Wodziński was an informal yet very close mentor of all my efforts. It is to him above all that I offer thanks for what I know about Jewish studies, and it is thanks to his help that I have obtained most of my foreign grants and that I have been able to take research trips, without which this book would not have existed.

The initial outline of this work was developed during my year at the Hebrew University of Jerusalem during the 2006/2007 academic year, when I had the privilege of discussing my reading and research thoughts with Professors Shaul Stampfer, Gershon Bacon, and Karol Szurek. After my return to Poland, an invaluable intellectual stimulus for me was the seminars of Włodzimierz Mędrzecki and the late Jerzy Jedlicki at the Institute of History at the Polish Academy of Sciences. A further opportunity for a foreign trip and the ability to focus solely on academic work arose during the 2008/2009 academic year, when a grant from Manfred Lahnstein at the Bucerius Institute allowed me to continue my research at the University of Haifa. There, I was supervised by Professor Marcos Silber, of whose help and intellectual guidance I was able to take advantage the whole time. Another very productive period of work for me was a four-month scholarship to the Institute of Hebrew and Jewish Studies at University College London, where I had an opportunity to discuss the outline of my whole work at that institution's academic seminar and benefit from the intellectual guidance of Professor François Guesnet. I finished the preliminary versions of chapters 3 to 6 of this book thanks to a one-month stay at Leipzig University in December

2012, taking advantage of the very favorable research conditions within the Religion and Law in Eastern Europe group, and also thanks to the help and guidance of Stefan Stach and Yvonne Kleinman.

I have taken away a great deal from discussions over the years with Rona Yona at Tel Aviv University about nationalism, socialism, and how these two phenomena were connected in most recent Jewish history. I am also grateful to her for most of what I have learned on the links between Zionism, the history of Yishuv in Palestine, and the Jewish diaspora in eastern Europe. During my first years working on my PhD, conversations with Scott Ury, as well as reading his doctoral work, were of enormous assistance to me. During visits to Israel, I discussed a great many current problems in my work with Ido Bassok, the author of a prize-winning doctorate on the psychological and cultural aspects of the socialization of Jewish young people in interwar Poland. Our stormy discussions and disagreements, which are evident on the pages of this work, played a key role in formulating and sharpening its arguments. Over the years, simultaneously writing my doctorate and the Polish version of this book, and some years later preparing its English translation, I discussed many of the issues raised in it with Ofer Dynes.

Elements of the work that led to this book were discussed at the Institute of History at PAN and at Professor Wodziński's seminars in the Department of Jewish Studies at the University of Wrocław, as well as at Grzegorz Krzywiec's and Karolina Szymaniak's seminars at the Jewish Historical Institute. I would like to warmly thank all the participants for reading an extensive part of the text and for their exceedingly valuable remarks. Marcin Wodziński and Grzegorz Krzywiec read the first manuscript in its entirety and shared their comments, which were very relevant in terms of its final form. I would also like to thank Marcus Silber, Helena Datner, Joanna Nalewajko-Kulikov, Natalia Aleksiun, Anna Motyczka-Spitzer, and Hanna Kozińska-Witt for discussions, consultations, and comments. Over the years I have been able to share all my ideas and doubts with Agata Rakowiecka, without whose encouragement, inspiring questions, and insistence I would not have cleared out my mental clutter, and this book would never have seen the light of day.

Thanks to my studies in Jerusalem and Haifa and a five-month scholarship at the Institute of the History of Polish Jewry and Israel-Poland Relations at Tel Aviv University, I was able to learn Hebrew. I took my first steps in Yiddish at a summer school at Tel Aviv University, which I financed thanks to the kindness of Professors Daniel Blatman and Israel Bartal of Hebrew University. On my return to Poland, I spent half a year learning to read Yiddish manuscripts under the patient eye of Małgorzata Kordowicz.

In 2007/2008 I took advantage of a scholarship from the Fondation pour la Mémoire de la Shoah in Paris. Thanks to a grant from the Rothschild Foundation and collaboration with the Association of the Jewish Historical Institute while preparing the Principal Exhibit at the Museum of the History of Polish Jews, I was able to travel for research to the YIVO Archive (today called the Institute for Jewish Research) in New York. During my time in New York City, Rivka Schiller, the author of the index of autobiographies of Jewish youth, shared her knowledge on my main source material. During the final months of working on the basis of this book, thanks to the help of Marcos Silber, I availed myself of a scholarship from the Zalman Hertz and Batia Cohen Fund.

In preparing a shortened, somewhat modified and augmented English edition of the book, I have been enormously helped by reviews of its Polish-language version by David Engel, Samuel Kassow, Izabela Mrzygłód, and Ula Krupicka-Madej, as well as critical comments from readers, above all Kenneth B. Moss and Daniel K. Heller. In more than ten years since the book's publication in Polish, a series of important studies have appeared dealing with the problems it tackles, including ones by Kenneth B. Moss, Wojciech Tworek, Naomi Seidman, Glenn Dynner, Gershon Bacon, and Daniel Mahla, whose important findings I have attempted to include in this English edition of *Modern and Radical*. Finally, I would like to express my thanks for the very critical and at the same time extremely insightful and very generous anonymous reviews commissioned by Indiana University Press. They have allowed me to make many important corrections to the English manuscript of this book, most notably to better emphasize its main theses and make them more accessible to English-speaking readers. This would not have happened without the consistent, generous support of Geneviève Zubrzycki and Mikhail Krutikov, who had supported the idea of translating and publishing this book in English from its very beginning.

This book was translated with a special grant from the chancellor of my home University of Wrocław. Jarosław Garliński has done a splendid translation. It would not have happened without the support of Marcin Wodzinski and Samuel Kassow. I would also like to thank Adam Stepnowski for all his hard and intelligent work with the transcription and transliteration of all non-English terms and names appearing in the text as well as Zachary Mazur for his meticulous work in editing the final version of the book manuscript.

MODERN AND RADICAL

INTRODUCTION

IN 1938, VICTOR ALTER—A LEADER of the Jewish labor Bund in Poland—published *Człowiek w społeczeństwie* (*Man in Society*), where he defined his own era as a quest for the "idea of freedom." This idea was to be used as a guiding light for a far-reaching transformation of life in the name of a much better future.[1] Although Alter opposed the kind of searching carried out by the Bund's principal opponents—communists, fascists, and Jewish and non-Jewish nationalist groups—he admitted that every movement, including his own, engaged in a kind of radical striving. Though they based their ideologies on Enlightenment-era concepts of progress, their ideas were defined through a distinct modernist radicalism, rejecting the present and looking forward to a future of freedom.

The aim of this book is to explain why the last generation of Jews who grew up in Poland before the Holocaust was so susceptible to radical ideas. The lives of Jews born and raised in the Second Republic, the Polish state established in 1918, differed greatly from those of their parents, who, before 1914, had been subjects of Tsarist Russia and the Austrian Empire. Unlike their parents and grandparents, in the 1920s and 1930s Jewish youth attended Polish public schools, lived in the new reality of a Polish national state, and were deeply influenced by both Polish elite and popular cultures. At the same time, various Jewish political, social, and cultural organizations—despite many difficulties in the Second Republic—thrived and developed dynamically, providing leadership and purpose to a rising generation. This book examines the processes of socialization: the ways in which children, youth, and young adults acquired the values and habits of the surrounding society, including an analysis of adolescence, education, and the participation of young people in elite and popular culture as well as their own youth culture. This book thus attempts to describe the most important generational traits of political consciousness of the last Polish Jewish generation before the Holocaust. As will be shown below, a particular mixture of factors—including increased Polish acculturation among Jewish youth, the experience of exclusion from a state and society they were taught to treat as their own, the remarkable development of modern Jewish culture and politics in interwar Poland, and, finally, broader political trends characterizing 1930s Europe—influenced the formation of a particular radical political consciousness among Polish Jewish youth who came of age before the Holocaust.

This book deals with the dominant mode of thinking about politics among Jewish young people in interwar Poland. The focus here is on youth from various backgrounds: the traditional petty merchant class (the so-called lower middle class), craftsmen, wealthy Orthodox Jews, or an acculturated urban bourgeoisie closely connected with Polish culture. As I will show, irrespective of young Jews' diverse and sometimes contradictory political sympathies or party affiliations, they shared a certain approach to the world around them, transcending the ideological differences that divided them. Young Jews in Poland, like most European youth in the 1930s, were convinced that they were living through deep economic, social, and cultural crises. They also felt a deep sense of imminent, unspecified but inevitable, catastrophe. What Jewish, Polish, and European youth had in common was the belief that this crisis could be overcome only with transformational change, achieved through dedication to disciplined, collective political action. This way of thinking about the world influenced how young people thought about politics and how they understood their own education and culture, as well as economic, social, and professional issues. Given all the differences between religious and secular youth, some elements of this thinking were characteristic even of the former group despite their conservative, religious, antimodernist tendencies. Regardless of the language in which they expressed it, Yiddish, Polish, or Hebrew, regardless of how they imagined the ideal state of the Jewish national culture and what cultural characteristics they possessed, young people were united in their mode of thinking. Regardless of whether young Jews in Poland in the 1930s remained religious as they entered adulthood—like their parents or grandparents—or abandoned religion during their adolescence, most were also united by a conviction that the traditional world was in an inevitable decline, that it was impossible to maintain its norms, values, symbols, and lifestyle in a dynamically changing world.

This feeling of imminent catastrophe, as an important thread of the political consciousness of young Jews, was connected to the particular political culture. The development of this culture was part of a general European phenomenon dubbed by Stanley G. Payne as "classical modernism." Its roots extend back to the end of the nineteenth century, peaking in the 1930s. In the sphere of European politics, modernism was unique in its time. In this era, Europeans experienced the revolutionary engagement of the masses, the widespread influence of propaganda, the polarization of opinions, millenarian convictions on the inevitability of massive social change, totalist conceptions explaining the current world, and complex dynamic change. For the last generation that came of age before World War II, all of their most formative moments coincided with the apogee of "classical modernism."[2] The rivalry between the extreme right and left dominated the final prewar decade. As Payne and others before him observed, the antagonistic movements fighting among themselves were characterized by many similar features. Bolshevik and Stalinist communism, Italian fascism, and German Nazism, along with their imitators and "fellow travelers," all shared an attachment to authoritarian forms of government, extralegal political activity, and invoking "the laws of history or nature." This specific spirit of the time made its mark on people born during World War I or just after it.[3]

In the present work, this dominant ideology is referred to as radical modernism—in contrast to the modernism of the end of the nineteenth century—thus emphasizing its high point in the 1930s. My aim is to examine how radical modernism manifested itself in the life of young Jewish people in interwar Poland. I therefore focus not on the relationship between modernism as an aesthetic-philosophical current and politics at the level of elite culture, literature, or ideological manifestos but rather on the relationship between modernism, political culture, and everyday life using microsociological analysis of egodocuments.

The Jewish experience of the interwar period was shaped by the near-permanent political, social, and economic crises of the newly established Polish state. Its establishment was announced in November 1918. This had become possible owing to the defeat suffered by Germany in World War I, the collapse of the Austro-Hungarian Empire, and the revolution and civil war that engulfed Tsarist Russia. The three empires collapsed that—at the end of the eighteenth century—had partitioned the territories of the Polish-Lithuanian Commonwealth. Between 1918 and 1921, the new Polish state was involved in numerous armed and diplomatic conflicts over borders and was on the verge of collapse during the Polish-Bolshevik War, when the Red Army was at the gates of Warsaw. Existential threats at the beginning of the state's existence and hostile relations with its two powerful neighbors, Germany and the Soviet Union, heightened the tenor of Polish politics, while a profound sense of insecurity spread throughout Polish society. The hatred between the left and right, and above all the propaganda campaign unleashed by the right wing against the first president in the history of Poland, led to the assassination of President Gabriel Narutowicz on December 16, 1922, just days after his election. Between 1918 and 1926, Poland was a weak parliamentary democracy. The elections of 1919 and 1922 were victories for a coalition of right-leaning parties, spearheaded by the National Democratic (ND) political movement. This was the name of the political grouping and the youth movements and other organizations that formed around it. Though the party's official name changed several times, in the popular consciousness it was always known as the ND or Endecja. This political ideology was characterized by increasingly extreme Polish ethnic nationalism, moral conservatism, hostility toward the left, and xenophobia, directed mainly against religious and national minorities living in Poland. Jews, however, were the main target of National Democracy and its leader, Roman Dmowski. Successive governments formed between 1918 and 1926, in which National Democrats played a central role, but these were unstable and quickly collapsed. Their policies were rejected by opponents from the camp of Józef Piłsudski, the first head of state between 1918 and 1921, as well as by the left, led by the Polish Socialist Party. A series of fundamental policy failures showed parliament to be ill-equipped to deal with the country's economic and social issues. As a result, citizens lost faith in parliamentary democracy as a system of government. The first years of independence did not lead to even a minimal consensus among political elites of the Second Polish Republic as to how it should function.

This state of affairs involving a lack of consensus and lack of faith in the system of parliamentary democracy was the basic context for the military coup d'état carried out in May 1926 by one of Poland's independence heroes, Józef Piłsudski. However, his personal dictatorship and the increasingly authoritarian system of state governance formed around it did not solve any of the country's key structural problems. These included the problem of discrimination and tamping down national self-development for numerous national minorities living in Poland, including Ukrainians, Jews, Belarusians, and Germans. Although Piłsudski's coup ousted the ND, which was openly hostile to minorities, the authoritarian so-called Sanacja regime quickly disappointed the national minorities' hopes for real equality.[4] The new political system in Poland also failed to cope with the enormous economic problems of the interwar period. They were exacerbated by the Great Depression, the disastrous consequences of which were felt in Poland much longer than in the United States or western Europe. All this contributed to the further radicalization of political sentiments in the Second Polish Republic. Beyond Piłsudski's natural enemies on the right, the Polish left and peasant parties also became increasingly hostile toward the ruling camp as a result of pressure from below, of the mood prevailing in society. The vast majority of the country's citizens, led by the largest social group in the country—the peasantry—lived in deep poverty. Prevailing unemployment, uneven access to education, and the protracted economic crisis minimized opportunities for social advancement among the rural and urban poor, leaving them searching for radical solutions. This was especially important for the youngest generation of Poles, Ukrainians, Jews, Germans, and Belarusians. This was the first generation to grow up in the Polish state and to receive universal, basic education. Thus, they had much greater ambitions than their parents and grandparents. Living as they were with structural poverty and economic underdevelopment, the modern ambitions of the younger generation could not be satisfied on a broad scale. This created a situation of deep socioeconomic tension, sometimes leading to violent outbursts of discontent and rebellion. Between 1936 and 1937, hundreds of people were killed in clashes between peasants, workers, and police. In the years 1935–1939, from the death of Józef Piłsudski to the outbreak of World War II, the rule of Sanacja evolved in an even more authoritarian and right-wing direction. This included the creation of the Camp of National Unity (Obóz Zjednoczenia Narodowego, popularly called OZON) in 1937, which used antisemitism as one of its many political tools.[5]

The intertwined political, social, and economic crises of the Second Polish Republic also deepened profound ethnic conflicts within the country. All this generated fertile ground for the development of modern radical antisemitism. The Polish-Bolshevik war of 1919–1921 served as a huge stimulus for the growth of antisemitic politics. It powerfully strengthened the myth of the special ties between Jews and communism, or so-called Judeo-Communism, the popularity of which was by no means limited to right-wing circles. National Democrats promoted ideas on the absolute incongruity of Jews and Poland and on their harmfulness in every aspect of life. After the election of Gabriel Narutowicz as president, pamphleteers proclaimed he had been elected as a result of a Jewish conspiracy to undermine Poland. This campaign inspired anti-Jewish riots on the streets of Warsaw and ultimately the assassin who murdered Narutowicz. Up to 1926, successive governments dominated by the ND introduced numerous practices targeting the Jewish population, despite the Jews' formal equality before the law as citizens of the Republic of Poland guaranteed by the constitution. Jewish politicians across the spectrum welcomed Józef Piłsudski's coup d'état in May 1926. Jewish leaders assumed that the new ruling elite would have a better attitude toward the Jewish minority. Indeed, in 1926–1930, although discrimination against Jews (and other minorities) did not cease, the attitude of the Polish government was at least not openly hostile. However, the May coup had other consequences that proved to be very dangerous for the Jewish population. Above all, it radicalized the right-wing opposition. With no chance of returning to power through democratic elections, and experiencing persecution, including imprisonment of leading politicians, National Democracy increasingly evolved in an authoritarian direction, looking to the example provided by fascist Italy and other authoritarian regimes in Europe. This was also associated with a further radicalization of antisemitic views, especially among the younger generation of ND members. Between 1931 and 1936, the right unleashed a campaign of boycotts and physical violence against the Jewish population. It was inaugurated at Polish universities, spreading over time to the provinces. It led, among other things, to a wave of pogroms and intensified anti-Jewish violence in 1935–1937. After the death of its leader, Józef Piłsudski, the Sanacja camp, which continued to lose ground socially, tried to save the situation by adopting part of the political program of the right-wing opposition. In 1935–1939, the government introduced laws and regulations aimed primarily at reducing the Jewish population through emigration, as well as weakening the economic role Jews played in the country.[6]

Amid the pan-European process of political radicalization in the interwar period, numerous political, social, and economic crises, and the ubiquitous Polish nationalism in public space was an excellent environment for the development of Jewish national politics in interwar Poland. A key context for its development was also the demographic, cultural, and social strength of the Jewish community. Jews had been living on these lands for hundreds of years in dense clusters. Jews had a strong traditional, ethno-religious identity that set them apart from their neighbors, as well as two distinct languages: Yiddish and Hebrew. The assimilationist tendencies, so strong in the nineteenth century among Jewish communities in western and central Europe, were much weaker in the vast majority of the lands that became part of the Polish state after 1918. The strength of tradition combined with the rising strength of a new national Jewish culture and the general ascent of nationalisms during times of crisis led to a tremendous increase in the popularity of Zionism in Poland during World War I. Both before and after the establishment of the Polish state, Zionists claimed, in addition to building a Jewish homeland in the Land of Israel, to fight for full legal equality and for the national and cultural autonomy of Jews in Poland. Zionism in the interwar period ranged from the far right to the extreme left. The most important Zionist parties and organizations in the Second Polish Republic were the so-called General Zionists, the religious-Zionist Mizrahi party, the left-wing parties Po'alei-Tsiyon-Left and Po'alei-Tsiyon-Right, Hitachdut, and finally the right-wing Revisionist Zionists. All these parties had their own youth movements. Ha-Shomer ha-Tsa'ir was also an important independent Zionist youth movement. Competitors of the Zionists saw the future of Jews primarily in Poland. These included Yiddishist parties such as the centrist Folkists and socialists from the Bund. They also advocated for the national and cultural autonomy of Jews in Poland. All these various parties challenged the traditional, conservative element of the Jewish community. Their interests were represented primarily by the Orthodox religious party, Agudat Israel. Despite the strength of antisemitism in interwar Poland and the discriminatory practices experienced by the Jewish community, its parties and social and cultural organizations all enjoyed a level of freedom not previously seen in that part of Europe. The unprecedented development of Jewish education was particularly important for the history of Jewish youth in this period. It competed with education in Polish state schools, which was attractive to many Jewish parents because it was free and was the best preparation for life in the Polish state. All of the political movements mentioned above developed their own school systems. The Zionists invested in the Hebrew-language Tarbut network of schools. Left-wing Zionists invested in the Hebrew-Yiddish Shul-Kult school network. Religious Zionists developed their own Yavne system. Anti-religious socialists from the Bund, as well as extreme left-wing Zionists from Poale Zion Left, were involved in the construction of the TsYShO network of schools. Agudat Israel developed Horev, an Orthodox education system, which included many traditional Jewish primary education institutions (i.e., heders).[7]

Difficult times, general processes of radicalization, a generational rebellion, and a wealth of opportunities to get involved led to an unprecedented level of political involvement on the part of young Jewish people in political parties and organizations devoted to the ideology of radical modernism. In short, modern Jewish politics enjoyed a flowering in the Second Polish Republic. The most important reasons for its popularity among young Jews were antisemitism, discrimination, and economic privation; the failure of tradition and religion to respond to those crises; and secularization and acculturation. Toward the end of the interwar period, for a young Polish Jew, membership in one of the numerous political organizations was often something quite natural, requiring no justification.[8]

In his groundbreaking book *An Unchosen People: Jewish Political Reckoning in Interwar Poland*, published a few years after the Polish version of this book, Kenneth Moss captured like no one before him the scale of the crisis in interwar Poland to which young Jews sought answers in countless political parties and youth organizations. He also noted the change that took place in a minority of intellectuals and some young people in the 1930s who lost faith in any collectivist form of modern politics. They no longer believed in the possibility of a substantial improvement in their situation in Poland, and as a result they began individual efforts to leave eastern Europe. In the 1930s, however, young Jews who lost hope that their lives in Poland might improve were a minority.[9] Indeed, as I will show below, young people could and often did doubt whether any of the movements and any of the political ideologies they had chosen could actually bring about an improvement in their situation and a new and better world. In interwar Poland, there were also many young Jews (as well as non-Jews) who were not interested in politics or the fate of the community, focusing instead on their own lives, financial well-being, careers, or entertainment. There is no doubt, however, that when it came to politics and the collective fate of the Jewish people, the absolutely dominant forms of thought were those I describe in this book.

To re-create this dominant thought pattern, I examine the generational aspect of Jewish politics in the 1930s from a new perspective, using sources that have hitherto been used only superficially. A wealth of knowledge is contained in hundreds of autobiographies of young people sent in to successive competitions at the Jewish Scientific Institute in Vilna (YIVO), organized in 1932, 1934, and 1939. Typical historical sources in the form of press, government documents, and the publications of political parties, as well as their associated youth movements, are more often evidence of a perspective from which the older generation saw the younger, rather than an expression of the latter's views. Memoirs written after the war are usually marred by later experiences—the Holocaust, postwar turbulence—which memoirists often had not spent in Poland. Similarly, not only did the reality of the Second Republic impact their memoirs, but so too did the new reality where they were trying to rebuild their lives. My goal then is to examine adolescence as well as the culture and political consciousness of young people from the perspective of the 1930s, avoiding teleological descriptions and explanations of them seen through the prism of later tragic events.

The merit of the autobiographical material used here is that it provides a window into the influence of politics on young people's general view of the world, their lifestyle, forms of socialization, and participation in culture. In descriptions and assessments of this area of their lives, political consciousness expressed itself no less forcefully than in explicitly political arenas—at party meetings, at demonstrations, and at youth movement meetings. An analysis of these young people's complete biographical constructs can help define the true scale of political involvement—exactly how politics fit into complex lives—which cannot be defined through analyzing party documents, leaflets, pamphlets, the press, or ideological statements from party elites. Young people were passionately involved in politics, but they were not politicians or ideologues. In their autobiographies we find views and attitudes inconsistent with those proposed by the political parties and youth organizations to which they belonged. I attempt to show which elements of the political ideologies promoted by the political forces fighting for influence on the "Jewish Street" operated in the daily life of young people involved in politics, and to what extent and how these ideas affected their identity, self-evaluation, worldview, family life, and immediate surroundings.[10] I deal with the ideological and organizational nuances of the parties and their youth movements only when this serves to explain real problems of youth socialization and political consciousness. However, that does not mean that I treat the YIVO autobiographies as "objective" sources or as providing an exhaustive description of the consciousness of young Jews during the Second Republic. I address their limitations in several places in this book.

This book is about a generation that was the first in history to come of age in a modern nationalist Polish state. Polish historian Roman Wapiński, referring to the studies done by sociologist Józef Chałasiński on young peasants growing up in the Second Republic, noticed that this group was distinguished by a fully modern national consciousness. In the 1920s and 1930s, these young Poles began to attend public schools, learning to read and write. Unlike their parents and grandparents, for them local identity was relegated to the background as they learned to see the world in national categories. As a result of this process, their non-Polish and non-Catholic neighbors, constantly present in the landscape of the countryside, ceased to be something "natural." Young peasants saw themselves as distant from their non-Polish neighbors in ways that their grandparents and parents had not. Young Poles internalized the conviction that the Second Republic was the homeland of the Polish nation in which all religious and national groups were secondary to the Polish-Catholic national interest.[11] Wapiński's observation has all kinds of consequences for the issues presented here. Above all, this conviction made rural youth, no less than city dwellers, susceptible to calls for the end of Jewish "domination" in trade, in secondary schooling, and at universities. In other words, many young Poles believed that Jews should be dislodged from their place in Polish social, political, and cultural life. These ideas, comprising the canon of so-called modern antisemitism, became widely popular in interwar Poland.[12] Thus, the reality of antisemitism, as a cultural code powerfully present in young Jews' closest social milieu, was a key influence on their experience of socialization.[13]

Young Jews, similar to all other minorities in the Second Republic, were subjected to the symbolic domination of the Polish national idea through education, socialization, and participation in public spaces. Young Jews faced antisemitism most often in public schools, where they had the most frequent and intense contact with non-Jewish adults and peers. The experience of antisemitism in the new social context of universal education was fundamental in the formation of identities and political consciousness among young Jews. No less important was the unquestioned conviction that the ethnically defined Polish nation was the sole sovereign of the Second Republic; the space around them seemed only to confirm this belief.[14] One of the aims of this book is therefore to show the influence of the Polish symbolic universe on the consciousness of the last generation of Polish Jews before the Holocaust. To what extent did they consciously accept it or adopt it subconsciously? And to what extent did this universe exclude them from the community of citizens of the Second Republic having full civic rights?

A key goal of this book is to show how the political consciousness of young Jews was influenced by a specific blending of the Polish idea of nationhood—its culture and language—and antisemitism. Through their education in Polish and Jewish schools (which also taught Polish language and Polish culture), as well as through exposure to everyday popular culture, they were subjected to an almost universal process of symbolic and linguistic acculturation. Usually without losing their strong Jewish national and religious identity, and deeply rooted in Jewish culture, they internalized the symbols of Polish culture, its heroes, its sites of memory, and its attitudes. Simultaneously, Jewish youth experienced varied verbal and physical manifestations of antisemitism, especially in places where this culture was passed on to them, such as schools or universities. Teachers and classmates carried antisemitic attitudes while also imploring young Jews to love and appreciate their culture. The high levels of linguistic and symbolic acculturation meant that young Jews in the 1930s felt antisemitism much more strongly than their parents. For them, this hostility came from people who were culturally and physically close to them. They felt it much more personally. And they felt a promise had been broken, since in schools they were taught that Poland was a homeland for all its citizens and that everyone enjoyed equal rights. Government officials may have hoped that funneling Jewish children through a state school system would result in docile, supportive citizens. Instead, the internalization of Polish culture combined with widespread antisemitism increased their political radicalism. Most young Jews felt their country had rejected and betrayed them and thus felt emboldened to contest the existing political order.

This book is also an attempt to write a subjective history of young Jewish people, of how they reacted and operated in the difficult reality of the 1930s. They were not simply the objects of actions on the part of the institutions of the Polish state and its culture. The history of the Jews in the Second Republic cannot be reduced to a reaction to the dominant Polish national culture or a reaction to antisemitism. Above all, this period was defined by the enormous dynamism of Jewish culture expressed in three principal languages (Yiddish, Hebrew, and Polish) and by the development of a whole range of sociopolitical Jewish institutions. From earliest childhood up to the moment of entering adulthood, this generation of Jews lived in a world of deeply rooted Jewish institutions, traditions, and culture. Many Jewish institutions that were significant in the lives of young people and were established or developed during the interwar period drew their strength from centuries-old traditions of eastern European Jewish society, from the Yiddish language, religion, demographic potential, and social and economic structure—what Gershon Hundert called the "genealogy of Jewish modernity" in eastern Europe.[15] The strength of Jewish historical tradition manifested itself in the daily political and social culture of Jews in the Second Republic. In the autobiographies of young Jews, the weight of history is frequently visible, as they studied in institutions that were decades or centuries old, such as heders, *beit midrashes*, or yeshivas, or in modern Jewish schools steeped in Yiddish, Hebrew, the Torah, the Talmud, or Jewish autonomy in the premodern Polish-Lithuanian Republic. This all led to the community's high level of national and cultural pride. No less important in this context was a dynamically developing Jewish "transnationalism"—that is, the strong links of the community of Polish Jews with other centers of Jewish life, above all in the United States, British mandate Palestine, and the Soviet Union. Many of the key institutions described below in the lives of young Jews operated in Poland as well as in these other countries. Many if not the majority of Polish Jews had family members living abroad. Many Polish Jews took advantage of aid from international Jewish institutions. The Jewish press in Poland provided daily information on Jewish life in other countries. Jewish inhabitants of Poland read literature created there and received letters from friends and family abroad, many of them wished to emigrate to the United States, and many worked in Poland on behalf of the establishment of a Jewish national homeland or a state in Palestine—the Land of Israel.[16] Polish Jews' horizon of culture, imagination, and political consciousness was simultaneously rooted in the Polish space yet extending beyond it. All this had an impact on the socialization, culture, and political consciousness of Jewish youth no less than the experience of antisemitism or Polish national culture.

This book aims to avoid the nationalism of traditional Jewish historiography, as well as the so-called assimilationist paradigm in studies of the history of Polish Jews. In contrast to classical Zionist historiography, I try not to minimalize the influence of local conditions, the Jewish community's relations with its non-Jewish milieu, and their mutual cultural and social intercourse. Despite this historical tradition, and some modern Yiddish scholarship treating the world of eastern European Jews before the Holocaust in a cultural vacuum, in effect deprived of outside influences (pogroms, discrimination, and political decisions could come from the outside, but not profound sociocultural influences), I show Polish Jews' deep roots in a multidimensional Polish reality. On the other hand, despite the assimilationist paradigm, implicitly present in modern Polish historiography, the history of Polish Jews is not solely defined by Poland, Polish culture, its attitudes toward the Jews, or the Jews' attitude toward it. Some time ago, Moshe Rosman splendidly outlined this perspective: "Was a Jewish culture embedded? Yes. Was it autonomous? Also, yes. This . . . approach to the relationship between two cultures appreciates the influence of one culture on another, but recognizes that not all is influence. One facet of the polysystemic quality of each culture is its own autonomous dynamic. Most importantly, the cultural interrelationship is fluid and requires description at various points of contact rather than one all-embracing characterization."[17]

This type of restrained postmodernist approach assumes that in some phases and dimensions of Jewish life it was subjected to various forms of domination or cultural appropriation from non-Jewish elites. However, despite certain applications by theorists of postcolonial criticism, I do not define Jewish culture as by definition and always a "colonized" hybrid under the domination of the majority culture.[18] This approach is evident throughout the book in understanding the sources used and explaining the processes of socialization and the development of cultural and political consciousness of Polish Jewish youth.

A FEW REMARKS ON THEORETICAL LANGUAGE

Throughout the book I employ categories developed in fields such as sociology and historical sociology as well as the research methods that come with them. First among them is the category of "generation." I see the generation of Jewish youth in the Second Republic as not only a specific age group of young Jews born between 1910 and 1923 but also an ideological community, linked by joint formative experiences, such as growing up in the conditions of an independent, modern Polish state. This was, at the same time, the first and last generation of Polish Jews before the Holocaust. The unique formative experience of this generation linked early childhood during the years of war and revolution in eastern Europe between 1914 and 1921 with adolescence and early adulthood during the years of the Great Depression and the general political radicalization of the 1930s, and it took place in a different historical moment than for their parents or grandparents.[19]

The second category is that of radical modernism. I see it as a dominant sociopolitical state of consciousness in the 1930s among Jewish (and non-Jewish) society, as a "total ideology" to use Karl Mannheim's term—in other words, as a collectively created knowledge, socially and politically intertwined, the source of which actors in these historical events are unable to fully comprehend.[20] Total ideology in the form of radical modernism linked various camps involved in a basic political dispute, despite the fact that they presented their views as a negation of those of their adversaries. Thus understood, the concept of ideology will be used to describe the worldview of YIVO scholars, Polish state institutions, and Jewish political parties and social organizations, influencing forms of socialization for young Jews. The concept of total ideology used in this work is very close to the concept of Weltanschauung and its definition formulated by Yaacov Shavit, according to which it represented "a comprehensive view of man, society and history as totality; it is a system of symbols and values; a code of behavior in every sphere of life. It is also a depiction of the historical past, a vision for the future. . . . A collective *Weltanschauung* therefore represents a comprehensive worldview of a certain public, its collective mentality as a part of the *Zeitgeist*."[21] Following Clifford Geertz, I treat ideology as a category appropriate for studying the social bases of human knowledge, "systems of interacting symbols as patterns of interworking meanings."[22] Accepting such a definition allows us to study ideologies not as systems of knowledge created in full consciousness by specific political elites but as complicated, not fully self-aware, socially created models of signs and systems of thinking, filled with internal tension. Ideology is not a given, created once and unchanging, a consistent knowledge system locked within the writings of ideologues. Rather, it is a conflicted configuration of continually changing meanings negotiated by people in constantly changing social contexts and having political consequences. The concept of ideology thus refers to these socially created meanings, thanks to which the social order is interpreted, and individuals and groups work in relationship to this order. In this sense ideologies are systems of culture, "maps of problematic social reality and matrices for the creation of collective conscience."[23] Radical modernism understood thus was not only the domain of the extreme left; it was also characteristic of the extreme right. Its basic feature in Poland and throughout Europe in the 1930s was that it weakened centrist political attitudes in favor of more radical solutions. This model of political consciousness prevailed among Jewish young people in Poland in the 1930s. As I emphasize several times in this book, the worldview of Jewish young people, defined by radical modernism, had a totalist character. This means that the political views of young people, which organization they belonged to, and from which ideology they drew inspiration determined in a decisive way their attitudes to politics and how they described their parents, family home, friends, and teachers from school, how they evaluated the literature they read, and how they viewed social, economic, and cultural issues. "Totalist," however, does not mean "totalitarian." The young communists did not know exactly what was happening in the Soviet Union; dreaming of a different Poland and a different world, they dreamed of something different from what was being implemented beyond the eastern border of the Second Polish Republic. Young right-wing Zionist revisionists, sometimes drawing inspiration consciously or unconsciously from the activities and symbols of the European far right, dreamed of a Jewish state in the Land of Israel different from those established in Italy or Germany in the 1930s. A certain authoritarianism, also present in the ideologies of centrist or left-wing Zionism or the Bund, did not invalidate the genuine ambitions of these movements to build democratic societies that had nothing to do with totalitarianism. The way in which young Jews were organized and acted in the parties and youth movements associated with these broader movements was very different from the way they functioned in the illegal, strictly centralized communist party, which was subject to directives from Moscow. At the same time, however, the supporters of all these parties and youth organizations, regardless of the differences between them, were united by a certain ideological totalism in looking at the surrounding world.

One of this book's central issues is the specific rivalry between Polish state institutions and various Jewish institutions in the battle for the "soul of young Jewish people." The rival sides arbitrarily imposed on them—by way of various educational practices—certain symbols and meanings. Following Pierre Bourdieu, I call this imposition *symbolic violence*: "Symbolic violence is exerted whenever any power imposes meanings and imposes them as legitimate by concealing the power relations, which are the basis of its ability to impose those meanings."[24] Young Jews, growing up in a modern national state, were, far more than previous generations, susceptible to the processes of acculturation to Polishness, being the result of symbolic violence on the part of state institutions and dominant forms of mass culture. I follow Itamar Even-Zohar in interpreting the influence on Jewish youth of Polish culture, its symbolic domination, and resistance to it by national Jewish institutions as a case of "cultural interference."[25] These intersecting state educational influences and those of rival Jewish institutions led to the penetration into the consciousness of young people of symbols and meanings drawn both from Polish and from Jewish (Hebrew and Yiddish) culture, creating a unique cultural hybrid. As I demonstrate in chapters 3, 4, and 5, Polish culture had a profound influence on the consciousness of many and indeed most of the autobiographers—both on those who realized it and those who did not, on those who acknowledged this influence and on those who attempted to minimize or even conceal it. It also affected their view of themselves as Jews.

The basic source material used here is young people's autobiographies submitted to YIVO. To understand the way in which the ideology of radical modernism, contradicting the forms of Polish symbolic violence and Jewish nationalism, affected the consciousness of young Jewish individuals, I have used Pierre Bourdieu's category of habitus. According to Itamar Even-Zohar's understanding of habitus in the work of Pierre Bourdieu, it is "a system of internalized embodied schemes which, having been constituted in the course of collective history, or acquired in the course of individual history and function in the practical states, for practice (and not for the sake of pure knowledge)."[26] In the course of recreating specific habituses, the objective order becomes an element in individuals' experience. My aim is to recreate and explain some of the political functions and meanings of young people's habitus. This concept serves to indicate the way in which intersubjectively distributed symbolic content operated at the level of individual experiences of Jewish youth, particularly in the way they were presented in the autobiographies. Ideological content, social values, and symbols forming a habitus never operate in the form of closed principles but are subject to reinterpretation and innovations introduced by actors struggling with ever-newer situations. Such an understanding of habitus as the basis of individuals' thinking and social activity aims to avoid explanations in which their behavior is completely guided by the social order, and also subjectivism, in which this order has no special meaning.[27] The theory of habitus allows us to observe the operation of social structures on the individual, as individuals conform to them and simultaneously interpret them, reacting creatively and transforming content imposed from above.

An excellent example of the function of habitus in the replication of social order is the school. School socialization and political institutions' pedagogical activities described in this work can be interpreted as "seek[ing] to reproduce the cultural arbitrary of the dominant or dominated classes."[28] Overlaying Bourdieu's class perspective, which captures the reality of postwar France, onto the reality of the Second Republic and its Jewish citizens' socialization problems, the arbitrariness of the dominant Polish culture collided with the cultural arbitrariness of the Jewish minority, or more precisely of its elite. Competing educational goals, Polish state schooling, private Jewish schools, mass Polish and Jewish culture, and the actions of competing Jewish political parties were central to the socialization and sociopolitical consciousness of young Jews during the interwar period. The general social habitus (composed of various partial habituses) developed in this objectively conflictual situation "accounts for intergenerational conflict because it instills different definitions of what is possible and impossible or what is natural and what is scandalous."[29] Being a structure of recognition and also a structure generating action, it assumes on the one hand an unconscious internalization of certain elements of the objective state, and on the other, conscious action against other parts of it. The concept of habitus allows me to study the conflicting influences on young Jewish people of such institutions as the family, traditional and modern Jewish educational establishments, Polish public schools, Jewish and Polish popular and mass culture, and political parties in parallel.

THE YIVO COMPETITION:
AUTOBIOGRAPHIES OF JEWISH YOUTH

The principal primary source base for this work is one hundred of the over six hundred autobiographies submitted to the competition of the Jewish Scientific Institute in 1932, 1934, and 1939.[30] Established in 1925 and operating in Vilna (present-day Vilnius), the Jewish Scientific Institute (YIVO) was one of the most important centers of Jewish thought and science in Europe before the Holocaust. Although YIVO established its image as a national institution, standing above partisan divisions, in reality it attracted academics mainly of center-left or left-wing views, proponents of Yiddish as the basis for a Jewish national culture, of secularization, and of ideas for transforming eastern European Jewry. These radical ideas placed YIVO in opposition to powerful Jewish milieux, above all Orthodoxy and Zionism. Fighting for the ideals of "diaspora nationalism," YIVO came out against all sorts of Jewish "assimilation" and thus attacked linking Jewish religious identity to Polish cultural or national identity; it opposed the polonizing impulses of certain state institutions and lamented the various processes of acculturation affecting the Jewish community. All these ideas and points of view were also close to Max Weinreich, the principal organizer of all three competitions and the director of an interdisciplinary project, launched in 1935, studying Jewish youth—known by the abbreviation *Yugfor*. These ideas influenced the organization of the competition; the scientific, social, and political goals set by the organizers; and the methodology of analyzing and interpreting the results of the studies.[31] Because YIVO represented a certain set of ideas in the Jewish community, there was some built-in bias as to who would be willing to participate in the competition and write an autobiography for submission.

Although YIVO was not a neutral institution in terms of its worldview, its announcements of the competition for autobiographies were directed to the general mass of "Jewish youth," and it tried to show itself as being a national scientific institution above politics. Thanks to this, the idea of an autobiographical competition appealed to different segments of the Jewish population with diverse viewpoints. An enormous merit of the autobiographies is that during all three YIVO competitions, emphasis was laid on authors' creativity, allowing them to write more or less about anything.[32] In 1934 authors were instructed to respond to the following list of issues: "Immediate family. Relations between family members. The war years. Teachers, school and what they gave you. Friends of both sexes, relationships with them. Youth organizations, political party life and what it has given you. How you ended up [taking part in a political organization]. Which events in your life have made the greatest impact."[33]

However, even these general topics were not imposed on the authors; they were to treat them only as "suggestions."[34] The actual announcements of the competition also did not suggest the views that the autobiographers were to express. It was emphasized that education, employment, authors' views and political activities, and "poor style" were not important.[35] The idea was to encourage young people to write works faithfully reflecting their experiences. In the invitations to the competition, we find the following guidelines: "Do not write about something that you have not yourself experienced, but which can appear 'interesting.' Do not, however, refrain from describing events, which, it might appear, interrupt the flow of the story. . . . Write to the point. Clearly explain every issue. Do not think that 'trivialities' are unimportant."[36]

Authors would remain anonymous, which helped popularize the competition among traditional and Orthodox communities, whose elites were very critical of YIVO. The authors could sign their works using pseudonyms, and their personal details were held in sealed envelopes that YIVO committed to secrecy and opened only at the end of the competition.[37]

However, the strategy adopted by YIVO for advertising the competition for autobiographies might well have been a form of subtle suggestion. The institute consistently mentioned the profound generational conflict and the loneliness of young people, for the most part brought up in a traditional world, which was unable to deal with modern challenges and the younger generation's concerns.

YIVO presented itself as the only institution capable of understanding them and showing a deep interest in their fate. This strategy can be branded as "youth populism."[38] On the one hand, young people were part of the Jewish nation, its hope of surviving difficult times; on the other, the nation, as YIVO saw it, was a recently formed community differing greatly from current Jewish society. Young people in particular were to play a key role in changing society, for which, as Max Weinreich emphasized, "one had to fight."[39] As YIVO saw it, this generation of young people was very different from those that preceded it.[40] One of the competition leaflets addressed to them ran as follows:

> Never have the fortunes of Jewish youth been as complicated as they are to-day. Material conditions are very difficult, educational systems have lost their former cohesion and strength; society is divided, yet it demands from young people a single direction. Today's youth has had dissimilar experiences than the older generation, and its place in society is also different. How exactly do these differences show? It is impossible to reply to this question unless we know the situation of young people. In order to understand this situation we must listen to their voices, who themselves must tell us about their psychological and social problems.[41]

YIVO was not stirring up generational conflict here; rather, it was appealing to views that were widespread in contemporary Jewish discourse. This affected at least some of the autobiographies written by these young people. It appears that some authors, despite coming from families in which the generations lived mostly free of conflict, assumed that they would increase the attractiveness of their work in the competition by emphasizing their revolt against the values of their parents' world. YIVO was not simply playing on the "usual" (ahistorical) revolt of a younger generation against an older one. Instead, YIVO appealed to the idea of "a Jewish crisis of modernity," with its roots in the Jewish Enlightenment (Haskalah) conviction that the traditional world was not up to the challenges of the present. As a consequence, a substantial majority of the autobiographies adopted a definitively critical, even score-settling attitude toward older generations.

All this does not mean that the ideology of the institute provided a basis for most interpretations of surrounding reality in the autobiographies. Few authors had access to Weinreich's or YIVO's publications; nearly all of them only had the information provided in the pamphlet, from advertisements in the newspaper, or from friends and instructors in youth organizations. The institute's success in drawing so many young Jews to the autobiographical contest was based on the fact that, with its announcement, it fit well with the dominant discourse of the 1930s, presenting the world as sunk in crisis. Though YIVO had pretensions of being apolitical,[42] it was clearly on the side of progressivism, promoting far-reaching changes to social, economic, and cultural relations in Poland and in Europe.[43] The institute's populist rhetoric invoked the language of political modernism, just like a great many Jewish intellectuals, most of the articles in the press, and the most important political organizations. The initiative was popular thanks to the perception that YIVO was, more so than any other institution, able to understand the predicament of young people. Autobiographies submitted to the YIVO competition were a kind of communal criticism from young Jews, convinced that they were living amid profound political, social, and cultural crises.[44]

As far as the authors' political views were concerned, the majority of them were Zionists. Max Weinreich and other YIVO researchers interpreted this prevalence as evidence of "psychological immaturity," an unwillingness to tackle immediate problems, and escapism into a dream realm of creating a Jewish state in the Land of Israel.[45] A large minority of the authors, clearly possessing other points of view, were Orthodox Jews. They came from religious homes and lived in accordance with Orthodox precepts, studied in yeshivas, received rabbinical instruction, and were connected to Orthodox sociopolitical institutions that YIVO and Weinreich openly criticized.[46] Communists, who also did not enjoy the sympathy of the director of the Yugfor project, formed another large group of authors. Despite the unrivaled Yiddishness of the institute, young people from acculturated urban backgrounds also responded to advertisements for the competition. We find among participants in the competition sons of sharecroppers, daughters of wealthy merchants, and children of industrialists, with a poor or nonexistent command of Yiddish, who most often wrote their autobiographies in Polish. At the ideological antipode from YIVO were polonized members of the right-wing Zionist party Betar, who represented a large group of participants in the competition. Students took part in the competition, as did young rabbis, as well as individuals who had completed no more than three or four classes of elementary school. In keeping with the social structure of interwar Jewry, the majority of the authors were the children of petty merchants and artisans, though people from wealthier backgrounds were also well represented.

There were at least three Jewish communities in the Second Republic who are not to be found among participants in the YIVO competition. One of these communities consisted of young people whose parents or who themselves identified as Poles and for the most part completely repudiated the existence of Jewish nationhood. The absence of these voices is balanced out to some degree by individuals coming from an assimilated background, knowing only Polish, educated only in non-Jewish institutions, who at some point in their lives became involved with Jewish nationalism in one form or another. Another missing group was Jewish youth from formerly German territories—from Greater Poland, Pomerania, and Silesia. YIVO's nationalist orientation, its Yiddishism, and its claim to be an intellectual hub for eastern European Jews clearly set it apart from "assimilated" Jews who grew up amid the strong influence of German Jewry.

Another important group absent from the competition were the ultra-Orthodox, who rejected all forms of contact with secular Jewish institutions. Although I quote the work of people from these communities later, they were exceptions among participants in the YIVO competition. Written in secret from their parents, rabbis, and yeshiva authorities, they are a testimony to experiences of young people looking for a way out of these environments, rather than "average" representatives. In the case of ultra-Orthodox and highly polonized Jewish communities, these sources provide a window onto certain trends existing at the margins of these two groups, having an influence on them, and "plucking out" certain young people, but not these communities themselves.

YIVO was an avid supporter of the idea of Jewish national and cultural autonomy in east-central Europe, expressing itself in the ideology of *doikayt*, which recognized modern, secular Yiddish culture as the basis of the Jewish nation's existence, and east-central Europe as its home.[47] The institute saw assimilation as the most important long-term threat to the existence and future of the Jewish nation in Europe.[48] However, YIVO used the term *assimilation* in a vague and highly judgmental way. Thus, anyone who did not use Yiddish on a daily basis or who simply gave too much of their time and heart to non-Jewish culture deserved criticism and the label of a traitor to their people. Some authors of autobiographies tried to hide their "not-too-Jewish" lifestyles, concealing or minimizing their participation in Polish culture, while their desire to succeed in the competition could also have had an influence on their eager declaration of attachment to the Jewish national cause, frequently affirmed in almost every autobiography. YIVO publications, as well as the young participants in its competition, frequently cited the nation's "good" and "future" as justification for actions and reaffirmed their dedication to "the national cause." Most of the authors also declared a readiness to make sacrifices on behalf of their community.

When assessing the representative nature of the autobiographies, the issue of the language in which they were written is extremely important. In the leaflets announcing the competition, YIVO assured potential participants that the language in which they wrote their work would have no influence on their chance of winning a prize. Indeed, most participants wrote their submissions in the language they were most comfortable with. But the institute's pro-Yiddish orientation was well known, and this fact influenced the choice of language of some authors. Over 70 percent wrote their submissions in Yiddish. Almost all of them doubtlessly spoke the language well and used it at home, in the heder, and in their immediate surroundings. However, only a small percentage of Jewish children had the opportunity to learn to write in Yiddish beyond learning the alphabet and taking short and simple notes. Traditional education did not teach this language for abstract philosophical or social concepts, while only a minority of children had access to secular Yiddish education. The consequence was that for the majority of young Jews in the 1930s, Yiddish was their first language, used at home, and yet at the same time many of them wrote better in Polish, which they knew less well than Yiddish. More than half of this generation (and a similar proportion of participants in the YIVO competition) went to public schools, and Polish was taught even in the majority of traditional Jewish heders. There can be no doubt that those who wrote their autobiographies in Polish knew Yiddish poorly or not at all. However, among those who selected Yiddish, many could have written their submission in Polish, and at least some of them might even have done it better.

The relatively lucrative prizes for the winners of the competition might also have influenced what and how the authors wrote. The winners of the first prize in the first and second competitions received 150 zloty, a relatively large sum at the time.[49] This fact sometimes influenced the choice of language in which the submissions were written and, to a much lesser extent, the political views expressed in them, as most of them differed greatly from YIVO's ideals. The institute's success in reaching a wide range of authors was apparent too in the varying motivations for participation in the competition. Some were compelled by purely financial aims, others had literary and political ambitions, and a few sought professional psychological help. Many of the contributors simply wrote because they could share their thoughts with someone for the first time.[50] However, most of them understood the YIVO guidelines, separating the composition of an autobiography from literary works, which they sent in together with their submissions to the competition.[51]

In total, 627 autobiographies and several hundred other personal documents (letters, memoirs, literary attempts) were submitted, coming mainly from Poland but also from other European countries, Palestine, the United States, and South America.[52] Among the 384 autobiographies made available to scholars between 2005 and 2012 (out of the 400 or so that by some miracle survived the Holocaust and in 1947 were brought to YIVO's new headquarters in New York City), 282 (73%) were written in Yiddish, 77 (20%) in Polish, 18 (5%) in Hebrew, and the rest in other languages.[53] Most probably those were more or less the linguistic ratios of all the submissions to the competition. Authors aged sixteen to twenty-two could take part in the competition, which, taken in relationship to the dates of the three competitions (1932, 1934, and 1939), gives us the generation born between 1910 and 1923. Among the submissions, there are also works written by people younger or older than the competition rules permitted, who had no chance of winning a prize. Women and girls are massively underrepresented among the sample, representing only 25 percent of participants in the competition.[54] Fortunately, those who decided to write autobiographies came from diverse backgrounds: Zionist, socialist, Orthodox, secular, religious, poor, wealthy, assimilated, and those who spoke only Yiddish on a daily basis.

I have selected one hundred of the nearly four hundred autobiographies available, choosing them in such a way that they represent the greatest variety of participants in the competition in terms of their political, social, and cultural viewpoints. Among the works under scrutiny, there are seventy-one by men and twenty-nine by women. Six of them were submitted to the 1932 competition, fifty-eight to the 1934 competition, and thirty-six in 1939. Sixty-seven of them were written in Yiddish, twenty-nine in Polish, two in two languages (Yiddish and Polish), and two in Hebrew. Fifty-two of them came from the central regions of Poland, twenty-two from former Galicia, and twenty-six from the Eastern Borderlands, the so-called Kresy. Three of the participants in the competition lived in the country, thirty-six in small towns or shtetls of fewer than ten thousand inhabitants, twenty-four in medium-size towns of more than ten thousand inhabitants, and thirty-seven in large cities of more than fifty thousand inhabitants. Thirty-three of the authors came from homes in which the main source of income was trade (ten itinerant or street traders; nineteen in medium-sized trade, owning their own shop or small business; and four who owned a larger business); in twenty houses the parents were mainly artisans; in nine of them the fathers were religious officials (rabbis, ritual slaughterers, synagogue vergers); eight supported themselves as workers; the parents of six owned factories, mills, or sawmills and other manufacturing enterprises employing people; the fathers of five of the autobiographers supported the family as melameds (teachers in a traditional Jewish educational religious establishment); in the case of five families, the parents were luftmenschen, meaning that they had no fixed occupation, worked odd jobs, were unemployed, or tried to support themselves by begging; the parents of two of the authors were usurers;

two were manual laborers; two held senior management positions in commercial enterprises; two had mid-range positions in similar institutions; and for six families there is no information.

There was a similar spread in the political views of the authors whose autobiographies and other documents are analyzed below. Almost half the authors, fifty-one, belonged to one of the many Zionist party youth movements or were at least sympathetic toward them (eleven, Ha-Shomer ha-Tsa'ir; nine, He-Halutz; eight, the revisionist movement or more specifically Betar; five, Gordonia; four, Po'alei-Tsiyon-Right or Frayhayt; three, Mizrahi; two, so-called general Zionist organizations; one, the Jewish National Party; and nine had unspecified Zionist sympathies). Three of the authors belonged to parties for adults or one of the Agudat Israel youth organizations. Seven supported Po'alei-Tsiyon-Left or were members of its youth organization Borochow Yugend, sixteen were associated with the Bund or its youth organizations, thirteen sympathized with the communist movement or belonged to one of its youth organizations, and nine declared no specific political preferences.

In terms of education, seventeen of the authors had not completed elementary education (that is, had not completed six grades of elementary school), and thirty had completed six grades. Eight of the authors were in secondary school, five had not completed that level of education, seven had left without a diploma, and fourteen had left with one; three of the authors were students, and two had completed higher education. In the case of two authors, their level of their education was unclear. A separate, twelve-person group were competitors who had not completed any formal secular education but were studying only in traditional Jewish educational establishments (such as a heder, beit midrash, or yeshiva).

Twenty-nine of the authors were artisans, thirteen were unemployed, eleven worked as tutors or private teachers, seven were still in secondary school, six were in service, six were workers, three held specialist positions in commercial or manufacturing enterprises, three were in *hakhshara* (preparatory training for departure to Palestine), two were religious officials, two were librarians, two were teachers, one worked various odd jobs, one worked in the family store, one ran a family production facility, one was a master craftsman in a factory, and one ran a family business. We have no information on another eleven.

The autobiographies' political, geographical, social, class, and cultural spread allows us to draw conclusions about the whole generation, especially since the same opinions expressed in many of these works transcended social and ideological differences separating their authors. Although it is impossible to verify biographical elements provided by the anonymous participants in the YIVO competition, what the authors chose to share and how allows us to understand the generation's social, cultural, and political sensitivities. The autobiographies and other materials submitted to the interwar YIVO competitions, like all sources, are not perfect, but at the same time they are the best of the available materials allowing us to describe the life experience and consciousness of the last generation of Jewish youth in Poland before the Holocaust. My aim is not to get at the "truth" of each of biography but to recreate collective frameworks of thought to understand the values and symbols behind them. Jewish national symbols were widespread in the interwar period, proclaimed daily by the majority of Jewish political, social, and cultural organizations. Not all the authors put into practice the norms and values of political movements and social organizations that they described in their work. Certainly, the authors were usually people who were deeply involved in politics. And not all young Jews were radical modernists. At the same time, however, radical modernism dominated their lives. Regardless of background, they described their experiences using radical modernist concepts and symbols. This influence of radical modernism as discourse and a form of totalist ideology on how young Jews comprehended their lives is the central subject of this book. The conclusions drawn from the YIVO autobiographies do not apply to all Jewish youth living in 1930s Poland, but to a majority. This majority consisted of young Jews who felt they belonged to a separate Jewish nation, of whom some were religiously indifferent, some decidedly secular, and some religiously devout. Members of this majority were deeply divided regarding where they envisioned their personal and national future. Most saw their future in the Land of Israel, some dreamed of emigrating to western Europe or the United States, and others still believed that it could be possible to stay in Poland.

THE BOOK'S CONSTRUCTION

The book's narrative thread follows the structure of the autobiographies, whose authors were invited to begin their narratives with descriptions of their parents and early childhood and then continue to successive stages of their socialization, sticking as much as possible to a chronology of events. I have tried to write a collective biography of an entire generation of Jewish youth growing up in the Second Polish Republic starting with early childhood and the family home, gradually moving to a description of the wider environment in which young people lived, and finally arriving at the moment when they began to become politically engaged. In chapter 1 I describe the immediate environment: parents, the family home, friends and neighbors from childhood, and traditional religious education. This chapter and the next differ from the succeeding chapters in that I attempt to comprehensively analyze some of the autobiographies presented in them, each time presenting the complete biographical structure created by specific authors. The way in which the participants in the competition connected specific facts of their lives, how they saw their childhood in the context of their later fortunes, is in itself one of the most important pieces of information on their sociopolitical awareness. Several of the autobiographies described in chapters 1 and 2 in more detail are meant to show the dominant biographical trajectory among the bulk of Jewish youth. In these chapters I present a typical sequence of individual fortunes, characteristic of the majority of YIVO autobiographies that could not be fully presented in the book. This approach has another advantage. In my view, it allows us to minimize the negatives of taking quotations out of context, unthinkingly replacing the narrative logic of a specific autobiography with the logic of a scientific deduction. Studying the autobiographies comprehensively allows us to follow the widely understood ideology of an era, the common threads of sociopolitical awareness transcending conscious party divides. It also allows us to describe the deep cultural and political fragmentation of the Jewish population in the 1930s, often showing a basic common semantic context for the majority of the autobiographies.

Chapter 2 focuses on the individual ambitions of the young people and the beginnings of their work lives. In chapters 3 and 4, I analyze educational experience drawn from Polish and Jewish schools. Chapter 5 deals with models of cultural consumption and the influence that competing ethno-state and Jewish institutions had on their complex identity. With this aim in mind, I also discuss the curricula both of public education and of various private Jewish school networks, as well as the ideologies on which these curricula were based. In chapter 6 I tackle the issue of the simultaneous proximity to and exclusion from Polish culture, as well as the serious problem of antisemitism as a generational experience. Chapters 7 and 8 deal with strictly political matters: youth movements in political parties and openly declared political views. Here I supplement the autobiographies with documents from Jewish political parties, the papers of their most important leaders, and analyses and reports from state institutions.

Using the work of contributors to the YIVO competition, I have attempted to respect their anonymity, using mainly their pseudonyms. I use authors' names only when they themselves did so. Most used pseudonyms, attaching a separate envelope to their competition submission containing their personal information. It was to be opened only in the event that a given autobiography was considered for a prize. Apart from several autobiographers who from the start spurned anonymity, I have also given the names of a few others who publicly claimed authorship of specific submissions years later.

ONE

—ᘛ—

TRADITION

Young People in the World
of Their Parents, Religion, the Shtetl,
and the Jewish Neighborhood

FROM THE FIRST PAGES OF the great majority of the YIVO autobiographies, it is clear that these youth defined themselves as the representatives of a generation formed by a new world, one very different from the world of their parents. The institute appealed to this key element of young people's generational identity. Young people took on this kind of identity above all by participating in politics and in the modernist discourse characteristic of the interwar period. Participants in the YIVO competition, using modernist symbols and narrative structures, gave their autobiographies a consistent internal form—they derived one set of events from another, and they explained their current situation and worldview in a holistic way, giving their life stories an overall, comprehensive, usually political meaning. Politics—as a network of social organizations, a context for social action, a lifestyle, a symbolic universe, and a network of ideas—is in fact present in every part of the autobiographies. Seemingly apolitical, neutral descriptions of family life, immediate milieux, schools, and work often say more about the authors' political views than the descriptions of their direct involvement in parties or youth movements. Politically significant symbols drawn from the ideologies of various movements begin to appear in the abovementioned contexts, for the most part unconsciously. Politics thus had an influence on descriptions of childhood, relations with parents, and conditions in heders, elementary schools, Jewish national schools, and so on—in other words, in seemingly nonpolitical areas of young people's lives. What links most of the autobiographies is a modernist perspective on childhood in a traditional world. Its institutions, like other elements of contemporary reality, were judged very critically. These judgments carried with them far-reaching demands,

26

sometimes for a revolutionary transformation of the surrounding world, a vision of how it ought to be.

THE FAMILY HOME

Let us first look at an atypical autobiography, whose author, unlike most of the others who entered the YIVO competition, had not completely abandoned the religious values of her family home and, at the moment of writing the autobiography, was not a member of any of the radical, political, and secularizing movements that were challenging these values. Juxtaposing this testimony with narratives by more radical individuals who were more critically attuned to their own immediate milieu allows us to consider a certain general generational model of awareness, linking youth from different backgrounds and representing various sociopolitical camps.

An autobiographer using the pseudonym "A Shtetleshe" was born and had spent most of her life in Ignalin, a small shtetl not far from Vilna, near the Polish-Lithuanian frontier. She wrote her autobiography in Yiddish, submitting it to the first YIVO competition in 1932. She came from a religious background, but this was not a typically traditional home. In addition to religious practices, the children and parents consumed secular literature. The author's parents wanted their children to receive not only a religious but also a secular, indeed formally secular, education. Undoubtedly, the author's immediate surroundings were not divorced from the secular or the non-Jewish world. A Shtetleshe's family was somewhat typical of modern Orthodoxy. It was quite well off; its members were involved in trade and traditional religious professions (the author's father was a shohet).[1] In A Shtetleshe's autobiography, there is no description—common in other authors' contributions—of an acute intergenerational conflict. Despite this, her comments reflect a modernist consciousness, a sense of difference, a way of looking at religion and tradition differing from that of her parents and grandparents. She did not subject the norms and values of previous generations to the withering criticism present in the majority of other submissions to the YIVO competition. However, she too questioned some of them. In the first pages, she describes her grandmother getting married at the age of twelve, when she was still a child and completely dependent on her parents (when she was a married woman, her father beat her because she had not taken care of the cow grazing in the field).[2] Thus, in a subtle and ironic way she criticizes one of the important Jewish traditions of the day. At the same time, A Shtetleshe praises other elements of tradition and the social roles deriving from it. We see this in her story her grandfather, one of the wealthiest *balebatim* (owners) in the shtetl,[3] who enjoyed wide respect since he shared his wealth and helped the poor.[4] The author's father, a pious shohet who spent his free moments studying Hebrew and Yiddish literature, also embodied the required fusion of traditional and modern social roles and associated personal attributes.[5] A Shtetleshe valued this modern rational Judaism, which was not opposed to the secular world and secular knowledge.

A Shtetleshe's personal role models were her beloved teachers from her private Jewish school. Before then, she had studied in a heder.[6] The very fact that such an institution could operate is an indicator of the modernization of the world in which the author was growing up.[7] She wrote that before life's obstacles led her to understand the impossibility of realizing her dreams, she wanted to become a schoolteacher.[8] In A Shtetleshe's description, a teacher combined modern secular educational values, as well as the imperative to transmit them to succeeding generations, with her grandfather's traditional philanthropy and her father's wide intellectual horizons. A Shtetleshe dreamed of having a similar social position, challenging the place of women in the traditional Jewish world. She saw herself as an independent, active person, working on behalf of society and freely gaining knowledge. She clearly did not wish to find herself in her grandmother's situation. The description of her parents' reaction to her birth also bears signs of criticism of the social roles assigned to women in traditional Jewish society: "My arrival brought no joy. I was their eighth girl."[9] Despite her attachment to the Jewish religion and to the world of the shtetl, she was able to take on a critical position regarding its attitudes toward women and secular education.

The unmodern elements of the traditional world, which in A Shtetleshe's autobiography were the object of subtle criticism, were subjected to radical criticism in other YIVO autobiographies. "Feygeles" (son of Feyge) submitted an autobiography to the 1934 competition, writing in Yiddish. He came from a traditional family and grew up in Lublin, where his father was a tailor. He wrote his autobiography at the age of twenty-three as an activist of Tsukunft, the youth organization of the socialist Bund—an anticommunist, Marxist political party committed to revolution and secularism. These biographical facts influenced how Feygeles described his own father:

> My parents: Father: physically weak. Exceptionally religious, a true fanatic. In no way learned in the Torah. He studied only from time to time, but was characterized by a timid reverence for Jewish wise men, for holy tales and in general for every "holy precept" [*frumen psuk*], if it had been noted even once[10] . . . no hero, a coward. Rarely cheerful, antisocial, complaining. He had little sympathy for other people and their feelings. He was inadequately interested in politics. Hence his total interest in business, financial matters, complete dedication to family matters, mother and the children.[11]

This statement is unambiguously critical. It suits the modern ideological vision of the traditional Jew—superstitious, cowardly, having no social predispositions or higher ideals. Characteristically, this stereotypical description links directly to the ideal of political activism and dedication to public affairs advocated by the new Jewish politics—in the case of the author, by the ideology of the Bund. Feygeles described his mother differently as "healthier than father." She could read and write in Russian; in her youth she had written poetry, and she loved literature. However, the son was critical of her religiosity and lack of interest in politics.[12] This assessment of his parents clearly corresponded with the author's socialist views, as was true in most other autobiographies.

"Heniek G" came from a traditional poor Jewish family in Warsaw. As an adult he was a convinced communist and remained on the margins of society, rubbing shoulders with the criminal underworld. He described his father as follows: "Father never had a steady income. At the time that I was born, father was a melamed [teacher], and taught older boys the *Torah* and the *Gemara* and earned *more* or less nothing for doing this. During my earliest years father wanted to fill me with the wisdom of which he himself was a specialist."[13]

Growing up in a small shtetl in the Nowogródek area, "Yud-Giml" was also critical of her parents: "Father, a broad shouldered well-built Jew, a carpenter by trade. Fanatically religious, devoting all his free time to religious studies.... At home he behaved like a tyrant. He was severe and firm towards his children. Mother, petite, rather intelligent . . . is never satisfied with her life, and is rather nervous. . . . From the description of my parents you can work out how I was brought up."[14]

Mendl Man wrote of his shoemaker father, "My father is a terribly unlucky Jew. He has a thick beard, he is calm, he never raises his voice, he sits all day at his machine engrossed in work, I never heard him yell. When he had no work, he would sit with one leg crossed over the other, stroking his beard with his right hand."[15] His mother was the opposite of his father, physically strong and energetic, and it was thanks to her creativity and enterprising character that the family did not suffer from hunger.[16]

The appearance in many of the autobiographies of better assessments of mothers was the result of their greater "modernity." This was true mainly in traditional homes and was the result of the traditional division of social roles in Jewish homes. According to participants in the YIVO competition, mothers were more interested in their children, understood them better, and knew what childhood was like. Unlike the fathers, they did not treat their children as small adults. The fact that mothers did not devote themselves to abstract religious studies made them more practical in daily matters and better able to understand the surrounding world. Not bound to the same extent by religious norms, they read more secular books and thus better understood their children's secular educational aspirations. It is striking that traditional gender roles were attacked with criticism of fathers, which was similar to that found in the literature of the nineteenth-century Haskalah.[17] Exceptional works among the autobiographies such as A Shtetleshe's show that criticism of traditional gender roles in Jewish families was very widespread among young people, irrespective of their geographical or social origins or the ideological perspective from which they were writing their autobiographies. Ideology in particular, however, decided whether this criticism was simply selective or in fact radical, totalist, and embracing the whole world of tradition.

LOST CHILDHOOD

The "old world" (world of tradition) was viewed negatively in almost every modernist political ideology popular among young Jews. The autobiography of "Mars" from Krasny in Eastern Galicia is a typical example of this generation's life trajectory. The author came from an Orthodox background, conscious of the secular dangers posed by the surrounding world and actively defending itself from its influences.[18] His break with his parents' way of life was accompanied by a critique of the world in which he was growing up: "In our family there was the 'law of the strongest.' . . . This lack of freedom of movement, lack of family warmth and open-heartedness, finally a lack of physical contact, which I never knew, formed my psyche in a certain way, making it not very resilient. . . . Discovering the injustice of the family structure, I wished to change it and this miniature 'social reform' became my first, clearly-defined demand."[19]

Another author, coming from Odziatycze in Volhynia, a future Bundist, began with recollections of his heder, children's games in the yard, and the physical punishments meted out by his father.[20] In his description all these elements combined to produce a basic picture of his immediate traditional world. At the same time, the author described a "scandal" involving his elder brother that resulted from his Bundist political views, which were unacceptable in his traditional Jewish family: "My elder [brother] 'W.' was 15 years-old and a Bundist. We treated him like an outcast. Mother took to saying that he brought shame on the family. Father took to shouting at him: 'disaster.' No one in the family sympathized with him, with the exception of his two older sisters, who were already studying in 'W' [Vilna] and were already also Bundists. There were daily rows at home; he did not want to say his prayers, and was beaten. . . . He put up with it all."[21]

The "lost childhood" was a leitmotif in most of the YIVO autobiographies. Poor parenting was blamed on poverty and the unfavorable conditions created by the world of Jewish tradition. The categories "poverty" and "tradition" were often closely connected.

"Ernst" came from a religious family living in Warsaw. In his autobiography he saw his traditional father's financial ineptitude as the principal reason for the pauperization and catastrophes that befell him and his family. When he was eleven years old, his mother fell ill, and the family could not afford treatment for her.[22] Owing to the difficult financial situation, as well as his father's egoism, Ernst had to go out to work at the age of twelve. He was taken out of Talmud Torah and apprenticed to a typesetter.[23] The rest of his autobiography is a description of working over ten hours a day, beyond his strength; his father's miserliness; and the lack of opportunities for further education and self-improvement.[24] In his account, poverty and his father's "traditional" financial ineptitude and egoism were the basic reasons for his mother's death and for the author's and his younger siblings' lost childhood.

"Moses S.," from Lviv, entitled his autobiography "A Young Jew's Life Today." He perceived his fate as typical of his contemporaries in his community and generation, and even of the whole "Jewish nation." He presented his story as exemplary of the "Wandering Jew" trope.[25] On the subsequent pages of his narrative, he related a series of misfortunes in his childhood, describing quarrels between his parents, his father's miserliness, his own illnesses, and accidents resulting from neglect.[26] Moses saw his teenage years as a struggle for secondary schooling and university education. Given the elite nature of these opportunities, it is doubtful the author's home conditions were actually that bad and whether his father really was all that opposed to his son's secular education. However, regardless of the author's "real" biography, which is impossible to verify, the opinions expressed are far more important. In addition to poverty, the obstacles to Moses's education were supposedly his father's exceptional miserliness and narrow horizons. All this supposedly handicapped the boy physically and psychologically, depriving him of his childhood.[27]

The account of Moses S., a university student—belonging to the relatively small group of educated people—converges in many places with the autobiographies presented above, whose authors had not even completed elementary school. Despite all the hardships described, his childhood was different from those of many other participants in the YIVO competition. This did not prevent Moses picking up the narrative of the "lost childhood" of young Jewish people growing up in the Second Republic. This fact testifies not only to the modernist narrative style but also to the modernist sociopolitical views of most

Jewish youth, irrespective of the backgrounds from which they came and of their actual fates. To be sure, at times the autobiographers described their lives in such a way to gain the sympathies of the competition judges. Lost childhood was, after all, a recurring theme in YIVO competition announcements. However, the regularity with which the motif of lost childhood appears in the autobiographies is testimony to the fact that these diverse authors generally shared certain sociopolitical convictions. According to them, the Jewish nation was in crisis. Its traditional social and religious customs were not suited to the contemporary world. The older generation forcing young people to live by its norms had disastrous consequences. Their parents' attachment to traditional standards was to a great extent responsible for the poverty and hopelessness in which their children were forced to develop into adults.[28]

I notice in the autobiographies a strong generational awareness of the basic difference between the young people's world and the adult world. Young Jews perceived themselves as a separate group in the Jewish nation. One consequence was an essentially modern demand for a right to childhood. The negative psychological and physiological influence of traditional customs and material poverty on childhood and adolescence was a central theme in the Jewish autobiographical literature of the day.[29] However, literature was certainly not the sole nor the most important source used by authors taking part in the YIVO competition. All contemporary secular political ideologies held the same attitude toward the world of Jewish tradition. What is important is that this kind of narrative thread appears equally among the Orthodox as well as those attached to certain Jewish religious customs, symbols, or rites. Understandably, the authors articulating these ideas the most strongly and drawing from them the most far-reaching consequences were those who had become actively involved with radical political organizations. Young people's criticism of their parents' world—which deprived them of their childhood—was not so much the result of the literary nature of their autobiographies and their supposedly exceptional individualism[30] as it was the consequence of the ideological impact of radical collectivism in political movements to which the authors belonged while writing their autobiographies.

THE HEDER AS A SYMBOL OF THE NEGATIVE SIDES
OF THE WORLD OF TRADITION

The autobiographies of young Jewish people are for the most part holistic. The narrative takes the reader through a logical process, tying all the stages of their lives and episodes into a cohesive whole. These young authors demonstrated a clear tendency to explain the reasons for their personal problems and defeats through social factors over which they had no influence. The consistency with which they did so says a great deal about the authors' attitudes toward the social order around them. In addition to the criticisms of their immediate milieu seen above, in the form of emotional depictions of their own experiences, participants in the YIVO contest referred to the situation of the whole Jewish "people" or "nation," or to a significant segment of it.

The most important influence in this type of holistic description of the young people's childhood world beyond the family home was the heder. According to these narratives, it was this institution that exerted the greatest influence on their childhood, and—since it symbolized the world of tradition—it was also the most widely criticized form of social life. When these youth attacked the heder, they did so to show traditional society's material poverty, its spiritual emptiness, and its intellectual backwardness.

The heder in its traditional form was no longer an object of veneration for the majority of Jewish communities in the interwar period. Even some of the Orthodox aimed to reform it. The new reality forced a revaluation of views on education on even the most deeply conservative and religious social movement, Agudat Israel (or, as the Ashkenazis called it, Agudas Yisroel)Since a section of the Orthodox also wanted to change the heder, proponents of secularism could have no doubts about its nature. Criticism of premodern institutions and norms of Ashkenazi Judaism, of which the heder was a basic element as early as the 1930s, had a long history. For one hundred years, it had been an important element in Haskalah literature and new genres of Jewish literature emerging during the time of its development.[31]

Books devoted to the fate of the individual, the difficulties of growing up in a traditional and oppressive milieu, and the youthful struggle for emancipation had been written by many well-known figures in the Jewish Enlightenment and during the birth of Jewish nationalist organizations at the turn of the nineteenth and twentieth centuries.[32] They were all united in their criticism of the heder. National and socialist movements recognized this institution as a bastion of tradition, as one of the most hated obstacles standing in the way of the construction of a new Jewish nation. This kind of total and absolutist criticism of the heder can be found in nearly all publications of the Yiddish and socialist network TsYShO (in Yiddish, Di Tsentrale Yidishe Shul-Organizatsye [the Central Jewish School Organization]), as well as the Hebrew Tarbut ("culture").[33] The YIVO world was also critical of the unreformed version of the heder.[34]

Participants in the YIVO competition placed their assessments of traditional Jewish education into the framework of historical logic, condemning it to inevitable oblivion. Even young Orthodox shared such negative assessments. They surrendered to the specific "symbolic violence" of political modernism and its concomitant critique of the traditional world. The Orthodox too found the material poverty, violence, ignorance, and lack of pedagogical preparation of the melameds teaching in heders offensive and their esoteric knowledge useless. For young people growing up in the interwar period, the heder represented the "ghetto wall" no less than for Haskalah luminaries of the eighteenth and nineteenth centuries. And just as the Maskalim did before them, young people growing up in 1930s Poland dreamed of a secular education.

The thread of scholasticism in this agency of traditional education, its detachment from reality, and its inability to come to terms with the modern world clearly appeared in the Feygeles autobiography mentioned above. For him the heder symbolized dogmatism, blind faith in impractical abstract religious principles, and the lifestyle of "living ghosts," people coming from another "ignorant" era, unsuited to their new surroundings.[35] "M. Schwarzklat" described his teacher in Talmud Torah: "A tall, dark Jew with sidelocks. He taught us the *Gemara*. He was completely indifferent whether we learned anything or not."[36] Another autobiographer, "A. Remez" from Horodenka, recalled his first melamed as a primitive person, "using his own finger to stir his tea."[37] He apparently inspired fear in all his pupils, doling out painful blows. Toward the end of the school week, on Thursdays, frightened mothers would gather outside waiting for their children while the melamed quizzed his students and beat ones who provided unsatisfactory answers.[38]

For centuries the profession of melamed had had low social standing. Seen through youthful eyes, the melamed was symptomatic of the declining traditional world. If the shtetl or a poor Jewish district in a city was the opposite of all things modern—the world of the city, the factory, the political party—then the traditional melamed was the opposite of the secular teacher or the political activist. In many of the autobiographies, it was precisely the teachers at private Jewish schools—ranging from the secularist TsYShO to the Orthodox Bais Yaakov (Beit Yaakov)—who represented a "new" life, filled with ideals. It was they, together with comrades in the new political parties, who most frequently served as role models for the youth. The melamed teaching Ernst was narrow-minded, sadistic, and occasionally ridiculous, stealing food brought by his young charges.[39] Gershon Pipe recalled that the house of his first melamed in Sanok, with whom he started studying at the age of three, "was on a Jewish street, the dirtiest of all the streets in the town." All that he recalled from the heder was fear, beatings, and humiliation.[40] Summing up his education in many heders and with many melameds, he wrote of the latter, "All of them were fanatical Jews unable to understand the modern world, they had no profession, they were all your typical wheeler-dealer."[41] Another author, "M. W.," one of the few autobiographers from among Orthodox elites—the son and brother-in-law of Hasidic rabbis in Dobre and a graduate of several Hasidic and Litvak yeshivas—summed up his experience in heders as follows: "My time in heder made a deep impression on my young soul . . . during long, winter evenings dozens of pupils, children aged six and seven, sat at tables consisting of two desks and barrels. . . . The lamps on the tables were weaker than those in a prison." What stuck in his memory most of all was the melamed's constant beatings.[42] Sensitivity to the general physical violence in traditional educational establishments was undoubtedly a new social fact, especially important, since the young Orthodox noticed it too.

"Z.G." was a Litvak. He perceived the superiority of his religious community over those of the Hasidim in an ability to reform traditional establishments so that they might function in the modern world.[43] As for the Hasidic heder in Ostrowiec, when he and his family were living as refugees during World War I, he had nothing but words of contempt and mockery:

> A small, poor house in which one went into straight into the heder. On coming in one saw four low benches, filled with children sitting from wall to wall . . .; they sat silently like little soldiers, awaiting orders from a mighty rabbi sitting at the table, whose massive body blocked the light from the window, making an already dim room darker. The rebbe . . . his melancholy face, devoid of compassion, inspired fear in our young hearts. We tried to avoid his gaze, staring above his head at a patch of gentle blue sky, that was visible through the windows. This lasted only until the rebbe suddenly ordered the children: "drop your pants!" . . . We watched as a small "yidele" [Jewish child], a poor little fellow, dropped his pants in front of all of us, was put across his knee with one hand by the rebbe, who then did the honors with his meaty paw. Ashamed, with frightened eyes, the poor little child quickly pulled up his pants and, sobbing, slid back to his place among the group of children. I too eventually earned the right to take part in the sacred ritual of the beating, though undeservedly.[44]

Among authors who had already left religion behind when they wrote their autobiographies, the heder was a microcosm of traditional Jewish society, in which the wealthy despised the poor. For "Shtoimeshan" (a supporter of Po'alei-Tsiyon-Left), this institution, in addition to violence and transmitting impractical and unnecessary knowledge, symbolized "class extortion" and the discrimination experienced by the children of the poor Jewish working class. Already at the heder level, the children of wealthy families despised the poor.[45] We find these same themes in "Drori's" autobiography. Despite having been sent to the most prestigious heder in town, he quickly observed the melamed's cruelty and trickery—beating the pupils and stealing some of the food provided for the children by the local Jewish community—and prejudice separating the pupils. Traditional class differences, in which the children of merchants and the religious elite looked down on the children of artisans, could not be overcome.[46] The same was true in the other heders that he attended. In them Drori became aware of general social injustice supposedly for the first time, and he developed a total and deep distaste for many traditional social norms and customs.[47]

The criticisms of the heder presented here were linked by a vision of this institution as a symptom of the crisis, or indeed the downfall, of the world of tradition. Many of the participants in the YIVO competition stigmatized their parents or other traditional people's blind faith in religious dogma and abstract religious principles. The melamed in the heder, in addition to his impractical knowledge and lack of awareness of the surrounding world, exemplified blind, irrational violence. The heder was one of many traditional institutions depriving children of their childhood. Some of the authors, equipped with modern ideological apparatuses for perceiving and analyzing society, pointed out that this traditional institution of Jewish education was an arena for class extortion and for reproducing social inequality. Most of the authors wanted the heder to be abolished. A minority wanted to reform it along the lines of a modern religious school. Nearly all agreed, however, that basic forms of Jewish life required fundamental changes.

THE WIDER SURROUNDINGS: THE SHTETL AND THE JEWISH NEIGHBORHOOD

The broadest context of social life described by young people when writing about the milieu in which they grew up was the local community of the shtetl, or the Jewish neighborhood of a larger city. Just as in the descriptions of heders, common threads emerge among autobiographers from different social worlds.

Born in 1913, "Ben-Tikva" (Hebrew: "Son of Hope") spent the first years of his life in Święciany near Vilna. On the first page of his autobiography, he included a typical description of his shtetl. It was "just like all the others"; its inhabitants were more or less evenly divided between Christians and Jews. The latter lived mainly from trade and irregular labor. While Christian children grew up in healthy contact with nature, Jewish children would spend days in "a dark room, toiling over the *Gemara*."[48] In his autobiography, Ben-Tikva linked his frequently expressed dislike of trade as the principal means of supporting the traditional community with the whole lifestyle of the Jewish shtetl. According to him, this was an unnatural and unhealthy world. Dislike of petty trade as a profession, of a mercenary attitude toward reality, or of the "unnaturalness" of Jewish life it conditioned is typical of a substantial majority of the autobiographies.

Another autobiography is the opposite of those quoted earlier, since the writer describes her happy childhood in it. One might imagine that since "Zhanet" recorded her early years with pleasure, she must have also positively assessed the milieu in which they had been spent. The fact that, according to her description, this "happiness" had come about as if despite the traditional environment says a great deal about the power of the modernist worldview internalized by the vast majority of Jewish young people represented in the YIVO competition. Apart from their personal experiences, the values motivating them while writing the autobiographies did not allow them to assess the world of tradition positively. Zhanet was brought up in a small shtetl, Ostryń in Nowogródek province, at the heart of the Litvak area of eastern European Jewry. She described her childhood as "heaven," in which her parents created the perfect environment for "physical and spiritual growth":[49]

> Conditions were the kind found in a small town that had just come through the war. Besides, what kind of changes could the war have brought? The shtetl still had the same five streets and a dozen or so "alleys," with the marketplace in the middle where, in autumn, one had to wear enormous boots so as not to drown, a pair of galoshes being nowhere near enough when venturing into the mud. Clearly, electric light was something one read about in the papers, which reached the town three days late. We had no road link with other towns. So, it took a whole day each time by cart to travel to Grodno (50 kilometers). Of course, newspapers obviously reached the shtetl "aristocracy," pharmacies and such places. Only then were they passed round from hand to hand.[50]

The author went on to state that the only entertainment in such a place, the only pleasure during breaks from hard work, was conversations with neighbors. She justified the conditions of life in the shtetl by its inhabitants' intellectual and cultural backwardness. Just like others, this autobiography is filled with modernist symbols, contrasted with the world of the shtetl.[51]

An autobiography by "Gamalielis" contains a novel generalization of the traditional world of the small Jewish town, or rather of its traditionalism already in decline. Gamalielis is a fascinating example of someone from a relatively wealthy home, placed between tradition and Orthodoxy. This graduate of various heders and yeshivas brimming with hermeneutic talent was working in the extreme left-wing Po'alei-Tsiyon-Left revolutionary party when he wrote his autobiography. Despite his radical political involvement, he had not completely abandoned religion. As a result, his description of his immediate surroundings and generalizations on the subject of the world of the shtetl, though critical, are at the same time original and subtle. An extensive quotation from his description of Brańsk Podlaski, where he was born and had grown up, displays this nuance. The following excerpt is the introduction to a description of his earliest years and opens the text:

> Surrounded by beautiful wheatfields, muddy pastures, small, damp woods and peaceful villages, next to a gently flowing stream, several kilometers from the railroad station lay the shtetl of Brańsk. . . . It is one of many "Jewish" small towns with no industry or major trade. The low houses, in which a few machines had once been assembled, the barely taller cottages, from which the endless sound of light hammers can be heard, the old huts of peasants from the surrounding villages, the stalls and booths with merchandise and foodstuffs. . . . Once this had all throbbed with life, and today . . . it still throbs but only feebly. A young generation . . . is growing up, its meeting places are no longer the *beit midrash* or the *kloyz*;[52] only fathers and grandfathers attend them. Party battles, lamentations and quarrels [*kine un shnae*] dominate,[53] even forcefully affecting the older generation, fathers and grandfathers. [Young people] start quarrels in the chevra kadisha[54] no longer recognizing any good deeds by the "*Lines ha-Tsedek*," they quarrel all day long.[55] . . . That is how the shtetl, in which I had the honor to grow up, lives.[56]

On succeeding pages Gamalielis describes an almost ideal childhood in a home combining traditional attachment to religion with an openness toward modernity. Just as in the case of Zhanet, his home provided him conditions to grow up in that were exceptional in the poor, backward world of the shtetl. Gamalielis, although himself educated in both religious and secular subjects to be a member of the future Orthodox elite, admitted that the shtetl did not allow for secular learning.[57]

The autobiographies of Gamalielis, A Shtetleshe, and Zhanet demonstrate the limits of acceptance of the world of tradition by those participants in the YIVO competition who did not completely reject Orthodox Judaism. For these writers, religion was a value. They saw it as the core of their identity and Jewish philosophy, as a pure form of faith. However, they criticized other sides of traditional religion, such as its dogmatism, inaccessibility, and irrationalism. For them, faith and the pursuit of secular education were not mutually exclusive but rather of equal value. Religious tradition was never presented as an alternative comprehensive sociocultural model. The beginning of Gamalielis's autobiography appears to suggest his own critical attitude toward the youth world that was skeptical and politicized and attacked tradition. The Jewish small towns of interwar Poland (not to mention the Jewish districts of large cities) ceased to be an undisturbed environment of traditional religious life but were being shaken by powerful social and cultural conflicts, running frequently along the fault line dividing generations. For autobiographers the "natural," conflict-free world of the shtetl was not what they themselves personally experienced. None of the writers, even the Orthodox, yearned for the "traditional" world, understood as quite separate from the modern one. None of the submissions to the YIVO competition idealized the past; instead, they turned to the future, seeing an opportunity for themselves and for the Jewish world in its modern transformation. A minority of writers, faithful to religion, were distinguished by the fact that they also saw the negative sides of sudden modernization, admitting at the same time that one could retain Judaism only on the condition that it be reformed. According to Orthodox writers, a return to tradition was impossible as an antimodern alternative.

The autobiography by "Greyno," presented below, represents an extreme example of radical criticism of his whole surroundings. It allows us to perceive the essential differences between the religious Orthodox and the secular radicals. Despite these dissimilarities, for the most part they grew up in similar milieux, attached to tradition. Juxtaposing this typical radical autobiography with the Orthodox or conservative autobiographies presented above allows us to observe a strikingly common element in their vision of their parents' world. Greyno's autobiography includes all the threads frequently present in other works. The writer begins with a criticism of his home environment, then makes a number of generalizations about his immediate environment and draws conclusions on how the world of the future should be organized.

Greyno was born in 1911 in a small town "in which some sixty to seventy per cent were Jews,"[58] and he grew up after the First World War in Kielce, where he wrote his submission to the 1934 competition. Although he never once mentions in which specific political organization he was working, the Marxist character of his sociopolitical vision, descriptions of party activity as illegal (party meetings in the woods, frequent arrests, etc.), and his glorification of the Soviet Union show that he belonged to the Communist Party. More than likely, the writer was afraid to admit his activities in a communist organization on account of potential repercussions. Further excerpts from his autobiography describing childhood experiences supposedly unconnected with politics, as well as conditions in his immediate surroundings, reveal symbols and frameworks of thought with political significance. In Greyno's work, just as in those of many other writers, symbolic ideology, consciously used to describe reality, mingles with descriptions in which the use of ideological categories was unconscious.

Greyno's work is distinguished by its decidedly teleological character. It is written from the perspective of an adult, a supporter of radical ideology. Events in early childhood appear in this tale inevitably to lead the writer to becoming a communist, the logical consequence of growing up as a minor "Jewish proletarian." He came from a traditional Jewish family, inhabiting one of the poor Jewish areas in Kielce. In Greyno's description these living conditions led to a "bad childhood." He also included a typical criticism of his parents: an exhausted and overworked mother, showing her children no warmth, and a father steeped in prayer and divorced from reality.[59] The primitive conditions of his family life, their economic impediments, the traditional social roles of his father and mother, and their resultant personality traits were supposedly the principal reasons for Greyno's unfortunate upbringing and his resulting demoralization. When writing about a later period in his life, he describes himself as a member of a criminal gang. He himself took on the general features of his immediate situation: "brutality and sadism."[60] A principal factor forming the mentality of Jewish society, as described from the Marxist perspective, was the constant, desperate battle for the masses to satisfy their basic needs. The autobiographer shows a clear distaste—at times even disdain—for the traditional Jewish world. This negative opinion refers not only to religion and religious culture but also to clothing, appearance, careers, and "personality types." "The masses' ignorance," ridiculousness, and contemptible ways of earning a living were, in Greyno's opinion, inextricably linked with the material circumstances in which they had to live. These factors combine to produce a comprehensive, unified vision of the "old" Jewish world, serving as a negative reference point. As the epigraph of his work, Greyno selected a quotation from Gorky: "The past belongs to the dead; the future to life."[61] The picture of the writer's life presented in the autobiography arranges itself into a unified continuum of an unambiguously bad childhood in a "past world" and a biographical trajectory leading toward ever-higher levels of illegal revolutionary activity. The result is a complete rejection of tradition, an abandonment of any illusions as to the existence of God, real knowledge of the world (principally through self-education and political ideology), authentic friendships, and a comprehensive understanding of the mechanisms governing the world. In addition to the writer's descriptions of his family, the excerpt best describing his disdained past is a description of his hometown:

> I can see before me those narrow, poorly-paved little streets with their low houses, most made of wood, and Jewish stores. . . . Here is the exchange, and here are the Jews, with their heavy beards and cloth coats. Their hats sit on

their heads like lids, once black, now faded to a reddish brown in the sun. They stroll with pieces of straw in their mouths, waiting, as always, for the car to arrive from the big city. And here it comes, honking in the distance to announce its arrival. The Jews quickly swarm about it, like flies around a lump of sugar on a hot summer day.[62]

Just like those of the majority of participants in the YIVO competitions, Greyno's biography is marked by total criticism of the world of tradition.

These aforementioned descriptions reflect the processes of secularization, which were taking place on a large scale for the youngest Jewish interwar generation in Poland. However, this does not mean that they affected all or even nearly all young Jews. In excerpts of the autobiographies from the religious, Jewish Orthodoxy appears to be accompanying the processes of secularization, adapting to the challenges of modernity, developing new lifestyles, and institutionalizing new forms of its political representation. The more religiously Orthodox were, however, a minority among participants in the YIVO contest. They—and their values—were on the defensive and had to respond to antireligious social discourse that rejected all religious symbols. The secularization of the younger generation was one of the basic reasons, more or less universally accepted, for the decline of traditional social life, so deeply rooted in religion.[63] The descriptions of shtetls and Jewish areas in large cities on the verge of disintegration were often a summation of the simultaneously described processes of inertia on the part of traditional parental roles, as well as of the crisis of traditional education.

Particularly striking in the autobiographies is the stagnation and the lack of any invigorating impulse in the life of small towns, the main feature of which was their complete inability to deal with the changes around them. Data drawn from more varied and more objective sources than the autobiographies contrasts with this picture. The dissonance between the image presented in the autobiographies and other data speaks volumes to the state of young people's social consciousness. A refusal to notice changes appearing in their immediate environment, which in contrast with the values and aspirations preferred by young people could indeed be seen to be inadequate, is testimony to a radical way of looking at social reality. Toward the end of the interwar period 25 percent of Polish citizens of the Jewish faith lived in the five largest cities—Warsaw, Łódź, Kraków, Vilna, and Lviv. A further 40 percent lived in towns of more than twenty thousand inhabitants. Between the wars the majority of Polish Jews no longer lived in shtetls. As Samuel Kassow notes, despite the fact that between the wars it was the town, and not the shtetl, that was the center of Jewish life, the old nineteenth-century motif of the decline of the shtetl continued as one of the central points of Jewish discourse.[64] The shtetl, as a place in which the decline of the traditional world and its inevitable disintegration when confronted with modernity could best be seen, occupied an important place in Jewish secular literature toward the end of the nineteenth century as well as between the wars.[65]

Young people had to be especially susceptible to this kind of discourse on the collapse of the world of the shtetl, given that, in contrast to their parents, they were growing up in a new reality of modernist culture, democratic and egalitarian ideals, and universal education that strengthened individual aspirations. Pluralism and political freedom were also important. The youth—susceptible to radical rhetoric—counted on revolutionary change in the world around them and must have been affected by the image of the decline of the shtetl as a symbol of a bygone era. Even though small Jewish towns increasingly continued to lose their previous character, and that their inhabitants (especially the youth) were migrating to larger population centers, they were still an important element of the social landscape of the Second Republic. They possessed a unified social space, a network of internal relationships, norms, and institutions that had survived for centuries and that, despite the assertions of the young people already quoted, were changing in the new world and adapting to the new situation. The basic social structure of the shtetl divided its Jewish inhabitants into *sheyne yidn* ("beautiful Jews," those learned in the Torah), *balebatim, balmelokhes* (artisans), and *balegoles* (people without a trade).[66] This hierarchy supported a dense network of traditional religious institutions, such as the beit midrash, the heder, the chevra kadisha, and the rabbinate. These continued to operate between the wars and were not distinguished simply by crisis and disintegration but also had, from the point of view of nationally oriented youth, positive contributions such as social intimacy and ethnic solidarity that prevented the process of assimilation.[67]

As we have seen, these facts escaped the attention of some young people, who perhaps preferred not to see them. Traditional institutions and positions of status were perceived mainly as obstacles to professional or intellectual emancipation. What is notable too is the near-universal absence of any mention of local Jewish communities, which played an important part in the sociopolitical life of the older generations. Despite the continual existence in it of traditional institutions, the shtetl during the interwar period was losing its autonomous nature. Conditions of life were increasingly defined by new institutions such as American mutual aid societies (landsmanshaften), branches of Gemilas Chesed, political parties, or youth movements.[68] Big-city culture, both Jewish and Polish, was increasingly reaching the small towns in the form of traveling theaters, press, or literature. Libraries were opened in large numbers.[69] In their autobiographies, young authors drew attention to only some of these new institutions that were changing life in the shtetl. They wrote a great deal about political parties, youth organizations, and associated libraries. They mentioned institutions advocating radical social change, almost entirely ignoring philanthropic or self-help organizations, which genuinely improved living conditions in small towns. Most of the autobiographers were employed in workshops or small businesses, often the recipients of assistance from the Gemilas Chesed Fund, the American Jewish Joint Distribution Committee, and other institutions. However, we rarely find any mention of them in the autobiographies.[70] The absence of these elements was thus an important ideological choice.

The image of the anomie of the world of the shtetl in competition works was very similar to an analogical vision of big-city anomie. The decline of small towns symbolized the broader decline of the whole world known to these young people. In the YIVO autobiographies, we are struck by the vividness of descriptions of immediate surroundings: dirt, pain, and suffering. The immediate milieu was presented for the most part as a degenerate world. At the same time, in this respect the shtetl did not differ from a larger city. Jewish young people, irrespective of whether they grew up in a small town or in the Jewish neighborhood of a large city, were presented as alienated from the world of nature and the healthy people living in harmony with it. Interestingly enough, especially among the authors living in shtetls, who had daily contact with the world of the countryside, their quite frequent delight in nature appeared only at youth camps or the camps of youth movements and political organizations. They were thus presented in contrast to the "unnatural" style of life of the traditional Jewish world.

There can be no doubt, then, that participants in the YIVO competition came down on the modernist side of the Jewish sociopolitical discourse. In the autobiographies, shtetls and the Jewish quarters of larger cities were associated with tradition, with all that was old, in modern times useless, and thus doomed to collapse or radical transformation. Of course, new social phenomena, such as the presence of political parties (particularly relevant in small towns), could not escape the attention of young people taking part enthusiastically in their lives. In these descriptions they appeared as islands of positive modernity in a sea of the old reality's stagnation and poverty. It was mainly political ideology that furnished young people this way of looking at their own environment. In most of the YIVO autobiographies, the old world was not changing, was not evolving (although this process was in fact taking place), and was not adapting to the modern world that could develop on the ruins of traditional reality. For most autobiographers presented here, only its demise could fulfill their own life aspirations.

Marcus Moseley, analyzing the YIVO competition works as an element of the genre of the Jewish autobiography, emphasized their uniqueness, clearly distinguishing this "autobiographical" generation in the Jewish world from previous generations, for whom such features had been the preserve of only exceptional individuals.[71] However, on the basis of such a way of describing one's own experiences, imposed after all by the competition rules, it is impossible to say a great deal about the world of values (both declared and perceived) as well as the young people's state of mind. Individualism, defined by Moseley as a critical approach to the symbolic contents of the narratives saturating one's own time and place, is a very rare feature of the YIVO autobiographies. In addition to their declared respect for collective values and norms, in the quoted excerpts, the authors strikingly use this same symbolic key to attack the world of tradition—an attack launched from a position of an imagined modernist social order, organized on the basis of rational, socially just, "productive" principles exemplified in modern institutions. This type of "holism," antitraditional collectivism, and political radicalism of social opportunities is a basic feature of the young Jewish people's autobiographies. It derived directly from instructions of parties and youth movements, in whose life the young people took part, as a rule declaring absolute and uncritical loyalty toward them. Thus, it is hard to call this attitude "individualism." It was doubtless an important indicator of the radical sociopolitical awareness of the last generation of young Jewish people before the Holocaust.[72]

TWO

—⚉—

YOUNG PEOPLE'S PERSONAL AMBITIONS AND WORLD OF WORK

IN THIS CHAPTER, I TRACE the personal ambitions of YIVO autobiographers. I focus on their real as well as their ideal educational paths, their plans for their own futures, and their daily realities, especially the world of full-time work.

This chapter provides further proof of how between the wars the broadly understood processes of modernization, in both the economic and cultural spheres, left no Jewish community in the Second Republic untouched. However, I am interested less in the processes themselves and more in the way they were perceived by young people. The pressures of the ideology of radical modernism and its influence on the consciousness of young people are just as visible in individual descriptions of ambitions and the start of working life as they were in the descriptions of immediate surroundings, of parents, the heder, the shtetl, and Jewish neighborhoods. To some extent this ideology affected Jewish youth from almost all social, cultural, and political spheres. It affected the ways in which young people defined their educational and professional ambitions and their plans for the future. Also, in these parts of their autobiographies, young actors revealed that they perceived the surrounding world to be characterized by a deep, all-encompassing crisis.

Perhaps the most emphatic proof of the power of total ideology and radical modernist influence on the imagination are the autobiographies of a minority of authors who remained religious at the time when they were participating in the YIVO contest. That is why this chapter begins with an analysis of these authors' writings. Contrary to the majority, they resisted the temptation to convert to a politically radical and antireligious ideology. Nevertheless, as this chapter demonstrates, they were also impacted by radical modernism. The

45

testimonies of these individuals prove that antitraditional ideological materials reached even the most closed traditional or Orthodox communities. The autobiographers coming from these circles were in no position to free themselves from a certain modernist symbolism or did not see this as necessary. Familiarization with the experiences of these communities allows us to understand the scale of the symbolic domination of the language and values of radical modernism in the Jewish world of the Second Republic. Therefore, it is with this group that I begin a presentation of the realm of young people's individual ambitions. Later, I turn to the experiences of the secularized majority of YIVO autobiographers.

The defense of faith in the face of the secularizing influences of modernity did not mean saving all traditional institutions. Some of them had to go. The "irrational" side of Jewish tradition, based on folk beliefs, was condemned. In their submissions, the young Orthodox tried to extract from religious Judaism the spiritual and ethnic essence, the strictly religious norms, the beliefs, the world of texts and knowledge, the strictly ritual, sacral, or philosophical domains. Shorn of certain unmodern elements not drawn directly from Talmudic tradition, religion was meant to conform to models of high nonreligious culture. These two cultural models, reflected in practices and institutions—the yeshiva and the secular high school, the synagogue and the theater, Talmudic studies and critical Haskalah literature, secular Yiddish literature, and Polish and foreign literature—were to supplement one another and not oppose each other. The traditional premodern world was the alternative that no one wanted.

Despite the commonalities between religious and radically secular authors, the term *secularization* can be applied only cautiously with Orthodox authors. Its common meaning can suggest a one-dimensional and one-way process of moving from a religious ideology to a rationalist and empiricist vision of the world. For Orthodox authors, the drive for secular education, the rejection of certain traditional beliefs (for instance, the literally understood date of the earth's creation), and the condemnation of certain norms of religious life did not have to go hand in hand with a rejection of belief itself or other principles of religious life such as kashrut or daily reading of the Talmud. An empiricist adherence to the laws of nature and the laws ordering social life, in line with positivist ideology, did not necessarily have to lead to a rejection of belief in God. These authors were distinguished by an Orthodox ethos. In analyzing their autobiographies, this last term is more helpful than the more commonly used *lifestyle*. Orthodox Judaism—defined as a modernized model of the traditional religious Jewish organization of social and individual life—was developed to defend against the threat of modernity and created an exclusive way of living, defining closely which spheres of Jewish social life could intermingle with their non-Jewish surroundings and which were to remain separate.

Young people's comments on labor are a key introduction to later discussions on their impressions of a desired social order. We must examine onto what professional path those closest to them were trying to steer young people, as well as study its course, the differences between it and young people's dreams and ambitions, and finally the ways and symbolism used to describe and assess their work environments. Apart from openly ideological and political models of thinking about society and its economy, the young people in these excerpts from their autobiographies often expressed their view of the Polish state. Directly or indirectly, they judged not only its economic policies but also its attitude toward the Jewish minority. Such seemingly apolitical areas of life as the personal ambitions of young Jewish people, their lifestyle, their language of daily use, and their entertainment were the object of political rivalry between various Jewish and Polish state and party institutions. Political entities competing for influence were correct to perceive a link between young people's private life choices—in the areas of education, reading matter, work, and so forth—and their political affiliations.

THE PERSONAL AMBITIONS OF RELIGIOUS YOUNG PEOPLE

"Esther" came from an Orthodox family of the Ger Hasidim and grew up in Grójec. From the very beginning of her autobiography, she indicated her attachment to religion and her roots in the world of Hasidic orthodoxy. When she was still a child, her father hired a private melamed for her, suggesting that the family was well off and emphasized their daughter's religious education more than was typical. A breakthrough in the earliest stages of her life was a visit from the famous Sarah Schenirer to her hometown on behalf of Agudat Israel. Schenirer established a network of primary schools for Orthodox girls called Bais Yaakov.[1] Thanks to Bais Yaakov, Esther's parents were able to provide her both a modern and religious education, insulating her from secularizing threats. The author, spending her evenings in the Bais Yaakov school, attended a Jewish public school—a so-called *szabasówka*—during the day.[2]

Despite her critical attitude toward public schooling and her involvement in the life of the Bais Yaakov school and the girls' Orthodox youth organization Bnos Aguda, Esther completed public school as a model student and wanted to continue studying at the public secondary school.[3] To her enormous despair, she had to abandon this idea, since she would have had to attend school on Saturday, which was a violation of the Shabbat laws. Understanding her father's opposition to breaking religious principles, she reacted critically to his prohibition on going to the movies or the theater or taking photographs. In secret from her father, but with her mother's quiet consent, she enrolled in the library to borrow works of Polish literature.[4] The autobiographer eventually became teacher in a Bais Yaakov school. Before she began working in a school for Jewish girls, she experienced another "life tragedy" in addition to the need to abandon secondary school. Owing to her difficult financial situation, she did not have the money to pay the high fees in order to study at an Orthodox teachers' college affiliated with the Bais Yaakov network. She described her pain in typical fashion: "'Why? Why?' a voice within me cried. 'Why do I have to suffer like this, when I have such a drive to learn? Why must I suffer within the narrow confines of my limited duties, when everything in me longs for broad horizons? Why must I content myself with conforming, when I know that, given the opportunity, I can accomplish great things?' These thoughts tormented me."[5]

Esther was one of the leading activists at the local branch of Bnos Aguda. Despite being a religious person, she criticized the negative features of her environment, such as the Orthodox community's isolation from nonobservant Jews. Very important too is the gender dimension of the criticism of her own milieu that she presents in her autobiography, complaining about the limitations on her life ambitions. Both Esther and A Shtetleshe, mentioned in the previous chapter, came from religious yet also quite elitist Orthodox homes. Both young women wanted to make crucial decisions for themselves and study both religious and secular knowledge. Esther opposed any kind of external control in this matter. The individuality of Esther's autobiography appears to contest—although in a somewhat oblique manner—the social role assigned to her by Orthodox norms. At the same time, Esther's and A Shtetleshe's fortunes differed from those of girls from more traditional homes. Both of them studied in modern religious schools, which were usually unaffordable for poorer parents. Their elite background—as understood within the shtetl environment—allowed them an above-average, religiously Orthodox education, providing at the same time greater access to secular knowledge and an exposure to modernist criticism of the traditional Jewish world.

In interwar Poland, Orthodox schools for girls represented an important social innovation.[6] Without breaking the traditional prohibition on girls studying the Torah and using modern teaching methods, they provided them with the most religious education possible. Taught along progressive or reformed lines, Judaism was meant to strengthen young Jewish girls' modern religious and national self-awareness. In this way Orthodox social movements—Agudat Israel, Mizrahi, or the many rabbis operating outside political parties—tried to prevent the growing acculturation and secularization of future Jewish wives and mothers. However, the Orthodox education of girls continued to be a conservative education, aiming above all to preserve the traditional social roles of Jewish women. Learning, religious as well as secular, still did not have any intrinsic value for them but was meant to preserve their attachment to religious society and help them raise children to be true Orthodox Jews. Self-fulfillment, an individual career, and ambitions were alien values not only for the traditional but also for the Orthodox woman. She was to subordinate herself to the interests of the religious community and on a practical level to the whims of men. A woman was unable to fill independent or leadership social roles.[7] Esther's and A Shtetleshe's autobiographies are examples of situations in which the Orthodox education of girls led to them developing modern ambitions, which were also turning against certain Orthodox norms and values. This critical and combative attitude to the world of tradition and Orthodoxy also characterized religious boys participating in the YIVO competition.

"Henekh" came from the northeast border regions of interwar Poland. He spent his early childhood in a closed Orthodox world. At the age of twelve, he was sent to a yeshiva in Grodno, and two years later he entered an elite yeshiva in Raduń, where the principal authority was the famous Chofetz Chaim.[8] Before leaving home and still during his first years at the yeshiva, Henekh fully respected the traditional norms and symbols of the religious world.[9] His first doubts as to the soundness of its basic principles appeared during his studies at yeshiva.[10] Seeking "rational"—that is, "modern"—foundations for social norms, according to which he wished to direct his life, he criticized the institution of the yeshiva from a utilitarian and modernist perspective. Henekh criticized the religious institution for developing passive attitudes in young people, psychological weakness, and a lack of practical skills. In his description, the yeshiva in Grodno perpetuated the negative sides of traditional society. Interestingly enough, and as testimony to the author's highly complex self-awareness, he appears to suggest that despite its deleterious features, the institution of the yeshiva and its Litvak rite, famous for its emphasis on intellectualism and rationalism, had developed within him a passion for critical and profound analysis that paradoxically led him to criticize the institution itself for its scholastic education bereft of important knowledge about the modern world.[11]

Eventually, Henekh's initial worldview collapsed after the start of his studies at the famous yeshiva in Raduń, which, despite his expectations, turned out to be much worse than the one in Grodno.[12] His personal successes at school paralleled his growing disillusionment and criticism of the whole system of social relationships existing in the Raduń school. He condemned the well developed "spy" network catching all sorts of transgressions among the yeshiva students,[13] as well as the glaring examples of economic inequality between the students and the establishment's administration.[14] As was typical, the successive stages of the author's secularization led him not to abandon the Jewish faith but to renounce the Orthodox way of life. Initially out of defiance but later with great interest, Henekh began to read *Haynt*.[15] His developing hunger for secular knowledge was for the time being satisfied by the Haskalah scientific encyclopedia and the religious philosophes of *Sefer ha-brit* (The book of the Covenant).[16] He gradually began to develop a reputation among his peers and was seen as someone with extensive knowledge. For that reason people "drawn close to Haskalah" sought out his companionship.[17] Meanwhile, he was ordained as a rabbi. At this time the group of yeshiva students gathered around Henekh and others set up a secret study group that met in the woods. Interestingly enough, the students undertaking this serious infraction against the rules governing the yeshiva described themselves as "maskilim," using the nineteenth-century term.[18] The group was uncovered by the spy network that monitored yeshiva students' adherence to Orthodoxy. Soon thereafter, Henekh abandoned the yeshiva, moved to Warsaw, and tried to start a new life.[19]

"Etonis," like Henekh, came from the northeastern region of the country from a small town in the Nowogródek province on the border with the USSR. He studied in yeshivas in Raduń and Baranowicze and spent the last stage of his life before writing his autobiography in Vilna. The boy began his education at the age of three in a modernized heder, in which Hebrew was taught as a modern national language. Etonis's Litvak and Orthodox milieu appeared to share a conviction on the basic compatibility of deeply religious attitudes and modernity in the guise of modern nationalism with the new Hebrew culture born in the nineteenth century.[20] Alongside his studies in the heder between 1918 and 1920, Etonis took lessons in Russian, arithmetic, and geography with a private tutor.[21] Probably under the influence of his family and teachers, his early readings came from the first generation of Jewish nationalists, such as Smolenskin and Berdichevsky, who treated traditional Judaism extremely critically.[22] Later, when Etonis began studying in the yeshiva, the rabbi pointed out to his father the harmfulness of these kinds of books. As he wrote, "Father, however, was not a fanatic," and continued to allow him to read this literature, although it emerges that both father and son were religious Jews in the full meaning of that word. The description of the environment in which Etonis was growing up suggests its relatively gentle adaptation to modern changes. Nonetheless, the society in which he lived was still deeply religious. While writing his autobiography, the author retained his loyalty to Orthodox Judaism despite many moments of doubt. In further sections of his account, he lists "threats" to his own religious faith and that of those around him. For Etonis and his friends, this was a major challenge. The modernization of the author's social milieu between the wars took on an added urgency.

At the age of twelve, as one of the brightest students in the heder and devoted to religion, Etonis entered the yeshiva in Baranowicze at his father's urging.[23] He wrote that the loneliness he felt in this strange place led him to return home and continue his studies in the beit midrash.[24] After spending a year at home and at the insistence of the local rabbi, who argued that young people living with their parents are likely to "be spoiled," he returned to the yeshiva in Baranowicze. He was already for the first time thinking of dropping his Talmudic studies in favor of a secular education. He did not abandon this idea during the next few semesters in the yeshiva, in which, under the influence of a friend studying there ("acknowledged to be a heretic"), he began to view the Orthodox world around him more critically, to read secular newspapers, and to become more interested in politics and secular Hebrew and Yiddish Jewish literature.[25] Etonis remained in the yeshiva in Baranowicze until 1926. During vacations he would return home, where attitudes had changed greatly. Some of his formerly religious friends were now in business; others had begun studies at the Hebrew teachers' college or at secondary school. The author himself remained a religious person despite peer pressure. At the end of his autobiography, he summed up his life thus:

> Several years passed. I became older, wiser, more mature. I experienced many inner struggles. More than once I stood on the brink of abandoning my faith, on the verge of crossing the threshold. And yet, at the last moment, I would step back and throw myself once more into the whirl of yeshiva life. I experienced a great deal during the years 1927–1930. I underwent more profound internal development. I had the opportunity to discover the great wide world. In 1928 I spent a few weeks in the bustling town of Sopot.[26] I saw with my own eyes what life is like in the world today. And after all these encounters and struggles, I still retained my deep religious convictions.[27]

One of the last passages in Etonis's recollections is a description of some recent life decisions and plans for the future:

> Finally, after much consideration and introspection, I did not return to yeshiva in the winter of 1931–1932. I stayed in our town, where I found a position teaching Jewish religion in public school. I began to study secular subjects on my own. . . . I wanted to complete the entire course of studies in secondary school [*gymnazjum*]. . . . I decided to move to the city. And so this past summer I came to Vilna, where I prepared myself for eight grades of secondary school, working hard all summer. Of all my studies, I most enjoyed the poetry of Mickiewicz, which often stirred my own suffering soul.[28]

Etonis's narrative is a description of changing life goals aimed at becoming a modern, self-reflective person, conscious of his own roots in the surrounding social reality and resultant conditions. Individualism and a critical attitude toward both the world of the yeshiva and the lure of modernity became important values for Etonis. The way to cultivate them was through knowing the world—knowledge of politics, literature, and so on—and, as he wrote, "seeing how people live today with my own eyes," which could be achieved by acquiring a secular education and working in the public school system. A modern, reflective attitude would enable Etonis to assess critically both the world of tradition and the threats of modernity while remaining an emancipated yet also a religious Jew.

"M. W." was born in 1916 in Dobre, a small town not far from Warsaw. Like most of the authors whose autobiographies I discuss in this part of the chapter, he came from a traditional elite. He was the son of the local rabbi.[29] His father's early death destroyed the family's happiness. His mother's resourcefulness (she opened a beer hall with which she supported herself and her children) saved the day, as did the family's traditional prestige (*yikhes*), as well as a vacancy for the father's position of rabbi. The autobiographer's sister, with this specific legacy in her dowry, was married off to a candidate for the position of rabbi, who became the next rabbi of Dobre. The family's relatively good financial position came to an end, however, with the outbreak of the Polish-Bolshevik war of 1920. Within a short space of time, three of his relatives died. In 1923, when M. W. was seven years old, his mother decided to move to Warsaw with her children in order to support the family. In the capital the boy began his studies in a heder, which he criticized mercilessly in his autobiography.[30] He then studied in a Talmud Torah, where he was one of the best students and enjoyed the title of *masmid*.[31] His experience of studying in this establishment was accompanied by observations of the elementary school next door: "We, the children in the heder, looked enviously at the students in this school, who attended for only a half-day, spending the rest at play, while we had to spend the whole day within the confines of the heder."[32] M. W. clearly yearned for a real childhood, for dances, for parties accessible to children from a modern world that was so distant from him. His new friends from the neighboring school impressed him enormously. Playing with them, he began to be ashamed of his traditional clothes and sidelocks. His mother severely punished him for exchanging his yarmulke for a school cap and once again when he ran away from the heder.[33]

At this stage in his life, the author was close to abandoning religion. The situation was saved by his mother's decision to move him from the Talmud Torah to the Hasidic heder Amud ha-Torah at Nalewki, a main street of the Jewish neighborhood of Warsaw. As he emphasized with pride, his friends were the smartest students among the Hasidim. In this environment, M. W. once again turned to his religious studies with a vengeance. They became his whole world, in which he could forget about his difficult material circumstances. He completed the four-year course at Amud ha-Torah in two years as a star student.[34] At the age of twelve, M. W. began his studies in "Mesivte Yeshiva."[35] Even before his fourteenth birthday, he began further studies with his brother-in-law, the rabbi in Dobre. The final stage of his religious education was a year in the Torat Chaim yeshiva, under the direction of the son-in-law of the famous "brisker rebe."[36] According to M. W., the underlying value of this stage of his studies was not religious knowledge per se but a mastery of the principles of "analytical thought," subjecting the religious texts and himself to "real-life" and "analytical" questions.[37] His studies in this yeshiva were a watershed moment in the author's life. There he met a friend, with whom he worked on his religious studies. However, with time their conversations and interests began to head toward other issues: "During our studies we began to talk about all sorts of things. We talked about science, technology and secular education, and in all these subjects my friend was seven times more competent than me. Over the course of a single month devoted in particular to biology my friend learned so much that I was quite simply jealous. It was then that a calling to [illegible] began to develop within me, so I would have to abandon [illegible] and enter another world of education and science."[38]

As a result of this ideological watershed, M. W. left the Torat Chaim yeshiva. At the age of sixteen, he received a certificate from the Warsaw rabbinate entitling him to teach religion in schools run by a local Jewish community. He had been judged the best of six students examined. He was proud of being a "certified teacher" and devoted himself to studying the secular subjects that interested him at the time. He ended his autobiography declaring that his principal goal in life was to become learned in the Torah and in secular subjects.[39]

This modern character of Jewish Orthodoxy clearly seen in the autobiography of M. W., the type that was born and was developing in the Second Republic, is splendidly portrayed in another autobiography whose author used the pseudonym "Damaszek." He was born into a family with rabbinical traditions in 1911 in "the small town of K" (referring to Kałusz, a county town in Stanisławów province, in southeastern Poland and today Kalush in Ukraine). His father and grandfather were kosher butchers, who also carried out various other duties in the local Jewish community. His mother and grandmother ran the home. Writing his autobiography as a young member of Agudat Israel,

describing his childhood and the attitudes prevailing in his family, he emphasized its harmony, based on patriarchal respect, obedience, and tradition.
Like those of most of the Orthodox autobiographers, his family was wealthy.[40]
At the age of three or four, he began his studies in the heder. From the start
he showed a great aptitude for religious studies, since at the age of barely five
he started studying the Pentateuch (the Chumash). Damaszek noted at the
same time, "My parents did not want to enroll me in a school, claiming that it
was not seemly for the son of a kosher butcher to walk around without a cap,
and since I was exhibiting signs of ability, they taught me at home to read and
write in Polish, as well as elementary mathematics, which I managed to master
quite quickly so that I was able to read and write fluently in Polish."[41] In his
elite (at least in terms of the shtetl) family circumstances, there was no specific
fear of non-Jewish studies but rather of non-Jewish secularizing institutions.
Eventually, Damaszek entered the third grade of a public elementary school
after the war, in 1918 or 1919 (he did not give a reason for his parents' change of
heart in this matter). After completing fourth grade of elementary school, he
began studying at a business school in Drohobycz, where he earned a diploma
in 1923. After completing this stage in his education, he successfully continued
his Talmudic studies.[42]

A watershed in Damaszek's life came in 1923. It was then that Rabbi
Hirschhorn came to Kałusz from Lviv with the aim of establishing a branch of
Agudat Israel and its youth organization Tse'irei Agudat Israel (Young Agudat).[43] Damaszek from the very beginning was one of the emerging leaders in
this latter organization. Summing up the role that this organization played in
his life, he describes well the secularizing "spirit of the age" with which young
Jewish people coming from traditional homes had to grapple (and which most
of the autobiographers were unable to resist): "Generally speaking, I'm grateful
to this organization for my mental and intellectual development as well as my
whole store of knowledge of old Hebrew literature, and thanks to it I became
a one-hundred-per-cent religious Jew, not allowing myself to be seduced by
the evil currents of the time, and thus I shall always be grateful to it and in the
future a loyal member of it."[44]

The author's religiousness had been saved by an Orthodox organization.
One of this institution's overriding aims was a modern reorganization of the
religious lifestyle and social forms of cultivating tradition. The organizing principle of Tse'irei Aguda called for a democratically elected board and a clear division of positions. One of them was that of treasurer, which the autobiographer,
a graduate of a business school, held for some time. The organization gave him
an opportunity to use his secular professional skills in the service of Jewish

Orthodoxy. Damaszek dreamed of further secular education and obtaining his high school diploma. His religious father opposed his son studying at secondary school. The final pages of his autobiography are a record of the years of struggling with the vagaries of fate and sacrifices on the road to achieving this dream. Damaszek completed the course on his own at a secular secondary school and earned his degree as an external student.[45]

Damaszek of course took his external state diploma in Polish. Between the wars it had become the national language, command of which was a key access point to secular knowledge. To what extent secular knowledge and culture were penetrating even communities trying to distance themselves as much as possible from them can be seen in "Yehezkel Twerski's" autobiography. Yehezkel, aged twenty-two at the time he wrote his piece, worked as hard as possible to conceal his participation in the competition. As he explained in 1959 to a YIVO employee in New York, his autobiography had been three-quarters true, although he "had added one or two things" in order to conceal its authorship.[46] He probably concealed his identity because in his milieu of Belz Hasidim, corresponding with a secular Jewish institution was viewed very critically.[47] Just as in other similar autobiographies, the veracity of specific facts is less important than the author's views.

Yehezkel Twerski was born in 1917 in Prague, where his parents had fled during World War I. He came from an eminent rabbinical family. His mother was a granddaughter of the Belz rebe and a devoted supporter of this branch of Hasidism.[48] A large segment of the autobiography is a description of his mother dominating the home, whose character had been conditioned at it were by Belz Hasidism. Unlike his father, who as a young man had also been interested in secular studies, his mother was opposed to all innovations coming from outside the Jewish world. In 1922, together with his family, he returned to Belz. Initially, his parents ensured that Yehezkel received a religious education and upbringing. The boy studied in heders and with a melamed, who at the instigation of the local rabbi taught the five cleverest boys (coming from the local traditional religious elite). The young children were intensively taught the Talmud, preparing themselves for a rabbinical career. What is important for my study is the first of several segments of autobiography devoted to the conflict between his parents on Yehezkel's educational path. When he was twelve years old (thus a year before achieving traditional maturity), his father wanted to employ an additional teacher to teach the state Polish language as well as the grammar and orthography of the Jewish languages: Yiddish and Hebrew. His mother protested violently. Despite the fact that Yehezkel himself supported his father's suggestion, neither for the first nor the last time this "daughter of Belz" carried the day.[49] Later his mother successfully blocked her son's studies in an Aguda school in Zamość.[50] Her main complaint about this school was that it taught Polish. The author presented his lack of opportunities to study secular subjects as a personal tragedy, for which intensive Talmudic studies were only partial compensation.[51]

A further long passage in his autobiography describes studying at the yeshiva in Trzebinia and the evolution of the author's personal religious affiliations from Belz Hasidism to Bobov Hasidism.[52] The author accurately recreated the stereotype of Galician Hasidism—irrational, less intellectual, less open to the world—from which he himself came. He wrote of the Bobov Hasidim that what attracted him was "their order, organization, especially their young people and how they stuck together. Among them were many of those who had returned to the path of faith."[53] The most important feature of Bobov Hasidism, which in the autobiographer's opinion represented a definite advantage over the Belz version, was its modernity and openness to the surrounding world. Just as the previously quoted authors did, Yehezkel Twerski protested at the strict supervision of yeshiva students. Despite seeing the yeshiva in Trzebinia as more open and modern than his home background, he also criticized this institution for aiming at too strict a control over its students. One of its students, Aaron Teitelbaum, the son of a rabbi from Częstochowa, was removed from the yeshiva having been caught in a nighttime conversation with his landlord's daughter. Reading secular books or even having "simple conversations" was seen to be sinful, as was listening to the radio or reading Jewish national papers such as *Haynt* and *Der Moment*.[54]

After completing the yeshiva and receiving his rabbinical certificate, Yehezkel returned to Zamość. The final piece of his autobiography is a significant description of the crisis of the traditional world and the mass abandonment of religion by young people. Yehezkel, a son under the immense influence of his anti-Aguda mother, tried to establish a local Agudat Israel branch in order to save young Jews' religion. Similar to his earlier adoption of the modern Hasidism of Bobov, he now believed the road to salvation was Aguda's "organization and order."[55] This participant in the YIVO competition, growing up in one of the most separatist Hasidic communities, tried to save Judaism just as the Orthodox Litvaks described above did—by the use of a careful and selective openness to elements of the modern secular world.

A NEW POLISH ORTHODOXY?

The group of autobiographies presented above represented a varied spectrum of Jewish Orthodoxy in the Second Republic. We encountered reports by people coming from a Litvak background, some of whom were engaged in religious and Zionist activities for the Mizrahi party, Hasidic Orthodoxy based on Agudat Israel, or, as in the case of Yehezkel Twerski, an ultra-Orthodox community that was hostile to the too-liberal Aguda. These different communities were characterized by different tempos and forms of modernization. As I remarked in the book's introduction, the young Orthodox described above who took part in the YIVO competition definitely did not constitute a group of average representatives of their milieux. They were critical of their own surroundings, often on the verge of breaking with them. Nonetheless, the common features of these religious autobiographers indicate the general direction in which some of the younger Polish Jewish Orthodox were headed. On the basis of an analysis of the YIVO autobiographies, it is impossible to state what percentage of young Orthodox growing up in interwar Poland were affected by this direction. Doubtless, however, it is possible to speak of an important trend straddling the borders of various Orthodox communities (including those in Galicia, central Poland, and the so-called Kresy, as well as Litvaks and Hasidim). In the 1930s this trend was barely beginning and was interrupted at the outset by the Holocaust.

The autobiographies of young Orthodox, like those of their secular and politically radicalized peers, were distinguished by a modernist consciousness. It represented a preference for social order and for institutions regulated along rational principles, which were to be generated by secular, institutionalized, scientific knowledge. Typical of the autobiographies of students in heders and yeshivas, rabbinical candidates, teachers, and tutors of religious subjects is a conviction that negatively assessed institutions of traditional religious education should adhere to these principles, thanks to which they were to be transformed into modern Orthodox institutions. As we have seen, this modernist approach also influenced personal life paths and educational choices.

What is striking in the majority of Orthodox autobiographies, or those by authors who continue to declare a personal relationship with religion, is the very high prestige of institutionalized, secular education. On the one hand, what was important for them was the maskilic, individualistic model of acquiring secular knowledge, based mainly on broad, unstructured reading. As we have seen, to achieve this model, they often had to break rules imposed on them by their traditional surroundings. On the other hand, they strove for or dreamed of acquiring a formal, secular education. Esther dreamed of studying in a secular secondary school (studying secular subjects in the Bais Yaakov teachers' college, which was like a secondary school). For Henekh and Etonis (both Litvaks) or Damaszek (a Galician Hasid), an important, if not the most important, stage on the road to forming their adult lives was the high school qualification (*matura*). M. W. was proud of his certificate from the Warsaw religious community permitting him to teach Judaism in elementary schools.

The ideal path to educating Orthodox authors thus embraced three systems of knowledge—for young people complementary, for the older generations often conflicting. They were the traditional system based on the Torah and Talmud; the Haskalah system based on the modern Hebrew language, national literature, and biblical exegesis; and the third, a universal system. We can add to the last one secular sciences, Jewish and non-Jewish secular literature, and non-Jewish languages being an important access point to secular knowledge, of which the most important for young Orthodox growing up in the Second Republic was Polish. The popularity of the second system, based on self-improvement in the spirit of nineteenth-century central European supporters of the Haskalah, the maskilim, is particularly striking. Although the Haskalah as an intellectual movement in eastern Europe had ended fifty to seventy years before the young Orthodox were writing their autobiographies (and in central Europe even earlier), what is striking in them is the popularity and resilience of a lifestyle model in the form of the maskil, already referenced by Henekh, Etonis, and M. W. It probably spoke to them so powerfully because, like the real maskilim preceding them by several decades, the young Orthodox participating in the YIVO competition for the most part were the first members of their own families to lay down a challenge to the traditional way of life, wishing to gain secular knowledge and to live differently from their parents. Of great significance here is opposition to the "ignorant" and "irrational" life represented by the world of their parents, which linked them directly to the principal current of the Haskalah wishing to "cleanse" Judaism of superstitions and nonrational beliefs.[56] This type of selective criticism of the traditional world was also undertaken by students of Orthodox yeshivas (M. W.), Agudat Israel activists (Damaszek), and Yehezkel Twerski, who did not see themselves as maskilim. Likewise, their attitudes, which they express in their autobiographies, were characterized by a modernist consciousness urging a criticism of selective elements of Jewish tradition, which were impossible to reform through modernity.

For the group of authors presented here, retaining their religion in its basically modern, Orthodox form required wide-ranging intellectual abilities and a critical and individualistic approach to the social and political ideologies of the day. It appears that this kind of individualism, based on a higher-than-average level of religious and secular education, broad reading, and hard personal intellectual development work, prevented the first group from being absorbed by one of the radical ideologies, unlike so many other contestants in the YIVO competition also coming from religious homes. Individualism, intellectualism, and a high level of secular and religious knowledge meant that they were no less critical toward radical, secular ideologies. In the autobiographies of young Orthodox, descriptions of the surrounding world were less apocalyptic, and the fulfillment of their individual ambitions did not depend on the success of a nationalist or socialist revolution. Politics and significant events, which were accorded great weight on the secular Jewish Street, were of burning interest to yeshiva students, girls studying in Bais Yaakov schools, and young people studying in beit midrashes. Nevertheless, broad cultural capital meant that political ideologies did not have special status for them, did not represent a way of living, and were not the dominant source for acquiring knowledge of the world. If this group of young people had any specific political sympathies, they oscillated between Aguda, Mizrahi, or centrist Zionism.

Of particular significance here too is the selection of professional paths by young Orthodox. Most people from this community who took part in the YIVO competition were hoping to become rabbis or teachers of religion in public or Jewish private schools. Working in these professions entailed an acceptance of the political system in which public and private Jewish establishments supervised by the state operated, thus precluding any questioning of it. It is particularly important that, on the one hand, these authors were determined to become acquainted with and internalize elements of Polish national culture, while, on the other, feeling themselves to be Orthodox Jews, they likewise did not question the ethnic character of this culture or the nationalist character of the Polish state. The subject of antisemitism and a sense of rejection arising from the ethnic nature of the Polish state and Polish culture occupied a central place in the vast majority of the autobiographies. The only autobiographers who did not mention antisemitism or a sense of rejection were the Orthodox.

Do the autobiographies of the minority of contestants in the YIVO competition who had remained religious add something new to our knowledge of interwar Polish Jewish Orthodoxy? What potentially new avenues of research on this society do these autobiographies indicate? In east-central Europe of the 1930s, being a religious Jew following Halakhic principles, fully acknowledging the authority of rabbis and religious tradition, was no longer a choice without any alternatives. Orthodox Judaism was a phenomenon born out of modern change, a response to secularization and competition in the guise of various alternative forms of Jewish identity. In these new times, to defend traditional Judaism, it was essential to establish new organizational principles for the world of religion and to build new de facto modern, institutionalized forms and social norms. As early as the nineteenth century, traditional Jewish elites had begun to transform themselves into a modern Orthodoxy. The difference between tradition and Orthodoxy lay in the fact that the latter was fully conscious of the modern changes occurring around it and tried to take advantage of certain elements of modernity in order to counteract its other negative effects.

On Polish lands the culmination of many attempts at a modern defense of tradition was the uprising in 1912 and the development of the Agudat Israel party. Aguda was a world organization of Jewish Orthodoxy, and between the wars its center was the Second Republic. The mass political party with its press, Orthodox schooling, and youth and children's movements was without doubt modern. Supervised by Aguda, modern institutions imitated the activities of similar secular and radical Jewish political parties and were meant to neutralize the latter's supposedly negative influence on Jewish youth. A quite separate element of Orthodox educational and social policy was the system of Talmudic higher institutions of learning—the yeshivas. Originating in the Middle Ages yet reborn only in the nineteenth century, these institutions of Talmudic higher studies had a modern character. Their aim was to educate future Orthodox elites. The yeshivas were to replace traditional forms of education in the beit midrashes (houses of study). Partly copied directly from secular universities, modern methods of teaching and organization (including cafeterias and residence halls) and supervision of young people were to weed out those who were not true believers and to strengthen faith and students' sense of exceptionalism and uniqueness. Only this future elite of new Jewish religious generations could ensure the survival of Judaism in its conservative, reformed, and traditional (in other words, Orthodox) form.[57]

The basic principle organizing social norms among the majority of interwar Polish Orthodox communities was their separation from the influences of their Jewish and non-Jewish surroundings threatening their religious values. Aguda and even more conservative ultra-Orthodox groups had bred a separatist type of eastern European Orthodoxy. The non-Hasidic Jewish Litvak elites from Vilna, Nowogródek, Białystok, Polesie, and Volhynia had a different character. The intermingling of complicated historical circumstances meant that the Litvaks were far more receptive to secular elements coming from surrounding cultures. In the nineteenth century, civilizational trends such as secularization and acculturation (to German and later Russian culture) had a strong impact, and various forms of Jewish nationalism were also more popular there. Between the wars the Zionist-religious Mizrahi party represented the open elements of Litvak Orthodoxy.[58] Its more conservative elements were breaking down their traditional dislike of Hasidic Aguda and in the 1930s were entering the ranks of the party. However, there also existed in Litvak Judaism an extremist wing, focused on the Musar movement, aiming at the ruthless separation of its members from the secular world.[59]

The principle of the activities of the Orthodox institutions dominating interwar Poland was based on building a wall of modern organizations conserving traditional values. To be sure, young people from Aguda schools (Horev and Bais Yaakov) also studied secular subjects, such as Polish, mathematics, history, and Polish geography.[60] Some Litvak and Hasidic yeshivas introduced into their curricula the study of secular subjects. However, what was meant to distinguish this community was control of all "foreign" contents.[61] Between the wars Agudat Israel promoted its ideology of the "Torah Worldview" (*Da'at Torah*). In the face of the collapse of traditional sources of rabbinical authority, the party announced a dogma of the infallibility of Torah wise men in subjects not only affecting religious law—Halakha—but extending also to all areas of private and social life (including politics). According to this ideology, being a member of an Orthodox community meant not only adherence to commandments and traditional forms of cultivating them but also subordinating oneself to the religious as well as the secular authority of rabbis.[62] Gershon Bacon pointed out that interwar Hasidism, conscious of secularizing threats—unlike in the nineteenth century, when only an adult, married man could become a Hasid in the full sense of the word—now began to actively include far younger people in its ranks, teenagers still in school and without families and even boys below the age of ten. This inclusion was carried out by the far more frequent participation of sons in their fathers' pilgrimages to the courts of the tsadikim, special supervision of young people studying in *shtiblekh*, and encouraging young people to combat the temptation presented by secular Jewish political movements.[63] All these features of Jewish Orthodoxy on Polish lands testify to the fact that despite the signs of modernity, they had an unambiguously separatist character different from the more open type (for instance, in nineteenth-century Germany). Its norms were formed mainly by religious elites personified by famous tsadikim, rabbis, and principals of yeshivas. They were the ones to create the sources on which we base all our current knowledge about interwar Orthodoxy.

The classical works of Gershon Bacon, Saul Stampfer, and Ben-Zion Klibanski, mentioned above, as well as the latest research by Bacon, Glenn Dynner, Wojciech Tworek, and Naomi Seidman show the durability of interwar Polish Orthodoxy or traditionalism more broadly and the innovativeness of its elite in the form of multilayered, planned adaptation to the challenges of interwar modernity. Their work has focused on the institutional dimension of these modernizing, adaptive processes, on the spheres of politics and education.

They show just how the Orthodox political parties, their youth movements, and their educational institutions (from the heder to the yeshiva) promoted a modern vision of Orthodox collectivism and an awareness of the importance for religious Jews to abide by Orthodox norms and not question the authority of the Orthodox elites for the survival of the community in times of a universal secularizing threat.[64] We still do not have any studies showing how these norms, promoted and imposed by modern Orthodox institutions, operated at the level of daily culture; whether, when, and how these norms were questioned; and whether Orthodox collectivism was not accompanied by the new generation's growing individualism.[65]

The YIVO autobiographies from the youngest generation of Polish Orthodoxy show that in the 1930s this type of separatist and collectivist model was being questioned with growing regularity and by those who still wished to remain Orthodox Jews. The young people described above criticized not only certain elements of the unreformed tradition but also at least some elements of Orthodox separatism. The fact that this was being done by young people from various Hasidic and Litvak backgrounds, coming often from very distant places, testifies to the generational change taking place within the Polish Orthodox Jewish community. A point of contention between some of the young generation and their parents, rabbis, staff in the yeshivas, and the Orthodox political parties or youth movements was the separation of the youngest generations from people, institutions, and lifestyle elements that could be expose them to secularizing threats. In all the autobiographies analyzed here, this kind of separatism was questioned. This opposition undermined one of the fundamentals of Orthodox ideology. Young people were modern individualists; they rejected the rabbinical authorities' absolute control over their lives and guidance extending beyond religious matters. Contestants in the YIVO competition clearly suggested that while they were religious people, abiding strictly by Halakhic principles and the Orthodox lifestyle, what they were reading, how they attempted to acquire an education, and what they were doing in their free time were private matters and should not come under the control of the religious authorities. These kinds of views, evident in the autobiographies, spoil the image of the unified separatist character of Jewish Orthodoxy in interwar Poland, testifying to a much greater openness to secular education, to work, and to moving in social space (e.g., public secondary schools) than we have hitherto known. Perhaps—and this problem calls for much more detailed research—in 1930s Poland, in addition to the separatist type, a new, more open sort of Orthodox lifestyle and identity was developing, but it was hitherto more associated with German or American Judaism rather than Polish Judaism.[66]

It appears that the somewhat exceptional features of the religious minority of contestants in the YIVO competitions say a great deal too about the conditions in which interwar Jewish Orthodoxy operated in Poland and about the size of the challenges facing it. Almost all the young people who wrote their autobiographies and sent them to Vilna came from traditional, religious homes. At the same time, however, at the time of the competition they had abandoned religion. Only the minority of young Orthodox described above still adhered to it. This testifies above all to the power of interwar secularization affecting the Polish Jewish community. The defense of religion now required equipping a young person with relatively high cultural and symbolic capital, with many years of education at expensive, superior heders and yeshivas, depending on the relative separation from the surrounding secular world filled with temptation. Providing such an educational path for their children was for the most part out of the question for minor Jewish merchants, artisans, and people without any specific profession. All the religious authors quoted here had been studying for over a dozen years (starting at the age of three in a heder), usually not taking on any paid employment before the age of eighteen. They were the children of wealthy merchants, rabbis, and synagogue vergers, people coming from communities associated with the traditional elite and the religious establishment. Only a very large investment in studies at elite establishments, as well as their parents' above average cultural capital, could get children to retain their faith. The professional literature, pointing to the successes of interwar Jewish Orthodoxy, draws our attention to the fact that, toward the end of the 1930s, for around thirty thousand Jewish students in secondary schools there were twenty thousand students in yeshivas. Considering the fact that religious girls could not study in yeshivas, this is an impressive figure.[67] Such a large number of students in yeshivas was a new phenomenon, characteristic of the interwar years. However, we must always remember that most Jewish children in interwar Poland attended neither a secondary school nor a yeshiva. The heder, in which they studied at a very young age, did not protect against secularization. None of the several dozen authors analyzed who came from traditionally religious yet poor homes were religious while they were writing their autobiographies. They all kept their distance from Jewish Orthodoxy. Of course, one hundred autobiographies written for a specific competition do not represent the whole religious Jewish community, yet they undoubtedly reflect a significant trend within it. The silent traditional majority of religious Jews in east-central Europe between the wars was turning into an Orthodox minority.

THE AMBITIONS OF SECULAR AUTOBIOGRAPHERS

The examples described above of Orthodox paths to fulfilling one's own life ambitions did not apply to most of the autobiography writers. An important feature of the Jewish community in the Second Republic, inherited from earlier times, was the social and economic distance between the traditional elites, where financial capital flowed smoothly into social capital (for instance, the daughters of wealthy men married candidates for rabbi), and the traditionally poor Jews. Children from poor Jewish homes began working at a very young age. Despite having the same educational aspirations as young people from wealthier homes, after a hard day's work they had neither the time nor the energy for individual self-improvement. These young people usually fulfilled their desire to acquire knowledge and achieve their life ambitions in the world of politics, as we shall see below.

The value of a secular education was important even for those whose material conditions frankly precluded any chances of achieving this goal. An extreme example is "Garner Borysław." He came from the socially most disadvantaged Jewish community, the luftmenschen—people with no steady occupation, from time to time taking on any work they could get. He was sent to the heder at the age of four. He went to elementary school at the age of eight, a year later than was the rule; he eventually did not even complete third grade. His school experiences, written in terrible Polish, without punctuation, filled with orthographic mistakes and Yiddishisms, show the tragic life of a child coming from the depths of society. The quotations presented below clearly indicate that the writer's everyday language was Yiddish. He wrote his autobiography in Polish, since this was probably the only language in which he had ever learned to write.

Recalling his first years of school, Garner described hunger, the lack of warm clothes allowing him to go to school in winter, and the lack of school supplies.[68] His father withdrew him from formal education in the third grade, since he needed his son to help him work as a porter. The writer's later fortunes were a sequence of humiliations associated with a series of short-term jobs and looking for them in Kraków and Lviv.[69] His autobiography is a textbook example of the reproduction of a generational life trajectory of someone born on the social margins. This also prevented him from taking part in Jewish youth organizations.[70] Even in his difficult situation, the author never abandoned his humble educational aspirations, requiring enormous sacrifice. At the age of thirteen, while looking for work in Kraków, he searched for something that could also give him a chance for an education, which eventually turned out to be impossible.[71] Garner Borysław, like his father, became a big-city luftmensch. What distinguished him from his parents' and grandparents' generations were modern ambitions, validated by graduation from a secular school. His social background and the financial circumstances in which he lived did not allow him to achieve this.

We find a similar theme in the autobiography of "Ben-Ish-Kal," a Litvak from Święciany, coming from a completely different background from Garner Borysław. Ben-Ish-Kal studied in heders and later in a Tarbut Hebrew Jewish secondary school. He described in a typical manner his own life and his own unfulfilled life ambitions. Thanks to his poor family's efforts, he managed to complete secondary school. Unable to count on any further education, he began to work as a clerk in a local Jewish bank, looking for a better life in the local branch of Ha-Shomer ha-Tsa'ir and working on behalf of the Jewish national fund (KKL—Keren Kayemet le-Israel) and the local Tarbut library. He wrote that his life was marked by general stagnation. He was disgusted by the corruption of his bosses in the bank and their cozying up to the local Sanacja elite. Ben-Ish-Kal was frustrated by the lack of means to help poor Jewish artisans and merchants, the inability to work for a better life for everyone, and the lack ways to achieve his own ambitions in the form of studying and finding a better job. Replying to his own dramatically phrased question—"Where to?"—he decided to leave for the Soviet Union, the one place that, in his opinion, represented the chance for a better life. Arrested immediately after crossing the border, Ben-Ish-Kal spent several months in Soviet and then Polish prisons. He did not find his holy grail in the USSR. He saw his only chance to change his drastic fortunes as a Jew and as a poor person in "real socialism" (or rather "real communism"), which did not exist in Poland and which he had not found in the USSR.[72]

Descriptions of the reasons for an inability to fulfill life ambitions are present in almost all the autobiographies. The basic obstacle for each was the writers' social background. Their difficult start in life was the result of tradition as much as of their position in the modern social hierarchy. Almost none of the contestants in the YIVO competition described themselves as happy or at least satisfied. Just about all of them were distinguished by pessimism and the realization of being representatives of a generation without a future. This type of description—irrespective of its veracity—of life ambitions and the reasons for not being able to fulfill them are yet more proof of young Jewish people's modernist consciousness during the interwar period. Behind these varied descriptions of individual fortunes lay basically a single vision of the contemporary world as one characterized by crisis and decay, as well as an expectation of the arrival of a completely different world. The most important value declared by young people, modernist in character, was secular learning. This feature of the autobiographies, like their attitude to the world of tradition, also had an important political meaning. The overwhelming majority of contestants in the YIVO competition, and among them almost all the supporters of radical political parties (who were a majority among the writers), did not believe in the possibility of fulfilling their ambitions within the framework of the existing social order. They gave their individual failures an unambiguous political meaning, seeing the cause of them in the injustice, irrationality, and backwardness of this order. This very same vision of the social world not allowing young Jews to fulfill their life ambitions emerges from their descriptions of the working world, which they were entering.

YOUNG PEOPLE'S PROFESSIONAL
ASPIRATIONS AND WORLD OF WORK

Apart from education, the main element of young people's personal ambitions was work. In the YIVO autobiographies, labor had both a symbolic and a political significance. The form and nature of a desired job would distinguish the writers from their parents, being key factors in transitioning from the world of tradition to the world of modernity. Descriptions of the working world included in the autobiographies present a fascinating collage of the realistic elements of paid work as well as the ideological desires associated with a working life. Descriptions of work conditions and the professional aspirations of young people represented a very important element in their vision of the future. They included visions of the society that was to come. They were for the most part presented using modernist terminology as a community of productive, educated, rationally organized people.

One of the most noteworthy descriptions of the Jewish working world is contained in the biography of "Chaim Berl." He attached to it a generalization of his personal experiences, an eleven-page report entitled "The Life of Young People in the Provinces." Chaim Berl presented himself as a typical representative of the "generation without a future."[73] This type of collective biographical trajectory was to determine his own tragic life: "My autobiography is the testimony of a young person, perhaps 'a superfluous person,' who had been born in order to endure suffering, drudgery and hunger . . . exploitation, chicanery, hatred, envy."[74] According to Chaim Berl, the cause of this state of affairs was a society that was immature and poorly organized.[75] The writer was born in 1917 in the country, the third child of very religious parents; he spent most of his life in Działoszyn, a small town lying at that time in the southwestern region of the country. Chaim Berl's father worked as a trader going around the neighboring villages. Chaim's parents dreamed of him one day becoming a rabbi.[76] These plans for the boy's religious education were cut short by the death of his father. His mother assumed the burden of supporting the family. Chaim had to help her with the business, and at the age of eight, after less than two years studying in the heder, having mastered barely "a few prayers and some of the Chumash," he had to abandon his formal education.[77]

When Chaim was eleven years old, his mother sent him off to learn tailoring. His description of the conditions of craft apprenticeship is typical of YIVO autobiographies. The writer worked ceaselessly and was endlessly supervised, bullied, and exploited by the master craftsman, who did not want to teach Chaim anything that might help him enter the profession. When he eventually mastered the trade on his own, his master fired him. He emphasized that this practice was common in his shtetl. Master craftsmen accepted pupils who undertook to work with them for free for two years in return for training. When this period ended, pupils usually had to leave, having no chance of employment.[78] The writer then experienced the bitterness of unemployment, looking for a long time for work with another tailor: "My mother found me a new master craftsman, with whom I earned two zloty a week working 15 hours per day. I went to work very early and worked until midnight, eating only bread, that I had to bring to work myself. In this way, days, weeks and years passed in dreadful exploitation in the midst of provincial poverty, misery and hunger. This was the time of my labor awareness. . . . This all awakened within me ideas of a socialist, economic and psychological nature about freeing myself from all this humiliation."[79]

With these words Chaim Berl concluded the first part of his autobiography. His life, as described in the second part, was now led under the banner of "so cialist struggle," which was interrupted by his short membership in the right-wing Zionist Ha-Shomer ha-Le'umi (National Watchman) and led him to the ranks of the KPP (the Communist Party of Poland) and finally the Bund. We shall examine later the political elements of Chaim Berl's memoirs. For the time being, let us focus on his report on the life of young people in the provinces, written in June 1939 and attached to his autobiography. In it, Chaim wrote,

> The fate of young workers is a spiritual and material tragedy. A young person at the age of twelve begins to learn a trade, he learns from a shoemaker [or] from a tailor, other trades are not really available in a small shtetl. Additionally, they must also pay the master craftsmen. Poor daddies and mommies fervently hope that their son will become a "professional," provincial parents have no other hopes. The antisemitic "drive" has forced them to their knees. They can no longer work in trade. When they try to do so they are met with stones. Peasants already have their "own merchants," trade is no longer in Jewish hands. Stall trading has also had to be abandoned owing to the great boycott, which has been felt painfully in the provinces. Parents have become "superfluous people," so they have shifted all their hopes onto their children. When a child is only ten or twelve years old he already must start earning.[80]

We can see clearly here the drama of the proletarianization of Jews, forced on them by boycotts and physical attacks but above all by economic forces.[81] In the consciousness of YIVO writers, the world of their parents symbolized by traditional trade was doomed to failure. Our attention is drawn in the quotation above to another very typical feature of the writers' imagination. Young apprentices, often without permanent employment or performing day labor in small workshops, saw themselves as working class or actually proletarian. According to Chaim, Jewish parents, often dabbling in trade, were also for the most part aware of the inevitability of the fall of Jewish trade. Other autobiographies also confirm this attitude of the older and younger generations.

In this report by a former communist and Bund activist, the theme of class clearly comes through—or, more accurately, an ideologized perspective that affects his perception of relations between master craftsmen and apprentices in terms of absolute division and estrangement. The writer of this report pointed out the lack of trade unions or other institutions that could have fought for the rights of young workers. What made the situation for young people even worse was that the master craftsmen effectively prevented them from taking professional examinations. Working for free or for starvation wages excluded the chance of fulfilling other life ambitions. In Chaim Berl's opinion, apprentices wanted to have the possibility of self-development and study. There was a lack of free libraries and theaters, and very few newspapers got through. Young people thinking about education, a worthy job, and self-fulfillment saw the chance to achieve this only in larger cities and left the shtetl for large industrial cities: Łódź, Częstochowa, or Sosnowiec. Just like the author, the heroes of his report also experienced failure there and returned to their small towns "with their eyes lowered," accepting further exploitation. In Chaim Berl's opinion, the "children of wealthy proprietors" were not better placed. Prepared from childhood to take over the family business, they suddenly realized that it was no longer making a profit. In Chaim Berl's report, there was no other path for young people than "proletarianization" and "socialism."[82]

We find a similar description of the world in "Chaja's" autobiography. Despite coming from Ostroh (Ostróg) in Volhynia, from a completely different background than Chaim Berl's, and despite having different political views (she was a Zionist), her description of the working world shows a basic similarity with the one provided by Chaim. Chaja, in addition to her autobiography written in Yiddish, sent in an almost-one-hundred-page diary (in Polish), written between 1930 and 1934. At the age of seven, she had been sent to a public primary school, which she completed with distinction. This ambitious girl dreamed of secondary school, just like a great many other writers, but her family's poor material circumstances (she was brought up by a single mother) stood in the way. At the age of sixteen, when she began to keep her diary, she was working as a tutor while at the same time learning to be a seamstress. In her diary, she described for the most part two opposing realities: the gray working world and a happy world based around activities in the Gordonia Zionist youth organization.[83] According to Chaja, the social circumstances in which she lived "made her unfriendly and aloof," just like the people surrounding her.[84] Her work day began at 8:00 a.m. in the sewing workshop. From 5:00 p.m. until the evening, she gave private lessons. The only alternative to the life she was leading became political activity, and the only solution capable of bringing a positive change would be to leave for Palestine. Just like all the other young people quoted in this chapter, she saw no opportunity for fulfilling her life ambitions in Poland, in the social conditions around her.

"Jerzyk Tomaszów" was five years old when his mother died from poverty and stress. He grew up in Łódź, and his family lived in poverty. Deprived of the care of his hard-working father and older sisters, he was brought up, as he wrote in his autobiography, mainly by the street. Jerzyk completed at the age of fourteen (fifth grade) both a traditional education in a heder and a secular education in an elementary school. He described in detail the conditions at home. He lived in a small apartment on the fourth and top floor of an apartment building together with his father, his sisters, and their families. The author's father died at the age of fifty-six. Jerzyk then moved in with his older sister, who had earlier rented her own apartment and supported herself by selling quilts she sewed. Describing his work for his sister, the autobiographer presented her as a "master craftsman" "exploiting" her workers.[85] While sewing quilts, Jerzyk dreamed of becoming an "intellectual." He wanted to read, speak better, possess a broader vocabulary, and write "stories and other things." He was inspired by articles he read in the popular Yiddish daily *Der Moment*. At the same time, work absorbed all his energy.[86] When he clashed with his sister, he took up a new trade—dressmaking. His new boss was a good friend of his. The work was hard, but it had its good sides. At work one of Jerzyk's colleagues sang hits from the latest shows. His comment about her is telling: "She was a rare beauty. We knew of course that she had a child. But she was working for her powder and lipstick, or simply for her reputation, for what they would say about her work. She would spend the nights with officers in nightclubs and dance halls. She worked without a break. The apprentices who worked with her were weighed down with obligations, and she treated them as if she was their lieutenant."[87]

From this description of his colleague, the author's socialist views come through. According to him, she was deluded by the illusory pleasures of contemporary bourgeois society. She had no idea what labor meant or should mean. She was unaware of her social role and did not identify herself with her colleagues in the misery of employment. Jerzyk wrote in similar fashion about other workmates. He wanted to be another person, as he wrote: "A free thinker not like them."[88] His method of becoming "truly" different was to quickly master a trade, make "better money," and use it for school. Therefore, he decided to look for a new job. He wanted to find one that would help him improve his professional qualifications. He was finally taken on in a large factory in the city center. The work was very hard, the workers had no breaks, and the master craftsman, despite having promised, taught Jerzyk nothing. However, this episode had great significance in the author's life. Two people working with him made a deep impression on him: the best craftsman in the factory, who was also the union representative, and the oldest worker, a Zionist. Not yet sixteen, Jerzyk already felt himself to be an adult. His own "evaluative" commentary on how he assessed his own "professional qualities" as an "adult person" is very interesting: "I have learned a trade and I am a worker. I have seen how hard it has been to obtain a qualification. I have seen qualified workers who earn nothing, and unqualified ones who earn good money. I have seen how people are forced to lie and to scheme. A person must be smart, no different from a trickster."[89] Like his description of his colleague, this description of his work experiences also serves as a sharp criticism of the social order.

A little later Jerzyk met a young activist of Po'alei-Tsiyon-Left. Under his influence he joined a trade union and began to be active in the party youth movement, Yugend. Over time his political views evolved toward communism. In a description of his further fortunes, various trends are interwoven: dreams of revolution, hard seasonal work, and "romantic" and "revolutionary" reading matter. Spending almost a year in prison, the result of being arrested after a May Day demonstration in Łódź in 1932, had a great influence on this autobiographer and fully committed him to the ideal of communism. Jerzyk's eventual departure from the Communist Party did not change his view of his own life, in particular his work and economic relationships. The author had to go back to working for his sister. His used his description of his immediate family to define "the nature of the bourgeoisie": "So, what is the petty bourgeoisie? My sister's business was doing badly, and as far as I could tell, was barely solvent. The whole business survived thanks to my sister, a born saleswoman from Nowomiejska Street. I wondered how she was able to get things done like that. I later discovered on what 'feet of clay' the whole world of business stood. I saw how my sister was constantly tormented by the thought whether she had sold at a profit, and if not, whether to pay or not to pay."[90]

The description of Nowomiejska Street in Jerzyk's autobiography is in reality also a description of the declining, degenerate "petty bourgeois" world: "Nowomiejska Street, full of petty traders, had only a single bourgeois [balebos], I shall call him 'a denizen of the street.' He filled the whole street, he would spend whole days walking among groups of brokers, rogues, money changers, pickpockets."[91] Jerzyk became friendly with one of them. His new friend, a former thief, had once belonged to the elite of his profession but had broken away from criminal activity. Very characteristically, Jerzyk assessed his qualities in the following words: "A good man, has good political sense, buys working-class newspapers." This person is contrasted in his autobiography with another denizen of Nowomiejska Street, an industrialist's son, "a typical bourgeois," "spending days thinking of nothing but prostitutes."[92] While writing his autobiography, Jerzyk abandoned communism. His sympathies transferred to the socialist Bund. He was a big-city worker who was dedicated to socialism and the Yiddish language, who had served a prison sentence and possessed all the features of a young Jewish radical.

The memoirs of a young female worker from Lublin describe in many places, just as Jerzyk's autobiography does, the power of the factory as a social context conducive to developing a radical consciousness. She was born on February 23, 1921. She came from a religious background, and her father supported the family as a trader going around the local villages. Her mother traded from a market stall in Lublin. The writer studied in a TsYShO Jewish school and dreamed of continuing her education at a secondary school, which was out of the question for financial reasons. Her parents were able to afford only a tailoring apprenticeship.[93] She wrote that work in a Lublin factory changed her life: "I was now in a new world. I joined a trade union (and became an active organizer), where I saw a great many young workers, who spent all day at work or in the union. I saw battles between master craftsmen and workers on the subject of longer or shorter work days, battles over wage increases, fights between young men and girls. This was all something new and unknown for me."[94] She continued, "I did not like the work itself and I still don't, but I understood that I had to learn and master a trade. I succeeded in becoming one of the workers (I adapt quickly to any situation) and I go to work willingly. Not out of any love for it, but out of love for the collective. To be in a line of workers, to sing together, to eat together, collectively, and chat a bit when the boss isn't watching."[95]

The writer became more deeply involved in trade union work, where the Bund was most influential. Like a great many of her peers with similar backgrounds, she was seriously bothered by the seasonal nature of her work and her income. Often, there was no work for four months. The new world, the arrival of which she was awaiting, was to be a world in which work and schooling would be available for everyone. She wrote, "Only one thing keeps me going, without which I don't know what would become of me. That thing is faith in a better more beautiful world, in which all the dreams of the old and the young will be fulfilled."[96] The only bright spot in her life was her activity in the trade union and the Bund youth organization Tsukunft.

The autobiography of a religious writer, an activist in the Zionist-religious Mizrahi party and its youth organization Bnei Akiva, shows yet another side of this perspective. "Galitsyaner" was born in July 1922 in Olesko, a small shtetl in former eastern Galicia, southeastern Poland, and today in Ukraine. He was brought up in a poor family. His father worked as a melamed, which was poorly paid and had low social status in traditional society. As Galitsyaner, remarked ironically, "My dad has the 'trade' of melamed."[97] Despite the family's poverty, the author's parents did everything so that he could acquire the best religious education. Standing in the way of his Talmudic studies and career as a rabbi was his father's illness and the family's catastrophic financial position. Galitsyaner had to abandon elementary school, and his father, dreaming of a career as a rabbi for his son, ordered him to learn a trade. In this decision by the head of the family, we can clearly see the changing socioeconomic context of the lives of Jews in Poland, the restratification, and the change in social values associated with work and one's place in the economic structure. Mastering a trade and living by the work of one's own hands, considered of low prestige in traditional Jewish society, now became the most certain means of earning a living: "Dad urged me to study tailoring. 'after all it's an ideal trade.'"[98] To pay the master craftsman and learn a trade, Galitsyaner began to give private lessons. Shortly thereafter, abandoning his apprenticeship in tailoring, he began training for the traditional trade of ritual slaughterer (*shoykhet*). He had to abandon this owing to problems with his lungs.[99]

Like many of his peers, Galitsyaner felt that the traditional world had not prepared him for contemporary challenges, at the heart of which was the need to do physical labor. It appears that, unlike several writers quoted above, he did not want a trade and physical work. However, like his predecessors, he recognized the need. Unable to support himself in the family shtetl, he joined his sister "in the big city," in which she found him work in a vinegar factory. Once again the work's physical demands overwhelmed him, in addition to the obvious exploitation. Galitsyaner began to cough blood and stopped eating. He was not fit for physical work, and private lessons became a lifeline.[100] On the final pages of his autobiography, he describes the hardships of life as a private tutor, the need to take on too many classes, the poverty of his students' families, and the lack of any income during the summer months. Despite the advance of his illness, Galitsyaner tried to devote all his efforts to his family, above all to keep his blind seventy-nine-year-old father alive.[101]

Galitsyaner's autobiography raises many of the themes appearing in the discussion of other authors' work. It points out, too, what connected the communities represented by the contestants in the YIVO competition. The autobiographer remained a religious person and loved his parents, yet he did not hesitate to criticize certain elements of the traditional world from which he came. Just like the Bundist, communist, or left-wing Zionist writers, he felt close to modernist categories of perceiving reality, such as the dichotomy between tradition and modernity, the conviction of the crisis and the disintegration of the surrounding world. Similarly, this religious author, a member of the Mizrahi party and its youth organization Bnei Akiva, believed in a central element of the current modernist discourse: the value of factory work and modern production methods. For him too, the "productivization" of the Jewish nation was essential. This successive modernistic element of the writers' social consciousness also had significant political meaning.

CONCLUSIONS

When writing their autobiographies, the young people did not conduct broader macroeconomic or sociological analyses. However, the autobiographies undoubtedly convey their economic and social-class sensitivities. According to Ido Bassok, many of the contestants in the YIVO competition (especially those from the lower classes), when describing the traditional social distances in the heders, yeshivas, and elementary and Jewish schools as well as in political organizations, treated them as innate and immutable phenomena. At times, they even openly identified themselves with these divisions, which is proof of their internalization of the traditional system of social stratification.[102] However, I maintain that both the autobiographical examples presented above and those quoted by Bassok prove something completely different. The fact that almost all the writers did not just write about social stratification but actually attacked it, using modern concepts such as class, excessive profits, exploitation, and bourgeoisie, proves that the traditional ways of perceiving social differences had been rejected by the majority of the youngest generation. Social distances themselves continued to operate as a legacy of the traditional order, yet the way of perceiving then took on a different, modern character. The rhetoric of class conflict took center stage in many of the autobiographies. As we have seen above, the fundamental change in this important dimension of social consciousness also did not pass by their parents' generation. Even those coming from the old Talmudic elite, by now more Orthodox than traditional, often brought up their children on secular lines, which some of them pursued in secondary schools, universities, others in nonbusiness professions.

Despite the sharp social and political divisions, young people were linked by key generational values, to which Bassok has added a consciousness of their own exceptionalism and distinctiveness (as young people) and a conviction of the need for deep sociopolitical engagement as well as the creation of new individual and collective models of life, such as the new man, the new family, and the new nation.[103] To this the radically modernist system of values and the resultant conviction of the deep crisis and the unreformability of the surrounding world, as well as the need for revolutionary change, can be added. This collection of sociopolitical values and symbols linking young people belongs under the heading of radical modernism.

This ideology was dominant and found many outlets in the work even of those writers whom one could not consider to be political radicals. We can see its power most forcefully in the autobiographies of writers coming from backgrounds of traditional Orthodoxy. Members of the Aguda or Mizrahi youth organizations attacked the older generation of Orthodox leaders for their dislike of modern forms of education and secular upbringing, for the "confusion" and "chaos" in traditional education, and finally for their opposition to institutions such as the cinema and the theater.[104] As we have seen, a great many young Orthodox looked unwillingly at the dominant traditional way in which the Jewish masses supported themselves by retail. In their consciousness the working world and social hierarchy were inextricably linked with modern knowledge. Even young people who had not decided to abandon the world of religion saw the unreformed sphere of tradition—the old type of heder and the traditional business occupations—as a world of dirt, chaos, violence, and disorganization.

The autobiographies confirm the violent process of the proletarianization of the Jewish minority in the Second Republic. Reading them shows how great a symbolic and practical meaning so-called productive trades—crafts or manual labor—had for young people at that time. Many writers coming from traditional Jewish lower-middle-class homes emphasized that their parents preferred that their children learn a trade. Minor Jewish merchants, trying at all costs for their children to become tailors, shoemakers, locksmiths, and so on, saw in this social promotion rather than demotion. Both in the Yiddish and the Polish autobiographies, the noun *beruf/zawód* (in Yiddish "trade," also "calling") was described as craft work or laboring. The fact that in practice parents' traditional business activities were not called a "trade" shows the symbolic power of the process of proletarianization of the Jewish minority. Intellectual occupations were also "trades" or "professions" mentioned by the autobiographers, mostly teachers or bookkeepers. In fact, only people coming from the traditional elites, where learning was connected with financial capital—such as Damaszek, Esther, M. W. and Etonis—aspired to them. Only the elites could afford to replicate their own social position, in which religious activity was linked with business and which was characterized by placing physical labor at the bottom of the Jewish social hierarchy. At the same time, we are able to observe here the collapse of the hitherto-unifying tradition of social stratification—the process by which a section of the elite tries constantly to replicate its own position, although now with the help of modern institutions, such as schools and diplomas, while the masses have ceased to believe in the old social hierarchy, valuing the practical and prestigious value of occupations based on physical labor. This type of productivization, though, did not affect everyone. Apart from the Orthodox elite, another path was chosen by children from acculturated families from wealthier circles of the big-city Jewish bourgeoisie. There, where it was possible, Jewish parents tried to provide their children with the best education and professional careers as white-collar workers. A great many traditional parents were not opposed to this type of career for their children, who had no choice. Work in a factory or a workshop in modern institutions was for them the only alternative. There was a widespread belief that the productivization (in this case the proletarianization) of the Jewish masses was for them the only way out, a belief shared by those who had to submit to this process, like the elites, who were productivizing themselves in another way by assuring their children a secular education and modern professions based on specialist knowledge and intellectual work.

Sensitivity to poverty and personally degrading living conditions as the main cause of physical, psychological, and spiritual degeneration were the central themes of the autobiographies. Furthermore, they saw the causes of this poverty in the poorly functioning social system. Many of the authors, not having any socialist or communist views, described the conditions in their immediate surroundings or at work in class terms, and even sometimes in openly Marxist terms. Of course, this is not proof of the sudden popularity of communist ideas among young Jewish people in the 1930s. It is more a phenomenon that I would call metasocialist consciousness, a way of looking at the social world not fully consciously or even unconsciously using categories of perception and description from the arsenal of Marxist thought. Among the young people, socialist or communist ideological systems did not dominate so much as did individual elements and symbols taken from them or mental images of them. Why was this system of knowledge useful? We can hazard the hypothesis that it was best suited to the modernistic consciousness characterizing young Jewish people between the wars. They criticized the world of tradition, the central symbols and models of their own parents' social life, and their ways of making a living. Young people operated in a defined system of modern, individual values, with self-realization through productive work and secular education as a goal of the highest order.

Bringing these values to life was not the automatic consequence of abandoning the world of tradition on behalf of modern urban civilization. This was also the domain of social pathology, unemployment, poverty, criminality, and difficulty in obtaining the means to support oneself and to get an education. The world of Jewish traders, merchants, and rabbis was not the only one consumed by crisis and degeneration. After leaving it, young people realized that factories, manufacturing facilities, and finally the state and its economic system were not free of them either. The modernistic character of young people's social consciousness assumed the possession of a clear vision of social order, the reasons for its pathology, and the future state of society, which would put an end to these pathologies. The kind of learning that young people valued the most, evident in the apparently least political elements of the autobiographies, was sociophilosophical learning, providing a modern and comprehensive explanation of the mechanisms of social life. This metasocialist social consciousness, connecting young people beyond sociocultural divides, was one of the central elements of the radical habitus of the last generation of Jewish youth in the Second Republic, created by the specific conditions in which they grew up.

THREE

—⚏—

PUBLIC SCHOOLS

The advent of the Second Republic led to a revolution in the field of education. The introduction of universal mandatory schooling meant that for the first time most young Jewish people came into contact not only with secular education but also with a curriculum imposed by the state. For thousands of young people, a Polish school was the first significant Polish state institution with which they interacted. It played an enormous role in the processes of acculturation. Inevitably, the Polish school and, as we shall see, the mixed experiences taken from it were key factors in forming the attitudes of young people toward the Polish state and Polish culture. The influence of state education policies was not restricted solely to public schools. The state permitted various Jewish community groups to establish schools with their own curricula. At the same time, over the years the Ministry of Religious Affairs and Public Education (MWRiOP) made ever-greater efforts to introduce its own curriculum into all private schools, both those teaching in Polish and those teaching in one of the Jewish languages.

Established toward the end of 1918, the Polish state had to quickly organize all matters within its remit, including education. Compulsory seven-year schooling up to the age of fourteen was introduced by a decree of the Head of State Józef Piłsudski, dated February 7, 1919. Schools were divided into three categories, depending on the extent to which they covered the full elementary school curriculum. Only category III schools, operating in the larger urban areas, provided a full elementary education. In the smallest category I rural schools, over the course of seven years of schooling children completed only four grades, and in secondary schools it was five grades.[1] Despite the fact that elementary education was free, this kind of structure of a universal education system was a serious obstacle to young people from the country or from small towns, who had no opportunity to acquire a complete elementary education. Children from this background usually did not have access to category II and III schools that would give them a full elementary education, let alone secondary or higher education.

The secondary education system—elitist and, unlike elementary education, fee-paying—was not integrated with the elementary system in the first decade of the Second Republic. Throughout most of the period between the wars in Poland, there existed an eight-grade secondary school (*gimnazjum*), the first grade of which one could enter as early as after fourth grade in elementary school (at the age of ten or eleven).[2] Although one could also start secondary school (in the fourth grade) after completing seventh grade in elementary school, the great majority of students who completed secondary school started right after fourth grade in elementary school. It was not easy to get into the fourth grade in secondary school after seven years of elementary school, a situation that additionally privileged students from wealthy families, who were able to pay for their children's education at the age of ten or eleven, usually in a school at some distance from their home.[3]

The 1932 reform changed the education system in Poland. It maintained the three types of elementary school while introducing key changes to secondary schooling. The eight-grade gimnazjum was abolished and replaced by a four-year junior high school, followed by a two-year specialized high school, after which one took one's diploma. This meant a new situation in which one could no longer enter secondary school after fourth grade but could enter only after completing sixth grade in elementary school.[4] Since this reform came into effect only in 1937, most of the autobiographies submitted to the YIVO competition were written by young people who were still being educated under the old system.

A key feature of the education system in the Second Republic was its elitism. The introduction of elementary education for all democratized access to culture for children and young people, but for those in the lower classes, access to a longer educational career leading to the possibility of earning greater cultural, social, and symbolic capital was made difficult. The children of peasants, small-town and big-city minor traders, less well-qualified workers, or the unemployed could only dream of any education beyond elementary school, with infrequent exceptions.[5] The state of educational development left a great deal to be desired (despite the rapidly increasing correlation of education with success in the battle with illiteracy), especially in the countryside and in provincial towns.[6] Many children of peasants and also of artisans, laborers, and minor merchants were unable even to finish seven grades of elementary school.[7] Such was the fate of many children of the Jewish lower social classes, among others. Peasant children, both Polish and minority, in the Eastern Borderlands (the so-called Kresy) were in a worse situation, since it was harder for them to obtain a secondary education. The eight-grade secondary schools, in operation until 1932, as well as the four-grade junior highs and two-grade high schools, which had been established as a result of the reform, were fee-paying. In 1934 the average fees for a state junior high school were between 200 and 300 zloty a year (poorer people paid half that), representing about six weeks' wages for a worker in a large factory or a qualified tailor in Warsaw, or more than three months' wages for workers in small factories and artisanal workshops. Private secondary schools, playing a greater role in the educational marketplace than elementary schools, were two or three times more expensive.[8] The annual fees for private secondary schools, which the great majority of young Jewish people in school attended, varied between seven hundred and thirteen hundred zloty. These were astronomical sums for most citizens of the Second Republic. Furthermore, most parents were unable to do without help on the farm or in the shop, or without the additional income brought in by their children going out to work at a young age. Schools in interwar Poland were thus elitist institutions, into which a majority of the youngest citizens were unable to enter, irrespective of their abilities.[9] Polish society between the wars continued to display a great many features of a quasi-estate system (largely inherited from an earlier feudal society), which the state education system perpetuated.[10] The ability to obtain a postelementary education was an unrealistic dream for a great many ambitious young people from the working classes and peasantry.

JEWISH CHILDREN IN PUBLIC ELEMENTARY SCHOOLS

Between the wars almost all Jewish children aged between seven and fourteen attended public elementary schools, which represented a significant generational breakthrough. The state's domination in educating Jews took shape as early as the 1920s. According to data from the Institute of Minority Affairs, 60 percent of Jewish children of school age attended public schools during the 1928/29 school year.[11] The 1929 crash additionally reinforced the domination of the public sector in Jewish children's education. The fall in parents' incomes meant that many had to enroll their children in or transfer them to public elementary schools, which were still the only free ones. During the 1934/35 school year, over 80 percent of Jewish children of school age attended public schools.[12]

These statistics did not account for the fact that a great many students were studying at the same time both in public schools and in private Jewish establishments in the evening. The percentage of students in Jewish schools out of all the Jewish children between ages seven and fourteen was higher than 20 percent. According to data from the American Jewish Joint Distribution Committee, during the 1934/35 school year 180,000 children attended Jewish private schools. Comparing that number with the 450,000 Jewish children of school age at the time, we obtain a figure of 40 percent of Jewish children studying in private schools. It emerges from the difference between these numbers that around 20 percent of Jewish children at this time were studying both in public and in Jewish private schools.[13]

The percentage of Jewish children studying in public schools varied enormously by region. In central Poland (the former Congress Kingdom) it was 81.9 percent, in former Galicia (the Austrian zone of partition) it was as high as 95 percent, and in eastern Poland (the former Pale of Settlement) it was only 58 percent.[14] The relative weakness of the public education system in this part of the country is explained by the region's historical traditions, especially in the Litvak area of Jewish culture (the northeastern provinces); by the power of secular and modernized religious education; and by the almost nonexistent polonization of the Jewish community before 1918.

In the 1920s a small number of Jewish children attended special public schools for Jews that respected religious tradition and did not operate on Saturdays. Public schools for children of Jewish faith were commonly known as *szabasówki*. They were introduced in 1923. They did not teach any of the Jewish languages, and Jewish political parties and cultural organizations had no influence over their curriculum. The only Jewish subject was religion taught two hours a week, while the rest of the curriculum did not differ from the mandatory one taught in the regular public schools. The overwhelming majority of the teachers in these schools were non-Jews. These schools had limited reach. In the 1920s only 15 percent of Jewish students in public schools attended this type of school. During the 1930s these schools were gradually phased out.[15] Since most Jewish children did not attend szabasówki but went to normal public schools, as early as 1923 they were excused from writing on Saturdays. They were obliged to go to school that day just like Christian children, but in that way, they were not forced to break Shabbat rules.[16]

Jewish children usually attended Judaism classes in elementary schools at the time when Christian children were having their religion classes, or they were arranged outside school. These Judaism classes were usually taught by acculturated non-Orthodox or graduates of Polish teachers' colleges having no interest in religion. This absence both of Orthodox religion and of other elements of Jewish culture in public schools was an important reason for both the Orthodox and the most important secular nationalist communities disliking them. Teachers of Judaism on the whole had a poor reputation in the Jewish community. Orthodox groups despaired of the fact that children coming from traditional homes would learn their faith from people who did not know it and who did not follow its precepts.[17]

PUBLIC SECONDARY EDUCATION
AND JEWISH BILINGUAL EDUCATION

The Jewish population, as an essentially urban community, was overrepresented among secondary school students. This overrepresentation was especially significant in the case of girls. During the 1927/28 school year, the ratio of Jewish boys to all boys in secondary schools was 17.7 percent, while for girls it was as high as 28.3 percent. This was the result above all of social principles of educating children, which had a long history and according to which boys received mainly a religious education, while girls coming from wealthy homes received a practical and secular one.[18]

Given that throughout the whole interwar period Jewish students were discriminated against in terms of entry to secondary schools, most of them studied in private secondary schools. In 1927 Jews represented around 25 percent of all secondary school students, but in the cheaper ones, also offering a high standard of education and at the same time good opportunities for entering higher education, that percentage was lower than 6 percent.[19] In 1930, out of 45,400 Jewish secondary school students, as many as 33,800 attended much more expensive private establishments, thus making it harder to pass the high school diploma.[20] In the 1930s the policy of numerus clausus (by which a limit on Jewish students was set ahead of time, irrespective of their results on entrance exams) was introduced not only in institutions of higher learning but also at the secondary level. The flow of Jewish secondary school students from public to private schools was accompanied by a gradual decline in their overall numbers. While during the 1921/22 school year the number of Jewish students in secondary schools reached 48,850 (23.7% of the total number), by 1936/37 it was only 33,320 (16.5%). That same school year, as many as 73 percent of all Jewish secondary students in middle and high schools attended private schools.[21]

Jewish private secondary education was varied. Besides schools associated with Jewish political movements teaching in one of the Jewish languages (in addition to mandatory subjects taught in Polish), there were also so-called utraquist (bilingual) schools with a half-and-half curriculum (Polish-Hebrew schools and Polish-Yiddish schools). The importance of these bilingual schools gradually rose. During the 1930s they came to dominate Jewish secular education at the secondary level. During the 1936/37 school year, out of 17,911 Jewish students in private secondary schools, only 2,059 were in Hebrew-language Tarbut schools and 184 in Yiddish TsYShO schools; the remaining 15,669 attended bilingual middle and high schools. At the same time, 15,301 Jewish students attended national and local Polish secondary schools.[22]

In the educational philosophy of these bilingual schools, Polish was not an equal language but the dominant one, which the students most frequently used among themselves. At the secondary level, therefore, Polish held decidedly the strongest position. The polonization of the curriculum, its conformity to ministerial demands, and its similarity to that in the public schools allowed Jewish schools the right to award the state diploma, which greatly increased their attractiveness in the eyes of Jewish parents. During the 1933/34 school year, the percentage of students who earned this type of diploma reached 82.8 percent for public schools, 78 percent for accredited private schools, and 47.4 percent for unaccredited ones, while in the eastern part of the country it was no more than 36.6 percent (children in these schools took the state diploma as external candidates).[23] These numbers to a great extent explain why bilingual schools dominated among Jewish private secondary schools.[24] Taking this into account, as well as the fact that during the 1930s almost half of Jewish students in secular secondary schools studied in public or locally run establishments, the Polish language dominated at this level of Jewish education in interwar Poland.

ELEMENTARY SCHOOL AS THE GATEWAY TO MODERNITY

As we have seen, the attitude of young people toward the basic institution of traditional Jewish education—the heder—was largely negative. The heder represented everything that the young people were rejecting. As Michael Steinlauf writes about the views of YIVO contestants, "School, whether it was Jewish or Polish, anything but the traditional heder, was venerated. In the autobiographies school is referred to as a second home, as better than home, as something magical, as a palace, as a temple, as the sun."[25] Many of the authors expected a school operating along the enlightened lines of modern pedagogy to bring back their childhood, of which poverty and the world of tradition had deprived them. School was meant to provide them with the opportunity to acquire a greatly desired secular education, and with it the cultural and intellectual capital that would facilitate social promotion and a different life from that characterizing previous generations. School was the first institution of the great outside world that the majority of authors entered from an area of tradition that they criticized.

The exceptional nature of school in the life of a Jewish child was symbolized by its physical attributes. "GW," an activist of the Bundist Tsukunft and a fervent supporter of Jewish cultural and national autonomy, wrote his autobiography in Yiddish. He recalled his delight at the appearance of the building of the public elementary school that he attended, its well-lit classrooms so different from the dim rooms of a heder.[26] An anonymous author coming from a working-class Lublin background before entering TsYShO schools, where she began a "new life" in the socialist nationalist counterculture of the Bund, had her first experience of the outside world in a public preschool:

> I went to a public preschool.... The building was very fine, tall ... large, the floors were red and shiny. It had a special "pantry" with shelves full of food. The city council had built it. There was also a dining hall.... We spent every day at a great many activities. We slid around on the shiny floors in shoes wrapped in cloths, we sang, we jumped, we played all sorts of games that we invented. In the preschool there were also large, beautiful dolls, clown and boxes with bricks.... We spoke Polish.[27]

Another participant in the YIVO competition had been studying in a Tarbut Hebrew school from age seven. This establishment did not have its own building, and the students used the facilities of local beit midrashes. After completing sixth grade, she transferred to a public school despite the fact that as a Zionist she criticized its non-Jewish character. Comparing it with her Tarbut school, she wrote, "Here, the school has two stories, high rooms full of light, a covered floor, a large hall to which all the children would go either for physical education, or in winter during the long recess. In summer we would play in the school yard, with trees and flowers growing all around."[28]

"Em. Tepa," the son of a tailor, was a councilman in Parczew and a Bund sympathizer. He wrote in similar vein about his school, contrasting it with the "dirty" and "unfair" heder:

> Even the preparations for the first day of school were something quite distinct and different from anything in the heder. After putting on a clean shirt and my Shabbos-best outfit (before going to school) I felt a kind of warm summer breeze on me. One sensed in these preparations a warm, tender hand, such a contrast with the one that my first "rebe" gave me, when he came to lead me for the first time into the "school." Only the strong contrast between that first "school" and the second, real one snapped me out of passivity. Seeing

the cleanliness of our classroom awoke within me repugnance towards the heder's dirty, smoky hut. The teacher's human appearance . . . led me to despise this other "teacher," in a dirty black smock, always wearing a cap and with little "specks" of food on his black, uncombed beard. What is interesting is that before I encountered this second school, the first one had not disgusted me. Only when I found myself in a classroom, when I sat down on a nicely planed bench, did this dislike and hatred of the heder, with its long tables and dirty benches, arise within me. I began to run away from there as often as I could.[29]

The actual physical appearance of the school appears to have been an attribute of its modernity. The large brick buildings, the spacious, sunlit classrooms, and the clean corridors contrasting with the dark and dirty heders made an enormous impression on the young people. Em. Tepa's statement touches on all the most important themes appearing in the majority of autobiographies by traditional authors, who between the ages of six and eight had begun their education at elementary schools. Independent of the intentions of the teachers, school districts, MWRiOP officials, and Jewish parents sending their children to public religious schools, it was a powerful element of secularization of the generation described here, and more importantly, the first significant institutional one.[30] There can also be no doubt that studying in a public school served to deepen the differences between the youngest generation and their parents. It alienated young Jews from their immediate environment. The norms, values, symbols, and models of daily life in this environment were for the first time no longer obvious and self-explanatory for them and, compared to other models, were becoming more unfamiliar.

The quotations above come from the autobiographies of young people from all walks of life represented in the YIVO competition. This fact points to the specific conditions of the interwar years. Earlier, studying in a Polish school had been a socializing experience only for young people coming from acculturated Jewish homes in Galicia or central Poland. In the 1930s the impact of elementary school extended to almost all Jewish communities and took on a revolutionary meaning since the large-scale effects of state educational institutions were something completely new. For different reasons, both secular and religious young Jews from Białystok, Vilna, Nowogródek, Polesie, and Volhynia attended those schools. Young people from humble, traditional homes from all over the country, and in some cases also the children of the Orthodox elite, began to attend public schools en masse.[31] The individual life ambitions of young people, together with their social and political imaginations, were being formed ever more strongly by Polish culture as well as by contact with state institutions—mainly school, which was the main transmitter of this culture.

ELEMENTARY SCHOOL AS AN OPPORTUNITY TO ACQUIRE
SECULAR KNOWLEDGE AND A CHANGE IN LIFESTYLE

Free public schooling was a breakthrough, especially in the lives of the poor and traditional Jewish social classes, who could not afford to send their children to religious or secular private schools or hire private tutors. The consequence was a certain significant paradox. As a result of this specific circumstance, a smaller percentage of children from more secularized, wealthier (acculturated or not), and for the most part nationalist-oriented homes attended elementary schools than young people coming from poorer traditional homes. Thus, the greatest percentage of Jewish students in elementary schools came from communities where the mindset and lifestyle were different from those instilled in public establishments.

An author using the pseudonym "Pionier" undoubtedly belonged to the latter, more numerous Jewish community. He was brought up in a traditional, religious home. He came from a small town in the eastern part of the country near Łuck in the province of Volhynia. This was an area where the footprint of Polish culture and institutions in the life of the Jewish community was the smallest. Pionier wrote that he was enrolled in an elementary school at age seven and, thanks to his eagerness to learn, was a member of the first Jewish generation from Volhynian shtetls to speak and write fluently in Polish. For him, school was the only accessible element of a different life, a "modern" life.[32]

Owing to his complete lack of knowledge of Polish, Drori's first day in elementary school was a miserable experience. However, he settled in quickly and appreciated the completely different atmosphere from the one he had known in the heder: "School made a good impression on me owing to the systematic nature of the teaching. Each lesson lasted 45 minutes, after which there was a break ended always by the bell. Here, I felt that a student had greater prestige, which I had not known in the heder. There was no rabbi beating children with a ruler here. When one of us stepped out of line, one glance from the teacher was enough for us to realize that we needed to buck up."[33]

Drori was delighted by the interesting Polish and mathematics classes, thanks to which he learned some completely new things. For him, classes such as physical education, singing, and above all his beloved drawing were a novelty. He was delighted by the availability of school educational aids, such as maps, geographical and scientific atlases, and a school library.[34] Drori quickly made up the deficit resulting from his poor Polish and became a good student. However, as he writes sadly, he encountered problems in the higher grades of elementary school. They were mainly the result of the incompatibility of the world of school learning with the one from which he came. The work became harder, while he had to spend a great deal of time in the heder and on daily prayers, which often clashed with his school hours. It became harder for him to make up the deficit resulting from the chasm dividing his home world and the world of knowledge transmitted in school.[35]

Extreme examples of how children coming from the traditional world perceived the public education system are accounts of teachers of Polish coming to give lessons in heders. Directives from the Ministry of Education demanded that traditional institutions of Jewish education cover the minimum elementary school syllabus, leading them to hire secular teachers for several hours a week.[36] Living in a small shtetl in the northeastern part of the country, Yud-Giml never attended a public school. She studied in a Talmud Torah, continuing in a TsYShO school. While she was writing her autobiography, she was an activist of the Kultur-Lige and her political sympathies were drifting away from Bundist socialism toward communism.[37] Therefore, the author is unlikely to have leaned toward acculturation, but she remembered one bright spot from all the many years of suffering in a Talmud Torah: the teacher coming in to give Polish lessons. According to her, he was the antithesis of the melamed in the heder; he did not hand out beatings and quickly established a rapport with the children. He was also their first point of contact with secular, modern learning.[38]

Another Zionist, coming from Lublin, "Basia R." had an equally ambivalent attitude toward public education. Basia was the daughter of a luftmensch, and it was her mother, taking on various casual jobs, who was responsible for supporting her and her three sisters. Owing to the family's low economic status, going to private Jewish schools was out of the question. Although she despised antisemitism and scorned "integrationists," the public school was also the only means of acquiring her desired education. Like many contestants, she began her description with a presentation of the misery, torpor, and hopelessness of growing up in her poor circumstances. Attending elementary school was for her a definite change: "Unfortunately, I don't recall anything good or pleasant from that time in my life. Things looked up when I began to attend elementary school. I would spend more time with the many children there and competed with them in my studies. At that time I was top student and our teacher held me up as an example to the other girls. I was very proud of her praise."[39]

Public education also played a large part in the lives of some of the Orthodox young people. An opportunity to acquire secular and at the same time practical knowledge was the reason for which Gamalielis abandoned his studies in the yeshiva and decided to study in a public vocational school in Białystok. His religious friends envied him such a daring step. The spirit of secular, practical knowledge swept through most of the students of the yeshiva in Grodno: "My plan was after all not a secret, since we had all been overcome by the conviction that nothing would come of our yeshiva disputations and that staying here was a waste of time. . . . I decided to leave the yeshiva and take the path of work and useful knowledge! Of course, I told my closest friends of this . . ., they were amazed that I in fact was able to impress them with my ability to learn and my consistent approach."[40]

To be admitted to school, Gamalielis hired a private tutor with whom he intensively studied arithmetic, Polish spelling, and grammar. Although he did badly on the entrance exam—probably worse than those studying in secular schools—he was accepted on account of his determination and "desire to learn."[41] Another author, "Yafet," a Ger Hasid and future graduate of a yeshiva, recalled his time in elementary school as follows:

> After seven years I received a school leaving certificate. By now I spoke and wrote Polish excellently. I had also learned German, Polish history and world geography. When in the heder we studied the Israelites leaving Egypt, as well as their wanderings in the desert I did not hesitate to tell my melamed about my knowledge. I also drew a map for him, thanks to which we could see what the journeys of the Israelites to the Promised Land looked like, and all this was thanks to what I had learned in school. I began to read different Polish books.[42]

As we have seen, other Orthodox authors quoted earlier (Etonis, Damaszek, M.W., and Esther) who had also tried to find fulfillment by contact with public educational institutions had had similar secular educational ambitions.

The attitude of young Jews toward public schools was not uniformly enthusiastic. It was also often ambivalent. For many secular authors with nationalist convictions, acquired usually after a period of study in an elementary school, public establishments were agents of assimilation. Many Orthodox authors could fear the secularizing influence of Polish schools, their tradition so remote from the world of the symbols and values of Jewish religion and tradition. However, almost none of them denied the role of the school as the most important and first source of secular education as well as of knowledge for the majority of Jewish youth.

JEWISH PARENTS AND PUBLIC SCHOOLS

Jewish parents were even more ambivalent toward elementary schools. Most of them were devout, traditional Jews. The great majority of them, especially those living in the areas of former Tsarist Russia, had no contact with public, non-Jewish schooling in their younger years. In most of the autobiographies, we do not find statements that traditional Jewish parents did not want to enroll their children in Polish public schools. At the same time, a considerable number of these autobiographies testify to their opposition. The local authorities forced many parents to enroll their children in elementary school. A refusal to follow the rules could lead to serious fines.[43] This administrative pressure was based on directives from the MWRiOP allowing district school authorities to decide whether a local heder was or was not the formal equivalent of an elementary school.[44] An even larger group of parents were justifiably extremely wary of public educational institutions.

What did these traditional Jewish parents fear from the public schools? Despite what the critical young people wrote about their immediate surroundings, traditional communities, more often than one might imagine, wanted their children to receive a modern education, especially one that would allow them to move freely in the real Polish world. As emerges from these autobiographies, their parents were for the most part interested in their children learning the following three subjects: mathematics, Yiddish, and Polish. The wealthier households often hired additional personal tutors to teach these subjects.[45] At the same time, Jewish parents often feared the alienating influence (including secularization and extreme acculturation) of school on their children. The values, daily norms, and goals as well as the whole world of symbols instilled in a public school were diametrically opposed to those instilled in traditional homes. Parents were afraid that public schools would sow in their children seeds of doubt as to the principles of faith and the widely understood traditional lifestyle. It was thus not an issue of parental opposition to their children breaking Halakhic precepts (mainly doing forbidden things on the Shabbat under the influence of their peers or eating nonkosher food) but above all of alienating children from older generations' lifestyle and thinking. Not everyone was reassured by officially excusing children from writing on the Shabbat. Parents' deep distrust was already aroused by the fact that the institution that Jewish children were to attend on that day worked on the Shabbat. As the autobiographies attest, many traditional parents did not know of the existence of the rule excusing Jewish children from writing in school on the Shabbat or did not believe that it would be applied. In YIVO autobiographies written mainly by secularized individuals, the prohibition on writing on the Shabbat was never actually a problem for the authors, but it was for their parents (of course, religious youth saw this differently).

Opposition on the part of Jewish parents to Polish schooling was not—apart from a few exceptions—absolute. The situation described above in which the mother of an ultra-Orthodox Hasid from Belz, Yehezkel Twerski, forbade him studying Polish and acquiring any secular knowledge belonged to the exceptions, even in the author's extremely conservative surroundings. Despite the dominant narrative among the young people of "ignorant" parents, unable to comprehend the world around them, the latter were not at all opposed to everything that was modern. They were not afraid of their children's actual connection with Polish culture and language. The social and intellectual capital acquired as a result of this connection was recognized to be valuable for their children's future success in life. However, more religious parents, not living in poverty but situated near the Orthodox elite, did indicate their unhappiness with public schooling. These parents usually had the financial means to educate their children in private Jewish schools or to teach them Polish without the agency of the non-Jewish community.

As we can see from Galitsyaner's autobiography, he was enrolled at the age of seven in elementary school (he had been studying for some years already in a heder) as a result of official pressure. This was despite the opposition of his father, who said angrily, "That school is turning Jewish children into goyim."[46] Proof that his father was not opposed to the study of secular subjects or to contact with Polish culture was the fact that when the boy had been going to the heder, his parents had hired a tutor to teach him arithmetic and Polish.[47] Moreover, his parents were afraid not so much of the different" Polish culture as of the secularization of their child. Total opposition to public education on the part of poor, traditional parents was very rare and was religiously based. "Yudl" came from the Kielce region, from an extremely poor and conservative family of an assistant to a melamed: "I was seven years-old. I wanted to go to elementary school but no-one would hear a word of this. My father said: 'Your older brothers don't go to school, nor do any of your sisters. Why do you want to go?' I begged him: 'Why do all the other children except me go to school?' Father replied that he did not want his child to sit bare-headed next to a crucifix."[48]

Yafet's parents had similar fears. From the start of his studies in the heder, which he began at the age of three, the boy showed signs of being a masmid—an exceptionally talented pupil able to aspire to a rabbinical career. When he was approaching his seventh birthday, his parents had to deal with a dilemma typical of the educational choices facing traditional parents in the Second Republic:

Now, when I was meant to enter elementary school, a row broke out between my father and mother. Father declared that elementary school was the road to abandoning the Jewish faith. In a dramatic voice he asked mother: "This child could become a rabbi and you want him to convert?" Mother replied that even if he wanted to become a rabbi he also needed to master Polish: "If he doesn't go to school, he won't be able to speak, read, or write in Polish." If she had the money she would hire a tutor, but since that was out of the question the boy ought to go to school.[49]

Yafet eventually went to elementary school, and later he studied in a yeshiva and became a rabbi. However, right after this he abandoned the Orthodox lifestyle, which was a great tragedy, especially for his father. It was elementary school that sowed the first seed of secularism within him.

The secularizing influence of public establishments was often feared less than the similar effect of secular Jewish schools. A conference of four hundred rabbis from all over Poland, held in 1926, forbade Jewish parents from sending their children to TsYShO or Tarbut schools, "which have the single common goal of extinguishing every spark of religious belief in children's hearts."[50] It emerges from a number of YIVO autobiographies that traditional parents enrolling their children in secular Jewish schools were often unaware of the antireligious nature of some of these schools, especially those in the TsYShO network. Yud-Giml's "fanatically religious father" enrolled her in just such an establishment. The little girl had already been studying in a Talmud Torah, and after some hesitation her father decided to enroll her in a "progressive school," as she wrote, "probably because I was a girl and also a cripple."[51] Her happiness at going to this school lasted only a year, up to the time when her father realized the secular and even antireligious nature of TsYShO establishments.[52]

Traditional Jewish parents had no idea what a public school looked like, since anything they knew about it usually came from their children studying in one. Therefore, their opposition often changed to grudging acceptance. This was the case with Drori's parents. As he wrote with the great irony typical of descriptions of a traditional community by someone who, as a teenager, had joined Po'alei-Tsiyon-Left while he was still studying in a heder, "Disaster struck moms and dads in Częstochowa! The educational authorities issued an order that all children between the ages of seven and fourteen were to be enrolled in a public school! They were not going to be taught love of 'Yiddishkayt,' nor any prayers, but what the goyim learned. Many parents, fearful of fines, enrolled their children. I was one of these 'unfortunate, poor children,' who had to go to such a school."[53]

Initially, although he was a good student, he was afraid to remind his parents of the need to buy textbooks: "At home I was not brave enough to raise the issue of money for books, since mother had said that she had not enrolled me in a school, from which she later wanted to withdraw me, to spend their last pennies on 'Polish' books."[54] However, with time, his mother saw the school's good side. It turned out that Drori's brother, who went only to a heder, was no more pious than Drori.[55] The boy's mother liked the fact that the children's work, including her son's, was displayed during exhibitions in the school. The mother and father were proud of their son's grades.

The autobiographies confirm that religious, traditional, and above all Orthodox parents were far more afraid of secondary schools' secularizing influence. The principal reason for their opposition was the fact that in secondary schools the rule on not writing on Saturdays did not apply. Of course, it happened that some teachers did not follow this rule even in elementary school, but given that following Halakhic precepts applied only to people considered to be adults in Judaism (that is, thirteen-year-old boys and twelve-year-old girls), the issue of going to school on Saturdays applied mainly to young people in secondary school.

There were also non-Halakhic factors causing parental opposition to their children's education in postelementary secular schools. If a child came from the provinces, he or she often had to travel to another city and live in a residence hall far from direct parental supervision. The elite educational level of secondary schools in the Second Republic exerted equally strong cultural pressure on students in the issues of manners, dress, way of speaking, and general lifestyle. The models instilled in secondary schools were different from those represented by the traditional or Orthodox Jewish world. Teenagers, though, tend to rebel against their parents and are more susceptible to peer pressure.[56] All these reasons (and of course financial ones) meant that a great many parents, while agreeing to their children going to elementary school, were opposed to secondary schooling.

This was the case with Feygeles's sisters. Unlike the author, they were enrolled in elementary schools. They later even enrolled in a public secondary school. What led to their father withdrawing them was precisely these schools' failure to abide by the Shabbat rules.[57] Esther, described in chapter 2, abandoned her studies in secondary school for the same reasons. The need to write in secondary school on the Shabbat meant that "Sara Kopyto's" parents were opposed to her studying there, although they had not opposed her attending elementary school.[58] Gershon Pipe, who was attending elementary school and Talmud Torah at the same time, wrote, "After third grade we could take the entrance exam to secondary school; it never even crossed my mind to do so! Heaven forbid that I should go to school on the Shabbat and write!" Young people who attended secondary school were not, in Pipe's circle, treated as Jews at all.[59] We find in a great many of these autobiographies examples of this lack of opposition (and even some satisfaction) on the part of parents to their children attending state elementary school, yet opposition to their children attending secondary school.[60]

There were also religious parents who tried to circumvent the prohibition on writing on Saturday in order to allow their children to study at a higher level of secular education. As one of the autobiographers wrote, "The issue of writing on a Saturday was given a serious airing at home: mother disagreed on principle: how could a granddaughter of Sura Mala write on a Saturday! My sisters were screaming for me not to leave school, for Ida had had to interrupt her education because of this Saturday writing, although she had passed splendidly into the fifth grade of a Russian secondary school, and Father, well Father found a way round it: 'I'm not allowed to say "yes," I don't want to say "no," so do what you want!'"[61]

Of course, parents from wealthier, secular, acculturated, and nationalistically inclined families did not experience these dilemmas associated with public elementary and secondary schooling. When they could afford it, they sent their children to Jewish schools rather than elementary ones. At the secondary level, they left their children in private establishments, and when these did not have the full privileges of public schools, they sent them to public establishments to improve their chances of obtaining a high school diploma. These dilemmas did not affect the majority of poor traditional parents. Only parents from the Orthodox, acculturated, or simply secularized bourgeoisie and intelligentsia could afford to send their children to expensive private Jewish schools accredited by the state and pay for at least seven years of education in them.[62] The indisputable basic obstacle to achieving children's and parents' educational ambitions was poverty. Most of the authors mentioned their desire for further formal education as an unfulfilled dream and, knowing that they had no chance of achieving it, did not consider what their parents might have to say about it.

The popularity of public education among parents and students worried Jewish nationalist circles. There were many reasons for the growth of interest in public schools, as well as in (Jewish and non-Jewish) private schools teaching in Polish. Some reasons were demographic, given the postwar rise in the birth rate; others were economic, such as the impoverishment of the majority of Jewish social classes as a result of the worldwide depression, which made it harder for them to send their children to expensive private schools. Another cause was the authorities' clear desire to weaken the Jewish private education sector. Private Jewish schools in the Horev, Yavne, Tarbut, TsYShO, and Shul-Kult networks, as well as the independent ones, were fee-paying. These schools, suffering from chronic financial problems, were unable to operate in a great many small towns. They were in strong competition with one another. Furthermore, the last three networks mentioned were secular. Their influence on children was often recognized to be worse than the acculturation encouraged by non-Jewish teachers. For all these reasons, to the dismay of Jewish nationalist politicians and educators, a great many traditional parents preferred to send their children to public establishments.[63] As the teachers in the Tarbut school in Łuck pointed out, when a szabasówka opened there in 1926, they lost 250 of their 300 students to it.[64] As can be seen, a state school following the Shabbat laws and charging no fees won over a majority of traditional Jewish parents. Many of the autobiographers quoted here emphasized such a preference.

Arie Tartakower gave financial reasons as the main cause of the public schools' success.[65] An analysis of the YIVO autobiographies shows, however, that there were additional reasons. Other important factors affecting the choice of Polish schools (public or private) by Jewish parents were pragmatic concerns. A good knowledge of the national language was key in work as well as in every other area of social life. In the smallest towns and villages, the only accessible educational establishment, given the lack even of heders in the area, was often the public school.[66] All these factors, and not just the poverty of the Jewish masses and discrimination on the part of national school networks, meant that Polish public schooling enjoyed great popularity on the Jewish Street.

CONCLUSIONS

Attending an elementary school was a modern phenomenon, distinguishing the socialization of the generation growing up between the wars from that of earlier generations, and was yet another factor intensifying intergenerational conflict. The public school was for this generation the source of new norms and values, new categories and reference points for perceiving the world, and its educational content did not augment but challenged the educational model received at home. In this way it alienated Jewish parents, while in a great many younger people it led to the development of a negative attitude toward the world of tradition in which their elders lived. On the other hand, the public schools ignoring any kind of educational content associated with the Jewish world was seen by many of the autobiographers as yet another example of their difference. In their interpretation, public schools represented the external world to which Jewish youth aspired but that did not accept them. This feeling strengthened the strong consciousness of economic, social, and class barriers to admission into the higher levels of education. Schools taught children the democratic promise, a conviction of the value and prestige of higher education and the professions associated with it. However, as we have seen in the descriptions of their immediate surroundings, employment opportunities, and aspirations, young people understood that the state did nothing to help them achieve these aspirations. Ambitious life goals that could not be realized, as well as feelings of discrimination, were further factors radicalizing young Jewish people. Elementary education indirectly contributed to this state of affairs. Nearly all the autobiographies revealed the enormous expectations young people had of the modern public school. It was supposed to provide the tools necessary for young people to change the contemporary world they perceived so negatively. Accounts of young people's educational experiences, like those of other areas of life, were characterized by a modern social imagination, serving as an important basis for young people's political radicalism.

Elementary school was for young Jewish people one of the most important sources of secular European culture. There, a majority of young Jews learned a modern lifestyle and new forms of social life. The cultural capital acquired in school allowed them to participate in Polish culture. Most of the authors, almost 80 percent of whom wrote their contributions in Yiddish, had spent at least a few years studying in public establishments and thus knew Polish too. The remainder knew it not only from the street but also from private tutors or private Jewish schools assuring the minimum state curriculum. Their Polish was now completely different from the one that their parents used. A lack of Polish, and even often the presence of a noticeable Jewish accent, no longer applied to the youngest generation. Polish school unified the experiences of young people coming from such different areas as the provinces of central Poland, former Galicia, or the eastern provinces, in which the processes of polonization began only in 1918. The influence of Polish culture was strengthened by institutions of the nationalistically oriented state, with its education system in the lead, as well as the growing influence of mass culture. These factors played an enormous role in creating a new type of political consciousness on the part of Polish Jews, which gradually began to cross the old Litvak-Hasidic and Russo-Galician borders. In this process of change of awareness, the attitude of the youngest generation growing up in the Second Republic was avant-garde. For most of the nonacculturated parents, ignorant of Polish culture, the Polish state was a new phenomenon, for the most part foreign, and which replaced another foreign entity. For young people the Second Republic was the only country they had known.

The situation described here was conditioned by the great dynamic of processes of acculturation occurring within this generation. It is impossible to overemphasize their role in the development of young Jews' political consciousness during the interwar period. Education did not provide their desired place in the outside world or allow them to achieve their individual ambitions; at the same time, schools led them to recognize Polish culture as prestigious while simultaneously feeling rejected by it, feeling discrimination and antisemitism more strongly than previous generations. After leaving school, young people usually ended up in the only social space in which they were accepted: radical politics.

FOUR

—~w—

JEWISH PRIVATE EDUCATION

WORLD WAR I AND THE OCCUPATION by the Germans of lands that would soon be Polish led to a true revolution in the area of Jewish private education there. The German administration and the Regency Council, installed by it for the administration of occupied Polish territory, legalized plans for establishing both Zionist Hebrew- and Yiddish-language schools. The dramatic growth in Jewish private schools between 1915 and 1918 reflected the enormous demand for modern Jewish education.[1] Earlier, secular forms of Jewish education in their Hebrew and Yiddish iterations had been firmly fought by the Tsarist authorities controlling most of the land of the future Polish Second Republic. After 1914 the situation of traditional religious education also changed dramatically. The provisional regulations on elementary schools in the German-controlled Polish kingdom dating from October 29, 1917, called for separate schools respecting the Shabbat or separate classes that would follow the rules and precepts of that holy day. At the same time, it was already recommended that the Talmud Torahs and heders introduce mandatory Polish classes.[2] This kind of policy was continued after the establishment of the Polish state. Educational policy throughout the whole interwar period leaves no doubt that the state was aiming to take over the basic educational program for most young Jewish people, whether through elementary schools or through Jewish private establishments (from heders to national private school networks), which also had to adapt their curricula to state requirements. At the same time, despite the imposed curricula, Jewish schools enjoyed great freedom. The main ones, such as Horev, Tarbut, Yavne, and TsYShO, operated under the patronage of political movements (respectively, Aguda, general and moderately left-wing Zionists, religious Zionists, and the Bund and Po'alei-Tsiyon-Left) and both

96

during and outside class openly and intensively pushed the political views of their patrons. The world of Jewish education therefore reflected the general political, ideological, and cultural pluralism of the Jewish Street of the day.

THE ORTHODOX EDUCATION SYSTEM

The largest private Jewish educational network was the Orthodox Horev, supervised by Agudat Israel. It represented the most important component of the Orthodox education system, which toward the end of the 1930s educated around 60 percent of children attending private Jewish schools.[3] The aim of this network was to save and strengthen traditional education based on the study of Jewish religious texts. It included heders of all levels, so-called small yeshivas, and Talmudic institutions of higher learning. In line with centuries of tradition, although religious texts written mainly in Hebrew (and partly in Aramaic, as in the Talmud) were studied in these establishments, the teaching was in Yiddish. Horev, under the pressure of state requirements that it introduce a curricular minimum in the form of basic secular subjects, as well as of competition from other networks of Jewish schools, also ran modern Orthodox schools for boys, Yesodei ha-Torah (Torah Basics), and for girls, Bais Yaakov (House of Jacob). Polish was also taught in traditional heders supervised by Aguda.[4] The establishment and operation of the Horev system symbolized a new Orthodox stage in the life of the Jewish religious community in eastern Europe—taking advantage of modern institutions in the battle to preserve tradition. As declared in a memorandum of the Orthodox Teachers' Seminar, basing religious education on "modern pedagogical foundations" was essential to "hold young people to the Torah and its commandments." It was planned to fight the competition of secular Jewish schools—that is, "anti-religious elements"—using their own weapons. In addition to the Bible, the Talmud, "the lives of the Greats of Israel," the history of the Jews, and the Hebrew language in its traditional version, the seminar declared "basic instruction in pedagogy and psychology to be a key element of our curriculum."[5] Through the establishment of a modern Orthodox Teachers' Seminar, Aguda attempted not only to compete with Jewish schools but also to introduce its own teachers of religion into the public schools. Care was taken in Aguda schools that children follow Orthodox norms, such as appropriate dress, hairstyles (sidelocks in the case of Hasidic boys), and modest behavior. Overall, the Aguda school system embraced fully traditional heders, not always following even the state minimum curriculum, as well as heders modernized to the extent that they earned the title of modern Orthodox religious schools.[6]

The Bais Yaakov school network for girls, established by Sarah Schenirer, was a quite exceptional venture.[7] The first of its schools was established in Kraków in 1917. Schenirer shortly thereafter set up several other establishments, linked in a network, which in 1919 came under the Agudat Israel umbrella, making it in 1923 part of the Horev system with joint control over the finances. Within the Horev system, the Bais Yaakov network enjoyed autonomy; from 1924 it published two journals, *Beis Yankev Zhurnal* and *Kindergorten,* and from 1925 it had its own teachers' college in Kraków. In most of the Bais Yaakov schools, the children studied after completing their classes in a public school. Day schools that opened in the 1930s, located in the larger cities, were distinguished by the fact that, unlike the Aguda heders, they followed the full Polish elementary school curriculum, teaching traditional Jewish subjects in after-hours classes.[8] The Bnos Agudah (Daughters of Aguda), Agudat Israel's girls' organization, was very active in these schools. Bais Yaakov schools taught the basics of religion and Jewish law (Halakha), breaking the traditional stereotype forbidding Jewish girls from studying the Torah, although doing so in a different way and much less extensively than for boys. These establishments were meant to make girls conscious of their tasks as modern Orthodox women, thus able to defend their future families against the influences of secularization.

The Horev system took over the great majority of heders from the former Congress Kingdom, many of these establishments being in Galicia, and it also had a growing footprint in the northeastern provinces. In 1931 Horev had 73,311 students.[9] In 1937 around 70,000 boys and over 30,000 girls, altogether 109,000 children and young people, were enrolled in all its establishments.[10] The Orthodox community was successful too in the development of religious schools for girls, hitherto unheard of in this part of the continent. In 1926 the Bais Yaakov network had 55 schools and 7,340 girls, in 1929 the corresponding figures were 87 and 12,000, and by 1937 it had 248 schools, with over 35,000 girls attending them.[11] According to Joseph Marcus's calculations, during the 1934/35 school year 60 percent of all Jewish children studying in Orthodox and traditional education were in the Horev system.[12] The Horev educational establishments, which were legal and accredited by local education authorities, ran alongside (accredited and nonaccredited) unaffiliated Litvak heders outside the system, as well as traditional (mainly illegal) Galician heders run by Hasidim not recognizing the authority of the Ger dynasty and of Aguda, which was dominated by it.

On September 13, 1923, Aguda succeeded in obtaining a decision by the Ministry of Education recognizing its heders as the equivalent of elementary schools and thus releasing the students in these heders from having to attend public school.[13] The extent of teaching in Polish and of teaching basic secular subjects was in fact regulated by the 1932 educational reform and an agreement between Aguda and the Ministry of Education, signed in 1935.[14] The heders under Aguda supervision had each time to be accredited by the local education authorities, providing proof that they were implementing the secular curriculum at the elementary-school level. The local authorities thus gained considerable leeway in assessing the heders' pedagogical and academic level.[15] If they did not judge the syllabus to be satisfactory, they could insist that children be enrolled in public schools. A great many YIVO autobiographies testify that this often happened.

Some of the modernized Litvak heders, the so-called *metukan* (reformed) heders operating mainly in the northeastern provinces, were quite unusual. A result of the greater openness of Litvak Judaism to secular affairs, as well as the smaller chasm between Orthodoxy and the less religious or secular Jewish groups, was an affinity for and involvement with the Zionism of part of the religious elite in that area. This allowed religious sympathizers with Zionism to establish metukan heders as early as the 1890s, mainly in the area of the future Polish northeastern provinces. In these establishments the traditional curriculum was supplemented by basic secular subjects and the study of a modern version of Hebrew (sometimes they taught exclusively in this language), and greater emphasis was laid on studying biblical texts.[16] Between the wars some of these institutions came under the control of the Zionist religious Mizrahi party and became elements in its Yavne school system. After 1918 even secular Hebrew Tarbut schools were established using a model based on several metukan heders. Some of these establishments continued to operate as independent, private institutions. Some of the authors quoted here from Vilna and Nowogródek provinces attended them.

Vilna occupied an exceptional position in the field of modern religious education. Between the wars, the official city Talmud Torah—consisting of three separate institutions—followed the Yavne schools' modern syllabus. In the 1920s six grades of the Vilna Talmud Torah were recognized by the state as the equivalent of a four-grade elementary school. In addition to subjects such as Hebrew, the Mishna, the Gemara, and the basics of Polish and Polish culture, they taught algebra, geometry, physics, natural sciences, Polish history, drawing, and singing.[17] In the 1930s the "general studies" curriculum in this establishment already covered a full six grades of elementary school. In line with the government's and the local school districts' general approach (the latter more interested in battling with secular Jewish national schools and supporting the religious ones), the Vilna Talmud Torah for most of the interwar period received a substantial grant from the Vilna city council.[18] Hebrew schools could only dream of this kind of support, not to mention the openly harassed Yiddish schools of the TsYShO and the Central Education Committee (Tsentraler Bildungs Komitet, TseBeKa) that operated in Vilna and the surrounding area. The Jewish religious schools of the Beit Yehuda (Judah's House) network, an autonomous part of the Yavne network, also operated in the city. This type of modern religious education, typical of the northeastern provinces, was not found in the majority of Talmud Torahs in other parts of the country. Importantly, at that moment in most yeshivas, and thus at the highest level of Orthodox education, nineteenth-century prohibitions on any kind of contact by the students with secular literature still applied. As the YIVO autobiographies show, this led to intergenerational tension within the Orthodox community.

The Yavne network, like the ideology of its parent political party, combined Zionism with a modernized version of Orthodox religion in its curriculum. Schools run by the Mizrahi party joined the Yavne network in 1927. Teaching was in Hebrew (apart from a number of mandatory subjects taught in Polish), and this network provided a full range of secular subjects as well as devoting a great many hours to religious studies.[19] The traditional methods of teaching the Talmud as well as rabbinical commentaries were combined with modern pedagogical methods. Girls also attended these schools, which meant that, unlike in the Bais Yaakov schools, they learned not only prayers but also the Torah and Hebrew, which was contrary to the prohibition on women studying the holy texts. At the same time, the full range of secular subjects taught allowed the girls to continue studying in secondary schools.[20] Yavne, like Mizrahi, held a strong position among the Litvak element of Jewish society, but schools in this network operated throughout the whole country.[21]

The Yavne network ran elementary and secondary schools. At the beginning of the 1930s, it had four secondary schools: in Białystok, Kraków, Łódź, and Vilna. Some secondary schools were also rabbinical seminaries for boys, such as the Tahkemoni establishments in Warsaw and Białystok. The secondary schools for girls were teachers' colleges. In 1937 it was a great coup for Yavne to open a modern teachers' high school, modeled on public institutions. Only with a diploma from such an institution could one be granted entry to university.[22] In 1933 around fifteen thousand students attended Yavne schools, and four years later this number reached almost sixteen thousand.[23]

The modernized establishments of Jewish religious education described here differed greatly from the unreformed traditional institutions. This is confirmed by a great many YIVO autobiographies. It emerges from the one written by Feygeles that thanks to the author's transfer at the age of seven from a traditional heder to a modernized heder that also taught secular subjects, he could attempt to gain admission to secondary school.[24] In Esther's autobiography, the Bais Yaakov school symbolized modernity, an opening to the world, and knowledge of this world as well as fidelity to Jewish tradition and religion, and it was meant to eliminate the contradiction between modernity and religious tradition.[25] Esther emphasized that she appreciated the evening Bais Yaakov school more than the state szabasówka, which she was attending at the same time during the day. Esther also valued the fact that thanks to the Orthodox girls' school, religious education was now accessible to her—admittedly to a lesser extent than for boys, but to a greater one than was foreseen for girls in traditional Jewish societies. She wrote, "I told anyone who would listen that there would soon be a school for girls . . ., where we would learn Yiddish and how to pray and, I concluded triumphantly, study the Bible. . . . To make a long story short, a Bais Yaakov school was founded. My father worked actively on behalf of the school often giving public lectures."[26] The Bais Yaakov school undoubtedly played a key role in keeping the young author in a normative and social circle of Jewish Orthodoxy:

> I didn't consider the public school to be "ours," even though we were taught by Jewish men and women[27] . . . they didn't observe the Shabbat and always spoke Polish. . . . I also felt that the way they taught religion was wrong. More than once I found myself in tears outside the classroom door as a consequence of challenging my teacher. I had no intention of making myself important; I only wanted to point out where the teacher had erred. I would explain that this or that in the school's teaching of history didn't conform to what we were taught in Bais Yaakov and therefore was wrong. For this I got paddled liberally. While I continued to protest at every opportunity, this didn't prevent me from getting straight 5s on my report card.[28] Father was very pleased and stopped talking about me becoming a *"shikse."*[29]

In the context of the issues under discussion, "Stormer's" biographical path was typical. He came from Opoczno and grew up in an elite, wealthy (although over time experiencing growing financial problems) family of supporters of Ger Hasidism. In line with the Orthodox model, every effort was made to provide him with an above-average knowledge of Jewish religious studies, as well as a basic knowledge of secular subjects. Stormer initially attended several heders, and at the age of seven he went to an elementary school, from which his mother soon withdrew him, enrolling him in the elite Yesodei ha-Torah School associated with the Horev system. The quality of this establishment's religious education assured its students high social prestige.[30] Restoring the prestige of religious education was a fundamental achievement on the part of the Orthodox between the wars, as well as a condition for their survival, since, as we have seen, the traditional heders were no longer able to guarantee this prestige.

Those who attended modern establishments of religious education wrote positively about them. Here, Ben-Tikva was one of the exceptions. Unlike Esther or Stormer, he was the son of a poor peddler who was later a luftmensch. The fact that while writing his autobiography he was an unbeliever, a left-wing Zionist, and working on hakhshara was influential in the boy's attitude to every institution that had a religious element.[31] As a child of poverty, living at the time in Vilna, Ben-Tikva attended a number of traditional heders and Talmud Torahs, spent a short time in a secular school, and ended up at the Vilna Beit Yehuda. This was a school for children coming from the lowest Jewish social classes in Vilna, associated with the Mizrahi party. Mizrahi activists prided themselves on providing children of poverty with high-level traditional and secular education.[32] The author saw his school quite differently. In his view, it differed little from the Talmud Torah he had attended earlier. Like in the heder (as he called his earlier Talmud Torah), "we live under the smack of the cane and the rabbi's glare.... The sign over the school entrance read 'a place of Torah and secular studies.' The cane was secular; the whip was the Torah." Just as in other traditional institutions, here too students experienced hunger, poverty, and corporal punishment.[33] Ben-Tikva formulated his attack on the modern school from the same ideological perspective as the authors who criticized the traditional heder.

This modernist approach on the part of young people to looking at institutions of traditional education is summed up by "Binyomin R's" autobiography. This son of a rather wealthy merchant from Bielsko Podlaskie, well versed in the Torah, attended elite heders for many years. In most of them, he assessed critically the level of teaching, the physical force used by the melameds, and the lack of a modern pedagogical approach. Everything changed when he entered a heder metukan. For him, the positive elements were the fact that Bible study also included Bible exegesis and that his teacher was a freethinker who engaged in discussion with twelve- and thirteen-year-olds.[34] Etonis also presented his heder metukan in a very positive light: "This educational institution bore some resemblance to a modern heder. The teacher, a local young man, was a 'progressive.' He taught us to read and write in Hebrew from a textbook, as well as to recite prayers.[35] We didn't sit at tables but on real school benches. Every Friday we would gather in the teacher's room and sing songs. Naturally, they were Hebrew songs, such as *The Little Room, Sleep, My Child, Mother, Mother*, as well as other children's songs, and at the end we sang *Hatikvah*."[36]

M. W. described the moment when he was very close to abandoning religion, which his mother prevented when she transferred him from a traditional Talmud Torah to the Hasidic Amud ha-Torah heder in Nalewki. M. W. now proudly emphasized that among his friends were the "cleverest Hasidim," since he had entered an institution educating the Hasidic elite. In this environment, M. W. was once again able to devote himself with a passion to religious studies. In his description of the Amud ha-Torah heder, what attracts my attention is his emphasis on this institution's modern features, its innovative pedagogical approach, and the teachers inspiring students to study, lighting their ambition, and encouraging them to study in pairs. This description clearly differs from that of an unmodern traditional heder.[37]

Likewise, the students of elite Orthodox establishments did not spare traditional heders sharp words, although they did not criticize religious education as such. Their own experience proved that it could be reconciled with the demands of the modern world. Hence, the quoted excerpts can be seen as attempts to defend the traditional—yet at the same time modernized—institution with the aid of modernistic language and prove that it could rise to the challenge posed by the modern value system. In a great many of the autobiographies, the authors emphasize the "organization," "efficiency," and "general good order" in the schools, contrasting this with the chaos of unreformed institutions. Some indeed wrote about the modern pedagogical thought prevailing in Orthodox establishments, thanks to which they were treated as children and not as "small adults." The cat egories of "childhood" and "adolescence" were alien to traditional educational institutions. Young people also positively assessed elementary schools as well as yeshivas not only on account of the secular element of the curriculum but also for their "rationalism," allowing the secular to be reconciled with the religious. However, at the same time, they rejected some views of the Orthodox community, denying the legitimacy of studying secular subjects and claiming for itself the right to control what young people read or indeed studied in their free time.

As these excerpts and Orthodox authors' subsequent fortunes show, modernized Orthodox educational institutions at least partly passed the test. Without a doubt they assured a high standard of religious education, as well as intellectual training allowing students to continue their education in yeshivas or public secondary schools. The autobiographies of Etonis, A Shtetleshe, Gamalielis, Damaszek, and Esther, quoted in this and previous chapters, coming from such different religious communities and places as Eastern Galicia, central Poland, and the northeast provinces, demonstrate that the authors had an opportunity to enter secular schools after studying in Orthodox institutions, even obtain their high school diploma and apply to college.

Among the participants in the YIVO competition, on the whole the children of the wealthier Orthodox elite attended the modernized, more expensive heders, which taught subjects leading to real Talmudic studies. This proves that in the case of the generation being described here, despite Agudat Israel's rhetoric, the Orthodox no longer belonged to the "silent majority" but were a specific minority group standing out against a background of their rapidly secularizing peers.[38] In the 1930s, Poland experienced a change in social tendencies. The poorest stopped being the most religious social class. Protecting religiousness required large financial resources as well as social and cultural capital. Furthermore, the effectiveness of Orthodox educational institutions was likewise limited. This can be seen, for example, in the biography of Ernst, whose studies in an elite and modernized Talmud Torah did not prevent him later joining the antireligious Tsukunft.[39] There were similar situations in the cases of Binyomin R., Gamalielis, and several other authors who came from rather elite Orthodox families. The analyzed autobiographies show that, to save a child from usually radical secularization, it was not enough to send them to an elite Orthodox school and keep them there to the age of twelve or thirteen; instead, they had to be educated further in yeshivas up to the age of twenty (and sometimes even longer), or in Orthodox seminars for girls. Most of the autobiographers from Orthodox families, who as children studied the Talmud at a level that was inaccessible to most of their peers, if later they did not go to a yeshiva or a college, abandoned religion in their teens. When that happened, they nearly always ended up in one of the radically secularized political movements. This shows how difficult it was for this generation to break out of Orthodox society. From this society's point of view, both the Jewish and the non-Jewish worlds were full of secularizing dangers.

Finally, politics played a different role in Orthodox schools than in Jewish secular schools. Politics was present but was completely different from that in the secular, national Jewish schools. The latter were radically ideological, and the teachers and activists did not hide the fact that political encouragement and ideological awareness were important elements in developing students' personalities. Orthodox institutions, although favorable to parties like Aguda or Mizrahi, were perhaps the only organized sector of Jewish education in which political ideologies were not a central element in the syllabus. This fact also explains the Orthodox authors' less ideological way of looking at social reality.

THE TARBUT HEBREW SCHOOL SYSTEM

The most popular of the secular Jewish school networks was Tarbut, under the auspices of the centrist and moderate-left Zionist parties. Tarbut put into practice the idea of modern secular education in Hebrew, in clear opposition to traditional Orthodox and Yiddish education. As the leading Polish Zionist Yitshak Grünbaum wrote, modern national schooling was supposed to replace "medieval heders and aim to replace them with a national general school [Polish public school]."[40] The Tarbut system, however, was not atheistic or antireligious, unlike the TsYShO system, and students were introduced to the most important works of Jewish culture, including the Bible, the Talmud, rabbinical literature, prayers, and religious customs, but from a nationalist and not traditional, religious perspective.[41] Despite the fact that Tarbut schools were supervised by their Warsaw headquarters, they were not all similar. A student's experience was different in a school operating in the east of the country, in Volhynia, Polesie, the Nowogródek area, or Białystok and Vilna provinces, from one in central Poland or Galicia. These differences were the result of the differing natures of Orthodoxy and Zionism and of the relationship between them in various parts of the country. In Warsaw and the surrounding areas, it was out of the question for a respectable Ger or Aleksander Hasid to send his child to a Tarbut school. Meanwhile, many autobiographers living in the eastern and northern provinces not only came from religious homes but later, after completing a Zionist elementary or secondary school, continued their studies in Litvak yeshivas. Religious teachers also worked in Tarbut schools in the eastern part of the country.[42] The schools' Zionist character meant that a great deal of weight was given to studies of the Bible, which was treated as the most important national work of culture and proof of the people of Israel's unbroken relationship with their land. From the second half of the 1920s, when the Zionist community began to realize the impossibility of implementing a program of Jewish cultural national autonomy and there was a greater consciousness of growing polonization, Tarbut schooling, like the whole Zionist movement, banked on popularizing emigration and the preparatory hakhshara.[43] Zionism and Palestine were at the center of the schools' message, strengthened by the ceremonial observance of anniversaries, such as Teodor Herzl's *yortsayt* (his death anniversary), the anniversary of the Balfour Declaration, and the establishment of the Hebrew University in Jerusalem. In teaching Hebrew, the local Ashkenazi pronunciation was rejected in favor of the Sephardic used in the Middle East.[44] Zionist current affairs were explained to children in classes on modern history and on Palestine.[45]

Just as all secular Jewish schools did, the Tarbut ones had to cover the state curriculum dictated by the Ministry of Education in addition to their own syllabus in Hebrew. Subjects such as Polish, the geography and history of Poland, and knowledge of contemporary Poland were taught in Polish. Although

Hebrew schools were not treated as harshly as those run by the TsYShO, they too occasionally suffered from crackdowns by the national authorities. In 1936 the authorities closed two Hebrew teachers' seminars in Grodno and Vilna.[46] Likewise, Tarbut schools often had problems with the annual renewal of their operating concession.

During the war and its immediate aftermath, the dramatic expansion of Hebrew schooling was overseen by the Zionist Organization's Education Office. In 1922, when the Education Office was closed down, a center of Hebrew education was established—Tarbut.[47] In 1923, 30,672 students attended the network's schools, and in the 1934/35 school year that number had risen to 37,000.[48] Tarbut prided itself on having the second-largest network of secondary-school educational establishments after the Polish-Hebrew utraquist bilingual schools. As early as 1924, Tarbut encompassed nine secondary schools, attended by 2,447 students.[49] Some of them had official accreditation (unlike, for instance, nearly all the TsYShO schools), which allowed their graduates to attend Polish schools.[50] Between the wars the number of these institutions was constantly changing, dependent as they were on the economic situation and national policies. The Tarbut network, like its other Jewish competitors, was strongest in the eastern part of the country. In 1925 the Vilna Tarbut region prided itself on running as many as four secondary schools (half the national total), thirty-five elementary-level schools, three preschools, several evening schools, and the one and only Hebrew teachers' college at the time, established in 1921. The jewel of the Vilna Tarbut was the Hebrew Secondary School (Gimnasia Ivrit), established in 1916 on the initiative of Yosef Epstein and renowned throughout the Zionist world.[51]

Children from wealthier families, whose parents usually harbored Zionist sympathies, attended these schools and especially the Tarbut preschools. Their fees were the highest of all the Jewish private education networks. According to a 1930 study on the social origins of students at the Hebrew secondary school in Białystok, as many as 60 percent of the parents came from the merchant class, and as many as 10 percent represented the liberal professions.[52] Toward the end of the 1930s in Warsaw in the five Tarbut schools, despite the significant representation of children of artisans, workers, and minor merchants, as many as 14 percent came from the homes of the Warsaw wealthy bourgeoisie, and as many as 20 percent were the children of members of the liberal professions.[53] The percentage of children from the Jewish bourgeoisie was much lower in other schools. The same was true among the contestants in the YIVO competition who studied in Tarbut schools. Most of them came from the northeastern areas of the country. Education in Hebrew schools, paying particular attention to encouraging a love for the Hebrew language as well as for the idea of building a Jewish homeland in Palestine, had an enormous influence on its graduates' later consciousness and behavior. Starting in the second half of the 1920s, an emigrationist tendency arose in the Polish Zionist movement, developing at the expense of the battle for civil rights and freedoms for Jews in Poland. This led to the following paradox: The Tarbut schools, operating mainly for the bourgeois elite, at the same time encouraged an objective lowering of their own children's social status. This was what came of propounding hakhshara, emigration to Palestine, work on the land, and the ideal of physical labor. The tensions resulting from this paradox appear in a number of autobiographies.

Numerous contestants in the YIVO competition confirmed the power of the Tarbut schools' message. "Yesh," from Stanisławów, had attended a Hebrew pre-school. She wrote, "Since it was a Hebrew pre-school, I learned a great many Hebrew songs and first encountered the language, which is still so dear to me."[54] The Hebrew language was also one of her favorite subjects in Tarbut secondary school.[55] While writing her autobiography, she was an adherent (earlier an active member) of Ha-Shomer ha-Tsa'ir. "Neri" was transferred from a Talmud Torah to the Pińsk Herzliya (a flagship Tarbut school).[56] He wrote that thanks to this establishment he transformed from a troublemaker into a diligent student. Entering a Hebrew school was also a revelation, a completely new experience:

> What I got from the Herzliya school is the best any child can get from school. Pastoral care, first-rate teachers, a spacious building, all this had such a great influence on me that within a few months I became one of the best sixth-graders. The school ran on cooperative principles: each teacher was also a co-owner of the school, and its success was in everyone's interest.... The teaching at this school was of the very highest level. For the first time in my education, I would go happily to school. The teachers tried to find the best in every student and helped them to develop.[57]

According to another contributor to the YIVO competition, the advantage of the Hebrew schools was their high level of education, the development in young people of a "spirit of enterprise," and the fact that children in them were not exposed to the antisemitism that they encountered daily in the public schools. Paradoxically, this led to a situation in which they willingly learned not only Hebrew but also Polish. In the Tarbut schools, students did not associate Polish culture with the daily violence from the "shaygets."[58]

The schools' ideological and political message was strengthened by visits from "great people"—distinguished Zionists from Poland and around the world. The cult of personality from the Zionist pantheon was one of the important elements of the syllabus. A significant event in Grodno, and specifically in the Tarbut teachers' college there, was a visit by the famous Hebrew poet Haylm Nahman Bialik. The date of his visit, December 31, 1931, was one of a few dates that Binyomin noted in his autobiography. For Bialik's visit, quotations from the national poet's works were displayed in the classrooms, while he, speaking to the young people, called on them to dedicate themselves to a single goal, "which was the reason why they were attending Hebrew secondary schools"—in other words, building a modern Hebrew culture and emigrating to the Land of Israel.[59] A great event in the Herzliya school in Pińsk was a visit by the well-known writer and theorist of Zionist education Nathan Bistricki, who at the time had already lived in Palestine.[60] These visits by well-known people in the Jewish world to Tarbut schools gave them added prestige. Conversations with famous Zionists undoubtedly strengthened these establishments' political and ideological message. This all meant that students for the most part used only superlatives to describe them.

The excerpt quoted below, coming from an autobiographer who grew up in Równe (Rivne), is a typical account from a proud graduate of a Tarbut school. When after great effort he had managed to leave the "hated," "nationally foreign" elementary school and entered a Hebrew school, he wrote, "It was if I had been reborn. . . . Hebrew, the teachers and students, my brothers and sisters all had an enormous influence on me. . . . Here was sown in my heart a deep love for my people and for my homeland [the Land of Israel], and in this way my enthusiasm for work on rebuilding our country developed."[61] Zhanet wrote about her first day in a Tarbut school "as the wide world." According to her, children were taught there what they needed to know, and they were modernized and turned into "serious" young people.[62] An excerpt from Yesh's autobiography also attests to Tarbut schools instilling in their students a sense of exceptionalism, of belonging to a national avant-garde. After completing a public elementary school, she entered a Hebrew secondary school. The basic division and rivalry among the students was between graduates of state and Tarbut elementary schools. The latter supposedly displayed a sense of superiority over the graduates of a "foreign school."[63]

Although the Tarbut schools were undoubtedly sympathetic toward Zionist parties and youth organizations, some teachers followed the principle that politics should not obscure their primary responsibility to the children—namely, teaching. In Ostrynia a teacher in a Tarbut school forbade his students from attending meetings of the local Ha-Shomer ha-Tsa'ir other than on Saturdays. He even had a spy report on cases of breaking this rule, and students were punished for not following it.[64] In the Tarbut secondary schools, the administration of which lay in the ideological center of the Zionist spectrum, some of the left-wing activities of students were not favorably viewed. A sympathizer with the moderate Zionist left, Binyomin R., complained of the "white terror" in the Tarbut secondary school in Białystok.[65] He wrote that the principal supposedly told young, expelled left-wingers "in my school there is no place for Stalin-lovers."[66] That was in 1934. The authorities of Jewish secondary schools doubtless recalled the famous case three years earlier of the closure of the Jewish Teachers' Seminar in Vilna for allowing communist agitation.

The most important ideological feature of Tarbut schools was their support for all things Hebrew. Trying to find their footing among processes such as the growing acculturation of the wealthier circles from which their students came, as well as sincerely propounding Polish patriotism (and at the same time trying to distinguish it from negative assimilation), Zionist educators saw Hebrew as an essential element in building the new Jewish nation. This is confirmed by a number of autobiographical excerpts. In his autobiography written in Polish, "Ajzyk Rozen" recalled, "I spend most of my time at school on Hebrew at which I am a star student. I recall reciting lines by Bialik or Peretz and the teacher invited in the principal to listen to me recite lines from our national bards. He frequently spoke of my success in my studies, and especially in Hebrew. My parents were very proud of this."[67] Hebrew poetry also played a central part in Neri's memories of a Tarbut school.[68]

As I have already mentioned several times, society in the Second Republic, including the Jewish community, was characterized by social and class distinctions. In the case of Jewish people, the traditional divisions (the religious and merchant elites versus people living by the fruit of their own labor) were overlaid by new divisions, not just financial ones but also ones of social status between the intelligentsia and the uneducated. In the area of school experience, one can see the power of interwar social and class distinctions most clearly in the autobiographies of students and graduates of elite Tarbut schools. An autobiographer from an acculturated, wealthy, Zionist home in Kowel described her happy childhood playing with friends, all of whom were from the local intelligentsia. She presented herself as an unusual child, as the sole member of her community who did not look down on children from poorer and less acculturated Jewish families:

> On the other hand, I loved playing with Brakha and Yenta, daughters of a shoemaker, whom I liked very much. I lived between these two worlds and with unusual skill was able to divide my time between them. It was obvious that my aristocratic girlfriends (to a certain extent imposed on me by my mother) looked oddly at these other girls, but I took no notice of this. Often, very often, when I was returning from that beautiful world, where everything was shining, dainty, "over-the-top" and beautiful I would go into the shoemaker's shop, where you could smell the leather, the dirt and the poverty, I would sit there and would spend a long time talking about the wonderful phenomenon and that there were two worlds and that both were beautiful.[69]

This excerpt, as well as others, show the enormous social distance and condescension toward the "lower" classes transmitted to children brought up in wealthier homes. If they did not attend non-Jewish private schools, for the most part they went to Tarbut schools. The writer quoted here began to attend one of them at age six. Emphasizing the supposed egalitarianism of the institution she was attending, she unconsciously also revealed the force of deeply embedded social class distinctions in it: "My new school friends were to be sure from all backgrounds, the children of the wealthy and the poor, intelligent and stupid, dirty and clean, nice and unpleasant."[70] Student circles were roiled by conflicts based on class. One of the writers, when she was a student in a Hebrew secondary school, went through difficult times owing to the collapse of her father's business. Her parents fell behind in paying the fees, and the school secretary kept putting pressure on the girl for payment. She began to be excluded from classes to motivate her parents to pay the tuition. For the author this whole situation was an enormous humiliation and also affected her increasingly poor relations with her school friends, who began to draw away from her.[71] Having the good fortune to come from a wealthy home, Zhanet also emphasized how in Tarbut schools children were treated according to their parents' financial status.[72] She wrote, "For the first time in sixth grade I began to put things together. When a student was doing better than others and when the teacher began to treat him or her differently from other children, this would attract dislike on the part of the poorer children."[73] Yesh also drew attention to the rivalry between friends of both sexes in a Tarbut secondary school.[74] Once again we can see how sensitive young Jewish people were to both the traditional and the new social divisions developing in a capitalist society. Yesh nearly always described them in class terms. A great many of such descriptions dealt with the reality of school and relationships between the students.[75]

THE TSYSHO SCHOOL NETWORK AND OTHER SECULAR YIDDISH EDUCATIONAL ESTABLISHMENTS

The TsYShO Yiddish schools had a completely different character, in terms of both the social and financial status of the homes from which they drew their students and their ideological point of view. Before 1914, secular Yiddish education was illegal in the majority of Polish areas within the Russian Empire.[76] The dramatic increase in the numbers of Jewish secular schools teaching in Yiddish occurred during the German occupation during World War I.[77] The most important network in the interwar period in the Jewish sector was the TsYShO Central Jewish School Organization, established in 1921 by a coalition of the Bund and the Jewish People's Party (the Folkists), joined later by Po'alei-Tsiyon-Left and Po'alei-Tsiyon-Right. From the beginning the Bund played a leading role; later, it was the Bund and Po'alei-Tsiyon-Left.[78] The domination of the left meant that TsYShO schools were not just secular schools but also ideologically atheist, aiming for a complete transformation of the traditional Jewish community. Only the Vilna community was able to break free of this secular radicalism. The Vilna TseBeKa, which was established earlier than the TsYShO (in 1919), joined it but retained its autonomy. Unlike their counterparts in other parts of the country, the Vilna Yiddish schools from the beginning also taught Hebrew and the Bible (from a "cultural and historical" perspective) and celebrated Jewish holidays in a secular manner.[79] Within the TsYShO system, there were also school subsystems associated with specific political parties; for instance, the Medem schools were openly pro-Bund, while the Borokhov schools spread the ideology of Po'alei-Tsiyon-Left.[80] Like all the other school networks, the TsYShO also followed the Polish curricular minimum dictated by the Ministry of Education.

In 1923 the network of schools (preschools, secondary schools, and teachers' colleges) had over 13,000 students. Over ten years later, during the 1934/35 school year, this number had grown somewhat to 15,486. In 1937 there were 16,496 students in all TsYShO schools (elementary, secondary, and vocational).[81] The Yiddish schools were most popular in the northeastern provinces, especially in Vilna and the surrounding area, their historical home.[82] This network's establishments also operated in the former Polish Congress Kingdom, but there were almost none in former Galicia.[83] They were attended mainly by children from the poorest urban Jewish classes, people without steady jobs, artisans, petty merchants, and industrial workers.[84] This school network also had an exceptionally high percentage of girls. They represented 62 percent out of 3,200 students in the Vilna TseBeKa, which was part of the TsYShO.[85] In line with the old distinctions between boys' and girls' education, poor parents, still under the influence of traditional convictions, were much more likely to send their daughters to secular schools.

On March 11, 1932, the Polish Sejm passed a law "on private schools and educational establishments." Minority representatives in parliament opposed the bill and labeled it the "muzzle act." It concerned mainly secondary schooling, more than half of which was in the private sector. In one of the act's articles, the state gave itself the right to remove teachers and principals and even to close down schools if they carried on educational activities in "a spirit disloyal to the state," attacked its "political and social philosophy," or spread "radical political views."[86] In the case of Jewish schooling in the 1930s, state officials often took advantage of this vaguely drafted paragraph, for the most part when dealing with TsYShO establishments.[87] Government circles' poor opinion of the Bund and Po'alei-Tsiyon-Left led to quite frequent provocations on the part of school districts and the ministry toward schools associated with these parties. The most frequent pretext for closing down the Yiddish schools was an accusation of carrying out communist agitation.[88] Only one, the Vilna Real Gimnasie of the TseBeKa network (an autonomous department of the TsYShO), was accredited by the state.[89] In the 1930s the TsYShO ran, apart from Vilna, only two secondary schools—one in Warsaw, the second in Białystok.[90] A number of attempts to set up TsYShO secondary schools in the provinces ended in failure.[91] In 1931, "for political reasons" the authorities closed the jewel in the crown of Jewish secular education, known both in Poland and abroad, the Jewish Teachers' Seminar in Vilna, with which leading members of YIVO were also involved.[92]

The Shul-Kult network was established in 1928 on the initiative of left-wing Zionist parties, earlier involved in setting up the TsYShO system. The radicalism of the Bund and Po'alei-Tsiyon-Left dominant in the TsYShO forced the Zionists to establish their own school network. Supporters of the Folkists, put off by the radicalism of the TsYShO, began to send their children to it. The teaching in Shul-Kult schools was conducted in Yiddish, but Hebrew too was taught, as well as Polish as a third language in some of them; a number were in fact trilingual—Yiddish, Hebrew, and Polish.[93] In Shul-Kult establishments, as in Tarbut schools, the Jewish National Fund (Keren Kayemet le-Yisrael) operated, collecting money for building a Jewish national homeland in Palestine.[94] A small number of children attended Shul-Kult schools. Like those attending TsYShO establishments, they came from the poorest elements of society. In 1930, two years after its establishment, the network ran twenty-five schools with 3,592 children attending them.[95] In the 1930s Shul-Kult felt the financial crisis affecting private Jewish schooling more strongly than other networks. According to the American Jewish Joint Distribution Committee, in 1937 only 2,343 students were attending Shul-Kult schools, and by the following year it was only 939.[96] This network operated no secondary schools; however, it did organize evening classes and in 1939 was proud of running nine "people's universities."[97]

For authors from poor homes, the TsYShO schools were for the most part a completely "new world," to a much greater extent than for their colleagues in Tarbut schools. This was the role a secular Yiddish establishment played in Yud-Giml's life. When for financial reasons the author had to abandon her schooling in order to go out to work, she wrote, "This was simply a day from hell. I couldn't eat or drink, and I just lay in bed crying. . . . I cried because of my unhappiness and that of the thousands of other children, who for financial reasons, are unable to acquire even an elementary education."[98] Only in a TsYShO school could "Kola" find an escape from heavy physical labor and his father's constant beatings and scolding.[99] Likewise, for Ben-Tikva, the Yiddishist Vilna Mefitsei Haskalah school, under the auspices of the TseBeKa, represented a new life. The author had earlier attended religious schools and wrote that he had "had enough of being fed the *Gemara*" and was convinced of the utter uselessness of religious education. He was withdrawn from a Beit Yehuda school after being severely beaten by a teacher, and after transferring to Mefitsei Haskalah, he was transformed. From an idle, unruly student, he became an attentive student, thirsting for knowledge.[100] Henceforth the tone of Ben-Tikva's autobiography changed completely. Hitherto he had described his life in dark colors; only when he mentioned his studies in a Jewish people's school did positive emotions, such as joy and contentment with life, appear.

Many of the authors emphasize in their autobiographies the deep impression graduation day made on them. It appears that the TsYShO school authorities laid special emphasis on that day and thus often organized ceremonies around it. Indeed, for the students it was a special day, since for those youngsters coming mainly from poor homes, few of whom would have any opportunity for further schooling, completing seventh grade meant the beginning of hard, adult life. This was often one of the hardest periods in their adolescence. Imprinted on their minds, the last day of school even more strongly reinforced the image of a friendly enclave in a hostile, brutal world.[101] Young people leaving TsYShO schools (as well as other secular Jewish establishments) took with them a modernist worldview and high life aspirations, which had little chance of being achieved in adult life. In Kola's school a special farewell ceremony was arranged for graduates. During this ceremony, one of the teachers wished him luck "building a future life in the ranks of the proletariat." Kola's very typical, accurate observation, and one well conveying the atmosphere of that day, was the fact that the teacher's uplifting words were accompanied by fear on the students' faces. The graduates were apprehensive about their future, and the prospect of starting an adult life outside school frightened them.[102]

The TsYShO schools' Yiddishism—teaching in a modern version of Yiddish and promoting modern Yiddish as the national Jewish language—was a new phenomenon, not something normal for a Jewish child coming from a traditional home. As Feygeles wrote in Yiddish, "I would bring my new 'language' home, as well as a great deal of knowledge of the new, modern world, because everything, or almost everything that I had learned I immediately recounted. All this was building within me an even stronger connection with 'the modern school.' which is called a 'Jewish people's school.'"[103] The radical atheism, both of the curriculum and of the actual teachers in the TsYShO schools, was typical. Feygeles's extremely religious father apparently never realized the atheism of the environment to which he had entrusted his own child. It emerges from Feygeles's autobiography that it was simply of the utmost importance to his father that his son, unlike himself, would have an opportunity to acquire a secular education. The situation in which an Orthodox father sent his son to a TsYShO school makes Feygeles's autobiography unusual. Studying in a TsYShO school almost always led to a break with the religious lifestyle. Feygeles wrote, "When I was thirteen years old and was at an age when a boy begins to put on a phylactery, I tried to conceal this from my school friends, because I was beginning to be ashamed of my piety."[104] Feygeles, like many other authors, emphasized that entering a TsYShO school meant for him an entry into "a new world": "Neither my parents, nor I myself realized that studying in this school would at the same time represent a step in the direction of an absolutely new world and that it would have an enormous impact on my future life."[105] Yud-Giml wrote that studying in a TsYShO school was the source of a complete change in her worldview, after which she could no longer listen to her father speaking of "a good God" while being unable to explain to her "the reason for the suffering of millions."[106]

In the interwar Jewish educational landscape, the Warsaw Khinekh Yelodim (Children's Education) School, described in Abraham Rotfarb's autobiography, was exceptional. Established in 1912, this school was one of the first two Yiddish day schools established in Tsarist Russia (in addition to the Vilna Dvoyre Kuperstein School). Its teachers wrote most of the first school textbooks for the teaching of Yiddish. In Tsarist times the school had operated semilegally, maintaining officially that it taught only in Russian.[107] Between the wars Khinekh Yelodim was a trilingual school, one of only a few to break out from the culture war between Hebraism and Yiddishism. Unlike the TsYShO schools, it was not characterized by radical secularism. It was the first place in which Abraham Rotfarb encountered a warm and understanding approach to students. As he was from a poor artisan home and knew Jewish tradition very superficially, solely on the basis of several years spent in inferior heders, it was only in a modern Jewish school that he had the opportunity to become acquainted with the Tanakh, the nation's history, and the basics of Hebrew. He contrasted the "foreign" elementary school, in which at age thirteen he had completed his education, with this establishment that was welcoming to Jewish children.[108]

For most of the contestants in the YIVO competition, secular Jewish private schools, despite critical voices, were unusual places, special islands of new, modern, and national life in a world defined by the stagnation of tradition and by economic poverty. The educational and political ideology transmitted to the children had an enormous influence on this image of secular national Jewish schools. The Tarbut schools, TsYShO, Shul-Kult, and Markus Braude's Zionist Union of Social Associations Supporting Jewish Secondary Education in Poland did not shy away from politics—quite the opposite, they tried to instill in their pupils a unified vision of the world, drawn directly from the policies of the parties supporting them. An excerpt from a resolution at a conference of Tarbut school principals could easily apply to all the other secular Jewish educational networks: "A school is not a factory of certified tires, but an institution preparing a new generation for specific national tasks, to achieve specific aims. The achievement of these aims requires the use of appropriate means, which means specific policies. A neutral school, an apolitical school is an oxymoron."[109] Jewish national schools were thus the basic places for political initiation and recruitment of the youngest members to parties such as Hitahdut, Po'alei-Tsiyon-Right, Po'alei-Tsiyon-Left, the Bund, and the youth movements He-Halutz Ha-Tsa'ir, Gordonia, Dror, Borokhov Yugend, Tsukunft, and He-Halutz organizing preparations for emigration to Palestine. Almost all the young members described joining these organizations as the beginning of a new life. For a minority of the authors, who had been sent to national Jewish schools, this new life began earlier, in school.

For traditional parents, the message of secular Jewish educational establishments often promoted values at odds with those with which they tried to instill their own children. Here the exceptions were only some Tarbut schools, located mainly in the northeastern provinces. Things looked different for bourgeois homes of Zionist views or working-class and artisan homes of left-wing views. Tarbut and Yavne schools in the case of the first group and TsYShO and Shul-Kult schools in the case of the second, while achieving their educational goals, brought up children in the spirit of the values instilled at home. However, the overwhelming majority of Jewish children in private Jewish secular schools, like those in public schools, came into contact with a message completely inconsistent with the traditional culture of their home environment. Very often, private Jewish schools deepened intergenerational conflict and strengthened the youngest generation's radicalism.

As we have seen, Jewish schools were also not free of the enormous social gulfs and resulting conflicts prevalent in the Second Republic. This is confirmed by research done by Ido Bassok, who draws attention to the fact that Jewish children at a young age understood very well all the social barriers and gulfs and recreated them themselves in their relationships with their school friends. In many private schools, these social differences and the often dramatic class resentments were often reproduced by the teachers working there.[110] Considering the trope most commonly encountered in the autobiographies—the "absence of a childhood" caused by poverty, oppression, traditional norms, the dirt and chaos of their surroundings, and hard work providing no prospect of material advancement or further study for the development of personal interests—class resentment takes on a specific meaning. Those resentments strongly suggest that the generation of young Jews entering adult life in the 1930s were far more politically radical than any generation that preceded them.

FIVE

—⚹—

PATTERNS OF PARTICIPATION IN CULTURE

Nationalism, Polonization, and Polish Jewish Culture

SELF-STUDY: READERSHIP AND PARTICIPATION IN ELITE AND POPULAR CULTURE

In the imagination of YIVO scholars, the young people they were addressing would in the future be the elite of the newly formed modern Jewish nation. As such, besides having a secular education and the knowledge needed to succeed in the world (such as knowing the official state language and the principles of political and social life), they would also be deeply rooted in Jewish culture, which meant, among other things, knowledge of Yiddish culture, religious tradition, and the Hebrew language. Unlike Jewish far-left circles, YIVO activists did not identify Hebrew culture entirely with the uniformly negatively defined culture of the bourgeoisie or "Jewish reaction." However, for Max Weinreich and the researchers around him, the core of the modern Jewish nation was to be secular Yiddish culture. Unlike the Zionists, they did not recognize Hebrew culture as the culture of Jewish everyday life, on which the future of Jews in east-central Europe could be built. Knowledge of Hebrew was not a necessary condition for participation in the new national community; it was participation in secular, modern Yiddish culture. The language itself, in its traditional version, spoken rather than written, was what most Jewish youth in interwar Poland knew from home. Yiddish schools and political and cultural organizations were supposed to teach the new generation to write in this language, read secular literature, become immersed in the whole secular Yiddish culture, and think using its modern categories. Yiddish was to be transferred from the world of tradition to the world of the modern nation. Referring to Chone Shmeruk's concept proclaiming the existence in interwar Poland of three modern Jewish

117

cultural universes (Yiddish, Polish, and Hebrew) next to a fourth (the traditional universe), we can say that the elite of the new generation, as envisioned by the organizers of the YIVO competition, was meant to move smoothly and easily in each of these universes but on a daily basis operate mainly in the Yiddish universe, with which it mainly identified.[1]

Researchers of the young people's autobiographies agree in their conclusions with the most important ideological assumptions of the competition's creators. In their opinion, Jewish youth in unprecedented numbers and with unprecedented intensity compared to previous generations read Jewish secular and traditional literature in both Yiddish and Hebrew, and they were characterized by an unprecedented hunger for pure knowledge and by initiative in creating a new Jewish national culture of the elite variety. Moshe Kligsberg (a YIVO graduate student working in 1939 on the third competition), Marcus Moseley, Michael Steinlauf, and to a slightly lesser extent Ido Bassok and David Shavit expressed their belief in the ubiquity of this young "Jewish reader." Regardless of their social background, education, and current economic situation, they supposedly devoured thousands of pages of Jewish, international, and least often Polish literature, became immersed in elite culture, and avoided contacts with Jewish *shund* fiction and other less ambitious products of mass culture in ascendancy at this time.[2] In contrast to Shmeruk, the researchers mentioned above, recognizing the growing Polish cultural competence of the youngest Jewish citizens of the Second Republic, diminish the importance of processes of acculturation taking place among the generation described. In addition to underestimating the question of acculturation, they have not, it seems, separated the social ideal from social reality. In this chapter, I discuss their findings. The social experience and political consciousness of Jewish young people were shaped by modern mass society and culture, Polish acculturation, and the politicization of the Jewish community in the interwar period. The real significance of reading in the lives of young people cannot be grasped using only the tools of literary studies. The following analysis shows a clearer picture of the patterns of cultural participation by Jewish young people and how important they were for their political attitudes.

Marcus Moseley, defining the generation studied here as a unique generation in Jewish history of "Jewish individualist readers," stated that in writing their autobiographies they drew models mainly from literature. Apart from Romain Rolland's *Jean-Christophe* and the classics of Yiddish literature, the works of Hebrew writers were the books most frequently cited by Jewish young people, according to Moseley, and they were to determine the shape of the competition submissions.[3] In drawing conclusions about the reading of Hebrew books by young people, this British researcher of Jewish literature did not ask what group, among the participants of the competition, mentioned them in their autobiographies. He failed to notice that it was a minority group, characterized by a unique social background and a unique educational path, against the background of both Jewish young people in general and the majority of participants in the YIVO competition.

HEBREW READERSHIP

Hebrew literature was read by a relatively small number of autobiographers, usually with an above-average education, proficient in both secular and traditional learning. This group included Binyomin R. During his studies in several heders and later for a short time at the secondary-school level, he read mainly books and newspapers in Yiddish, sometimes also turning to Polish books. The period in which he devoted himself almost entirely to Hebrew literature was his time studying at the Tarbut teachers' seminar, and it was only this elite Hebrew school that awakened in him a love for literature in this language.[4] Gershon Pipe possessed very similar, relatively elite social and cultural capital. As the brother of Shmuel Zanvil Pipe, a young YIVO ethnographer sharing his enthusiasm for Yiddish culture, and at the same time as a supporter of the Zionist Ha-Shomer ha-Tsa'ir, he wanted to master the Hebrew language as well as possible in order to read the books of Mapu, Smolenskin, Lilienblum, and Fayerberg in that language.[5] Like everyone, even Orthodox authors growing up in elite schools, he did not have Hebrew as his first language. He had to devote many years to mastering it. The basic levels of heder education, learning Hebrew as a foreign language in TsYShO schools, or even taking it in the first grades of the basic Tarbut Hebrew schools did not assure an advanced enough knowledge of the language to be able to read secular or traditional Hebrew literature.

Binyomin R. and Gershon Pipe came from the traditional but at the same time modernizing elite. In these circles, a high level of traditional education was combined with a great deal of emphasis placed on secular education. Also unique was the Hebraism of this milieu, among whom even the religious harbored Zionist political sympathies. Both authors had abandoned the world of religion, but the patterns of their socialization meant that they could move freely in the worlds of both religious and secular Hebrew literature. As with most of the other contestants quoted below who cited Hebrew books, the determining factor in their attachment to this type of literature was their activity in Zionist organizations. The fact that Hebrew literature was read at home only by authors from richer and intelligentsia homes (most often those from the northeastern provinces, Jewish Lithuania) is also confirmed by the autobiography of "Hanzi." Her first readings were chosen by her father, an intellectual and a teacher in Hebrew schools who, separated from her mother, did not live with his daughter. As she recalled, the first book she read (probably her first book in Hebrew) was the biography of Theodore Herzl by Samuel Leib Tzitron.[6]

In other circles, only education in expensive and elite Tarbut high schools or Polish Hebrew secondary schools in the Union of Social Associations Supporting Jewish Secondary Education in Poland under the leadership of Rabbi Dr. Markus Braude could assure sufficient knowledge of the Hebrew language to read very difficult Haskalah or national literature. Only members of a rather narrow circle of above-averagely wealthy Jewish bourgeoisie could afford such education.

"Margalit" belonged to a small group of autobiographers who spoke Polish daily (the language in which she wrote her autobiography) and who could actually boast of a good command of the Hebrew language, acquired thanks to studying at an elite and expensive Hebrew secondary school. Previously, she had learned the language in a Tarbut evening elementary school; even earlier, she had been taught the language at home. The author's Hebrew reading interests were in fact conditioned mainly by her involvement in the Zionist movement.[7] Margalit was a Ha-Shomer ha-Tsa'ir activist and a participant in hakhshara preparing for the journey to Palestine. However, for her, too, Hebrew was a third language. She spoke Polish and Yiddish much better. At the same time, quite a few autobiographies of youngsters from Zionist and at the same time rich and acculturated homes among the contestants in the YIVO competition (more or less reflecting the scale of representation of this type of environment in the general population) show that not all of them read Hebrew. "Prowincjał," a student at the prestigious Hebrew La-Or school, admitted to having a poor command of it.[8] The same was true of other Polish-speaking Zionists writing for the YIVO competition. As we shall see below, the literature they read was Polish or Polish Jewish literature. They read books on Zionist subjects only in Polish translation.

Another group, all of whom read Hebrew literature, were Orthodox and studied Hebrew (and Aramaic) religious texts in heders and yeshivas for many years. The group of people who read Hebrew fluently, including secular literature, consisted of Litvaks, Hasidim, and Orthodox, who did not belong to either of the former two categories. The Hasidim, unlike the Litvaks, did not come into contact with secular literature at home, but they could get to know Hebrew well, because they studied it for no less than fifteen years—in a succession of heders (from the age of three) and then in yeshivas or beit midrashes. Only in this relatively small group did the authors from the northeastern provinces not stand out from those from the south and center of the country. Reading secular Hebrew literature, however, was forbidden in many Hasidic and Litvak yeshivas.

Henekh came from the border between the provinces of Vilna and Nowogródek. Although his father died very early, which greatly worsened the family's financial situation, his mother and older sister prepared him from a young age for future studies in the yeshiva. The sister was supporting his older brothers, who were already studying there. Henekh's older sister was active in the local Zionist organization, and she brought home Hebrew children's literature and got her younger brother interested in it.[9] Etonis, who came from a virtually identical background from the same part of the country, encountered secular Hebrew literature similarly early. He learned to write in Hebrew (which was not taught to children in ordinary heders) from the age of four in a heder metukan. There he used modern textbooks designed for language learning and sang Zionist songs. Later, he studied the modern version of Hebrew, including grammar, with a private teacher. As an eight- to ten-year-old, he passionately read children's books in this language.[10] When he was ten and eleven years old and studying in a small yeshiva, against the recommendations of the local rabbi, he was able to read modern, national Hebrew literature, including books by authors such as Peretz Smolenskin and Micha Josef Berdyczewski.[11] The same was true in the case of Z. G., another Litvak. He learned to read and write Hebrew from an early age in a Litvak heder in Ignatówka near Łuck. His first Hebrew reading matter was the Bible. The boy dreamed of becoming a Hebrew writer ("I thought at the time that they were built differently from ordinary people"), which would be seen as a sacrilegious wish in many other Orthodox circles. At this time, his father bought him a textbook to learn modern spoken Hebrew. His first poems were inspired by stories from the Bible. The whole family was proud of his Hebrew writing attempts.[12] He also continued them while studying in the yeshiva. Thanks to his passion for Hebrew literature, this young Mizrahi activist, who was not interested in the traditional professions of rabbi or ritual slaughterer, managed to get a job as a teacher at the local Hebrew school. Although, as he declared at the end of his autobiography, he stopped believing that he would become a writer, he did not give up creating poetry inspired by Jewish religious literature, as shown by the diary and literary attempts attached to it.[13] The first literary attempts of Gamalielis, another autobiographer who had studied in a great many yeshivas, were poems inspired by late Russian Haskalah literature about the hardships of life and study in the yeshiva.[14] It was in Hebrew Haskalah literature that his path toward full secularization and abandonment of the Orthodox environment began. Galitsyaner learned to read and write the modern version of Hebrew and its grammar not in a heder but only after joining the Zionist-religious youth organization Bnei Akiva.[15]

The above examples prove that only a relatively narrow elite of Jewish young people in Poland had an advanced knowledge of Hebrew. Of course, much wider circles came into contact with the language. In addition to the heder, the Zionist movement played a very important role in the spread and teaching of the language in its modern secular version. Hebrew was taught in Zionist libraries, youth organizations, and party offices and during hakhshara. However, as dozens of autobiographies testify, belonging to the Zionist movement was often not an adequate basis for developing a good mastery of this difficult language. To become immersed in Bialik's poetry or Smolenskin's or Lilienblum's prose, one needed long years of study in yeshivas or secular Hebrew schools. Most of the autobiographers did not have such an advantage, finishing their education at the latest at the age of thirteen or fourteen and going to work. Nor did all the children of the richer Jewish bourgeoisie, which sympathized with Zionism, speak Hebrew fluently. Thus, the battle for the language of modernity, including the language of politics, in the Jewish community in the Second Republic was between Yiddish and Polish.

Summing up the place of the Hebrew language and literature in the life of Jewish young people, it is necessary to dwell for a moment on its gender dimension. Girls did not have an opportunity to learn Hebrew as part of the Orthodox educational track. Bais Yaakov schools and Litvak religious schools for girls, according to old Jewish tradition, taught Jewish religion and culture in Yiddish. Girls did not study in higher heders and yeshivas. The abovementioned authors Esther and A Shtetleshe, young women who were unusual among the contestants in the YIVO competition—religious, educated, reading secular national literature—did not list Hebrew books among their reading material. Thus, the only educational path and social milieu in which they could learn this language was to study in secular schools associated with the Zionist movement. This was yet another factor limiting knowledge of Hebrew among Jewish young people. It was also not noticed by the researchers mentioned above, who overestimated the role of secular Hebrew literature in shaping the consciousness of the participants in the YIVO competition. Reading this literature was certainly not one of the key biographical experiences of an entire generation. In interwar Poland, the modern version of Hebrew still had not liberated itself from traditional male dominance.

YIDDISH READERSHIP

Secular Yiddish literature was potentially available to most of the autobiographers. Only young people from acculturated families growing up in Polish-speaking environments could not read it. For most Jewish youth, Yiddish was the first language they spoke at home. Turning to secular literature in this language, however, was not at all guaranteed. In traditional society, there was no category of secular literature. Parents were often suspicious of potentially seditious books, which made up by far the greatest part of the secular Yiddish canon. As is also known, traditional Yiddish in its written version had the low status of a language read by women and uneducated men who were unable to read Hebrew writings Many Zionists, as well as all circles promoting the integration of Jews into the Polish nation, disliked Yiddish, including national projects for its secular revival. All this meant that the autobiographers encountered secular Yiddish literature more often in Jewish schools (mainly TsYShO and Shul-Kult), in political organizations (the Bund or those belonging to the left-Zionist camp), or in local Jewish libraries (most often also associated with one of the political camps) than at home.

Works of secular Yiddish literature are among the most frequently cited in the autobiographies. The titles provided by the authors say a great deal about the nature of their cultural consumption. Contemporary twentieth-century Yiddish literature is mentioned in the autobiographies very rarely, giving way to nineteenth-century classics by Sholem Aleichem, Mendele Moykher-Sforim, or Yitskhok Leybush Peretz. Young people on the whole were unfamiliar with the poems and works of Perets Markish, Melech Ravitch, Moyshe Broderzon, or Uri Tsevi Grinberg (who later became a radical right-wing Hebrew poet), who were well known in Yiddish avant-garde literary circles. Even among the works of young people from the northeastern provinces or from Vilna itself, we do not find mentions of Avrom Sutzkever, Elkhonen Vogler, Chaim Grade, or Leyzer Volf, who were members of the Yung Vilne group, which was riding the crest of a wave at that time and had a permanent audience in its hometown.[16] Contestants in the YIVO competition were not part of it. This fact is further proof that, contrary to what the researchers quoted above write, the reading tastes and literary interests of young people were shaped mainly by school and political movements, not by sophisticated texts and literary environments. The generation described here was not at all a well-read generation of writers.

The autobiographies suggest that the Yiddish literary avant-garde operated rather within a specific Jewish subculture—namely, the Yiddishist secularized left centered on cultural organizations such as the Kultur-Lige, the members of which sympathized with the Bund, Po'alei-Tsiyon-Left, or the KPP. Very few authors familiar with twentieth-century Yiddish literature had become acquainted with it mainly in TsYShO schools, which were attended by a relatively small number of Jewish children. Besides, even among the graduates of these schools, authors such as Feygeles, whose first literary attempts were inspired by the poetry of Avrom Reyzen, were rare.[17] The autobiography of this interesting author is proof that modern Hebrew and Jewish literature was not the first reading option for most Jewish young people. The first books he read himself when he was still studying only in heders and that he bought with his brother were *mayse-bikhlekh*—popular literature considered by Orthodox as frivolous and intended more for women and by nationalist circles as low-level shund—a term used to describe so-called trashy literature. A major reading breakthrough in his life was enrolling in the Jewish workers' library operating in the same area as his school. After graduating from the TsYShO school and when starting out on his adventure with the Bund, he began to read the daily press, the *Literarishe Bleter*, and "critical and philosophical works" from the classics of Jewish socialism and Yiddish writing (including Chaim Zhitlovsky, Shmuel Niger, and Vladimir Medem) as well as Zionists (Max Nordau).[18] The exceptional Binyomin R., a Zionist who had received an above-average education at elite heders, from tutors, and in a Hebrew teachers' seminar, also read a great deal in Yiddish. His reading matter, in addition to the Yiddish press (*Der Moment* and *Dos Vort*), included, for example, *Pinkas*, edited by Niger.[19]

Another of the YIVO contestants, the exceptionally well-read Galitsyaner, also began by reading mayse-bikhlekh. When he was studying the Chumash, the Gemara, and Rashi in his father's heder, in his spare time he secretly read books such as *Graf Potocki* (a fictionalized Jewish legend about the conversion to Judaism of one of the counts Potocki). When his father caught him reading another book of the mayse-bikhlekh genre, describing the adventures of the famous Jewish apostate Jacob Frank, he gave the boy a stout spanking. He even moved him to another heder, so as not to expose him to contact with friends who would bring him *treyfe psuken* (dubious, nonkosher extracts).[20] However, his father could not find a way to prevent his son from reading seditious literature. After the mayse-bikhlekh, the next group of secular books that the boy read were cheap books in Yiddish published as part of a series of *groshn biblioteken* ("penny libraries"). They were tossed to him by a Jewish friend from the public elementary school, who obtained these books from his brother, who borrowed them from the Peretz library in their native Olesk.[21] Like most other authors, he encountered highbrow literature only in the Zionist-religious Mizrahi party and its library. In addition to Hebrew Zionist literature, the boy read "all the works of Mendele Moykher-Sforim, Sholem Aleichem, Sholem Ash, [and] the great history of the Jewish people by Professor Heinrich Graetz." He boasted that in half a year he had read its entire collection—two hundred books.[22] In the light of his autobiography, described in more detail in chapter 2, this number seems to be greatly exaggerated. Nevertheless, this pattern of reading certainly did not apply to most of the YIVO competition contestants or to the majority of their generation.

The reading interests of Feygeles, Galitsyaner, and Binyomin R. are exceptions. Much more often we are dealing with autobiographies like the one by Yud-Giml, who, when describing literature classes in the last grades of her TsYShO school, mentioned only nineteenth-century Yiddish literature and the Russian classics.[23] Another author, A Shtetleshe, lived in an environment where only Yiddish was spoken on a daily basis. Hardly anywhere in Poland at that time was Polish as marginalized as in the shtetls of Nowogródek province. This does not mean, of course, that the area (like other similar ones) was the sole fiefdom of secular Yiddish literature, where its classics were widely read. Modern social institutions—imported from big cities, established by intellectuals, and spreading modern, secular national culture—played a large role in this. In the case of A Shtetleshe, such an institution was the modern religious school for girls.[24] For this author, acquiring modern Yiddish cultural competencies was a key element of political consciousness and self-development. Her self-awareness and consciousness of the problems of the surrounding world were obtained in parallel—through national politics and the secular culture associated with it. Jewish literature played an important role in this process: "My favorite class was Yiddish. My interest in writing on literary topics continued to grow. . . . I wrote a piece entitled 'Jewish craftsmen in the classics.' . . . I wrote about their protest against the traditional order. I finished my piece expressing the hope that the sense of hatred towards workers would eventually disappear and that a new ideal of helping the workers, of alleviating their hard lives, would become established."[25]

The turning point in Greyno's life allowing him to free himself from a world of poverty and tradition was his older brother joining a trade union, thanks to which he began to bring home Yiddish classics: Mendele Moykher-Sforim, Sholem Aleichem, Yitskhok Leybush Peretz, and Shin An-sky.[26] Greyno then broke with the "bad company" of backyard troublemakers and devoted himself to reading books during his free hours. Educated only in a traditional way, the boy could not read in a language other than Yiddish. For people like him who had no education in Polish—relatively rare in their generation—the first and most important source of secular knowledge was Yiddish literature. As in many other autobiographies, for Greyno the library and avid reading meant "emancipation," liberation from the constraints imposed by his immediate environment. By reading secular Jewish books, the author could become a "civilized" person. For him, as for many other authors, until the beginning of his political activity, the only escape from the "evil," "gray" world was the Jewish library. It was thanks to the library that Greyno left the world of tradition and later entered the world of radical (communist) politics.

The future writer Mendl Man, who came from a traditional home where Yiddish was spoken, also did not read modern Yiddish literature during his first years at school. He studied in a heder and then in an elementary school, finally completing his seven-grade education in a szabasówka. He was encouraged to read modern Yiddish literature by his older brother, a graduate of the Vilna Teachers' seminar associated with YIVO, a teacher at a TsYShO school, and therefore a convinced advocate of Yiddish culture. Mendl wrote, undoubtedly using ideological slogans, that only this type of reading allowed him to get closer to his own people, to understand their soul and needs. From this place, a straight path was already leading Mendl into the ranks of the Marxist and Yiddishist Po'alei-Tsiyon-Left.[27] Often, Yiddish literature also played the role of arousing political consciousness in elite Orthodox circles, completely different from the ones in which Greyno and Mendl Man grew up. Reading secular Yiddish literature was no less an act of transgression against yeshiva Orthodox norms than were the cases of clandestine study of usually Haskalah Hebrew literature mentioned above. Yeshiva student Gamalielis started with the latter. The first secular book he mentioned reading was Fishel Shneurson's Yiddish novel *Avrom Itshe der Kushner*.[28] When the boy broke with religion and became a political radical, his reading interests focused on the literature and press of his party—Po'alei-Tsiyon-Left. For Gamalielis, entering the world of completely secular Yiddish culture meant breaking with the religious tradition in which he had grown up. Secular Jewish literature was the beginning of a life trajectory that also led another author, Yafet, holder of a rabbinical certificate and a graduate of Warsaw's Mesivta, to break with Orthodoxy. He first began to read it when he was conducting independent higher Talmudic studies in a beit midrash. He borrowed books from the local I. L. Peretz Library. Caught reading *Shtrayml* (Yitskhok Leybush Peretz anti-Hasidic satire) in the beit midrash, he was seriously reprimanded by the son-in-law of the local rabbi.[29]

These examples clearly show that secular Yiddish culture was at the heart of left-leaning Jewish national circles' life—the anti-Zionists, such as the Bund; the Zionist but at the same time revolutionary and far-left groupings such as Po'alei-Tsiyon-Left; and the Folkist and regional ones. But even taken together, all these groups do not represent most of the Jewish Street. Yiddish was spoken daily by the traditional masses, certainly by most of the older generations of Jewish citizens of the Second Republic, including the Orthodox and many Zionist sympathizers. The high-circulation secular Jewish national press was read in Yiddish, with *Haynt* and *Der Moment* in the lead (although reading them did not yet mean participating in a secular, highbrow version of Yiddish culture on a daily basis). However, Yiddish was not taught in the largest of the secular Jewish private school networks—the Zionist Tarbut. What is even more surprising is that in these schools, or at least according to some of their syllabuses, although the works of Polish and German writers were read in the original, the classics of Yiddish literature were quite absent, even in Hebrew translation.[30] Taking into account the above and the facts that most Jewish children attended Polish public schools and that secular literature in Yiddish was banned in most Orthodox institutions, it turns out that secular elite Yiddish culture was dominant in only one of the most important Jewish circles.

This does not mean, however, that the influence of secular Yiddish culture, and especially literature, did not extend to other groups. As we have seen, secular books in this language were read, often overcoming the resistance of the milieu and of many Orthodox. The same was true of the avowed Zionists. Zhanet began to read books in sixth grade at a Tarbut school, borrowing them from the local Jewish library named after Sholem Aleichem (therefore not Zionist but associated with the Yiddishist movement), which her father also used. She described herself as "a regular reader of Jewish and European literature." Given the basic nature of her Jewish education and the fact that she used a library associated with the Yiddishist movement, we can assume that the "Jewish and European" books she read were mainly in Yiddish. Many books in Yiddish were also read by other Zionists mentioned above: Binyomin R. and Gershon Pipe.

In writing about the Yiddish books they read, as already mentioned in chapter 2, the autobiographers emphasized the value of gaining secular, science-based, modern knowledge of the world. For those who had to interrupt their education and start their work life very early, reading literature, including Yiddish literature, available through a diverse and rich network of cultural institutions, became the primary way of acquiring this kind of knowledge. Its mastery was an elementary condition of individual emancipation from the world of tradition. The existence of serious, ambitious secular literature in a language traditionally considered to be the language of women was in itself a challenge to this world. Reading in Yiddish was much more common than reading in Hebrew. The autobiographers mentioned represented broader Jewish circles, and far more of them came from lower social classes and backgrounds than readers of Hebrew literature. However, contrary to the dreams of Yiddish activists representing YIVO, the Bund, Po'alei-Tsiyon-Left, school networks such as TsYShO, Shul-Kult, or organizations such as the Kultur-Lige, secular Yiddish literature was far from being ascendant. Highbrow Polish literature, popular literature, and Jewish shund competed successfully with the works of Yitskhok Leybush Peretz and Sholem Aleichem, Yiddish translations of international literature, and *Literarishe Bleter*, not to mention the twentieth-century Yiddish avant-garde.

In this situation, the huge role played by Yiddish school networks in promoting Yiddish literature is all the more evident. Characterizing the readership of Yiddish literature above, I quoted mostly autobiographies written by graduates from such schools. They represented less than 10 percent of Jewish school-age children. The second important group of institutions that promoted the reading of national literature in Yiddish were political organizations and related cultural institutions. However, compared to the Zionist movement (from the right through the center and the moderate left—Po'alei-Tsiyon-Left was a Yiddishist party) and to Orthodox circles, all these organizations represented less than half of Jewish young people. Yiddish literature was also read outside these circles and—unlike Hebrew literature—on a truly mass scale. However, it was far from dominant.

INTERNATIONAL LITERATURE

A large percentage of the books read in Yiddish were translations of world literature. As a rule, it is impossible to establish which translations young people read. Undoubtedly, Polish translations were the most widely available, but at the same time Yiddish groups engaged in admirable translation activity. In 1923, 20 percent of all books published in Yiddish were in fact translations.[31] This was an impressive achievement for a community seeking to modernize its language and to make it a full member of the European linguistic family, so that it could describe every element of human experience. Yiddishism, as a fully developed cultural and national ideology, at the end of the decade described was only thirty years old (taking as its birth the 1908 conference in Czernowitz). The vast majority of autobiographers read freely in both Yiddish and Polish. The fact that more than 80 percent of them wrote their works in Yiddish does not mean that they read foreign works only in that language.

Probably the most popular writer mentioned in the YIVO autobiographies was not any of the Yiddish or Hebrew classic authors but Romain Rolland, the author of *Jean-Christophe*, beloved by young people. Marcus Moseley compares this "novel about growing up" (bildungsroman) with the autobiographical books of Jean-Jacques Rousseau, Leo Tolstoy, Solomon Maimon, Moshe Leib Lilienblum, and Peretz Smolenskin, suggesting that young people had literary awareness. However, the autobiographies do not confirm this. In showing Rolland's Rousseauism and Tolstoyism, Moseley wrongly assumes that the reading of his book by teenage and uneducated authors meant acceptance of the entire literary tradition behind it. Rather, the autobiographies are proof of the prosaic fact that young Jewish people simply read fashionable literature written specifically for people their age, just as their Polish and European peers did. In dozens of autobiographies, *Jean-Christophe* is mentioned in both Yiddish and Polish translations, while references to Tolstoy (read in translation), not to mention Hebrew authors, are much rarer. This fact speaks to the normality rather than the uniqueness of the Jewish young people represented in the autobiographies.

The avowed communist Greyno ended his autobiography with a phrase from Romain Rolland.[32] Knowing no other written language apart from Yiddish, he was able to become a well-read person thanks to the Tarbut library in Kielce. He read in Yiddish Marcel Prévost, Guy de Maupassant, Upton Sinclair, and Maxim Gorky, among others.[33] "A. Remez's" first beloved book was *The Adventures of Robinson Crusoe*, by Daniel Defoe, read in a Yiddish translation.[34] The same book was one of "Gina" from Kolomyia's favorites, who read it in Polish, as well as *Gulliver's Travels* by Jonathan Swift.[35] Speaking only Polish fluently, Prowincjal, like most young people his age, loved to read the novels of Karl May, Thomas Mayne Reid, and of course Romain Rolland.[36] The latter was also a very important writer for Ludwik Stöckel, another acculturated author, who read books only in Polish.[37]

Among some of these adolescent young people, literature on puberty was of great interest. Autobiographers quoted only serious scientific works on it, which most likely was related to the fact that they were writing for the competition. Eighteen-year-old Ajzyk Rozen, having stated "that he was still an innocent," began reading this type of literature when he moved out of the house and started training at a Łódź barber's shop.[38] The fact that the authors referred to psychological literature or literature on sexual adolescence and relations between the sexes could also have been influenced by the nature of the YIVO competition, the organizers of which did not hide the fact that the works collected would serve psychological research. The exceptionally widely read "Tor," who lists about a hundred authors in his autobiography, devoted a disproportionate amount of space in his work to the experiences of reading the book *Sex and Character* by Otto Weininger.[39] Interestingly enough, despite emphasizing the anti-Jewish character of the Polish translations of Shakespeare's *The Merchant of Venice* and an unambiguously similar judgment on the original, Tor did not devote a single sentence to the antisemitic thrust of the work of the young Viennese psychoanalyst. He noted, however, that the work, along with "Dr. Glicksman's critical introduction," had made him "a different man."[40] As a result of reading this work, Tor acquired a "negative attitude to the female problem." As he wrote, he later took a long time to rid himself of a misogynistic aversion to women, internalized by also reading other authors, such as Baudelaire and Nietzsche.[41]

The canon of "Bronka's" "universal" readings went far beyond what the school offered. This author was one of a small number of people who lived in the world of literature. She came from perhaps the most elite of circles represented in the YIVO autobiographies. Her father, and later her aunt, who raised the author by herself, owned a factory. Growing up in Warsaw, the girl, unlike other authors, at the age of seven did not go to elementary school or any other educational institution. She stayed at home under the care of a nurse and a governess. At the age of nine, she was already reading works by Shakespeare, Homer, and Tolstoy in Polish translations at home. The way she was raised and the interests she acquired through this are a rare example of the real cultural universalism of the elite world in which she lived, a world that was accessible to Bronka through Polish culture.[42] Polish made international literature available primarily to acculturated young people, but not only to them. It was an important means of gaining knowledge and information about the outside world also for the Jewish poor, handing over their children en masse to free public schools, who, even if they spoke Yiddish at home, systematically learned to write and read only in Polish.

International youth literature was probably the easiest literature for young people to understand, the most attractive, but no longer the most accessible. This is evidenced by the places of origin of the authors quoted above, coming mainly from large and great cities. Most likely, translations of Daniel Defoe, Karl May, or Romain Rolland were often available only in metropolitan public or school libraries.

There was a special place in the young people's autobiographies for "more serious" Russian literature, but this was read by a minority of participants in the competition. The Russian writer most frequently mentioned was Leo Tolstoy, whereas Fyodor Dostoyevsky, who did not appeal to nineteenth-century radicals, was, understandably, mentioned much less frequently. The former's popularity was probably connected with the populist ideas contained in his books, important especially for left-wing Zionists but also for many other Jewish socialists. For the same reasons, some left-wing autobiographers mentioned Maxim Gorky as their favorite author.[43]

POLITICAL READERSHIP

The linguistic competence of a relatively small number of autobiographers allowed them to read both Hebrew and Yiddish literature. Even the latter, accessible to most young people, was often not read in all its diversity. A large role was played by the politicization of young people, the fact that they belonged to organizations that usually had far-reaching, sometimes quite authoritarian ambitions in shaping their members' consciousness. The fact that the parties of the day fought not only a political battle but also a no less fierce cultural battle, not leaving out the greatest classics of Jewish literature, escapes the attention of scholars with rather idealistic visions of interwar Jewish culture. For example, two of the three greatest authors of Yiddish prose—Yitskhok Leybush Peretz and Sholem Aleichem—incurred the Bund's displeasure. The party also had a low opinion of Sholem Ash, who was very popular among the Jewish masses as well as some of the Zionists and Folkists. Yitskhok Leybush, who was associated with Jewish socialism, was especially criticized for the essay "Hope and Fear," written in 1906 and warning against the potential oppression of a future revolutionary regime, and for the neoromantic turn in his work in the first decade of the twentieth century. The composer of the party's official anthem, "Di Shvue" ("The Oath"), the famous Jewish ethnographer and social activist Shin An-sky (in reality Shloyme Zanvil Rapoport), was on the Bund's blacklist for the same reasons. The Bund's attachment to Yiddish that had been growing since 1905 also influenced the language's gradually growing politicization. In the interwar period, the party criticized Yiddish literature and cultural organizations for the fact that their aesthetics, activities, and ideological message did not directly serve the cause of socialism.[44]

In many autobiographies it is clear that the emergence of reading patterns among young people was often influenced by party organizations and youth movements. Thus, the contestants in the YIVO competition did not have the characteristics of individualist authors or of individualist readers, but for the most part they simply revealed the cultural preferences of specific, strongly antagonistic organizations. In the world of authoritarian ideologies dominating in the 1930s, what was read, where and with whom literature was discussed, and, in fact, the entire nature of cultural consumption had political significance and was often a declaration of membership in a specific camp. Scholars who rightly emphasize the enormous role of the library in the lives of young people often miss the fact that most of these institutions were associated with one or more political parties.[45] Tarbut, Shul-Kult, or TsYShO schools were also not ideologically neutral, which must have affected the contents of libraries and the ways of using their collections.[46]

Contemporary scholars Ido Bassok, Marcus Moseley, and Moshe Kligsberg, quoted here, have drawn attention to the phenomenon of literary trials of individual books put on by young people during discussions devoted to criticism. Such trials were held mainly within the framework of political organizations—or youth organizations of a political nature—and served, at least in part, the goals of young people's ideological socialization. As Yesh wrote, "Literary evenings were particularly interesting. After everyone had read a novella or a novel, we would hold such evenings. One or two people defended, others accused, and then there was a discussion. Such trials really gave great satisfaction and enriched our minds."[47]

For most secular authors who abandoned old customs and traditions and underwent a radical ideological conversion, political ideologies were often the highest form of knowledge about the surrounding world, explaining how society worked. Max Nordau, one iconic figure of the Zionist right, was the favorite writer of the Zionist "Reflega." The influence of Nordau's *Degeneration*, one of the most famous fin de siècle treatises on the collapse of Western civilization, is evident on many pages of his autobiography.[48] *The House on the Hill* (*Dos hoys oyfn burg*), by Simon Horenczyk, the works of Karl Marx, and a report from a trip to the Soviet Union by Peretz Hirshbeyn were read by a sympathizer of Po'alei-Tsiyon-Right and He-Halutz, Binyomin R.[49] Working as a traditional private tutor, in the evenings he would read in Polish Jan Berson's *New Russia*; *Kostya Ryabtsev's Diary*, by Nikolai Ogniev; Rodion Markovits's *Siberian Garrison*; and Arnold Zweig's *The Case of Sergeant Grischa*.[50] As a conscious political activist, he wrote that he no longer "took into his hands any rag of a newspaper or previously unknown book"; he did not want to be an "ass" reading everything that he came across.[51] Like many other authors, he took the party's policies and ideological precepts deadly seriously. This also applied to the high-mindedness of the literature he read.

Greyno, who had previously read Sholem Aleichem and Yitskhok Leybush Peretz in a communist trade union, focused on reading other types of literature, such as *The Origin of the Family, Private Property and the State*, by Friedrich Engels; *The General History of Socialism and Social Struggles*, by Max Beer; *The Origin of Religion and Belief in God*, by Heinrich Cunow; and *Woman and Socialism*, by August Bebel.[52] Another author recalled how in 1938, in the Tsukunft offices in Mińsk Mazowiecki, the book *Lenin and Gandhi* was distributed to young activists.[53] On March 1, 1933, at a meeting in Płońsk, held as part of the courses for workers organized by Po'alei-Tsiyon-Left, Mendl Man discussed Upton Sinclair's novel *The Jungle*. According to the boy, the book's most important message was the author's demonstration of the "reactionary nature of capitalist power in America," the theft and careerism of the elites.[54] Also, a fragment of a note sent in by Mendl Man with his autobiography from a party course is proof that often not only the selection of readings but also their interpretation was determined by ideology and political orientation rather than by literary interests.

In addition to schools and political organizations, it was the press, not literature, even at its loftiest, that was the most important source of knowledge about the world, especially for young workers and artisans. As seen from the autobiographical trajectories above, most of the young people worked several hours a day and had neither access to books nor time to read them, let alone institutionalized forms of learning. The press mentioned in their autobiographies most often represented the Yiddish daily press: the clearly Zionist-sympathetic *Haynt*, the Folkist (and later also a tribune of the Zionist right) *Der Moment*, or the press mouthpieces of individual political groups, such as the Bund's *Naye Folkstsaytung*, *Dos Vort* of Po'alei-Tsiyon-Left, or Aguda's *Ortodoksishe Yugend Bleter*. Typical examples include an excerpt from the autobiography of Kola, a locksmith's apprentice who, with his cousin, a young baker, tried to read the press together every evening. They took this very seriously, not as entertainment but as the only form of self-improvement available.[55] The same was true of A. Remez. During the time he belonged to the communist Pioneer, the most important source of knowledge about the world was the party press, literature on "wars, revolution and revolutionary work in Russia." His favorite heroes during this period were "Mishka Yaponchik" (Mishka the Japanese) and the literary figure of the son in Maxim Gorky's *Mother*.[56] This author's literary interests were also mainly motivated by political involvement.

As Nathan Cohen notes (contradicting the thesis of Marcus Moseley and other researchers of the YIVO autobiographies), in the interwar period "hunger for the press" among the Jewish population far outweighed "hunger for literature." Indeed, highbrow Yiddish literature and literary magazines were, with the end of Tsarist censorship, at the peak of their popularity in the early 1920s. However, with the development of mass culture and entertainment, polonization, and the phenomenon today called the tabloidization of the press (together with its growing politicization), print runs of highbrow Yiddish literature and serious literary magazines were already dramatically declining in the early 1930s.[57] This was also influenced by the Great Depression. Like most readers, young people were looking for sensationalism, quick political information, and entertainment that did not require philosophical and literary reflection. On the basis of the autobiographies, it is impossible to establish why young people in the 1930s were so radically different from older generations.

Ido Bassok has rightly noted that Jewish young people's reading in the interwar period "was an expression of ideological totalism."[58] It was just this kind of totalism that to a great extent shaped such negative descriptions of the traditional world and its institutions, as well as the attacks to which even those of the older generation who were the closest to young people were exposed. As we have seen, it also conditioned the type of knowledge sought by young people and thus often also the way in which they selected and interpreted literature. This knowledge was to help in understanding the surrounding social and political reality in a holistic, total way. Almost all political parties operating in the interwar period, both right-wing and left-wing, Polish and Jewish, had typically modernist ambitions to describe and explain the social world's mechanisms. So I agree with Bassok that among young Jewish people there existed a powerful norm in the form of intensive reading; I even agree with the statement that within this group there actually was a subculture boosting this norm.[59] As I have written, it covered those with a broad education, recalling the ideal of the young Orthodox maskil, some secondary students (both those who were receiving a parallel high traditional education and those who were not), and a small group of self-taught people able to break down all life's barriers. However, most of the authors, and thus certainly most of the Jewish young people in general, were more impressed by the politically "aware" (Yiddish *bavustzinike*) than by writers. Much more often than Bassok admits, and even more so Moseley or Kligsberg, the contestants in the YIVO competition chose literature for themselves according to a political key and interpreted it using the same key, rejecting any that did not fit the ideological dictates of their home political movements. Thus, the vast majority of participants in the YIVO competition were certainly not individualist readers for whom literature was an autotelic value and reading their most important daily activity.

THE EXCEPTIONAL READER AND A CRITIQUE OF THE THEORY OF THE "GENERATION OF READERS"

Summing up the description of the patterns and importance of reading in the lives of young people, I will stay for a longer time with a completely unique autobiography, that of Tor. He is probably one of the most cited contestants in the YIVO competition, quoted by Moseley, Kligsberg, and Bassok in order to confirm the theory of an intense, thematically comprehensive, and multilingual readership that characterizes the generation in question and in this sense makes it exceptional.[60] Tor had to be close to the ideal type of young man promoted by YIVO. The problem, however, is that his socialization was characterized by the specific conditions described above. Tor also had an exceptional personality. For him, recalling the title of Moseley's article, "life" really "was literature," in contrast to most young Jewish people growing up in the Second Republic.[61]

Tor up to a certain point in his biography belonged to the exceptional young Orthodox, fascinated by the Haskalah model of the maskil, described in chapter 2. This model was characterized by individualism and a critical and nondogmatic attitude toward both the world of tradition and radical political ideologies. Against the background of the autobiography as a whole, the latter attitude was particularly unusual. It is fruitless to seek a critical attitude toward modernist political systems among the testimonies of secularized young people who came from traditional homes, who did not study in yeshivas, and who entered the path of political radicalism during their adolescence.

Unlike most other autobiographers from traditional backgrounds, Tor emancipated himself from the traditional world not through politics but through literature, borrowing books at the Bresler Library in Warsaw's Nowolipie district.[62] Then his "new life" began. Notable is Tor's model of individual self-realization, which differs from that of the majority and demands a critical attitude toward the all-encompassing politicization of the 1930s. The adolescent took a job in a knitwear factory. Because of the seasonality of his work, which provided employment for only five months of the year, Tor, in order to "kill time during his periods of unemployment," enrolled in an unspecified Zionist organization. However, he quickly left it and developed an aversion to the dominant forms of politics on the Jewish Street. This "organization filled with empty words" suppressed individual thinking on the part of its members. He had expected from it education and wide-ranging discussion but had encountered nothing but speeches and hostility toward all antagonists.[63]

The further description of Tor's life is a testimony to his very extensive literary interests. He read Lermontov, Pushkin, Yesenin, Tagore, Rilke, Baudelaire, Heine, Yiddish proletarian poetry, and the poetry of Bialik. He mentioned the names of writers often found in other autobiographies (Tolstoy and Rolland), those found very rarely (Dostoevsky), and those unheard of in other autobiographies (Knut Hamsun and Ernst Toller). "Universal authors have shown me a world full of light," he wrote. He presented his reading experience as a process of individual ascent, the development of personality. Another period was the resurgence of his interest in "proletarian literature, all written in Yiddish." He mentioned the following authors: Avrom Reyzen, Rosenfeld, Winczewski, Leyvik, Shvartsman, "new Jewish-Russian literature," Heftman, Barik, Fefer, Kvitko, Markish, Bergelson, Broderzon, Mani Leyb, "etc., etc."[64]

He supplemented his reading of poetry with the prose of Ash, Opatoshu, and Peretz. The latter's books became a "personal guide to life" for Tor. These descriptions are reflected in both the autobiographer's Yiddish-proletarian and Zionist-Hebrew interests, which at the level of political involvement may seem contradictory but are natural in terms of reader individualism. His politically contradictory tastes seem to be united by a Haskalah desire to get to know all sides of the Jewish world, and at the same time by an attachment to the idea of *klal Yisroel*. Tor expressed this by declaring his fascination with the works of Zalman Shneour, which were able to reflect the whole of Jewish life of the time, "in all its colors," "in a small shtetl, as well as in a large city": "I could not live a week without Shneour, just as a Jew cannot live without prayer . . . I felt the same way when I wasn't reading Shneour. The Shabbat was profaned to me when I did not delight in 'Shneour's bastard.'"[65]

Which of Tor's unique social and personal attributes influenced how uniquely well read he was? What do they say about the reading patterns of young people in general? The author came from a family aspiring to be part of the traditional elite; his parents, despite poverty, stubbornly educated him in successively superior heders and sent him to study at one of the most prestigious in Poland, the world-famous Torat Chaim yeshiva. Tor, despite his aversion to the Orthodox world (expressed retrospectively in his autobiography), left the yeshiva at age fifteen, only then entering the path of total secularism. More than ten years of very intensive, elite Orthodox education had allowed him to gain a perfect command of Hebrew. At this point in a biography, it was natural for almost all young people to join one of the political organizations. Tor did so too. However, he quickly left, which was unique compared to other autobiographies. He was put off by the order to subordinate everything to ideology, including what one read and thought about the books one read. Thus, Tor indirectly confirmed what other works stated—the politicization and ideologization of his generation, and not his generation's individualism or literary nature. Thanks to his stubbornness and sacrifice, he even learned German, mainly to be able to read books in the original. Tor belonged to a relatively small group, described above, of Orthodox young people who had the richest repertoire of intellectual tools allowing them to read and understand literature from three or rather five cultural universes: traditional and secular Yiddish, Hebrew-Aramaic religious literature, New Hebrew national literature, Polish literature, and world literature translated into Yiddish or Polish or read in the original. He stood out from elite Orthodox young people by virtue of his resolute secularism and aversion to religion, and he exemplified criticism of radical secular political ideologies. His uniqueness in not complying with the universal norm of political activity and an ideological view of reality, including literature, made him able to read Bialik, to be a Yiddishist and yet appreciate the famous poet's Hebraism, while at the same time allowing him to read revolutionary and avant-garde Yiddish poets such as Perets Markish. Tor's autobiography is a testimony to the norm of intellectual self-improvement through reading literature that undoubtedly operated in Jewish society (and probably not only there). The author stood out from most others in that he actually implemented this norm. His autobiography is also a testimony to the tension between this norm and another, adopted by political organizations claiming the right to determine what books their members were to read. Tor opted for the first of the norms, almost all the rest of the authors for the second. For them, life was not literature but politics.

Tor, Gershon Pipe, and Binyomin R., who are frequently analyzed by scholars, often complained that many of their friends read hardly anything or not at all. Kligsberg (co-organizer of the third autobiography competition in 1939, previously a Bund activist and a TsYShO teacher in Warsaw), when writing a kind of postwar requiem for the generation destroyed during World War II, ignored the differences between the various types of intellectual development represented by these three autobiographers and those characterizing most of their generation. He saw no difference between a critical intellectual, declaring his independence from all isms and pressure groups, and the majority of young people educated in political groups that brought forth an intellectual message addressing the winds of change in the surrounding world. All the scholars quoted here have also ignored the discrepancy between the very early interruption of education for the majority of young people caused by the need to take up paid employment, and the fact that the intellectualism, polyglotism, and literariness of authors such as Tor required comprehensive intellectual capital, developed over many years and in many institutions, as well as financial resources and free time. The aforementioned scholars have also failed to take into account the social issue indicated above, that modern Hebrew literature could be read only by people from defined, relatively narrow backgrounds, characterized by a specific educational trajectory and unique cultural capital. Contestants in the YIVO competition described a typical workday lasting over twelve hours, which clearly shows that they did not have much time to read and study on their own. If, to top it off, most of the authors were self-taught (as Moseley and Kligsberg have of course noted), how could the profound literary self-awareness that they attribute to them have been formed? The problem of financial and cultural obstacles and lack of time on the bumpy road to becoming an intellectual is perfectly illustrated by a quote in Kligsberg's work from one of the autobiographies, which in his opinion is intended to illustrate the unique dedication to cultural issues that characterizes the generation described here: "I earned 6 zlotys a week at the shoemaker's. I was left with only a single zloty, because I gave the rest to my parents. I had to live on it for a whole week. I gave 15 cents [grosze] to the party, 25 cents to go the movies . . . 10 cents to *Yugend Veker*, and with the rest I bought a piece of bread and a single herring."[66]

Apart from the impossibility of verifying whether the author demonstrated such meticulousness and dedication in his actual life, let us ask whether this was possible for the majority of Jewish youth. Of course it was not. An example is a fragment of the autobiography of one of the most consistent readers. Her working day began at 6:00 or 7:00 a.m. and lasted until 6:00 p.m. Up to 8:00 p.m., the autobiographer helped her younger sister with her schoolwork, and she devoted the next hour to a walk. She had the last two hours of the day between 9:00 and 11:00 p.m. to read.[67] Another author wrote, "There are moments when I give in to the sad thought of how empty is the most beautiful period of youth. Every day, young people are stuck in poverty, in the gray reality of hard work. They treat the few free hours only as ersatz."[68] The author meant a substitute for "real life," in which young people would also have time for their own intellectual development. Another author, working twelve hours a day in a workshop, wrote that in her position it was very difficult to engage in serious reading.[69] It would be impossible to defend the assumption that all the autobiographers were so consistent. In addition, we must remember that people determined to devote a few hours of free time to education were undoubtedly significantly overrepresented among the participants in the YIVO competition. Therefore, the enormous, authentic intellectual ambitions and striving for self-development so strongly expressed in the autobiographies are not to be confused with the supposedly daily, general, and intense intellectual activity of the majority of young people. Even among the above-average reflective and self-educated participants in the YIVO competition, only a minority had real opportunities to follow the lifestyle attributed to an entire generation by the scholars cited above. However, even those few could not read with the intensity assumed by Kligsberg. Completely improbable data contained in his classic work on Jewish young people in the interwar period are still to this day in academic circulation. Kligsberg calculated that in the 1930s there were about 450,000 Jews aged fourteen to twenty living in Poland. According to the scholar's "own experience," two-thirds of this group read an average of one book per week; the number of people who read little or not at all was balanced by people reading several books a week. Following the YIVO researcher Marcus Moseley, Michael Steinlauf and David Shavit have repeated the claim that

Jewish youth supposedly read fifteen million books annually.[70] In light of the above arguments, this figure is certainly much inflated.

Young people had not necessarily read all the books they referred to in their biographies. They might simply have heard about many of them at school or in the organizations in which they worked and boasted about their knowledge in their autobiographies. It is no coincidence that among the books that the authors not only referred to but quoted or whose content they described, what cropped up most often was not highbrow literature but popular works or ones known to young people from school. Moreover, many of the YIVO autobiographies not only described their reading matter but also included their complaints about the fact that in their peer environment hardly anyone read, or most were reading lowbrow literature.[71]

READERSHIP IN POLISH AND
PARTICIPATION IN MASS CULTURE

In academic studies of the YIVO autobiographies, what is also striking is the marginalization of the role of Polish culture in the lives of Jewish young people. Public school, which about 80 percent of young Jews attended, contributed greatly to the intensive reading of Polish books among young people. It is worth noting that, as in the case of the Yiddish classics, the most frequently cited Polish authors were those whom young people read compulsorily in elementary school. For example, Prowincjał in several excerpts of his autobiography clearly indicated the sources of his literary inspiration, undoubtedly formed under the influence of elementary and secondary school. Describing school life, as well as his own family tragedy, he recalled two Polish national poets, Juliusz Słowacki and Adam Mickiewicz.[72] Prowincjał belonged to the group of acculturated contestants in the YIVO competition, but similar examples are provided by autobiographies of young people from traditional or Orthodox backgrounds, who spoke Yiddish on a daily basis.

The favorite book of an autobiographer growing up in Maków Mazowiecki, a future member of Tsukunft and a convinced Yiddish woman, was a popular young adult novel entitled *Janka* by Gabriela Zapolska.[73] It was in fact her friends from Tsukunft who persuaded her to read Yiddish when she was fifteen years old. Previously, she had read mainly Polish books. The same was true for A. Remez, a future Bundist writing in Yiddish—his first literary canon, apart from Daniel Defoe's novels, was determined by the Polish school readings he loved. At this time, the greatest influence on his literary taste was a teacher of Polish from public elementary school.[74] Testimonies to the prestige of the

Polish language and Polish reading matter were provided even by the autobiographies of Orthodox authors. Esther, in accordance with the rules in force in her milieu, read mainly books in Yiddish borrowed from the library of the Bais Yaakov school, but at the same time she described her fascination with Polish nineteenth-century historical novels.[75] Tor, belonging to a minority of authors who had no contact with public education, read in Polish in translation, among others, the poetry of Byron and Shakespeare.[76]

In 1933, Borys Temkin analyzed the book-lending statistics of fifty Jewish libraries in Warsaw: 50 percent of the titles were in Polish, 25 percent in Yiddish, 9.6 percent in Hebrew, and the rest in other languages.[77] Nationwide research on the largest Jewish libraries, conducted by scholars from Yiddish circles, emphasized that as early as 1926, alongside 43.4 percent of borrowed books in Yiddish, 41 percent were in Polish.[78] These statistics were collected in the first years of independence, so they do not apply to the generation described here, which was powerfully influenced by the public education system. In the following decade, in 1937, 76.1 percent of all books borrowed from the TseBeKa library in Vilna were in Polish and only 20.8 percent in Yiddish.[79] Let us note that, contrary to the theory of the generation of readers, books in Hebrew were not actually read even in Vilna, a quite unique place in terms of the strength of modern Yiddishism and Hebraism. Toward the end of the 1930s, even in "Litvak Jerusalem," the Polish language became the basic non-Jewish language of the local Jews. In the area of former eastern Galicia, where secular Yiddishism was much weaker, the dominance of Polish books was beyond doubt even in private Jewish libraries. In the Y. L. Peretz Institution in Czortków in 1935, 70 percent of its 805 readers declared Polish to be their preferred reading language.[80] Jewish youth also used the libraries of public schools as well as city libraries. The latter most often had a larger selection of books, and their book collections were also used by regular customers of Yiddish and Hebrew libraries. Statistics based on data on loans only from Jewish libraries do not give a complete picture of young people's reading.

By attentively reading the autobiographies, one can trace the pressure exerted on young people by their political organizations in terms of their reading. This fact should be considered when comparing the number of Yiddish and Hebrew titles referred to in YIVO autobiographies with the number of titles in Polish. The competition organizers' as well as the entire Jewish national elite's dislike of popular culture undoubtedly also influenced how frequently young people mentioned Jewish pulp fiction or similar Polish-language books.[81] Direct evidence of this pressure can, of course, be found in very few autobiographies. An example is the autobiography of Mendl Man, who began reading modern Jewish literature only under the influence of his older brother, a teacher at a TsYShO school and an avowed Yiddishist. Thanks to reading the works of Peretz, Sholem Aleichem, and An-sky, the boy began to change from a carefree backyard troublemaker into an aware secular Jew "interested in social life." He condemned his Jewish peers for their lack of interest in "their own" literature dealing with the problems of the Jewish people or the problems of the class struggle of the proletariat.[82] One of the female participants in the competition described how at Tsukunft meetings members were made aware that "you can't read everything, and you also need to know what not to read." Undesirable reading matter included popular, frivolous books that did not have an adequate ideological message, especially those written in a non-Jewish language.[83] This kind of political pressure as to what a good Jewish socialist should read made her feel seriously remorseful. At home, both she and her Yiddish-speaking parents read Polish popular literature.[84]

This autobiography is one of the few that directly show what other authors try to conceal or downplay and what must have been the experience of the majority of Jewish young people of the interwar period. On the one hand, young people were subjected to the ideological pressure of Jewish political organizations, and on the other hand, they succumbed to covert but probably even stronger symbolic violence on the part of Polish culture. Defining Jewish young people as not entirely "our people," at the same time through school and mass culture Polish culture invaded their everyday language and literary, social, and political imagination. Many young people read books in at least two languages: Yiddish and Polish. Even if the latter language did not have a dominant position, its role was certainly large, because reading Polish literature united autobiographers from all social spheres.[85] It is also worth noting that although most of the young people came from homes where only Yiddish was spoken, in the interwar period several hundred thousand Jews in Poland spoke mainly or only Polish. People coming from this environment constituted between 10 and 20 percent of the contestants in the YIVO competition. Due to the specificity of the competition, it can be assumed that the percentage of this type of person among all young people in interwar Poland was even higher. While almost every autobiographer who wrote in Yiddish could read Polish, it was much more unusual for acculturated authors to be able to read in Yiddish or Hebrew. The autobiographical testimonies quoted here are a strong argument for the fact that Polish literature and Polish translations of world literature, even if not the most read, were the area of culture available to the widest segment of young people.

Of course, Jewish young people had contact with culture not only through books. Other media, such as the movies and theater, came up less frequently in the autobiographies. To a large extent, this was certainly determined by most authors' poor financial situation, as well as the lack of daily access to these cultural benefits for young people in small towns. Cinema in the interwar period had the status of lowbrow culture, not much different from pulp fiction. The fact that in autobiographies it comes up quite rarely was also influenced by the fact that the autobiographies were written for a competition and their authors often wanted to boast of their high cultural capital. The interwar period saw the unfettered development of Polish mass culture and, above all, the absolute peak of Yiddish mass culture. In the 1930s, in which young people wrote their autobiographies, Yiddish cinema experienced rapid development in Poland, with such hits as *Yidl mitn Fidl* (Yiddle With His Fiddle) in 1936 and *The Dybbuk*, which came out a year later. Warsaw Jewish theater occupied an important place on the cultural map of the Second Republic. Amateur orchestras and theaters performed in smaller cities and shtetls throughout the whole country. However, we find evidence of this in a relatively small number of autobiographies. It is striking that among the works written for the competition of a national Yiddish institution such as YIVO, there are few examples of Yiddish or Hebrew cultural involvement other than reading books, participating in the life of Jewish schools, or attending party lectures devoted to culture. We find almost no accounts in the autobiographies of visits to the Jewish theater, which operated daily only in Warsaw, or to the movies to see Yiddish films. Young people loved mass and popular culture, but this was available to them mainly in Polish. If autobiographies mentioned visits to the movies at all, it was almost always in the context of foreign or Polish films, but not Yiddish cinema, even though in the 1930s Poland was its center. This is further proof that in the reality of a modern twentieth-century state the national language inevitably dominated in the field of popular culture. Even autobiographies written for a competition organized by an institution that fought against this phenomenon indirectly prove this.

FROM LINGUISTIC TO SYMBOLIC ACCULTURATION

The theme of acculturation to Polish culture runs through all the previous chapters of this book. Jewish children became acquainted with Polish culture and the Polish language in elementary school, heders, and all secular Jewish schools. The Polish language and culture reached young Jews from various sources: through independent reading, contacts with peers and neighbors, wall posters, the Polish and Polish-language Jewish press, and movies or theatrical performances. Its presence in such dimensions of everyday life as homeschooling, self-study, vocational training, and work appears in almost all autobiographies written in Yiddish and written by authors from traditional backgrounds, where Yiddish was spoken at home. Even when writing only in Yiddish, authors wrote some words, often those concerning spheres of life in which they encountered the non-Jewish world, in Polish.[86] No wonder, then, that not only Weinreich and the YIVO community but also many other Jewish nationalist activists raised the alarm because of the pace of Polish acculturation, which was especially rapid among Jewish young people. One of the leading activists of Hebrew education, Alter Druyanov, who lived permanently in the Land of Israel, wrote as follows in 1932 about his fresh impressions from a visit to Poland: "Linguistic assimilation is gaining so much strength among Polish Jews that it seems that before our eyes they are forgetting the language that has been their language for hundreds of years. . . . Who knows if in the next generation or in two generations, it will be possible to speak Yiddish to a Jewish audience in Poland, just as it is no longer possible to speak this language to a Jewish audience in Germany."[87]

It is not easy to speculate just how credible Druyanov's predictions were. Ten years later, the futures of millions of Polish Jews were destroyed by the Holocaust. Regardless of whether these predictions were exaggerated or whether there was a high probability that they would be fulfilled, they flowed from real experience, from the cultural reality of interwar Polish and the impact it was having on the Jewish community.

POLISH LANGUAGE AND CULTURE IN JEWISH SCHOOLS

Polish culture influenced Jewish young people not only through participation in the outside world but also through institutions of the Jewish world, such as religious and secular-national Jewish schools, which were ostensibly bastions of the fight against acculturation. The content of teaching was influenced by the Polish state. However, the policies of the schools themselves were also not without significance. Their ideological approach assumed building a Jewish religious, religious-national, or secular national identity. At the same time, they tried to educate students who could function freely in Polish society and thus who knew its language and culture.[88] Activists and teachers in Jewish schools, like the YIVO community, had to deal with a difficult question: Where does knowledge of the Polish language and culture, seen in a positive light and crucial for the success in life of young Jews living in Poland, end, and where do assimilation and losing one's identity begin?

Since the First World War, the teaching of the Polish language had been gradually introduced into all institutions of basic religious education operating in the Aguda Horev network.[89] The educational reform of 1932 required religious schools to provide a minimum of 112 hours of school subjects taught in Polish during the school year.[90] Three years later, the arrangements between the schools of the Horev network and the government established that in one year students would take no fewer than 112 classes conducted in Polish, of which 38 were in Polish language and literature, 8 in history, 10 in geography, 10 in physics and biology, 22 in mathematics, 8 in needlework, 5 in drawing, 5 in singing, and 6 in physical education.[91] From the very beginning of the operation of the Bais Yaakov Orthodox religious schools for girls, Polish was the language of instruction for all Polish and general (mathematics, physics, biology, etc.) subjects.[92] The same was true of Litvak establishments. In the Rabbi Rubinstein religious school for girls in Vilna, half of the subjects were taught in Yiddish (religious subjects) and half in Polish (secular subjects).[93] In the 1930s, this establishment was the equivalent of a seven-grade elementary school.

The situation was similar in modern religious schools in the Yavne network. The Vilna Talmud Torah, which followed the network's syllabus and was the largest institution of traditional Jewish elementary education in the city, was in the 1930s equivalent to a six-grade elementary school. Its graduates could take the entrance exams to secondary school. This meant that children in this institution studied in Polish almost all subjects taught in state elementary schools, including Polish literature, history, and geography.[94] The same was true of another establishment in the city, operating since 1902: the Tora Emes national-religious school, in Tsarist times an ordinary heder metukan.[95] In a document from 1937, the Yavne network emphasized the importance of teaching the history of Poland, the historical evolution of Polish society, and a good knowledge of the country's economic and social issues.[96] In the most important educational establishment associated with the Mizrahi party, the Warsaw Tahkemoni Rabbinical Seminary, secular subjects were taught based on the full curriculum of an eight-grade secondary school, with an emphasis on knowledge of contemporary Poland, its people, and its history. The syllabus of other secular subjects was also taught in Polish.[97]

The Polish language and, above all, the cult of Polish literature were important elements of the educational mission of many Tarbut schools. Zionism, dominated by the middle class, together with its acculturation acquired an increasingly Polish character. This is also confirmed by the linguistic distribution among the authors in the YIVO competition, as well as Jewish memoirists writing after the Holocaust, coming from polonized homes and at the same time studying in Tarbut schools, who emphasized the great role played by education in the spirit of Polish patriotism and attachment to Polish national symbols.[98] Testimony to the presence of the Polish language and culture in Tarbut schools, which were supposed to teach mainly in Hebrew, was also the curriculum of the network's leading secondary school, Hertzliya in Vilna. This curriculum is all the more significant because it was implemented by an establishment operating in the least polonized of the metropolitan Jewish communities. The Polish language (dictation, reading, discussing selected excerpts from the primer) was already taught in *mechina*, preparatory class.[99] Attempts were clearly made to improve knowledge of the Polish language among students who had previously studied in institutions where attention had not been paid to teaching it to an appropriate level. The Vilna Tarbut school was characterized by the true philosophy of bilingual (utraquist) schools teaching Hebrew and Polish to the same level. In the first grades, children intensively studied grammar, spelling, and vocabulary, so that in the next grades they could read highbrow literature in these languages. At the same time, talks about the history of Poland began. Polish history as a separate subject began in third grade. In the next grade, getting acquainted with Polish literature, children read the works of its most important authors, including Adam Mickiewicz and Henryk Sienkiewicz. There were many more Polish books at this level of teaching than works of world literature. In fifth grade, children read, among others, the most important Polish national epic, Mickiewicz's *Pan Tadeusz*, in its entirety, as well as Sienkiewicz's major novels, and they studied a textbook on Polish style geared for the seventh grade of public schools. In the same grade, they also took a detailed course in the history, geography, and issues of contemporary Poland. In the subsequent grades, until the end of secondary school and a diploma, the Polish language and literature curriculum was based on textbooks used in similar grades in public school. The literary canon transmitted to the students in a Tarbut school was the same canon in which the Polish elite was educated.[100]

The syllabus "Hebrew History," published by the Tarbut head office in Warsaw in 1934, also laid emphasis on considering the role of the history of Poland and the Polish nation in the history of the Jews. In this program, the world history of the Jews in the nineteenth century was dominated by the history of the Jews in Poland, including the history of Jewish participation in Polish national uprisings.[101] The aforementioned list of topics affected the history of the Jews taught in Hebrew. The course on Polish history was held separately and was the same as in Polish schools. It was taught using the same textbooks. How Jewish history was taught was far removed from the Zionist metahistory of the day, which focused on the relationship between the various

communities of the diaspora and the Holy Land, seeing local non-Jewish contexts as something of a sidebar, and was certainly not interested in emphasizing the participation of Jews in other nations' struggles. This kind of "Polish
deviationism" by the Tarbut schools exposed them to devastating criticism
from Zionist activists visiting interwar Poland from Palestine.[102] In its emphasis on the Polish context and Polish patriotism, Tarbut was much more like
its local adversaries than the Hebrew schools then developing in Palestine.

Likewise, in the TsYShO schools probably fighting most fiercely against
linguistic assimilation, many subjects were taught in Polish.[103] In transmitting
Polish culture to young people, Yiddishist teachers went much further than
state regulations required. Chaim Shloyme Kazhdan, one of the leaders of the
TsYShO and an outspoken opponent of linguistic assimilation, wrote in 1926,
"We have proved that children attending secular Jewish schools [the TsYShO]
know Polish no worse than those who study in public schools. . . . We instill
in our children confidence and faith in themselves, in their friends . . . a love
and respect for Polish culture."[104] In this network's elementary schools, all the
classics of Polish literature were read. Polish culture also played a huge role
in the curriculum of the teachers' seminar in Vilna, as well as in other educational establishments in the city operating under the aegis of TseBeKa.[105] Max
Weinreich, who in 1934 sat on the matriculation committee of the Vilna Real
Gimnazye—which, as the only TsYShO secondary school, was fully accredited
by the government (as a category A, with its diploma granting admission to Polish universities)—wrote that in general the students knew the Polish material
better than the Jewish subjects.[106]

In Shul-Kult schools, language, literature, history, geography, and civics
were taught in Polish. Moreover, general subjects such as arithmetic, geometry,
algebra, world geography, botany, physics, chemistry, anatomy, and personal
hygiene were also taught based on the "Polish national curriculum."[107] Of
course, the same was also true of private Jewish utraquist schools, which were
not affiliated with the abovementioned networks.[108]

Most of the autobiographers attended several types of school during their
lifetimes, most often both public and private Jewish schools. The fact that
young people almost never wrote about the difficulties of moving to public
schools resulting from differences in curriculum or an inadequate knowledge
of the language (except when children from traditional homes went to first
grade, having previously attended only heders) proves that the number of hours
allocated to subjects taught in Polish must have been considerable. The important place and high level of teaching of Polish culture in Tarbut schools
are confirmed, for example, by the autobiographies of Binyomin R., Neri, and
an anonymous female graduate of the Hebrew secondary school in Kovel.[109]

Information about teaching Polish in heders and Orthodox schools can be found in the works of Abraham Rotfarb, Stormer, Binyomin R., A Shtetleshe, Gamalielis, and "Orient-Vostok," among others.[110]

The Polish educational content provided in Jewish schools was to instill in young people a cultural canon that would allow them to move freely in Polish social, cultural, and ideological reality. A condition of this freedom was to think and feel using the same symbols as did non-Jewish citizens of the country. Elements of Polish culture became part of young people's identity. In the process of symbolic acculturation of this kind, Polish culture ceased to be a foreign, external culture for them, and they were not indifferent to it.

THE SCOPE AND NATURE OF ACCULTURATION

What was the final extent of the acculturation processes taking place in Jewish society and to which its youngest generation had to be most strongly subjected? In answering this question, it is necessary to refer in advance to two censuses conducted in the Second Republic. Celia Heller, using the results of the 1921 census (when respondents were asked about both nationality and religion), accepted 270,000–280,000 as the number of assimilated Polish Jews—less than 10 percent of the total population. She considered as "assimilated" those people who declared Polish nationality and Jewish faith.[111] In the next census in 1931, the question of nationality was replaced by a question on language. Of those who described their religion as "Mosaic," 80 percent declared Yiddish as their native language, 12 percent declared Polish, and 8 percent Hebrew.[112] The data of both censuses are not necessarily reflections of reality. During the second one, Jewish political groups, as part of their opposition to the removal of the question on nationality, called for declaring Yiddish or Hebrew. There is no doubt that the number of Jews for whom Polish was the most natural language of communication was much higher.[113] The uncritical use of census data may lead to situations in which communists declaring Polish as their mother tongue, coming from the lowest social classes with a poor knowledge of the language and culture, and operating only on the Jewish Street will be considered assimilated or polonized, while polonized members of the Jewish intelligentsia advocating for Jewish nationalism will be excluded from this group. Therefore, the census data can be treated only as political declarations, with reservations as to identity declarations, but at the same time telling us little or nothing about the actual processes of acculturation or polonization taking place in Jewish society.

A perfect example of how nationalistically motivated declarations on the census can distort the real cultural landscape of interwar Poland was YIVO's research on Jewish middle school students in Warsaw conducted during the 1936/37 school year. At this time, not a single Tarbut or TsYShO secondary school operated in Warsaw. Most Jewish middle school students attended public schools or private institutions teaching only in Polish; the rest attended utraquist institutions, where Polish dominated. Despite this, as many as 53 percent of Jewish secondary school students declared Yiddish as their native language. Even more peculiar, among the subgroup of students attending Jewish (utraquist) junior highs, among whom there should have been more supporters of national parties, this percentage was only 33.2 percent. These declarations had little to do with the everyday language of Jewish junior high students. Moreover, the increase in the declaration of Yiddish as a mother tongue among Jewish college students, from 28 percent in the 1922/23 academic year to 50 percent in 1929/30, resulted from an increase in the popularity of the nationalist option, progressing in parallel with the process of acculturation.[114] The observations of Alter Druyanov also say a great deal. When in 1931 he went to Poland and visited the best Tarbut junior highs in Pińsk, Vilna, Grodno, and Białystok, he noticed that in their free time, outside class, the students most often spoke to each other not in Hebrew but in Polish.[115]

In the professional literature, when scholars reflect on the scale of the acculturation of various Jewish circles in the interwar period, the situation in Poland is sometimes too easily contrasted with the situation in the Soviet Union. Comparing Soviet data with Polish census data from 1931, as well as with the already-cited YIVO research statistics on the language of Jewish junior high students, David Fishman has pointed to a much slower pace of Polish acculturation and the success of Jewish autonomists in maintaining Yiddish as the basic language of not only the Jewish masses but even the future elites.[116] This contemporary statement, however, clearly contradicts the anxieties of interwar social activists, politicians, and YIVO experts, who emphasized the rapidly advancing polonization of Jewish young people, especially those in secondary schools. Fishman attributed the much slower pace of acculturation mainly to factors that hindered young Jews' access to higher education, such as widespread antisemitism or the numerus clausus. He failed to notice, however, that the dislike of Jews and discrimination against them had a much stronger influence on their nationalist pronouncements and political affiliations than on cultural processes. One side of the Jewish situation in interwar Poland compared with that of Jews in the USSR was the antisemitism existing in the public space; the other, however, was the freedom of activity of Jewish national parties, which channeled young people's opposition to discrimination into unrestrained activity in these parties. Identification with and involvement in Jewish national politics required specific cultural declarations, which, however, did not automatically translate into real patterns of cultural consumption or into the language and culture of everyday life. The conclusions quoted here drawn from census data by postwar and recent research are contradicted by the statistics already mentioned of borrowing books from Jewish libraries and the reach of public education on the Jewish Street. Census data have yet another drawback, which is that some groups were subject to the process of acculturation while others were passed over. Undoubtedly, it had a different character in different environments, but it occurred practically everywhere.

One of the best models describing the complex cultural universe of the Jewish community in the Second Republic is the model of the trilingual polysystem introduced by Chone Shmeruk. As the Israeli scholar has correctly pointed out, specific sociopolitical subcultures formed around each of the three languages spoken by Jews (Yiddish, Polish, and Hebrew). Although their publicly active representatives were often involved in fierce rivalry, undermining the legitimacy of their political opponents' subcultures, in fact many Polish Jews in different social contexts moved in various cultural universes. Shmeruk's great merit is also in leading the discussion about the culture of Polish Jews out of the sphere of a declared native or national language and introducing into it the problems of mass consumption of works of literature, stage performances, cinema, and all the products of popular culture, and finally the influence of the public education system on it.[117] Although Shmeruk pointed to the distinctiveness of Jewish young people's socialization experience and thus their cultural participation, his article refers to all citizens of the Jewish faith of the Second Republic and does not analyze significant generational differences in more depth. Furthermore, and what is probably justified in the case of most of older generations, the Israeli scholar, although he has suggested situations in which they lived in several subsystems—Polish and Yiddish, Polish and Hebrew, and finally three at once—drew a clear division between them. This divide, despite a few "excursions," ran between people, who, in his opinion, can generally be attributed to a specific system. Most young people, however, lived on a daily basis in at least two of the polysystems he mentioned, one of them almost always being the Polish polysystem.

SHORTCOMINGS OF THE TERM *ASSIMILATION*:
SYMBOLIC VIOLENCE AND THE SYMBOLIC
DIMENSION OF ACCULTURATION

So, what is the process whereby young people acquired Polish elements of identity, political consciousness, and culture called? Contemporary Jewish historiography draws attention to the vagueness and often unconscious ideological

entanglement of concepts that had previously often been used quite unthinkingly. One of them is the term *assimilation*. Testimony to the confusion of the
meaning of *assimilation* is the attempt to define this term by Tod Endelman,
the author of the entry in *The YIVO Encyclopedia of Jews in Eastern Europe*.[118]
He did not give a concise definition of it but only pointed out that the term was
often (unthinkingly) used to describe four distinct social processes: acculturation (the adoption of the social and cultural patterns of surrounding societies),
integration (bringing Jews into non-Jewish circles and non-Jewish spheres of
activity), emancipation (equality), and secularization (abandoning Jewish religious beliefs and practices). Endelman also points out that various scholars
often use the same term to describe two different means of change: political
programs and social reforms aimed at the amalgamation or integration of Jews
into their surroundings, and the spontaneous processes of a minority adopting
the values, symbols, and patterns of life of their surroundings. Many classical
studies devoted to the history of the Jews in Poland get entangled in this kind
of ambiguity, putting under the same category of assimilation such different
processes as completely blending into the dominant culture and erasing one's
own Jewish roots, or acquiring only selected elements of this culture while
retaining strong elements of Jewish culture and a strong Jewish identity.[119]
Among other things, for the above reasons as well as because of its ideological
entanglements, the use of the concept of assimilation in the description of Jewish relations with modern Jewish culture in the second half of the nineteenth
and the first half of the twentieth century is questioned by Ezra Mendelsohn,
Marcin Wodziński, and Agnieszka Jagodzińska.[120] According to these scholars,
the term *acculturation* is much more helpful.

Most of the Polish studies dealing with the issue of the acculturation of
Polish Jews, including those listed above, focus on the planned activities and
ideas of both supporters of Jewish integration and its opponents building various models of a Jewish national culture. Meanwhile, the various processes of
acculturation, like most profound social processes, could not be fully submitted either to the political will of the organizations fighting it or even to the
conscious control of the individuals concerned. In the context of Jewish youth
in interwar Poland, processes of acculturation should therefore be studied at
the level of the autobiographers pondering identity, and to understand them
more deeply, one should carefully look at the descriptions of home life, parents, friends, school, or ways of spending free time. This will allow us to free
ourselves from the level of ideological declarations by many autobiographers,
created under the influence of the political circles to which they belonged or
with which they sympathized, most often ordering them to declare a decidedly

negative attitude toward assimilation. An analysis of acculturation must also include the study of spontaneous social processes, both those that go against the identity declarations of those subject to them and those outside their consciousness. Participants in the YIVO competition certainly underwent these processes and therefore defined themselves in the nationalist or nationalist-religious sense as Jewish. The study of acculturation processes from a programmatic or declarative perspective ignores their very important emotional aspect. People and environments that were acculturating were concerned not only on the formal level with knowledge of the symbols of the dominant culture but also with the patterns of emotional reaction toward them. The internalization of symbols must be followed by the internalization of values. In adopting the language, dress, and lifestyle—elements of the Polish cultural canon—Polish Jews, including supporters of various Jewish nationalist options, could not have had an indifferent attitude toward it. The acculturation of young Polish Jews in the interwar period therefore could not have had only a pragmatic, purely linguistic character. It had a symbolic dimension too. The use of the Polish language by Jewish young people had a significant impact on their consciousness, mentality, and collective patterns of thinking. Although most Polish Jews considered themselves to be part of a separate nation—in fact, just about all participants in the YIVO competition did so—they lived in a country that, through universal education, the mass media, literature, art, popular entertainment, and so on, spread the culture of an ethnically defined nation. It also had a major impact on all young people, regardless of the fact that both Polish and Jewish young people saw the latter as functioning outside the boundaries of the former. Symbols associated with the Polish nation left a deep mark on the collective consciousness of Jewish young people. They not only served to describe and understand Poland and Poles surrounding young Jews but also significantly influenced Jewish national self-definition.

In the Second Republic, state institutions reproduced and upheld the Polish symbolic universe, at the same time exerting a strong influence on the consciousness of the minority, subjected—especially through elementary schools but also to a greater extent through the entire official and mass culture—to "symbolic violence."[121] This violence consisted in the fact that a truly multiethnic state was successfully promoting the vision that it was de facto the state for the Polish nation, and that other groups, even if they had the right to be nations, must submit to this vision. In elementary schools and in their own schools implementing the state curriculum, during classes on Polish language, history, and geography and on contemporary Poland, Jewish young people were taught a thousand years of history of the Polish nation, worship of nineteenth-century

Polish uprisings, and national legends and myths that they were supposed to love but that for many reasons they could not fully recognize as their own. At the level of their social and political consciousness, as well as of attitudes not fully considered, they submitted to the Polish national narrative through this symbolic violence. Therefore, the symbolic dimension of acculturation can be defined as a process of not fully conscious acquisition of elements of Polish culture. These elements functioned mainly at the level of practical consciousness, in spontaneous thinking and acting; at the same time, they did not find a place in the ideological programs of parties and movements with which Jewish young people sympathized. In the autobiographies of YIVO contestants, their presence was often revealed unconsciously.

PATRIOTISM AND THE POLISH HISTORICAL NARRATIVE IN PUBLIC AND JEWISH SCHOOLS

Gershon Pipe wrote in the introduction to his work, "I was wondering in which language to write my autobiography: in Yiddish, in Hebrew or simply in Polish? There are things that I think about in Yiddish, in short, they are issues relating to my everyday life, I think about Eretz Israel and matters related to Zionism in Hebrew. There are also a few things I think about in Polish—school, Polish history and general history, world geography, etc. I finally decided to write my autobiography in Yiddish because at least half of it would be about my daily life."[122]

Behind the choice of Yiddish was not only the everyday life taking place in this language but also the nationalist views of the author and the nature of the institution to which he was submitting his work. At the same time, however, Gershon Pipe raised the idea of the influence of Polish culture and its symbolic universe on Jewish patterns of thinking about public life, history, and politics. Of course, school played a leading role here. When he was studying in secondary school, he was particularly proud of his hard-won 4 and 5 in Polish and Polish history, as well as his involvement in the activities of student interest groups devoted to these subjects.[123] Similarly, coming from a much poorer traditional home, the future Bundist A. Remez, when he went to public school, most of all enjoyed his history, geography, and Polish classes. He was so good in these subjects that he was called on to respond during a visitation from the school board.[124] An autobiographer from Ostróg, a committed Zionist, wrote that her favorite subject in elementary school was Polish history. She recalled from it above all the public holidays, to which teachers attached enormous importance. At one of them, she was instructed to give a speech in honor of Marshal

Piłsudski, who ruled the country at that time—a task that she approached with great emotion and commitment.[125]

The educational aspirations of Esther, an Orthodox teacher at a Bais Yaakov school and a Bnos Aguda activist, were also shaped by Polish elementary school. In addition, studies at this school left Esther with an attachment to Polish national symbols and patriotic literature. Although she wrote her autobiography in Yiddish, she kept a personal diary in Polish: "I kept a diary in Polish. I was becoming more and more immersed in the Polish language . . . I idolized the Polish Romantic poets Mickiewicz and Słowacki. Polish history was also a subject I loved and learned easily. I was enthralled by everything connected to Polish history. I was consumed with the great martyrdom of Polish heroes in their struggle for Poland's independence. I venerated Marshal Józef Piłsudski."[126]

Testimonies to Polish patriotism can be found even in the autobiographies openly hostile to the Polish state. Growing up in Bereza Kartuska, one autobiographer attended a TsYShO school that was very critical of the political reality of the Second Republic. Previously, he had studied in a Talmud Torah. He had no contact with public education. In the 1930s, he was a committed Bund activist strongly condemning the oppressive actions of the state toward the lowest economic classes and ethnic minorities. Despite this, he remembered the following event from his time at the TsYShO school: "On the day when Polish Marshal Józef Piłsudski died, no classes were held. In all beit midrashes there were prayers for the Marshal's soul. Schools also organized events that lasted throughout the day. Individual students read their works. Others beautifully recited poems [in honor of Marshal Piłsudski]."[127]

Abraham Rotfarb, praising the Khinekh Yelodim nationalistically oriented utraquist school for giving him a grounding in Jewish culture and history, at the same time described school performances at which he recited aloud Polish poetry. When the author wrote about pride in the heroism of biblical figures whom he had encountered in Jewish school, he examined them largely from the perspective of the heritage of Polish Romanticism.[128]

During the interwar period, a very important element of young people's patriotic education was school trips to places connected to the country's history. This type of local history was especially important in the case of a young state. Hardly surprising are descriptions in the autobiographies of school trips from public elementary and secondary schools. However, visits to places important in terms of Polish national ideology were organized even by TsYShO schools, which were often accused by official circles of antistate activities. As one of the authors wrote, students graduating from his school organized a long-awaited trip to the capital. The Warsaw trip included a visit to TsYShO headquarters, a meeting with one of the most important activists for education in Yiddish, Shlomo Mendelsohn, and visits to Warsaw's palaces and parks that represented some of the most important symbolic places in Polish national history.[129]

Another author, a graduate of the Tarbut network secondary school in Stanisławów, also described his school trips:

> At the beginning of eighth grade, we were given a big surprise. Suddenly, a trip for almost two weeks through Silesia and Western Poland to Gdynia had been organized . . ., we sped off an express train to Cracow. It was a really wonderful trip. We visited a number of cities such as Cracow, Katowice and Sosnowiec in Silesia, where we visited mines and foundries. Then we visited Bydgoszcz, the whole Hel Peninsula, Gdynia, and Warsaw on the way back. In addition to the impressions experienced when visiting cities and monuments, seen for the first time, this trip had a lot of charm. . . . I was particularly impressed by the port of Gdynia and Warsaw."[130]

In addition to the most important symbolic places connected with Polish history, students at private Jewish schools also visited places of some importance in terms of the country's current propaganda policy and occupying a central place in the governing elite's nation-building narrative. They included the places mentioned by the student from the Tarbut school in Stanisławów, and they symbolized modernity and the industrial power of the young state. This belief was internalized by Jewish school students, just as it was by their classmates in elementary schools.

THE SYMBOLIC DIMENSION OF THE ACCULTURATION OF JEWISH YOUNG PEOPLE

Jewish young people were characterized by Polish patriotism. They knew the history of the Polish nation and its most important symbols. They were sympathetic toward the Poles' past struggles for independence; they celebrated Polish holidays, books, and paintings. Young people were patriots, regardless of the fact that their patriotism was put to the test not only by Polish right-wing political movements with their antisemitism but also very often by state institutions. This patriotism also distinguished the Jewish national elites, who wanted the new generation to prove their connections with the Polish state. Only their constant declarations could bring recognition by their Polish fellow citizens and above all bring de facto equality in the eyes of the law for the Jews. Patriotism brought with it the internalization of Polish national symbols and ways of thinking about history, what makes a nation, what are a national culture and literature, and attitudes such as heroism and sacrifice. These elements of collective consciousness naturally also applied to the sphere of politics. They partly defined the attitude of young people both to the Polish nation and state and to themselves. As we shall see in subsequent autobiographical quotes, they began to perceive themselves more and more through a specific image of the Polish nation. This, for those who declared themselves to be Jews and only Jews, became their most important point of reference. The Jewish nationalism of the generation described here saw itself in the mirror of Polish nationalism. At the same time, this did not in any way mean national assimilation. The Polish acculturation of Jewish young people did not go hand in hand with breaking with Jewish nationality, and it did not mean the disappearance of Jewish cultural and social distinctiveness. A new situation was developing in which the generation of Jews born and growing up in interwar Poland in new dimensions of social life was exposed to the influence of Polish national symbolic culture, so that its elements became part of its own social consciousness. These elements served to give value to the surrounding world and represented an important context for the internalization of one's own Jewish norms, for thinking and acting, including in the political sphere. On the one hand, young people were succumbing to acculturation processes in many areas of life, from the professional to the private, becoming part of Polish urban culture. On the other hand, they increasingly adopted a reluctant or hostile attitude toward the state and its patterns of social life. As we shall see, this set of attitudes was significantly influenced by antisemitism, which was widespread at the time. In addition, young people had a hitherto unprecedented scale of access to Jewish political organizations emphasizing national and cultural distinctiveness. Paradoxically, in the specific conditions of feelings of rejection and discrimination, this access could be accelerated by these very processes of symbolic acculturation.

Chaja had spent her whole life in a Jewish setting. Other national groups very rarely appear on the pages of her autobiography and the much larger attached diary. Chaja wrote her memoirs alternately in Yiddish and in Polish, but in the diary the dominant language was Polish. For many years she had been active in Zionist Gordonia. Her sadness and the hardship of her daily life were best expressed by the words of the Polish national poet Juliusz Słowacki, whom she quoted in her work.[131] The Ha-Shomer ha-Tsa'ir activist Gershon Pipe did the same, describing his romantic first love for the Polish national epic *Pan Tadeusz*.[132] "Żeń-ka," describing her difficult childhood, filled with poverty and humiliation, quoted Juliusz Słowacki just like Chaja.

A secondary school student from Kowel recalled her family garden as follows:

> Just before sundown, when the sun was going down somewhere there in the west, all of us used to go there. . . . I imagined that it was not Poland, not the Diaspora—but that dearly beloved (using the language of Kasprowicz [one of the most important Polish poets of the turn of the nineteenth and twentieth centuries]) Homeland, Palestine. At that time, I wanted to endure a thousand times worse poverty and work on my own Jewish soil. I thought then that I was going through "hakhshara" or that I was protecting this piece of the national garden from the enemy."[133]

A member of Tsukunft described how impressed she had been reading *Potop*—the famous Polish novel describing the Poles' struggle against the Swedish invasion in the mid-seventeenth century: "I have just finished *Potop*. Sienkiewicz awakens the courage of Poles. He calls for the struggle for an independent Poland . . . he gives you a weapon with which you can fight for the liberation of Poland."[134] Poland, with its recently regained independence, its outward signs of military strength and social solidarity (inflated by contemporary Polish state propaganda), was a key point of reference for many Zionists writing autobiographies, evaluating their own progress in efforts to revive the Jewish people. Mars, for example, wrote about his jealousy of members of the Polish paramilitary organization Strzelec, who, unlike him, a Zionist, in their songs could sing of love for their own homeland.[135] Acculturation provided young Jewish nationalists with an important new point of reference from which they looked at themselves. "Refleg" was a supporter of the right-wing Betar. He embellished the description of his own life philosophy and Zionist views with quotations from Adam Mickiewicz's "Ode to Youth" ("Oda do młodości").[136] Although Refleg, as a right-wing revisionist, believed deeply in the "pure spirit" and the original "national genius" of the Jews, he depicted their bright future in Palestine using categories taken directly from Polish culture. On the path of symbolic acculturation, Polish national history and its symbols became important elements of the self-image of the youngest Jews.

As the autobiography of Drori, who came from a traditional, deeply religious home where only Yiddish was spoken, shows, the symbolic dimension of acculturation was not limited to a knowledge of Polish history and its symbols. Through acculturation, the general cultural code was internalized, allowing young people to interact with non-Jews at completely new levels of social intercourse. The most interesting example of this is the description of a situation in which Drori, working for an insurance agent, went to the local notary public.

He found him and a colleague hotly discussing the question of the conversion of Jews. The two of them also unambiguously suggested the author change his religion. The boy, proudly rejecting the suggestion, got into a dispute with his adversaries about the nature of Judaism and, importantly, also the Christian religion. He refuted his opponents' arguments in a way that betrayed a good knowledge of the history of their religion. He recalled, inter alia, the situation of Palestine under the Romans, the persecution of Christians during the time of Nero, Charlemagne, the history of the Crusades, and medieval pogroms. In passing, he explained to his interlocutors the Jewish belief in the coming of the Messiah.[137] Undoubtedly, Drori's parents would not have been able to enter into this kind of dialogue with a Częstochowa notary public. It required an empathetic understanding of an adversary's culture.

An author from an Orthodox home, for whom Polish was a second language learned only in elementary school, chose some words by Mickiewicz as the epigraph to her autobiography.[138] In the fifth and sixth grades of elementary school, she began to attend Hebrew school in the afternoons. At the same time, she encountered antisemitism. The context in which Zionist beliefs first appear in her work is important for my analysis:

> In the fifth and sixth grades, I went to Hebrew school in the afternoon and learned Hebrew with great enthusiasm. I felt then that this language connected me with Palestine, to which we were being sent. It seemed to me that by using this language, we were resurrecting our whole great and dormant past. At school love for Poland was drummed into the children; they were taught that one should live and die for her. Something like a feeling of jealousy was awakening in me at that time. Why are we Jews not allowed to have our own country? . . . The thought of Palestine did not arise within me because of scientific books, dissertations or propaganda; oh no! It came about as a reaction to the love for Poland drummed into us in school.[139]

An author using the pseudonym "Zyg. Hor." wrote,

> [Polish] friends I grew up with in the same yard consider me a stranger because I am Jewish. I had nothing in common with Jewry outside of Zionism. I treated Hebrew as something amateurish, I thought only in Polish, I had come to love this nation, its language and its history. Even today, I delight in Sienkiewicz's *Trylogia* whose characters live and are one with the reader, and who—despite the events being in the distant past are, it seems, here with us. Jewish history, however, is distant events, something that smacks of legend, at least for me, brought up far from the atmosphere of Jewishness. I was partially assimilated and was converted by the organization.[140]

Zyg. Hor., despite his undoubted linguistic and symbolic acculturation, patriotism, and emotional attitude toward the most important symbols of Polish culture, felt alienated from it and from Polish society, just like almost all the contestants in the YIVO competition. He became a convinced Jewish nationalist, but at the same time his life path created a situation in which he looked at the world from the perspective of Polish symbols, language, and culture.

Polish culture in this and other autobiographies had the status of being the closest non-Jewish culture to these young people. At the same time, however, almost none of the autobiographers, even a declared "assimilated person" such as Zyg. Hor., considered it his or her own. Nobody wrote about "our struggle for independence" in the nineteenth century or in the years of World War I; no one wrote of "our" Mickiewicz, "our" Marshal Piłsudski; no one wrote "we" Poles. Thus, Polish culture played an ambiguous role among Jewish youth—it was very close and simultaneously foreign. To no less an extent than students in Jewish private, secular, or religious schools, this also applied to students in Polish elementary and secondary schools. The most important direct cause of this state of affairs was the experience of antisemitism, which was very strongly felt in the 1930s. However, the above passage, as well as many other quotations mentioned, suggests two other deeper and less obvious reasons for this alienation. The first reason was the cultural content—namely, the ambiguous vision of the (Polish) nation transmitted to Jewish children during classes at school and in Polish school textbooks. On the one hand, young people learned that they were full citizens of the Second Republic and were encouraged to participate fully in the life of the country, to take pride in its achievements, patriotism, and love of its history, and so on, but on the other hand, the Polish state, implicitly if not explicitly, turned out to be a state for the ethnically and religiously defined Polish nation. The Jews lay outside its borders. The second reason for the feeling of alienation lies, in my opinion, in the ambivalence of Jewish discourse. Young people received contradictory guidance from their political patrons. This contradiction was based on the previously mentioned difficulty in establishing the boundary between positive and desirable integration, Polish patriotism, and knowledge of the country's language and culture on the one hand and negative assimilation or even abandoning one's roots on the other. The process of acculturation, especially its symbolic dimension, often went unnoticed by the autobiographers. There was an unconscious convergence not only of cultural and social habits but also of the adoption of the dominant majority's patterns of thinking and political actions. There was an unusually dramatic process of internalization of the "Jewish problem" (as an objective, structural problem—impossible to solve within the existing social order but solvable only on the basis of radical solutions: mass emigration or social revolution) by the Jewish minority itself. Another aspect of this process was thinking about Jewish symbols, such as the national liberation struggle in Palestine or the Jewish soldier, according to the examples known from Polish history—that is, according to the models of the Polish national narrative, which was the basic point of reference of Jewish young people socialized in the Second Republic. This process took place not so much in the sphere of conscious, recognized cultural symbols, of choices concerning, for example, language, clothing, or patterns of social life (marital, professional, etc.), but in the sphere of social practice and patterns of group action, in which cultural symbols affect people in a way that they do not realize. The adjective *symbolic* emphasizes the fact that the process of acculturation, not recognized by the social actors affected by it, was a consequence of the domination and symbolic violence of the modern, nationally oriented Polish state.

The presence of Polish culture in the consciousness and everyday life of Polish Jews of the interwar period, especially young people, is best described by the term *Jewish Polishness*, discussed by Katrin Steffen.[141] It was shaped by participation in public life as well as in mass culture dominated by the Polish language and culture. Through this participation, the symbols of this culture were deeply internalized. At the same time, however, Jewish Polishness had quite its own character. It was not just a case of copying or assimilating the contents of the dominant culture but rather synthesizing these contents and elements of the Jewish national culture. In this way a genuine Polish Jewish culture was created and developed in the Second Republic. One of the participants in the YIVO competition, as we have seen, described herself as a halutz working in Palestine using lines from poems by Jan Kasprowicz. Another autobiographer, a revolutionary from the Bund, sought inspiration for her heroic attitude in Sienkiewicz's *Potop*. This kind of cultural fusion could be manifested both in Polish and in the Jewish languages. In the interwar period, the new Polish Jewish culture developed dynamically, despite the fact that it was not fully recognized by its spreaders, and many of its manifestations seemed to be the assimilation so widely condemned by the Jews of that time.

SIX

—∽∾—

SYMBOLIC EXCLUSION
AND ANTISEMITISM

SYMBOLIC EXCLUSION: THE AMBIVALENCE
OF POLISH CULTURE AND OF THE PUBLIC
EDUCATION SYSTEM'S INTEGRATION POLICY

An important element of the new state's strategy of political unification was the adoption of a specific direction of education for its youngest citizens. In the interwar period, there existed a clear tension between various forms of antisemitic rhetoric and action ("taking the Jewish out" of Polish culture, "strengthening the Polish middle class," discrimination in hiring for the civil service, and state monopolies) and state discourse and its efforts at modernization.[1] The need for modernization forced Sanacja, and up to 1926 even right-wing political groups, to take certain steps in favor of the political integration of minorities, including the Jews. The national government, through some of its actions, promoted not only narrowly understood acculturation of the ethnic minorities but also some forms of national (and, as we will see later, de facto ethnically Polish) patriotism. As part of state education aimed at building the loyalty of non-Polish ethnic groups, actions were taken that are commonly attributed to civic nationalism. At the same time, the homogenizing modernization project, which in the case of the Jews consisted in promoting Polish patriotism and knowledge of Polish culture at the expense of Jewish identity and culture, was carried out in parallel with activities aimed at excluding entire groups of the Jewish minority from important areas of social life. In the second half of the 1930s, the Polish government tried to facilitate the emigration of the Jewish element;[2] however, with the exception of extreme nationalist radicals, no one seemed to believe in the possibility of removing most of the Jews from

160

the country. The need for their integration into Poland appeared to be a necessity. Education played a key role in the state's policy of integration of ethnic minorities, including the Jewish minority.

The central value of education in the interwar period was patriotism.[3] The main goal of schooling was to produce citizens of a modern nation, which was just being formed after 123 years of partition. Throughout the interwar period, the public school system promoted Polish national culture as the only state culture, superior to the languages, literature, customs, and traditions of minorities. As Włodzimierz Mędrzecki writes, the state "was commonly defined as a nation-state where the Polish people were its only sovereign and master."[4] Instilling in minority students a belief in the exceptionalism and superiority of Polish culture over other cultures was an important element in national integration policy.[5] The public school system reproduced the social and ethnic hierarchy of the Second Republic. Therefore, its actions were a form of symbolic violence. For our purposes, the most important questions are, How were Polish and at the same time national culture taught? Was acculturation in the spheres of language, imagination, and Polish patriotism that spread among young Jewish people accompanied by real integration by building within them the conviction that they lived in a state that accepted them and that treated Jews and other minorities no differently from ethnic Poles?

Throughout the entire interwar period, Polish politicians failed to separate the concept of patriotism from the ethnically and religiously understood idea of the Polish nation. Although many Polish scholars point out that especially between 1926 and 1935 the ruling elites in Poland tried to build a civic educational ideology and build a Polish national community in which national minorities could find their own place,[6] there was a constant tension between their theoretical, ideological efforts and educational practice. In interwar Poland, regardless of whether we are talking about the years 1918–1926, when the country's democratic governments were dominated by the political right, or 1926–1935, when it was molded by the rather mild authoritarianism of Marshal Piłsudski, or 1935–1939, when after his death this authoritarianism deepened, national educational policy was not able to build among its minorities a sense of full equality and of belonging to a civic community. This was not possible in a situation where in the government's educational practice and the dominant discourse the Polish state and its institutions functioned as the property of the ethnically defined Polish nation, of which Jews and other national minorities simply were not part.

It is worth asking the question, What symbolic resources were used to achieve the goal of integrating ethnic minorities? The answer clearly explains why this integration failed. On the one hand, the authors of textbooks and school curricula were aware, of course, that more than one-third of children attending public schools did not belong to the Polish ethnic group (in schools in the east of the country, they constituted the majority of students). Therefore, from the very beginning the curriculum in elementary schools, focusing on "awakening love for the homeland," preaching "national spirit," and the nation's heroic past, did not use any clear definition of Polishness.[7] On the other hand, throughout the whole period of the Second Republic, the country's leaders did not create the concept of a civic community in which ethnic minorities could feel like equal, not inferior, members in relation to the state's only real host— the Polish people. Anna Landau-Czajka, analyzing the content of textbooks for teaching such subjects as Polish language, geography, civics, and religion in elementary school and in the lower grades of secondary school, has stated, "In the overwhelming majority of textbooks there was no mention of the existence of representatives of other national groups in Poland apart from Poles. This was especially true of books intended for the youngest children. In no primer or in the initial reading books for first and second grades in elementary schools can one find any mention of this issue, even tangentially."[8]

Textbooks for third grade covered this issue to a small extent, but then again in a very marginal way.[9] When the curriculum of a Sanacja school did include figures of individual Jews, Russians, or Germans (I mean the positive heroes of the school historical narrative)—as in the case of Berek Joselewicz, a traditional Jew who at the turn of the eighteenth and nineteenth centuries fought alongside the Polish elite against the Tsarism—they were mentioned only in the context of playing second fiddle to the Polish ethnic group, participating with it in its struggles, in its history.[10] In practice, the entire public school educational policy was based solely on Polish culture. Owing to the lack of other symbolic resources, the school was condemned to focus its efforts at integration exclusively on Polish national symbols.

The content of school reading materials made it difficult or even impossible for young Jewish people to imagine themselves as part of the Polish national community without completely giving up their own national-religious identity. Many Jewish elementary school students were probably no strangers to Leopold Infeld's school experience: "At the time I identified so much with the Polish nobility that I imagined that my forefathers, locked in heavy armor, fought with the Teutonic Knights. The smiles of the class reminded me that my ancestors probably studied the Talmud or lent money to the nobility. . . . That smile was a lesson for me that I was not to identify my family with the family of a Polish nobleman."[11]

We must remember that the vast majority of Jewish state elementary school students came from backgrounds far more rooted in Jewish tradition, language, and culture than the one in which Infeld grew up. For them, imagining themselves as descendants of the knights of Grünwald (the site of a great battle in 1410 between the Polish state and the German Teutonic Order) was even more difficult—all the more so because school textbooks usually emphasized the deep, inseparable connection between the heroes of Polish history and the Catholic faith.[12] Moreover, in textbooks for the higher grades, Jews were unequivocally portrayed negatively in religion classes. In a textbook published in 1939, they appeared as a nation of God-killers: "The Jewish people not only stubbornly demanded Christ's death, but also took responsibility on themselves and their children for Jesus's innocently-shed blood. Therefore, the Jewish people lost their homeland. The sons of this once chosen people of God have scattered throughout the world. The Jewish people have been burdened with the crime of the Savior's innocently-shed blood."[13]

It was also the case that during geography or civics classes Jews were presented as "a separate, hated, parasitic entity," as "cut off by their religion and fanatical superstitions" from the Polish nation.[14] This kind of message was consistent with the prevailing beliefs in the Second Republic about the economic role of Jews in the state. Milder authors of Sanacja textbooks on the subject sometimes postulated the emigration from the country of at least part of the population of the Jewish faith. In civics textbooks Jewish figures never appeared as friends from the same school bench.[15] One also seeks them in vain holding important civic roles as engineers, doctors, or politicians.

The situation was different in Polish classes, where the romantic and positivist literary tradition sometimes presented the Jew as a patriot and always proclaimed the necessity of enlightening the Jewish people. This enlightenment was equated with assimilation. Behind this kind of construct was the belief that Jews were an inferior class in terms of civilization. The only way for to them to change their status was to abandon their ethnic and religious identity in favor of Polish identity.[16] In school textbooks there was not even a hint of information about Jewish culture, religion, traditions, or languages. There was no question of recognizing the latter even as potentially equal to the only national language. Even positive messages did not create any basis for feeling oneself both Jewish and Polish, reconciling ethnic Jewish identity and the pride resulting from it with becoming part of the political, historical, and cultural community of Poland. Being a Jew in school meant being inferior, marginalized, someone whose existence in the country was not entirely legitimate. Only assimilation, understood as a complete obliteration of negative Jewish features, would allow this to change.

Meanwhile, most young Jewish people (and therefore most of this group) came from traditional homes and entered school with a strong sense of their own ethnic distinctiveness, a deeply internalized distrust, and often a blatant dislike of non-Jews. Educational content based on the principle of the Polish ethnic and Catholic national community did not have a positive impact on reducing strong traditional distances between Jews and Poles. Regardless of the negative, neutral, and even positive overtones of Jewish themes in school education, the Jew appeared as a stranger. Its content did not recognize the civic category of a Jewish Pole. Rather, it suggested that the student, and therefore the citizen, was simply a Pole. The public-school historical narrative represented only the Polish ethnic group, and no attention was paid to the different historical processes, features, traditions, and customs of other nations. The latter were mentioned only in relation to the history of Poland and the Poles, as playing supporting roles in their history and struggles, or as hostile to them. In Sanacja education, the Polish nation was still a coherent community of ethnic Poles, hierarchical, and subordinate to the elites and the "national interest" as defined by them.[17] There was a lack of an educational ideology and a broader national ideology so that minorities wishing to preserve their separate identities could be part of the nation and also participate in its political life. All this helps us understand why Jewish students, aware of their separate ethnicity and additionally influenced by Jewish national groups, had no chance to feel part of the Polish community. Contrary to integrationist goals, the Polish historical narrative alienated young Jews. The impact of this communal narrative lay in the impossibility of imagining its addressees or their ancestors as potential heroes of the historical story. This was not easy, if indeed possible, for those living by the traditional historical memory of the "people of the Book," a modern vision of a nation of the diaspora, of a nation fighting for a return to the Land of Israel. This educational experience created for young Jews the phenomenon of a simultaneous sense of inclusion in the form of symbolic and linguistic acculturation, and at the same time alienation. This symbolic exclusion, combined with manifestations of openly antisemitic attitudes on the part of classmates and teachers, was undoubtedly another very important generational experience for Jewish young people, significantly influencing the development of their radical political habitus. It is a paradox that the sense of exclusion was also reinforced by the public education system, which was after all supposed to integrate young Jews and diminish their political radicalism.

THE AMBIVALENCE OF THE JEWISH NATIONAL DISCOURSE

The self-awareness of the generation described here was not shaped only by the Polish discourse or the Polish state's educational policy. At the same time, it was subjected to pressure from Jewish political parties, youth movements, social organizations, and schools. The Jewish discourse, albeit in a different way, was also unable to cope with the definition of a Jew as a Polish citizen and at the same time a representative, no less than in the case of the Poles, of an ethnic, religious Jewish nation seen in exclusivist terms.

Education in autonomous Jewish schools was the focal point of all programs of national or religious revival. At the same time, the Zionists, the Bund socialists, the Folkists, and even the Orthodox Agudat Israel were all fully aware of the necessity of at least a partial integration of Jews into their surroundings. Likewise for the Zionists, who declared the goal of preparing the Jewish people for emigration, it was clear that most of them would not emigrate in the foreseeable future. The issue of professional integration remained indisputable. Jews were to be given opportunities for equal access to professions related to industry or intellectual professions, to go beyond trade and crafts, which had hitherto been their main sources of income. Economic and social integration was impossible without knowledge of the basics of the language and Polish culture. The burning problem for all Jewish parties was therefore the question of the degree of concessions to the necessary Polish acculturation and the meaning of the entire symbolic sphere, the internalization of which required learning the language. At what point did adoration of Sienkiewicz's prose or veneration of Romantic poets become a dangerous deviation toward assimilation? Is it possible to establish the desired proportions between knowledge of Polish culture and sensitivity to Polish values, symbols, and historical narratives on the one hand and the system of Jewish values on the other? Jewish politicians and social activists could not find a clear answer to these questions.

This was influenced by the fact that the models of the new national Jewish culture in their Zionist and Yiddishist versions were formed before 1914, in the completely different reality of the Habsburg Empire and Tsarist Russia. Polish Jews—or, more precisely, supporters of national and Orthodox parties— lived in constant fear of assimilation. They defined desired Jewish identity in terms of integral nationalism, with its emphasis on cultural monism. The ideology of the Zionist groups recognized Hebrew as the only national language. For Folkists, Po'alei-Tsiyon-Left, or the Bund, the only national language was Yiddish. Their supporters were to speak only in the national language on a daily basis and to associate mainly with the products of national culture, with "their" theater, art, or literature. Of course, knowledge of other languages, including the state language, was useful according to these ideologies, provided that it did not violate the sphere of identity. This kind of understanding of the concept of national culture continued to be in increasing contradiction to the reality of a modern twentieth-century state. Although the Jewish cultural polysystem based on three languages was a reality in the Second Republic, it did not actually have any defenders. The most important Jewish political currents promoted national identities based on the dominance of one language (Yiddish or Hebrew) as the only one expressing the true spirit of the nation. This was in contradiction to the reality in which children and young Jews participating in the mass culture of the young state had at least a dual cultural identity and thought and felt in at least two languages, including one non-Jewish one. The nationalism of the diaspora, Zionism, or Orthodoxy proclaimed demands for full equality and the integration of the Jews but at the same time did not want to recognize that learning the Polish language and associating with it in the pluralistic world of mass and high culture had to bring with it the internalization of non-Jewish symbols, norms, and values. From their greatest authorities—politicians of national and Orthodox parties—young people therefore received contradictory signals just like the ones they experienced in public schools.

In the Second Republic, it was impossible to fight legally and publicly for one's rights without at the same time declaring ardent Polish patriotism. All Jewish politicians declared their commitment to the cause of Polish independence. Jewish elites tried to include in the ethnically Polish story of the Polish people's struggle for independence threads emphasizing Jewish involvement in it.[18] Despite very harsh criticism of the situation of Jews in contemporary Poland, Jewish politicians believed in and spread many of the basic symbols and narrative outlines of Polish national history. In the introduction to one of the most important interwar publications intended to show the enormous positive contribution of Jews to Polish history and the present, the Kraków Zionist leader Yehoshua (Osias) Thon wrote,

> Poland's recovery of its independence, almost within its extensive historical borders, was a powerful and joyful experience for the Jews of the Polish state . . .; there was probably no Jew with even a minimal knowledge of history, who was not convinced that Poland would immediately join the ranks of free democratic states. Had Poland ever been different? When the whole of Europe and its proud West were up to their necks in despotism, Poland had been governed by a parliamentary system, and freedom was for a Pole a manifestation of life as natural and necessary as air for a bird or water for a fish.[19]

The myth of premodern Poland as open and tolerant perpetuated the patriotism of Polish Jews. This faith was also not alien to Orthodox environments.[20] Orthodox circles too had to face the contradictions resulting on the one hand from a desire to build a culturally and socially separated community, an ethnoreligious community *am segulah*—"the chosen people," "a nation that lives alone"—and on the other from the need to integrate with a twentieth-century nation-state. The latter required not only a continuous public declaration of Polish patriotism but also, through its internalization, a certain degree of submission to the Polish national historical narrative. Orthodox elites also had to face the problem of drawing a line beyond which acculturation threatened the Orthodox model of Jewishness.

This dilemma for secular and religious elites had consequences for many dimensions of social life. Possibly its greatest impact was in the sphere of education of the youngest generation. In the 1920s, the most important Jewish political leaders, led by Itzhak Grünbaum and Jakub Wygodzki, denounced public elementary schools as "factories of illiteracy and assimilation."[21] This "illiteracy" obviously referred to Jewish languages and Jewish culture. Grünbaum informed the non-Jewish public that "assimilation has long ceased being an ideal, and if it still is a process, the demands of Jewry are heading in the direction of weakening or completely destroying this process, removing the political, economic and cultural conditions that cause or reinforce it."[22] The Zionist leader was referring to much more extensive processes than consciously renouncing national Jewish identity. The removal of all "political," "economic," and "cultural" factors of assimilation was akin to a demand for maximum national autonomy in the form of its own school system teaching in the national language, with secularized and democratized Jewish local communities having very extensive authority, their own social institutions, and their own culture. Thus, Grünbaum's demands for the economic and symbolic integration of the Jews, their real equality, clashed with a program of autonomy based on social and cultural separation, because only it could eliminate the threats of assimilation and acculturation coming from all sides. This contradiction can also be seen in Grünbaum's other actions. During his time as secretary of the Tarbut network, he spoke of the nationalizing influence of the public school while fighting all manifestations of assimilation. On the other hand, he protested discrimination against Jews in access to public high schools and universities.[23] This internal contradictory discourse appeared beyond the political space. Words encouraging integration but at the same time threatening complete polonization and assimilation were spoken not only by leading politicians. They can also be found in many documents of the Jewish school networks, and they were addressed to parents deciding on the choice of school for their children. Many participants in the YIVO competition rejected anything that could threaten assimilation.

The signs of ambivalence toward the status of Polish culture in the life of the Jewish community also marked the battle of private Jewish school networks with the popularity of public education. As part of it, national-Jewish schools presented themselves as a remedy for the young Jews' progressive loss of national identity. The Lviv Zionist newspaper *Hinukheynu*, which focused on educational issues, appealed to parents in a characteristic way: "The day will come when a curse descends upon those unhappy children, who through their fathers' fault have abandoned their God, and having found no refuge under other protective wings, wander aimlessly and joylessly through life. And then a spark will awaken in them at the bottom of their souls and will overturn all their heretical parents' plans."[24] Tarbut, trying in another publication to convince parents from more acculturated and financially better-off backgrounds, frightened them with loss of national identity and antisemitism.[25] The negative impact of the Polish school was based on the acculturation processes taking place within it. These publications did not distinguish between the positive and negative sides of the influence of public school but reduced it to antisemitism and the loss of national identity, making no distinction between integrative acculturation and assimilation in the form of erasing Jewish identity.

The contradictions associated with teaching the Polish language and promoting partial Polish acculturation and patriotism also could not be solved by Aguda education, especially for girls. In line with the Orthodox principle of practical education for girls, teaching them the national language had played a much greater role than in the education of boys starting in the nineteenth century. On the one hand, in Bais Yaakov schools, children were taught Polish, and some other subjects were taught in it. On the other hand, there was a great fear that linguistic polonization would be a simple way to abandon the Orthodox way of life, and it was fiercely opposed. Speaking Yiddish daily was promoted, the meaning of which, as in secular school networks, was defined in modern nationalist terms as "an expression of the Jewish soul, of Jewish aspirations and desires, of Jewish sorrow and joy."[26] Bais Yaakov guidelines for female teachers in 1931 recommended that they ensure that children avoid adopting non-Jewish customs associated with celebrating days such as New Year's Day or April Fool's Day.[27] Speaking Polish during recess or free time or going to Polish films or Polish theaters, among other things, were considered to be signs of assimilation. Every Bais Yaakov school was meant to have a sign saying, "Speak only Yiddish."[28]

Zalmen Reyzen, a leading Yiddish philologist and one of the leaders of YIVO, called the Polish public school a "foreign school," "not in the interest of the Jewish child" and "not corresponding to the needs of its soul." In this institution there was nothing Jewish; there was no Jewish language, games, or songs. The child could only "suffer and assimilate" there. Very significant is Reyzen's generalizing opinion expressed in the same place: "In this way the Jewish people in France, Germany, England and Italy were destroyed." In this way, "entire segments of it in Poland, Russia and America" were now being destroyed. "Russification, Germanization, Polonization, Americanization—all are brutal means used by the ruling nations." Without national Jewish schooling, in complete control of its curriculum, teaching the history and culture of the Jews in Yiddish, a sovereign national life was impossible.[29] Reyzen's work *Der kamf far der yidisher shul iz der kampf far undzere rekht* (The struggle for Jewish schooling is a struggle for our rights) was published by Vilna TseBeKa in 1933 and was addressed to the broad Jewish masses. It perfectly illustrates its author's misunderstanding of the reality of a modern twentieth-century country, the need for it to influence the educational content of all schools operating on its territory. A modern country had to work for a unified national culture, for the promotion of a single state language and a cultural code integrating its various citizens. The fact that Reyzen did not mean the exclusivist character of Polish national culture described above but was objecting to polonization and Polish acculturation in general is evidenced by his diatribe also directed against "Germanization" and "Americanization." The Jewish philologist seemed to advocate a far-reaching national and cultural separation of the Jews, for only this could counteract broadly defined assimilation. In this statement one can clearly see the definition of Jewish identity in the spirit of integral nationalism. All "foreign" influences and emotional attitudes toward "foreign" books, films, plays, and historical symbols were understood to be negative manifestations of a gradual loss of identity. Meanwhile, in a modern country, in the era of mass culture and universal education, the "Polonization," "Germanization," and "Americanization" condemned by Reyzen were inevitable phenomena. It is also significant that the YIVO activist did not explain how it was possible to combine his far-reaching national and autonomous demands with those that included granting Jews unlimited access to universities and employment in government offices, hospitals, schools, and public and private enterprises.

Proof of how nationalist circles defined negative assimilation is their attitude to utraquist education, which was supposed to teach Jewish children in Polish and one or two Jewish languages. A 1934 internal information document from Tarbut headquarters deplored "the actions of the school authorities, clearly aimed at destroying the Hebrew character of our establishments by introducing utraquism, or closing our schools by not granting accreditation for various reasons." Ministerial efforts to "utraquize" them, which simply meant an increase in the number of subjects taught in Polish, were considered to be a greater threat than the closure of a few Tarbut schools.[30] In response to the "repression of TsYShO schools," which was state pressure to introduce more subjects taught in Polish, the authorities of this network in 1925 issued a "Protest," in which they wrote, "Our school, teaching in our native language, is a legitimate demand on the part of Jewish society, which refuses to modify it."[31] The head of the TsYShO, Chaim Shloyme Kazhdan, considered the order of the district school board in Łuck to teach Polish in Jewish folk schools from the first grade to be an example of state repression.[32] Circles of nationalistically oriented educators attacked utraquist initiatives, even those originating from their own political circles. In December 1927, the Third National Conference of the Tarbut Network recognized utraquist Hebrew-Polish and Hebrew-Yiddish schools as the idea of "inconsistent Zionists" and called on all "true" Zionists not to participate in this initiative. The schools of the Association of Polish-Hebrew Utraquist Schools, headed by the avowed and distinguished Zionist Rabbi Dr. Braude, were also attacked by the leading Hebrew pedagogical magazine *Ofakim*.[33]

A vigorous debate between Yehoshua Thon, one of the founders of the Hebrew Tarbut school network and its first chairman, and at the same time one of the leaders of Polish Zionists, and Nathan Bistricki, an activist of the Jewish National Fund and the world's leading ideologist of Zionist education, by now living in Palestine, exemplified the ambivalence of the position of Jewish nationalist circles, unable to indicate how to be a nationalist Jew and at the same time a patriotic citizen of the Second Republic freely moving in Polish culture. During it Bistricki attacked the teaching model of the Tarbut schools and de facto stated the impossibility of Jewish national existence in the diaspora. According to Bistricki, regardless of the quality of Hebrew education in these schools and their Zionist patriotism, the parallel internalization of Polish culture by young Jews was to mean their assimilation—that is, the objective loss of their identity. His concept of the nation as a community based on "one language and one national soul" was also shared by the Polish Zionists who remained with him in the dispute.[34] Their ambivalent attitude toward Jewish identity discourse is perfectly illustrated by the words of Arie Tartakower, when he was an associate professor at the Institute of Judaic Studies in Warsaw and, more importantly, a leading collaborator of the government's Institute of Minority Affairs, an institution working for the civic integration of national minorities. In his *Outline of the Sociology of Jewry*, published in 1938 in Polish, Tartakower wrote,

> The Hebrew language imbued with the brilliant flair of ancient Jewry has always been and has become in recent years even more a fount of thought and great creative culture. How disturbing in comparison is the infertility of

Jewish spiritual life growing on foreign linguistic soil! . . . The Jewish general public, who speaks a foreign language is usually stuck in a swamp of banality, which has little to do with spirit and creativity. The famous Jewish polyglotism, this ability to use many languages, in only a few cases testifies to a flight of the spirit and the ability to delve into the cultures concerned; all too often a shallow Levantinism hides behind it, imbued with the opportunism of life and far from the spirit of the languages spoken by an individual. The barren type of a Jewish full and half-intellectual is the true product of this linguistic assimilation, like a cage weighing down Jewish life.[35]

The excerpt quoted above can be analyzed on many levels. What is striking, for example, is a certain symmetry with many antisemitic critics of the day, accusing the Jews of shallowness and the inability to be fully acculturated or to understand the cultures of the people around them. It is all the more significant because these words came from the pen of a very deeply polonized author, whose first language was Polish. Tartakower's piece is an important sign of the times. In beautiful, expressive Polish, the author warned the Jewish masses and young people against polonization, or thinking and feeling in more than one national language, which he considered "shallow Levantinism," a feature of the diaspora testifying to the sterility of its Jewish culture. This piece perfectly illustrates the contradictory pressure that the national identity discourse exerted on young people. Probably the most important effect was a sense of alienation. Most often it was directly revealed by the young people writing about antisemitism. However, the examples of symbolic acculturation already mentioned show that it was not only about that. One of the few authors who directly expressed what in other autobiographies one had to read between the lines was Abraham Rotfarb. The following quotation reflects all the problems raised in this work: the forcible acculturation of young people growing up in a traditional environment and speaking Yiddish on a daily basis; the construction of the category of a nation talking about a single national "soul" or "psyche," suggesting that one cannot be authentic while being stuck in two separate national cultures; and a vague category of assimilation, dictating condemnation of almost everything that linguistic and symbolic acculturation brought with it. As the author's life trajectory attests, the intersection of all these interactions was an important factor in young people's political radicalization. Rotfarb, fleeing from the evil world of tradition, sought a new home in the Communist Union of Polish Youth (KZMP; often abbreviated as KZM), eventually finding it in the Zionist movement and dreams of Palestine:

I believe that a Jew, for example, is different from a Pole, not only superficially, but also internally. I am a Jew! This I feel today. Once I believed deeply in this.

Then, I called myself a citizen of the world and did not believe at all in national-ity, more recently, I "was" a Pole. But today I know that I am a Jew and that I am far from calling myself a Pole. I've become convinced, by being somewhat assimilated—I write and read Polish, I know Polish history, and so on—that I characterize myself as a true, twentieth-century Jew of the diaspora. Forgive me for writing in Polish instead of Yiddish—this is not my fault. Everywhere I am surrounded by Poland, and I have fallen under its influence. However, I want to feel closer to my Jewishness, so that Polishness will eventually be something with which I am familiar but is not a part of my psyche.[36]

Despite all their patriotism and undoubted knowledge and deep sense of Polish culture, Jewish nationalist activists and modern Orthodox elites lived in fear of its assimilative influence. This ambivalent attitude caused them to pro-mote a model of participation in the life of the country, including the language, which young people were supposed to know for utilitarian purposes, but the symbols of which were not to affect their daily lives, thinking, tastes, or political imagination. Young Jews' intimate spheres of identity were to be powered only by their own national culture. This model was pure utopia. It did not contain the essential guidelines to follow in order to combine both worlds: the Polish and the Jewish. The Polish public school carried a no less ambiguous message. The meta-ideology of the Second Republic in the form of ethnic nationalism did not match the reality of a twentieth-century, multinational state. The situ-ation described here led to a symbolic contradiction between Polish and Jew-ish nationalist discourses, between antisemitic prejudices and the need for integration, and finally between Jewish national-religious solidarity and Polish patriotism. Both traditional Judaism and Jewish and Polish nationalisms were based on a strong ethnic historical narrative. Both nationalisms referred to pre-modern communities, symbols, and traditions and proclaimed a quasi-organic connection with the history of their ancestors, thus excluding the possibility of imagining ethnic others within their framework. In the modern Polish state, Jews were supposed to imagine themselves in these two generally mutually exclusive narratives: Polish and Jewish. As a result of acculturation processes, "Poland" became both a positive and negative, a conscious and unconscious point of reference for young Jewish people. Jewish politicians and social in-stitutions, under pressure from the state but also voluntarily, cocreated these processes, at the same time condemning them as negative assimilation. This contradiction reinforced the sense of insecurity of the inevitably polonizing young people; it became an element of their radical habitus. The ambivalence of Polish and Jewish culture of the interwar period was therefore a factor of political radicalization.

ANTISEMITISM AT SCHOOL AND YOUNG
PEOPLE'S POLITICAL CONSCIOUSNESS

Before we move on to an analysis of the school as a new space for the formation of both Polish-Jewish relations and the attitude of Jewish young people
toward the Polish state, it is worth considering with what baggage of beliefs,
associations, and stereotypes Jewish young people encountered their Polish
peers when entering elementary school at the age of seven or eight. From the
autobiographies above all an image emerges of a very large ethnocultural distance, with which most of the young people growing up in traditional homes
approached their Christian peers. Abraham Rotfarb, at the time of writing
his autobiography a Zionism sympathizer already liberated from the world of
tradition, previously an activist of the communist Pioneer, recalled as follows
the years of his childhood and the distance that separated him from his non-
Jewish peers and the entire non-Jewish world: "I had always lived in a Jewish
neighborhood; I mostly saw Jews and rarely saw a gentile on the street. Therefore, I thought there were more Jews than non-Jews. Since the gentiles were
a janitor, a maid, a gardener, or had other similar, demeaning jobs, I thought
them to be beneath me. What could they know? The gentile knows nothing;
he doesn't think, he just beats the Jews. And while I thought Christian boys
were wanton savages, I was terribly afraid of them. I divided the world into
Jews and gentiles."[37]

Mendl Man, describing his childhood as a small shtetl troublemaker, re-
called quite brutal games and conflicts taking place in his native Sochocin.
The most common of these were stone-throwing fights between Jewish and
Christian children. The former fought among themselves only when there were
no children of the goyim, who were always the enemies.[38] "M. Sheynberg"
wrote that one of the reasons for his parents' move from a village near Kielce to
Łódź was the desire "that the children should not grow up among peasants."[39]
Growing up in Sanok, Gershon Pipe recalled the unambiguous distance that
separated Jewish and Christian students even in the public secondary school.
How much this distance was rooted in his environment was indicated by the
sharp social ostracism of those Jewish children who spoke Polish, did not wear
headgear, "ate ham," or went to school on the Shabbat.[40]

Interethnic divisions stood in the way of building relationships with Christian friends, even for young Jews coming from polonized and acculturated
homes. A Lviv high school student described a holiday with a family in the countryside. This acculturated author, professing communist views, felt a great ethnic and cultural distance from Ukrainian young people despite her friendship

with them. She felt this distance both as an educated Polish woman and as a Jew, as well as a resident of the city.[41] Such distances played a significant role in and ultimately contributed to the rupture of the intimate relationships between Jewish and Christian young people, rarely described in the autobiographies.[42] These autobiographies say a great deal about the social boundaries of acculturation of Jewish young people in interwar Poland. Acculturated young people grew up not so much in the Polish world as in a specific middle-class Polish Jewish subculture, in which the distance from non-Jews did not completely disappear, and the factor of status played an additional role. The child of a polonized Jewish intellectual or merchant could treat the child of a Christian worker, peasant, or minor merchant often not only with reserve but also with superiority.[43] That is why an acculturated student of the Hebrew secondary school in Kowel treated her transfer to the seventh grade of the public elementary school as social demotion.[44] Ludwik Stöckel, who came from a Galician family of landowners, wrote that from the first grades of elementary school, his closest playmates were Jews. Even in the public secondary school, Jews and Catholics kept a clear distance from each other:

> Although we got along fine with the Catholics, we didn't involve them in our "social life." . . . I had a peculiar attitude toward my Catholic classmates. As a rule, I conversed with them, helped them out sometimes just as anyone else would, played soccer with them, etc. At the same time, however, I tried to keep them at arm's length, and in doing so, I wasn't always on my best behavior. After all, I made a certain distinction between them and us Jews. If, for example, one of "ours" hurt my feelings or insulted me, I always tried to "have it out" and resolve the matter, and then things would be fine. Yet I remember that when one of the Catholics started to get under my skin and eventually called me a "dirty Jew," I punched him in the face. Though he didn't repay me in kind, we didn't speak to each other for a long time. Eventually he did apologize to me and admitted that I had been in the right. Having been successful on that occasion, I became aggressive towards some classmates that I disliked, and sometimes I was, perhaps, even responsible for provoking them.[45]

Equally polonized "Kitka," attending elementary school in Drohobycz, wrote, "We organized the most elaborate games and entertainment. There were frequent battles. Jews on one side, the rest on the other."[46] Distance, and sometimes acculturated people's belief in their own ethnic superiority, further hastened their adoption of nationalist views. This is perfectly shown by Margalit's autobiography. For her and those who thought like her, traditional barriers of consciousness played a smaller role, and national Zionist views played a much greater one. The girl wrote about her Christian girl friends from the state teachers' college with a clear sense of superiority.[47] The nationalism of acculturated authors made them behave particularly badly toward polonized individuals like themselves who, however, did not emphasize their national distinctiveness and who entered into too close contact with Christians. This may also have been influenced by a conscious or unconscious sense of discomfort due to the level of their own acculturation. The student in the Hebrew secondary school in Kowel quoted above described the brutal pressure that she and her peers put on an unpopular classmate whose greatest offense was that she "went out" with Christian boys. The author stated that at that time she "hated non-Jewish boys."[48]

These are the words of a young person writing her autobiography in beautiful Polish, using the language that she undoubtedly spoke at home. This excerpt is proof that acculturated Jewish circles were also not free of nationalist-motivated resentment and even hatred. To some extent, this was certainly the result of the antisemitic rejection of the day, so strongly felt by them, along with the resentment of those who were culturally closest to Poles. As the author continued, "I cannot forget how in my childhood I witnessed fights, knife fights between antisemitic militias and Jewish lads. I remember when I witnessed how an enraged 'narnik' (they were the organizers of these militias) beat our neighbor's boy, wounded him, and slaughtered the calf led by the boy only because it was Jewish. I remember smashing a vase over this thug's head drawing blood."[49]

The following account by Ajzyk Rozen shows that in his experience the true antisemitism of his classmates was combined with the prejudice against Catholics held by Jewish students, with which they came to school rather than acquiring it there. The author undoubtedly internalized early on the traditional hatred of goyim. Also influencing what he wrote was the fact that before going to elementary school he had studied at a Tarbut school, which had largely shaped his views on national issues. The boy stopped his studies at the Zionist school when it was closed for financial reasons:

> I took no pleasure in looking at my future classmates with whom I was
> to spend several years at school, who were 90% Catholic with a clearly
> antisemitic attitude, and the rest were Jews. After the first days they started
> mocking me and throwing ugly epithets my way, this was the prologue to my
> future life in this school. I slowly began to get used to this life. This does not
> mean that we Jews were all supporters of passive resistance, oh no! Although
> Catholics were in the overwhelming majority, when they messed with us,
> we responded with logical arguments showing up their idiotic antisemitic

hatred, which very rarely worked, but we also often reacted with our fists. There was never any solidarity with them. On the other hand, us Jews, when one of us was in trouble with a Catholic, we always came to each other's aid.[50]

BETWEEN LOVE AND HATE: ANTISEMITISM, PATRIOTISM, AND A SENSE OF RELATIVE DEPRIVATION

Elementary schooling was an opportunity to weaken interethnic stereotypes. Certainly, at least officials of the Ministry of Education saw such a role for it in the process of integrating the Jewish community. However, in addition to the obstacles mentioned above—the ethnic vision of the Polish nation, the lack of any civic ideal—Jewish students faced widespread antisemitism in schools and universities. In shaping the sense of alienation of Jewish young people from the Polish state and nation, it played probably the most important role.

As noted above, the influence of the Polish school cannot be reduced to the experience of antisemitism alone. School created an opportunity for a secular education and for getting to know and love Polish culture; it promoted patriotism and an attachment to the idea of the Polish state. However, the simultaneous rejection experienced by the Jews studying there meant that these factors could paradoxically have a radicalizing effect on them. In the Jewish young people's autobiographies, school and university antisemitism was the principal leitmotif. It appeared more often and was described more extensively and accurately than were the positive aspects of the educational experience. It was mentioned by almost all authors attending elementary schools or Polish secondary schools. What is very important is that this issue appeared regardless of the year in which the autobiography was written—it was noticed by participants in the 1932, 1934, and 1939 competitions.[51]

Antisemitism was most painfully felt by acculturated young people, who most deeply identified with Polishness and the Polish nation. It undermined their identity, the way they were raised, and the values imparted to them by their parents. This fact also explains why so often acculturated parents chose to send their children to private Jewish schools, including those with a Hebrew Zionist profile.[52] For people from this group, antisemitism played the greatest role. To be able to define them, let us take a closer look at the autobiography of Ludwik Stöckel, who described his experiences from studying at a public secondary school as follows:

We also got a new teacher for Polish, a dignified and even-tempered man. As for his views, we had the feeling that he was an Endek, although he never disclosed anything about himself to us.[53] By now our Catholic classmates had all but openly adopted the ideology of the right-wing hoodlums who were on the loose in Lviv at the time.[54] However, they treated us with the same civility that we showed them. Then, there was an explosion during one of our discussions of a paper.... During the discussion, one of the "greens," as we called the Endeks, openly stated that the only way to deal with us was to use a club.... After that, personal relations with our Polish classmates grew much cooler and even more formal. There were only a few first-rate fellows—and they were "free-thinkers" or socialists, after all—with whom we continued to be on good terms.[55]

In Stöckel's story, two issues occupy a central place. One is the almost completely Polish character of the cultural reality surrounding the author.[56] The second issue is antisemitism, felt by the author especially strongly due to deep acculturation, education, high social status, aspirations, and associated high self-esteem. Despite his nationalist-Jewish views, Stöckel was also a Polish patriot. Despite his Zionist belief in the "impossibility of assimilation," he did not give up on Poland as a country of "Catholics," "Russian Orthodox," and "Jews." However, the attitudes of both Catholic students and teachers unequivocally excluded the realization of these dreams.[57] Another example of how much acculturation strengthened young people's feeling of antisemitic rejection is an anonymous (not even pseudonymous) autobiography numbered 3740. The author's entire education was spent in Polish public schools. This girl with high social and intellectual ambitions was very sensitive not only to open or drastic forms of antisemitism but also to any messages betraying or even only seeming to betray condescending behavior toward her as a Jew.[58] Such was also the experience of Bronka, whose autobiography won an award in the second YIVO competition. She represented an environment that did not attach much importance to its Jewishness. She came from the highest social class and lived in Warsaw, surrounded by books and raised by a nurse and a governess. It was only during her secondary school education that Bronka paid more attention to the fact that she was Jewish. After one of her first classes, she was insulted because of her origins, got into a fight, and was beaten up.[59] As with many other acculturated writers, her self-awareness of her Jewishness was reinforced by antisemitic rejections. It was the same with "G.S.": "I myself don't exactly know how it happened that, despite my upbringing, such a strong feeling of Jewishness awoke within me, but the strongest influence was the antisemitism that flourished in schools at that time. My sister and brother also became ardent Zionists at the time, and this had an influence on our parents. To the extent that they could, they began to contribute to Jewish causes, shop in Jewish stores, and socialize in Jewish circles. Today, a portrait of Herzl and a map of Palestine hang over Father's desk."[60]

At the beginning of the establishment of the Second Republic, Jews, as a famously urban population, frequently inhabited the higher bourgeoisie and the urban intelligentsia and constituted over a quarter of all college students.[61] This group was most often recruited from the richest sectors, the best educated (secularly), and the most polonized, with the deepest roots in Polish culture. But by the beginning of the 1920s, it experienced discriminatory practices aimed at limiting or even fully "taking the Jewishness out of" Polish universities. Demands for a numerus clausus—that is, limiting the number of places in universities for Jewish students—were submitted by the nationalist movement as early as 1919. In fact, every year riots broke out in universities about this, and they only intensified after 1931. There were numerous cases of Jewish students being beaten up; some even were killed. At the end of the interwar period, many universities introduced formal "ghetto benches."[62] As Roman Wapiński emphasizes, an important distinguishing feature of Polish young people of the last decade of the Second Republic was the much higher incidence among them of the most severe forms of "obsessive antisemitism," the intensity of which in 1930s Poland was unprecedented.[63] Antisemitic excesses were widely reported in the press; numerous resolutions, strikes, and rallies organized by Jewish institutions protested against them. State agencies drew attention to their intensification in the mid-1930s—the beating up of Jews at fairs, at colleges, or simply on the street.[64] All these events, combined with the economic crisis and the discrimination against Jews practiced by state institutions, resulted in a steady decline in the number of Jewish students. From 24.3 percent of all university students in the early 1920s, this number had fallen to 18.5 percent by 1930/31, to 13.2 percent in 1935/36, and in the last year, 1938/39, to just 8.2 percent. In the last academic year, it was already lower than the percentage of Jews not only among the urban population or intelligentsia but among the entire general population.[65]

Those few participants in the YIVO competition who managed to enter university belonged to both the Jewish and Polish elite. They were the group of young people best integrated into Polish society not only in the social sense but also in the cultural sense. Regardless of their political views—whether they were supporters of Jewish nationalism or not—almost all of them spoke literary Polish on a daily basis and graduated from Polish schools, most of them spoke this language at home, and in practice they felt and thought no differently from their Polish colleagues. Thus, they must have felt antisemitism the most. Their autobiographies contain the greatest number of expressions of pain, disappointment, and powerful resentment toward those who were rejecting the accession of Jews to Polishness and their attachment to the country. This resentment was felt all the more strongly the more culturally close these Jews were to ethnic Poles. Paradoxically, therefore, Polish universities, probably the most important institutions representing Polish high culture and what it had to offer, instead of being spaces for integration were spaces of exclusion for young Jews.[66] Gershon Pipe belonged to a small group of authors who, despite growing up in a traditional, poor Jewish environment, managed to obtain a high school diploma. He wrote that when he was in the last year of secondary school, he knew that no matter how well he earned his high school diploma, he still had no chance of getting to college because of antisemitism. He meant both the difficulty of getting into college and harassment from other students and lecturers.[67] Although he did not even try, his belief in the impossibility of studying at university was confirmed by what he read in the newspapers and what the entire Jewish population lived with in the 1930s. Ludwik Stöckel, one of several Jewish college students among the participants in the YIVO competition, recalled his law studies in Lviv and the anti-Jewish excesses unleashed at the university there:

> The city looked as if it was under siege: there were hordes of police wearing helmets on patrol, broken windows, subdued conversations. People slunk past each other; it seemed that no one dared look his neighbor in the eye.... I was walking with some classmates.... A moment later I saw eight people coming toward us (I was walking with Celek). We were calm since they didn't have any sticks. Suddenly, right in front of our noses, one of the fellows in front pulled out a club from under his coat. Without waiting, I gave him a shove in the stomach and elbowed the other aside, dragging Celek after me. We escaped the attack, but it seems that the hooligan wasn't after us, because I could hear the sound of blows, and I saw him start to beat up an old man. The guardian of order and public safety [a policeman standing by] appeared to be deaf and blind to this.[68]

As I have mentioned, it was at this time that Stöckel's political views fully crystallized. For the first time abandoning his studies, he returned to his native Tłuste and strengthened his ties to friends from the Zionist-socialist youth group Gordonia.[69] After returning to Lviv, he joined Po'alei-Tsiyon-Right and became involved in the activities of its student union. However, he quickly abandoned his studies and decided to emigrate. At the end of his autobiography, he formulated his life plans, in which his personal creed blended harmoniously with the ideology he had adopted. He could achieve self-realization, both the individual kind and that manifesting itself in working for the nation, only by emigrating to Palestine and "living according to socialist principles and working as a pioneer in one's own country."[70]

University students were the most educated among the participants in the competition. They understood the legal system and thus more than others demanded that the state safeguard the rights of citizens. Their experience of antisemitism shaped their hostility not only toward the supporters of the National Radical Camp, the National Party, or the antisemitic part of Polish society but also toward the institutions of the Polish state breaking the promises that it had made. Even during their studies or after graduation, elite young people felt that they were in a hopeless situation and asked the question, "What shall I do?" Like graduates of elementary schools or heders coming from completely different worlds, who could not find their footing in the traditional social space of Jewish districts of large cities or shtetls, they filled the void by joining political organizations proposing radical solutions. The cases of Ludwik Stöckel and other high school graduates who decided not to go to college show that in the 1930s the children of the elites were often ready, despite their parents, for the far-reaching social demotion that joining a radical political organization brought. Undoubtedly, abandoning their studies, living in difficult conditions in agricultural collectives, and doing physical work in preparation for departure to Palestine must have been considered social demotion. Turning to this radical alternative represented not so much demotion as destratification. Those who did not want to leave did not believe in Zionism, and because as students they had high aspirations, they often opted for communist ideology proposing the most comprehensive solution to the situation—that is, a complete restructuring of the existing order and society.

Modern antisemitism had been hitting acculturated Jewish elites hard since at least the 1880s. It was felt in a completely different way by the Jewish masses, who experienced instead sporadic acts of violence and resentment motivated most often by traditional superstition. Both modern and traditional antisemitism was for them dislike of a foreign group living outside their world. One lived next to the goyim, one entered into various economic and social relations with them, but their worldview was fundamentally alien. Until 1918, most Polish Jews had just this kind of experience. The situation changed with the advent of the Second Republic and the new levels of Christian-Jewish contacts established within the framework of a modern state, with a system of universal education in the lead. This fact was particularly important for the generation now growing up in the new reality and thus the most strongly subjected to its influence. Polonization and public education also brought on the universalization of the experience of modern antisemitism. The autobiographies are full of testimonies to this process. They were written by people from traditional families who almost always encountered for the first time new forms of resentment and even hatred toward Jews in public school.

"Gitman N." entered elementary school from a szabasówka. For the first time, he was studying with Christian children: "The Jewish children were placed in both of the two fourth sections and had a hard life with their new classmates. They were all antisemites.... There were those among us who often 'complained' about Christian children to the teachers, who took no notice."[71] Radical antisemitism, which was also spreading in schools at that time (often unchecked), contributed to deepening the permanent divisions between Jewish and Christian students. Analysis of the autobiographies clearly indicates that, contrary to their integrationist goals, schools most often did not integrate but antagonized Jewish and Christian students. For the former, their school experience was proof that they had nothing to look for in the non-Jewish world. Not wanting to return to the traditional world, they found that the only way out was radical Jewish organizations. Most of the young autobiographers wrote about antisemitism beyond that of their classmates. Discrimination, dislike, or even contempt coming from teachers cut even deeper. Although those authors who were consciously and deeply connected with Polishness devoted the most space to antisemitism, references to it also appear in other memoirs. Elementary school teachers, and less often those in secondary schools, were the first representatives of the state with whom Jewish young people came into contact in their lives. Stormer, a young Hasid studying in a small local yeshiva in Opoczno in parallel with his studies at the elementary school, wrote,

> From my school years I also recall a whole gallery of teachers of various types. One teacher, Mr. Fachalczyk, sticks in my memory.[72] He caused me a great deal of trouble and used to make fun of my sidelocks and my long coat. He taught history and Polish. Today he is the leader of Endek Party in our area and is known to be very antisemitic. I was very fond of the school principal, Mr. Kowalski, who in his time had gained a reputation as a great humanist. I had wonderful conversations with him (in the seventh grade) about the Bible and the Talmud, which pleased him quite a bit. On the whole, I remember him as a very refined person with great pedagogical abilities. However, he too has now moved over to the antisemitic camp, although he still holds the same post.[73]

This excerpt shows how the radical antisemitic policy of the 1930s affected all the youngest Jewish citizens of the Second Republic. In schools, Jewish young people found that not only did the state not defend them but also many teachers implemented or praised this policy.

After graduating from elementary school, Moses S. entered a Hebrew secondary school in Lviv. In his opinion, the most important advantage of this institution was that one did not experience antisemitism there. As a result of family disagreements, the author had to leave Lviv after a year and return to public school.[74] In his account of his studies in this establishment, antisemitism, from both its students and its teachers, stood out:

> Some antisemitic teachers arrived, for whom their greatest joy was abusing Jewish students. I remember that I was beaten many times with a belt on a stool on the teacher's orders by a classmate, a Catholic, based only on false reports from his Catholic colleagues. During recess I just sought a good corner where I could protect myself from the fists of the Catholics. In turn, at the end of the day, at the gate, usually we were awaited by several real "shaygets" who treated us to their fists usually armed with wooden "boxing gloves." I would get home from school beaten up, covered in bruises, with no desire to learn or live. In winter, we usually "got it" from snowballs, in which there was often a stone, and many a head was broken. The school authorities were deaf to all our complaints, indeed they seemed quite happy. In this state of affairs, when I was supposed to get up after a sleepless night, during which all the blows I had received during the day caused me to cry as I dressed, to go like a convict to school, to be tortured both by classmates as well as teachers.[75]

We find such dramatic descriptions in many autobiographies. Ajzyk Rozen wrote about the constant fights at school between Jewish and Christian students, as well as the teachers' hostile attitude toward the former. When one of them hit Ajzyk's younger brother hard in the face, and he stood up for him, he was expelled from school.[76] The author again encountered manifestations of antisemitism as a nineteen-year-old when he began his education at a public evening vocational school. Once again, the Christian students often beat up the Jews, and the teachers and master craftsmen teaching classes at the school did not react.[77] Mendl Man described his experience in elementary school in a similar manner. In his account, Christian children were even encouraged by some of the teachers to beat up Jews.[78] In Zhanet's autobiography, as in a number of others, teachers and priests in religion classes excelled in spreading antisemitism among the students.[79]

School appears in the autobiographies as a harbinger of discrimination on the part of the state and society, which Jewish young people would encounter throughout their later lives. It was the most important place where young people experienced disappointment with the Polish state and the attitudes of Polish Christians. Esther, the "Hasidic daughter" whose idols were Mickiewicz,

Sienkiewicz, and Piłsudski, who taught her about the "heroism of the Polish nation," wrote in 1939,

> Relations between Poles and Jews had deteriorated significantly. This, too, had a powerful impact on me. The loyal Polish patriot in me suffered. Now I, whose soul was so bound to Poland, had to give up my cherished dream of Poles and Jews living together in harmony. I had drawn such a pretty picture of it. The impassionate patriotic thoughts expressed in my youthful speeches were genuine. And now all of this had vanished. Every day the newspapers brought fresh, grim news of the persecution of the Jews. My faith in Poland's "heart" was tarnished. I no longer saw a nation with brotherly feelings for all its citizens, as Poland had been in prewar dreams. The situation for Jews in general upset me, especially as I had experienced it personally when I lost the opportunity to study in a *gymnasium*.[80] Now I began to look for a home in a Jewish milieu.[81]

Coming from a completely different background, Abraham Rotfarb wrote,

> I'm a poor, assimilated fellow. I'm a Jew and a Pole, or rather, I was a Jew, but, under the influence of the environment, language, culture and literature, I evolved into a Pole—I love Poland. Most of all its liberation and the heroism of its battles for independence thrill my heart. But I don't love the Poland that hates me for no reason, that tears at my soul, that has pushed me into apathy, melancholy, and dark aimlessness. I hate the Poland that doesn't want me as a Pole and sees me only as a Jew, that wants to chase me out of the country in which I was born and raised. That Poland I hate—I hate its antisemitism. You, antisemites, I blame you for my inferiority complex and for the fact that I don't know what I am: a Jew or a Pole. Poland has made me unhappy. It has made me into a dog, who shamelessly begs not to be left alone in the wilderness but to be led along the path of Poland's cultural life. Poland raised me to be a Pole but brands me a Jew who must be chased out. I want to be a Pole, but you won't let me. I want to be a Jew, but I can't; I've moved away from my Jewishness. I don't like myself as a Jew. I'm already lost.[82]

Rotfarb did not come from an assimilated environment; he lived mainly in the Jewish world. His autobiography shows a very important social trend that affected young people regardless of their social background. Linguistic and symbolic acculturation included the Orthodox, the traditional poor, and young people growing up in secular, both Zionist and socialist-Yiddishist homes. It did not weaken but in fact reinforced the feeling of antisemitic rejection. In the specific conditions of the Second Republic, this had far-reaching political consequences.

CONCLUSION: THE SCHOOL EXPERIENCE AS AN ELEMENT OF JEWISH YOUNG PEOPLE'S POLITICAL SOCIALIZATION

The generation described here was the first generation of Jews to both speak the national language and function freely in non-Jewish culture. One of the greatest paradoxes of the Second Republic is the fact that the modern institution of the school—which was supposed to integrate ethnic and national minorities—had a hidden function that contradicted its official mission. Instead of bringing young Jews closer to the state and counteracting political radicalism, it eventually antagonized them even more.

Processes and events taking place outside school, relating primarily to the growing wave of antisemitic violence and the accompanying discourse, influenced young people's reaction to antisemitic experiences gained at school. Schools, by promoting reading and involvement in public life, created opportunities to encounter patriotic content. The greater cultural competence and higher life aspirations gained from the school system made Jewish students particularly sensitive to antisemitic attacks. Thanks to school, young Jews read Polish newspapers and books, and thus they felt anti-Jewish insults more deeply. Through school and the influence of mass culture, the antisemitism of the 1930s became a universal experience, transcending class, social status, and cultural divisions in the Jewish community. Alienation was felt more strongly than by previous generations because it fell on those experiencing antisemitism in a new, internal way. It could be felt by people who were already thinking in terms of Polish culture, who were close to its symbols. Unlike their grandparents' and parents' generations, young people experienced hostility from members of the symbolic community to which they themselves belonged. Antisemitism ceased to be the attitude of somewhat abstract strangers, goyim living outside, but became a manifestation of rejection by close friends, classmates, and authority in the form of teachers. Modern antisemitism, which attacked those who were polonizing themselves and struck at the foundations of their identity, had appeared as early as the end of the nineteenth century. But the public schools made this experience universal.

The modern institutions of the Polish state had a strong impact on the youngest generation of Jewish citizens: on the one hand, they aroused within it ambitions that were personal (higher education and work in a respected profession) and collective (national emancipation on the Polish model); on the other hand, they made it feel humiliation and exclusion more strongly than had previous generations. Young Jews in interwar Poland were much more likely to look for far-reaching solutions to stamp out antisemitism once and for all.

Symbolic acculturation was therefore also an important basis for the development of Jewish political radicalism during the Second Republic.

The interwar public school, which was the most common and accessible place of secular education, also transmitted to young people the basic symbols and values of the era. At that time, aesthetic and ideological phenomena closely related to political radicalism, such as futurism, catastrophism, and political modernism seeking radical solutions in various forms of communitarianism, statism, or militarism, were taking center stage in the sphere of politics, not only among Jewish groups, not only in Poland, but on the entire continent and in the Western world. In schools, young people had access to a cultural code that allowed them to follow these trends and become influenced by them. Not only Jewish parties and radical antisemites but virtually all sides of Polish political discourse—Polish socialists, the peasant parties, and the ruling Sanacja camp—believed in the depth of the "Jewish problem." In the 1930s, a solution to this problem for all these groups was possible only through far-reaching social change, socialist transformation, and the assimilation of Jews, or by the departure of nonassimilating or "nonassimilated, "economically harmful" members of the Jewish community. Access to Polish culture meant access to this kind of discourse. It did not leave much room in the country for the majority of young Jews, who felt themselves to be Jews in the national sense but at the same time had a unique Polish Jewish identity. Besides, in the 1930s, antisemitism attacked even people of Jewish origin who felt themselves to be exclusively Polish.

The discourse of Jewish political groups also played a huge role in the political interpretation of the problem of antisemitism. Young people encountered it in private schools, youth movements, political parties, and other social organizations. Jewish political ideologies gave traditional ethnoreligious consciousness its modern, nationalist expression. They also provided a sense of national pride and tools to interpret the meaning of antisemitic events. These tools were a set of symbols that made up a description of the world, thanks to which many authors could interpret the facts of their autobiographies as exemplifications of the collective fate of the Jewish people. A sense of national pride led to a sharp reaction to antisemitic rejection. The model of ideal national Jewish culture associated with this feeling, internalized by young people, called on them to feel ashamed of symbolic acculturation, feeling and thinking in terms of a foreign culture that despised and rejected Jews. It was precisely from the perspective of this model that Abraham Rotfarb, living in a Jewish environment that spoke Yiddish on a daily basis, called himself an "assimilant" and hated those who, drumming Polish culture into him, at the same time rejected him. The vast majority of authors were already entering school with a strong sense of ethnic distinctiveness, separating them from Poles, Catholics, Ukrainians, or Eastern Orthodox. Both antisemitism and the Jewish discourse of national pride only perpetuated these ethnic prejudices. It is also no coincidence that anti-Jewish attitudes were most strongly felt and most expressively described by two groups of authors. The first were students at university and secondary school, usually the most acculturated, often consciously applying to join the Polish nation, and thus feeling antisemitic rejection more strongly. The other included supporters of the Jewish national parties who were also subjected to acculturation but did not see or were unwilling to see its impact on their consciousness, and thus interpreted antisemitism as a constant feature of the Jewish people's fate.

The antisemitism experienced by interwar young Jewish people went hand in hand with their high educational and civic aspirations. The school system and the culture of modernism played key roles in instilling young people with these hopes that could not be realized in the political climate of the Second Republic. This volatile mixture of modernist aspirations, Polish cultural content, ethnic and national resentment, and a sense of rejection created the radical habitus of Jewish young people. This habitus was shaped by strongly inter-related phenomena: the experience of alienation at school, a sense of relative deprivation that came from public school, and finally the ideological offerings of national and radical Jewish parties. Youth radicalism, however, did not mean the adoption of some comprehensive systematized ideology represented by a particular political movement. What united young people who often belonged to hostile Jewish camps was a specific modernist, aesthetic, and symbolic sensitivity, as well as a tendency toward attitudes contesting the functioning political and social order.

Shulamit Volkov, in her essay on the differences in the perception of events such as the Russian pogroms of 1881–1882 and the emergence of so-called modern antisemitism in western Europe, attacking the legal emancipation of Jews already undertaken there, draws attention to a fundamentally different reception of these events by eastern and western European Jews. The former, more rooted in their ethnic culture and for the most part not identifying with the Russian (or Polish) people surrounding them, were inclined to treat modern antisemitism as an external, threatening thing, but not one to undermine the foundations of their own identity. The situation was quite different for the majority of German Jews, who deeply identified with Germanness and for whom antisemitic attacks were a blow to the intellectual and spiritual foundations of their existence. The eastern European Jews, who relatively quickly and painlessly switched to modern national positions, seemed to have a better understanding of the universality and inevitability of antisemitism and could come to terms with it, put it to one side, or make it another piece of the political puzzle on the way to the implementation of the program of national self-emancipation.[83] The situation and attitudes of Jews in the Second Republic—that is, the transition of the vast majority of traditional Jewish society to Orthodox or nationalist positions—seemingly suggests that the Polish Jewish community of that period should be included in the eastern European type of reaction to modern antisemitism analyzed by Volkov. However, the autobiographies suggest a more complicated picture. Young people who wholly identified with modern, national Jewish politics and considered themselves part of only the Jewish people, because of the depth of the acculturation processes, perceived antisemitism very much like nonnational German Jews. The autobiographies are full of descriptions of how antisemitic rejection undermined the very foundations of individual identity. In fact, it was never described dispassionately, as a situation with which to become reconciled. Even young Zionists, whose parties and ideologies most often proclaimed such a belief, perceived anti-Jewish attitudes in moral terms as terrible, undeserved, and personal harm done to them.

SEVEN

POLITICAL ACTIVITY

THE FACT THAT ALMOST ALL the autobiographers were involved in a political party or youth movement certainly does not reflect the extent of such involvement in Jewish society as a whole. It is difficult to assume that even in the extremely politicized 1930s, as many as 95 percent of young Jews (as was the case among the participants in the competition) belonged to nationalist, socialist, or Orthodox political movements. However, the literature is in agreement that the level of political engagement of the generation under discussion was exceptional and that it was certainly one of the strongest social norms in the last decade of the interwar period. The purpose of this chapter is to describe and analyze the significance of this norm for relations within Jewish society, for Jewish youth culture, and for relations between the Jews and the state, even if, contrary to their declarations, the authors quoted below did not always implement it. Proof of the power of its influence is both the amount of space devoted to politics in the young people's autobiographies and the structure of almost all their pieces. The whole iron logic of individual authors' fortunes, descriptions of their transition to subsequent political movements, associated hesitations, doubts, and their "discovery of the truth" are undoubtedly self-creations. Various ideas drawn from political ideologies impacted the way the autobiographers narrated their life stories. According to most autobiographies, it was the ideas, the "truths" explaining the meaning of the world around them, and the various recipes for its improvement that were decisive in the authors' finally joining one of the parties or youth political organizations. In fact, there were many more reasons for this, and they were often much more prosaic or accidental. More important, however, as I have emphasized in the previous chapters, is not the verification of individual biographical facts provided by the authors but the intersubjective pattern of self-creation used by most participants in the YIVO competition. It says a great deal about the world of their own imagination and the environments they represented.

HOW DID YOUNG PEOPLE END UP IN POLITICAL ORGANIZATIONS? SOCIAL ORIGINS AND POLITICAL AFFILIATION

Participants in the YIVO competition joined political organizations (or youth organizations associated with political movements) early, most often between the ages of twelve and sixteen. Entering adult life, young people usually found themselves in a situation of double alienation—they felt alienated both from the world of their parents and from society. Most young Jews from poor social backgrounds were convinced of their own class and ethnic discrimination. The surrounding state, the language and symbolism of which were so familiar to them and personally close to them, was foreign or even hostile. Contestants in the YIVO competition entered adult life with a sense of deep resentment toward the state and its economic and sociopolitical system.

The coherent autobiographical narratives offered by most of the works analyzed here owed a great deal to politics. The autobiographies were written by committed political activists, and from this perspective the participants in the competition described their home environments, neighbors, schools, or work. However, as I have tried to show in the previous chapters, it is possible to extract elements of these young people's authentic experience from this first ideological layer of autobiography. Political and social alienation was undoubtedly a fact, and young people experienced it before most of them joined political organizations. Regardless of different ideological interpretations, young people actually experienced a lack of prospects for further education and the need to go out to work young. This usually meant a very long working day, low pay, and no chance of economic advancement. All this clashed with young people's high aspirations (compared to those of previous generations), which the state was unable to satisfy, even if there had been no anti-Jewish discrimination. This issue, moreover, affected not only the Jews.[1] Aware of their otherness, desperate and deeply disappointed with the surrounding reality, this generation was accepted into political organizations. How did young people describe the moment of joining an organization? Who or what was the cause of this? Most often they joined an organization despite their parents and, in general, despite their initial milieu's entire universe of values. Situations in which the values of their parents' world and the world of politics were partly compatible with each other were the rarest, and from them I shall begin to analyze the paths that led young people to different political movements.

HOME ENVIRONMENT

Perhaps the rarest events described in the autobiographies are those where joining one of the political movements was nonideological. This was the case for an author from Kolno, whose testimony does not reveal any Zionist views but only shows the belief that in Palestine she would have a chance for a better life than being condemned to the fate of a small-town seamstress. Her older sister met her future husband thanks to hakhshara, left with him, and began a new life in Palestine. The author, not yet eighteen years old, could not join He-Halutz. So, to increase her chances of getting into hakhshara as soon as possible, she enrolled in the strongest youth organization in the left-wing Zionist movement (the one offering the largest number of exit visas)—the Frayhayt youth organization. It was only there that she became somewhat interested in politics ("I started reading the press and various political books"), but she was interested in it only insofar as it gave her a chance to leave for Palestine.[2]

The few authors whose parents had any deeper political sympathies or were involved with one of the Jewish parties almost always ended up in the same organizations as them. Margalit's autobiography shows that the daughter of a wealthy Tarnopol merchant ordained as a rabbi and the granddaughter of a religious activist in the first Zionist movement in Tsarist Russia, Hibbat Zion, had virtually no alternative but to become a Zionist herself. Unlike most of her generation, Margalit's involvement in politics was not a rebellion against her parents and the values they represented but a continuation of them, complementing them. The girl, who was studying in elementary school, was sent by her parents for parallel classes in a Tarbut evening school. Finding herself in a peer environment similar to home, Margalit developed her Zionist interests. Eventually, as a teenager, she joined one of the youth organizations representing this movement.[3] A writer with the pseudonym Yesh grew up in Stanisławów (present-day Ivano-Frankivsk). She wrote her submission in Polish and came from a relatively wealthy, acculturated home. Her parents sent her to a Hebrew kindergarten and later to a Tarbut evening secondary school, which she attended while also enrolled in a public school, suggesting Zionist political sympathies and the family's wealth. Her social background clearly predisposed her to join Ha-Shomer ha-Tsa'ir, which often attracted pupils from elite secondary schools. Yesh wrote, "The holidays after graduating from first grade in secondary school were memorable for me. My sisters belonged to Ha-Shomer at that time, and the eldest Frydka [was] even on the board. Even before that, I often went to the evening get-togethers, which I enjoyed very much. The shomer organization was then experiencing its heyday. Led by older people with very good organizational skills, it was attracting a growing circle of young people. They were young people still at school, and mostly from secondary school."[4]

It is no coincidence that the authors mentioned here who ended up in the Zionist movement came from wealthy, mostly bourgeois homes. Until the 1930s, Zionism was mainly a middle-class movement. Youth organizations operating within it, such as Ha-Shomer ha-Tsa'ir, Gordonia, and to some extent Frayhayt (associated with Po'alei-Tsiyon-Right) were, despite their radical ideologies, elite organizations, often preferring secondary school students in their ranks.[5] They demanded from their members high moral standards, absolute sacrifice, and, above all, a Zionist spirit. The latter had to be associated with knowledge of the Hebrew language. The situation was changed by the evolution of the Zionist movement in the 1930s. David Ben-Gurion's Mapai gained dominance in the World Zionist Organization and in Palestine. In the diaspora and in its most important center, which was Poland, the policy of turning it into a mass movement in the form of hakhshara—preparing young people to go to Palestine— began. Hakhshara was based on the idea of work and life in a commune. Belief in this ideal was the sole criterion for joining, and only then did the young people become familiar with the ideology of the movement. In this way, hakhshara and less elite youth organizations assured entry into the Zionist movement for young people from poorer homes.[6] However, the Zionism of home was still mainly the Zionism of the children of the wealthy. This factor meant that, unlike young people from traditional homes joining left-wing or radical left-wing groups, their involvement in right-wing, centrist, or moderately left-wing Zionism was not always a radical break with their parents' worldview.

The mechanism for young people joining Orthodox parties was very similar. It also owed much to their new members' home environments. Orthodoxy was a way of life with specific patterns of raising children and its own education system, focused on separation from the negative secularizing influences of the environment. This fact is clearly shown by the autobiographies of such authors from Orthodox homes as Gamalielis, who ended his political trajectory in one of the most radical and antireligious parties, Po'alei-Tsiyon-Left. Interestingly, this yeshiva graduate, who was living with his parents at the time of writing his autobiography, carefully hid his membership in this organization. He came from a religious home, which stood out from the traditional environment by the fact that it encouraged a keen interest in politics. As in many religious Litvak homes, pro-Zionist sympathies were cultivated in Gamalielis's home (although his father was an Aguda activist). Certainly, however, his family did not exhibit the signs of political activism toward which some children drifted:

> He [the author's elder brother] was the first to introduce literature into our house. In his free time, he thought, composed rhymes, which he later turned into poems on various issues. In his notebook he had poems and elegies about the Hebrew University, Borokhov, Trumpeldor, Herzl and many others.... Politically, he was not very active, but he officially belonged to Po'alei-Tsiyon-Right. My sister Chaya, an enterprising person of the highest order, ran the whole household. Her proletarian nature led her straight into the proletarian ranks and she has become a left-wing activist, where she can display her enormous political commitment. Joining the workers' ranks required from the daughter of bourgeois landlords a great degree of idealism, also because of the specific sense of honor and pride of the petty bourgeoisie that prevailed in its homes. She had a huge impact on me.[7]

However, before Gamalielis completely succumbed to the influence of his sister the revolutionary, he followed the sacred path of tradition. In the first of the yeshivas where he studied, he became involved in Agudat Israel's election campaign. His rebellion was born later, in a yeshiva in Słonim, where students were harassed for focusing on secular subjects. When Gamalielis switched to the Talmudic academy in his hometown, his political involvement was gradually ignited by the Po'alei-Tsiyon-Left publications passed on to him by his sister, despite their confiscation by their father, who was worried about his ideological evolution.[8] His parents' protests against Gamalielis's decision to abandon the yeshiva were to no avail. The author was already a "different man." After returning to his hometown, he joined Po'alei-Tsiyon-Left. A huge role in this was played by his older sister, who in fact herself had left for Palestine.[9] Gamalielis's autobiography shows how politics, in its radical form, entered the life of even Orthodox circles in the interwar period and pulled many young people out of them. Traditional, and often more modern, Orthodox environments were not always able to counter politics with a competitive alternative in the form of an attractive lifestyle and by fortifying young people with self-esteem. For this reason, the path of most authors to politics that challenged their parents' world appears as something natural. That is why the minority who did not join radical movements and persevered in religious faith described this in terms of "fighting," of "struggling" with an ideological crisis.

However, regardless of where they were at the time of writing their autobiographies, young Orthodox ended up in political organizations mainly thanks to the influence of home environments. If their peers drew them into an organization, they came from the same environment in which young people did not radically challenge the norms and values of previous generations. This was the case with Damaszek, described in chapter 2, who was an Aguda activist; with Esther," a member of the girls' organization of the same party; and with Z. G. and Galitsyaner, supporters of Mizrahi. Damaszek joined Tseirei Aguda when it was being established on the inspiration of Rabbi Tzvi Hirszhorn, who for this purpose visited the Orthodox inhabitants of Kałusz. Esther, whose father was an Aguda activist, attended a Bais Yaakov school run by this movement, where she was enrolled in the Bati girls' Orthodox youth organization. Z. G.'s father was an important community and social activist in Ignatowo and at the same time a person with religious, Orthodox beliefs. When his son decided to stop studying in the yeshiva, he was more or less condemned to join a Mizrahi cell that had just been established in town. As another author, Galitsyaner, wrote, the religious youth organizations Bnei Akiva and later Tse'irei Mizrahi were established in the town especially for children from a religious background. Even if young Orthodox were recruited to a political movement at school or during political meetings organized in a synagogue or yeshiva (as was the case with Gamalielis), they were always supported by their home environment.

These experiences of Orthodox young people confirm Gershon Bacon's findings regarding the defensive nature of Jewish religious political movements in interwar Poland. Although their youth organizations modeled their institutional forms on secular movements, they recruited new members in a completely different way. They focused primarily on maintaining the social and normative cohesion of the Orthodox environment and thus recruited children of members of Orthodox parties, local community elites, and people praying in synagogues and shuls, whose Orthodoxy was never in doubt.[10] The youth organizations of Aguda and Mizrahi did not risk entering new areas of already secularized young people and consequently exposing their own Orthodox youth to a decline in religious zeal. They were not interested in restoring the faith of religious apostates. With only a few exceptions, yeshivas also did not do so, tending rather to get rid of students whose piety was questionable. In all the autobiographies analyzed here, authors who abandoned religion never returned to it. Even Ajzyk Rozen, who described how a whole group of secular youth with Zionist views became for a short time ardent supporters of Ger Hasidism, was not an exception.[11] All the people described by Rozen eventually abandoned Hasidism and religion.

Not all young Orthodox people were drawn to radical politics, as happened in the case of Gamalielis or Ajzyk Rozen. An alternative to both the former and the traditional politics-free life was Orthodox politics, mainly in its Aguda or Zionist-religious Mizrahi version. However, even when they chose this life option (because it was not limited to strictly political attitudes), young people were not free from dilemmas. This is perfectly illustrated by the case of Orient-Vostok, a young Lubavitch Hasid from Drujsk. His autobiography, although having a different ending than Gamalielis's, is a testimony to very similar social processes. In the case of Orient-Vostok, too, numerous safeguards against the dangers of secularism in the form of a network of Orthodox institutions proved inadequate to defend him against doubts, against the sense of malaise that would be life in a traditional community. The boy was sent to study at a yeshiva in Breslav at a very early age. He was proud that his studies there would enable him to become a "Torah sage" and join the ranks of the Orthodox elite. He was one of the best students there. When, in parallel with his Talmudic studies, he studied in elementary school, like many of his yeshiva classmates, he dreamed of studying at a Jewish teachers' college or secondary school and even of going back to school later.[12] Although Orient-Vostok emphasized the gap between secular and religious knowledge, between elementary school and the yeshiva, and was aware of the tensions associated with being in two parallel worlds, in the period under description this did not yet cause a crisis in his social and religious identity. When he realized that there was no point in dreaming of attending a secular secondary school, he was glad that thanks to the yeshiva he had a chance to receive rabbinical ordination. Later, he studied at three other Talmudic schools: an unspecified one in Vilna, another in Prużany, and finally one in Pińsk. Although he still dreamed of studying in a secondary school, and although he came into conflict with the mashgiach and the authoritarian regulations of the institutions in which he studied, he persisted not only in his faith but also in the conviction of the rightness of the traditional way of life.[13] However, over time, this belief was increasingly undermined due to the weakness of traditional and Orthodox institutions and their inability to provide the author with a decent standard of living or to create attractive life prospects. Orient-Vostok described how hard and even somewhat humiliating it was for him to sleep in a beit midrash (the yeshiva did not have a dormitory) and to eat modest "teg" (there was also no cafeteria) consisting of herring and potatoes.[14] He became increasingly tired of the life of a *batlen*. When a fire broke out in the yeshiva, he and his friends lost not only a place to study but—more importantly—an entire social world in which they could live following the existing Orthodox norms. As the author wrote, this situation bothered him more and more: "It was impossible to live in this goles."[15] Finally, he enrolled at the Talmudic school in Prużany. There he studied for two years, and "a youngster became a man." He still doubted whether he was right to live outside the "modern" world. Nothing changed after he moved to the yeshiva in Pińsk (one of the yeshivas in the Beth Yosef network, supervised by the radical branch of the Musar movement from Nowogródek), despite his pride at the high level of studies there.[16] His doubts caught the attention of his superiors and eventually caused him to leave the yeshiva. In 1932, as a seventeen-year-old youth, Orient-Vostok returned to Drujsk, having previously obtained the certificate of ritual butcher. He wrote his autobiography while working in this profession and dreaming of escaping to the "great world." In his Orthodox world, he wrote, "it's hard to do nothing, to suppress your youthful fire, to waste your energy for no reason, to look at a wasted day every night."[17] In the end, he found the only attractive way out, which was to join the Zionist-religious Mizrahi party and its kibbutz operating near Vilna. Only in this way "could he get rid of his pessimism," "use his energy," and "direct all his actions towards participation in the construction of a great defensive wall for the Jewish people."[18] Only in this political way could he satisfy his youthful thirst for activism.

Orient-Vostok's autobiography, despite its author's Orthodoxy, is characterized by the same crisis of the world of tradition as the works of people who had undergone a radical ideological conversion. This crisis raised doubts as to many traditional norms and values and the resulting lifestyle. What saved Orient-Vostok's religiousness was the modern Orthodox policy of the Mizrahi party. Although the author did not say a word about what or who had urged him to join this organization, his autobiography clearly indicates that the impulse came from his peer environment among yeshiva students looking for both the meaning of life and a more practical occupation.[19] To save young people from the clutches of political radicalism and the inevitably accompanying secularization, Orthodox political organizations had to begin to organize their lives in a holistic or total dimension, just as radical organizations did. As for the role of home upbringing and the political views of parents as factors conducive to joining a particular political movement, it is characteristic that they almost never led to joining leftist revolutionary organizations.[20] The Bund, Po'alei-Tsiyon (and later Po'alei-Tsiyon-Left), and the Social Democracy of the Kingdom of Poland and Lithuania and its successors—other ephemeral radical parties and organizations—experienced brief moments of triumph during periods of particular social upheaval, such as the revolution of 1905–1906, the Russian Revolution, and the subsequent eastern wars fought also on future Polish territory. However, at least until the 1930s, they were generally not popular among the Jewish masses. For this reason, then, hardly any participants in the YIVO competition grew up in families sympathetic to them. As we shall see later, the situation was changed by the generation they represented.

SCHOOL

Another important factor influencing the selection of a particular political organization was school. All private Jewish school networks in the Second Republic had explicit political profiles, but many parents never became fully aware of these profiles. Hence, the influence of their children's schools did not necessarily align with their value systems. In recruiting for youth organizations associated with the Bund, the network of TsYShO schools, dominated by the party, played a decisive role.[21] Most often it was the lowest Jewish social classes—the children of luftmenschen, petty merchants, craftsmen, and workers—who joined them. The fact that they were joining the Bund or Po'alei-Tsiyon-Left, which focused on a certain type of socialist Jewish nationalism, and not the communists was most often determined by a biographical episode of studying at a Yiddish school. For example, for Feygeles, after growing up in Lublin, attending a TsYShO school, and spending long hours in the reading room of the Jewish workers' library, joining the Bund was a natural development, stemming directly from his life experience: "*I shall be a socialist—a Bundist.* In sixth grade I lived only for politics. Previously, I read daily newspapers, but as I look at it from today's perspective, I did not understand the political information contained in them, I was interested only in sensationalist stories, nothing more. I also read publications on literature, writers. . . . At that time 'SKIF' was being established there and I was one of the first to join the organization, which became a field of new activity, new experiences that school did not provide.[22] I was one of SKIF's founding members."[23]

The first leader of the Lublin SKIF group was a Yiddish literature teacher from a TsYShO school. As Feygeles wrote, at that time it was fashionable at school to belong to the Bund's children's organization.[24]

Another author grew up in a traditional, apolitical home. A Tarbut school attracted him to Zionism. There, children from the highest grades clamored to go on vacation to camps organized by He-Halutz, a nonpartisan organization preparing young Jews to leave for Palestine. The author and his friends returned from camp as convinced Zionists.[25] Ben-Tikva joined Bin (Little Bee), a Jewish scout organization started by Max Weinreich himself, in the Mefitsei Haskalah Vilna school. Bin, like school, was a very important element, he wrote, in the "complete" transformation of his personality: "My brother and I became good students, the teachers were pleased with us . . . we applied ourselves to every school requirement."[26] There, the boys experienced real friendship with their peers for the first time, and they had the opportunity to develop their characters and gain practical knowledge about life and the world: "The organization gave us what we badly needed, what the students in the heder were missing."[27] Hanzi, feeling lonely in metropolitan Vilna, where she had to go away to secondary school, ended up in the right-wing Zionist youth organization Betar through her classmates.[28] This happened at a time when the author was beginning to lose her previously very deep religious beliefs. The youth political organization gave her much-needed support: "I got closer to people from my grade, who belonged to 'Betar.' Of course, they wanted to recruit me, and the idea of Jewish national politics attracted me very much. When I asked to be assigned a task, I was made responsible for organizing the Betar youth organization. When the members of our cell greeted me on the street with a shout of 'Tel Hai,'[29] I felt very confident. For the first time in my life someone paid attention to me."[30]

PEER ENVIRONMENT

In the context of the social space in which the political initiation of young people took place, the school can be treated as a specific form of peer environment. It was the most important factor determining which organization the participants in the YIVO competition joined. The act of joining was often also a complete break with their home milieu's value system.

"Ludwik B." was born in a small town near Kraków. He was brought up by a single mother. Very early on he had to help her at work, which caused him to interrupt his education both in the heder and in elementary school. He worked as a waiter in a beer hall, and finally he went to a locksmith's workshop. One of the young people he met there brought him into Ha-Shomer ha-Tsa'ir. His account is important because he came from a poor, uneducated background— people who rarely joined Ha-Shomer. Ludwik B. recalled,

> Sometimes, having nothing to do, we sat down and talked. I spoke until the topic of the organization came up. I was a complete layman on the subject. They talked about Palestine, about some sort of socialism or other, they imagined their future life in a *kvutsa*,[31] they talked about ideal relationships in some cooperatives or other, and I sat quietly. I didn't know what they meant. . . . From that day on, every day during the break at work, they gave me lessons to make me aware of all these previously unknown things. At their urging, at the age of fifteen, I joined a shomer organization. When I joined the organization, I knew that I would find something completely different from what I had seen in my life so far. My sadness got lost somewhere, it disappeared.[32]

The primary reason for joining political organizations was the social emptiness felt by young Jews that pierced through almost all their descriptions of their initial surroundings. These were complemented by reports of a "gray," "monotonous" twelve-hour day of hard work. The experience of emptiness affected not only young people from small towns but also those from medium-size and large cities. The poor there did not have the material resources or the social and cultural capital to take advantage of all the opportunities for spending time and for establishing new, interesting contacts. Living in Częstochowa, Drori (whose pseudonym most likely came from the name of the youth organization Dror, associated with Po'alei-Tsiyon-Right), after completing only five grades of elementary school, worked as an insurance agent's assistant while struggling to complete a bookkeeping course; in his free time, he liked most of all going to the movies. He emphasized that he differed in this from most of his peers, whose greatest passion was soccer matches. The cinema alone, however, could not be enough for a young man looking for the company of his peers and a goal in life. Everything changed when, during a lecture organized as part of a people's university run by Po'alei-Tsiyon-Right, Drori met a former friend from the heder, a member of Frayhayt (the youth wing of Po'alei-Tsiyon-Right), who strongly urged him to join the organization. As the author wrote, "I joined it for social reasons, but once a member, I began to take a strong interest in the movement's ideological goals."[33] Further pages of his autobiography are a record of ideological faith, of a new understanding of the surrounding world, an expression of the hope that radical ideology provided, as well as a testimony to finding a new social space that finally filled the emptiness surrounding him.

Young people from the poorest traditional backgrounds most often ended up in the most radical left-wing parties—from the least antiestablishment Bund to the most antiestablishment Communist Party of Poland (KPP).[34] The children of the unemployed, of manual workers, of luftmenschen who did not have a permanent job, or of craftsmen found themselves most at home in these parties. Among the authors working in the KPP, we can also find the son of a melamed. Young people from the lowest classes and groups most often occupied the same social position as their parents. However, like their whole generation, they stood out by virtue of their individual ambitions and expectations. Acculturation and the promise by the Second Republic of equal treatment for all its citizens, regardless of their ethnic origin or religion, were influential. This was a promise that elementary school gave to young people, meaning that their expectations and ambitions were no less than those of their wealthier friends, who tended to go to moderate left-wing, centrist, or right-wing Zionist organizations. On the other hand, young people from poor homes felt the weight of the question the most: "What should I do?" For those young people starting their working life early, the world of the shtetl or the Jewish district of a larger city reeked of social emptiness. Politics was everything to them, because it alone could fill this emptiness.

A textbook example of this kind of biographical trajectory, leading directly to a radical left-wing political party, is provided by Mendl Man. This son of a usually unemployed shoemaker and a street trader graduated from a seven-grade szabasówka in Płońsk. He did not see any life prospects for himself and his peers. In his autobiography, he expressed a deep fear that he would share his father's fate, alternating between an unemployed and hard-working craftsman, a quiet Jew enduring everything with traditional "Jewish fatalism." Mendl claimed that he was becoming the same as his father, having no influence on his own fate. The only thing that could cut him off from the sad fate of preceding traditional generations was his work for the revolution and the complete transformation of the Jewish people. To this end, he joined the Yugend, the youth wing of Po'alei-Tsiyon-Left.[35]

Gitman N. was persuaded to join the Bund, or rather its children's organization SKIF, by a friend. In his artisan milieu, the traditional awareness of belonging to the social class that performed physical work (*balmelokhes*) was combined with the modern language of class struggle ideology. Gitman recalled his political initiation as follows:

> The summer of 1929 . . . a Friday evening, the first day of Shavuot, I go with my grandfather to the shtibl to pray. We prayed, some of my friends came over, but this time not with stupid jokes. . . . With a sincere and joyful expression on their faces, they said, "Gitman, since you are already a worker, you can enroll in a children's organization that is currently being formed. There they're going to be teaching reading, writing and how to become a man, today after the Shabbat dinner we'll be meeting on the street. "OK," I replied . . . I said yes because I had been called a "worker," a word that made me raise my head higher and instinctively conveyed to me what was yet to come.[36]

The main reason for joining the party was undoubtedly the author's working-class background. But the symbolic value that the Bund had for him is also interesting. The socialist party had made a "worker" from a tailor's apprentice with traditionally low social standing. The tailors' shtibl, where the author would go to pray with his grandfather, the traditional environmental values, and the ties between the balmelokhes smoothly transition into a new form of organization for craftsmen—the socialist party and its children's organization. Elements of traditional and modern symbolism also combine in his description of the initiation of young Bundists: "Among all our friends, young workers, we walked across the pasture towards the bank of the stream. We all sat down, I saw my comrades around me—older Bundists, whom I had previously envied for being self-aware people heading through life in a specific direction."[37] The initiation by the stream was accompanied by speeches by more experienced Bundists, who ran SKIF.[38]

Gitman N.'s autobiography is a perfect example of the biographical trajectory that characterizes almost all activists of the most radical political organizations: the Bund, Po'alei-Tsiyon-Left, and the communists. The author came from the traditional poor. From the age of three, he studied in a heder; when he was seven years old, he was sent to elementary school, and no one bothered about his religious upbringing anymore. Four years of study in the heder had been quite enough for previous generations of craftsmen like him. His family's educational strategy was focused on the boy finding paid employment as soon as possible. No one in his immediate milieu was counting on the boy's Talmudic or any other intellectual career. Growing up in a world of tradition, he received very little traditional cultural capital that (as was the case with young people from elite Orthodox homes) would have saved him from losing his religiosity. In the traditional social hierarchy, craftsmen had very low status. This stratum was often characterized by a dislike of the traditional merchant or religious elites. Advancing secularization, modernization, and the difficult economic situation further reinforced traditional interclass animosities. All this made it so easy for the child of balmelokhes, who was to become one himself, to reject the traditional world and join political organizations that condemned it in the most radical way. The attractiveness of these organizations was reinforced by their proletarian symbolism, especially relevant for young people doing manual labor, who were despised by the traditional world and rejected by the modern one.

Similarly, in the case of Abraham Rotfarb, his social background increased the likelihood of involvement in a socialist or communist movement. He grew up in Warsaw in a poor family of artisans. Little was known there of the Torah or the Talmud; his parents' religious education (or rather his father's) was probably limited to a few years spent in a heder. Youngsters from this type of background were therefore most affected by all radicalizing factors, such as acculturation combined with a strong feeling of antisemitic rejection, secularization, pauperization, limited employment opportunities in industry, and the lack of prospects. All these processes led Abraham Rotfarb to communism and left their mark on his autobiography.[39] The author came from a large family. His father was a "practicing" Jew, but "he did not wear a long coat." The description of difficult living and working conditions in the autobiography is part of the model of an unhappy childhood and typical of the distorted relations between children, parents, and siblings.[40] When the author was not yet fourteen years old, his mother died, so he left school and began working in his father's workshop. Radical politics, communism, and then left-wing Zionism were, according to him, the only chance to break out of the isolation, ignorance, and superstition of the world of tradition.[41] Rotfarb, as a typical representative of the poorest young people, was drawn into the communist organization Pioneer by a friend from the same background. For some time he resisted invitations and was afraid to attend a communist meeting. However, as he grew older, he became secularized, and as he experienced more and more social and ethnic alienation, his resistance weakened:

> But once, Chaskiel ran into me during my "Alone among the Waves" period, and joining the organization seemed like a natural thing for me to do. This was after my mother had died. I didn't have any friends at all, but, more importantly, I was reading and had acquired some knowledge and a sense of justice. Although it still frightened me somewhat, that word "communism" meant to me (although not completely consciously) a consistent, continuous, and fearless struggle for justice. Communism was an authority that I held in esteem as being forceful and just. These two motives—the appeal of communism's authority and the need for community—propelled me to join the Pioneers [members of the communist youth organization], rather than any intellectual conviction.[42]

Gitman N. ended up in the Bund and Abraham Rotfarb in the KPP by way of youth organizations recruiting young people from the poorest Jewish communities. Other very important loci of political initiation into these parties and into Po'alei-Tsiyon-Left were metropolitan factories (if young Jews managed to find jobs there at all) and most often larger workshops employing several workers. The Bund, the KPP, and Po'alei-Tsiyon-Left organized Jewish trade union life and were very active in metropolitan factories and workshops. The Bund dominated the Jewish Union of Class Trade Unions. The second force here were the communists (at the peak of their union power in 1934–1935, they constituted as many as one-third of the activists), and the third were activists of Po'alei-Tsiyon-Left (10% of the members that same year). Individual regional and local branches of the Jewish Union of Class Trade Unions were usually dominated by one of these three parties.[43] Thus, trade union activity was also very heavily politicized. It was yet another sphere of life in which Jews operated in relative separation from the non-Jewish population.

"M. Sheynberg," like the abovementioned authors, belonged to the Jewish poor, which was traditionalist and at the same time far from Orthodoxy. For several years he attended a heder, where he experienced violence and a low academic level. He also studied in elementary school, where he experienced strong ill will on the part of the teachers and violence from Christian students. Almost his whole autobiography is a record of various odd jobs done by his father and himself, his painful poverty, and his lack of hope for a change in his own fate.[44] M. Sheynberg encountered the same life problems as many other authors from the Jewish poor, trying to find a job in a craft workshop, dreaming of working in a factory, despising his parents' traditionalist generation, unable to find his footing in an unfriendly big city, and convinced of his double discrimination as a Jew and as a member of the exploited lowest class. The only person who became interested in his fate was an acquaintance, a local trade union activist and a member of the Polish Communist Party. Having earlier avoided "party affiliation" and despite honestly describing the problems of his KPP cell, such as the large number of careerists and opportunists as well as sharp internal divisions, M. Sheynberg saw for himself no other way in life than to become an "activist and comrade."[45]

Greyno's biographical trajectory was very similar, likewise leading him to communism. His adolescence was also marked by poverty, unhealthy family relationships, social handicaps, and national alienation. The breakthrough in his life came during the feast of Yom Kippur when a friend took him from the synagogue to an "anti-religious rally":

> I remember, it was Yom Kippur. I stood in the synagogue among the worshippers. It was dark. The men, with *tallitim* draped over their heads, wailed, cried, and beat their breasts, as they asked their God for forgiveness for the sins they had committed during a life that was so brutal and wicked. . . . And suddenly, there was Yankl! . . . He had some harsh words for us, especially for me, saying that we ought to be ashamed of ourselves for staying with the old folks, who didn't understand life the way we did. "We are now going," he said in his optimistic tone, "to be with our own kind." And so, we set off. . . . He led us to the hills outside town. A large group of young men, who were older than we were, had already gathered there. Some of them were dressed in traditional Jewish clothes. There were young women there as well. They were eating rolls and sausages, fooling around, and joking about the holiday. . . .[46] A young man standing in the crowd came forward and addressed us. He was wearing traditional Jewish clothes. A rabbi's son, he began to explain in simple words the point of religion, which enslaves the individual and prevents him from rising to a higher level of life. This is especially true of workers who toil all year long. They are exploited by the very men who are now beating their breasts for their sins, in order to continue tomorrow with their exploitation of the weak and helpless, who possess nothing but their own ability to work.[47]

A similar biography and social origins also characterized the son of a melamed from Nalewki, "Heniek G.,"; a craftsman from Działoszyn, Chaim Berl; and a Łódź worker, Jerzyk Tomaszów.[48] The autobiographies of all the communist activists listed here are a record of violent secularization processes and anomie, especially affecting the lowest Jewish social classes. It seems that the greatest decline of their Jewish world caused them to seek the most radical denial of it, which was communism. At the same time, another important feature in common is striking in these people's autobiographies. Both the recruitment of these authors and their activities in political organizations, proclaiming a complete break from the shackles of "traditional Jewishness," took place exclusively in a Yiddish-speaking Jewish environment. This is also evidenced by the extensive autobiography of Kola. I quote many parts of it later; here, I look only at the ending, in which the author shared his reaction to the dissolution of the Communist Party of Poland in 1938. This event was a huge personal tragedy for communist authors. He described it in terms of a cataclysm, as the end of the only world in which young people found support:

> In the midst of unfortunate events, in all this darkness, one light guided me. The Party. But in 1938, that light was extinguished. We were told that the organization had been dissolved. We took the news with our eyes wide open, frightened and asked, "What did dissolved mean? Where would our struggle go now? What about democracy? All was lost, all was destroyed. Who would defend our rights? Who would defend national minorities? There would be no one to speak up for the equality of the Jewish masses." They say that only Jews are communists. But why is that? Because we are constantly humiliated . . ., we are sick, we do not have the right to work in state institutions, we are not allowed to work in factories, so we must fight against reactionary forces for our rights. We must fight and ally ourselves with the Polish and the international proletariat. We must have all the rights that are our due as citizens. Why do the Jewish masses of the Soviet Union have the right to fly in the heavens, at the same time to go as deep underground as possible, working in the mines, to be both janitors and engineers, while we have the right only to hunger and unemployment?[49]

An extremely important element of the struggle for the support of the poorest, urban Jewish classes were the communists' protests against antisemitism. From its very beginnings, the Polish Communist Party had tried to use the meetings of Jewish trade unions and other noncommunist institutions to demonstrate and to recruit new members.[50]

The autobiographies of communist authors from traditional Jewish homes suggest an ambivalence as to their own individual identity. On the one hand, they wanted to get rid of the negative stigma of their own Jewishness, and on the other hand, they did not cease being Jews, of which they were accused by the traditional environment. From the perspective of Poland of the 1930s and what they knew—or rather did not know—about the Soviet Union, they felt the Communist Party to be defending them as Jews. They believed that it did not force them to abandon their cultural and ethnic distinctiveness. Most of the descriptions of KPP cells appearing in autobiographies speak only about the Jews operating in them and about the fact that only Yiddish was spoken there. Abraham Rotfarb, describing extensively his activities in Pioneer and the Communist Union of Polish Youth, never once mentioned a single person who was a non-Jew. Communist activity in Warsaw's Murdziel, contrary to what one might think, was in no way a complete break for him, an abandonment of his Jewish environment.[51] Rotfarb still lived among the children of the poor, supporting himself by manual labor.[52] Greyno, describing his activities in a communist Jewish trade union over several dozen pages, mentioned his non-Jewish comrades only once. He would meet them only in prison.[53] Kola grew up in the Soviet Union and came to Vilna around 1930 as a teenager. Even this boy, called "a Ruskie" by his schoolmates, described his communist activities only in the context of the Jewish Street.[54] For him too, the only point of reference for political activity was the Jewish community. Young communists were de facto breaking only with their parents' value system and lifestyle while remaining within a familiar Jewish environment.

The theme of a separate Jewish subculture existing in some of the metropolitan structures of the KPP has not yet been fully described in academic works. Dealing with the problem of Jewish involvement in communism, Polish academic and memoir literature draws attention to two groups of young Jews joining the Polish communist movement in the interwar period: They were supposedly either Jews from strongly "assimilated homes" or people from traditional homes trying to erase the stigma of their Jewish origin and seeking to be released from it.[55] The young people's autobiographies analyzed here contradict these findings. In their radical criticism of everything that the Jewish tradition implied, in the autobiographies of the communist participants in the YIVO competition we undoubtedly find traces of ambivalence in relation to their own national identity. However, it is difficult to say that everyone sought unequivocally to erase their own Jewishness. As communists, they operated only in their own ethnic (and class) environment. They addressed their political message only to Jews, usually in Yiddish. Of course, they believed in the international brotherhood of the proletariat, but in their daily party work it was most often an abstraction that had little to do with reality. In the KPP in the 1930s, Yiddish officially had the status of just a tool that was used to rile up the Jewish masses. However, at the very base of this illegal party, the situation was often quite different, and Yiddish played a much more important role. This is attested to by the autobiographies of Binyomin R., Greyno, Kola, and M. Sheynberg quoted in this book. In this regard, the work of the last-mentioned is the most evocative. It was his work in the KPP that led him to appreciate the modern version of Yiddish culture, which he had previously intended to abandon. In the last pages of his autobiography devoted to politics, he wrote,

> The fact that I am writing in Yiddish is a sign that I am no stranger to the problems of the Jewish masses, of which I am a part. I identified Yiddish with party affiliation. There was no Yiddish movement for me, no party, because I felt disgusted with parties, so the Yiddish language itself seemed alien to me, you can say that I had got over Yiddish like a runny nose. To be more specific, I was ashamed at the time that Polish was not spoken in our house and that all I heard around me were Hasidim muttering in Yiddish.[56]

His negative attitude toward Yiddish culture changed radically when he joined a KPP cell, when he understood that this culture was the culture of the Jewish proletariat to which he himself belonged.[57] Speaking Yiddish daily and reading the party press and literature in this language were inextricably linked to his new communist life. Communism did not have to mean the complete abandonment of Jewishness. The nationalist self-identification of young communists, as well as the similarity of their social world to that in which other young Jews lived, is also evidenced by their large representation among the participants in the nationalistically oriented autobiographical competition. All this proves that the activity in KPP metropolitan cells, operating mainly on the Jewish Street, in no way deprived communists from traditional Jewish homes of their ethnonational Jewish identity.[58] As we shall see below, some of the communist-leaning authors who took part in the third competition in 1939, a year after the dissolution of the KPP, had very quickly joined other political movements. These were always secular Jewish nationalist movements. Less surprising is the choice of a party like the Bund or Po'alei-Tsiyon-Left, but, as we shall see, young communists also quite easily switched to less radical Zionist organizations.[59]

Contemporary research by historians proves that in the communist movement in the Second Republic, apart from the most famous polonized Jews or simply people of Jewish origin, who were particularly numerous at the upper levels of the party hierarchy, most of its Jewish members came from the lowest social strata, who in Isaac Deutscher's words can be described as "Jewish

Jews."[60] The subculture created by them and operating within the communist movement has not yet been described. A breakthrough in this respect is the work of Joanna Nalewajko-Kulikov, done on the occasion of the biography of one of the creators of the Polish version of Yiddish communist culture ("Nusekh Poyln"), David Sfard. But it also out of necessity focuses on the elite of this subculture, the writers and editors whose work and socialization experience were different from those of the autobiographers.[61] People from the Yiddish-speaking traditional poor began to flow into the communist movement only in the interwar period. Although the ethnic proportions in the Polish communist movement were subject to fluctuations in the interwar period, people of Jewish origin accounted for about 25 percent of its members. This percentage was higher at the leadership level. Examining the KPP's nationalities policy, Piotr Wróbel described it as "an unsuccessful attempt at integration."[62]

The communist leaders' attitude to the "Jewish question" was ambivalent. The KPP called for a war against antisemitism, against all forms of discrimination against Jews, and demanded the possibility of using Yiddish in the civil service and even public schools with Yiddish as a teaching language. At the same time, it did not recognize the Jews as a separate nation and rejected demands for Jewish cultural autonomy in a future socialist republic. The communists also attacked private Jewish education as represented by the TsYShO network associated with the Bund. Propaganda in Yiddish, institutions such as the Jewish Department, the Jewish Bureaus, and even "Jewish" district cells that were supposed to be only temporary—all the activities of these institutions were only a tactical move to facilitate the recruitment of supporters from among this group of the population. The same effects were to be produced by the sometimes short-term cooperation with Jewish revolutionary groups or by communist pamphlets created during the so-called People's Front, published in Yiddish, and addressed to all opponents of "fascism."[63] Ultimately, the communist Jews were to merge with the non-Jews in a single centralized organization, of course getting rid of all signs of separateness. Activists repeatedly stressed that party members, and even its leadership, were not free from antisemitism. There was a mutual reserve, a reluctance to take joint action, a tendency to separate along ethnic lines. The overrepresentation of people of Jewish origin in the leadership and among the rank-and-file members of the party was a constant, clearly articulated issue for it. There were complaints that the proportion of Jews to the rest of the party was too great, that they were too visible.[64] The issue of this visibility had to translate into an attitude toward all forms of manifestation of Jewish identity and culture. What at the level of top-down decisions was supposed to be only a tactical solution, in some party cells, almost entirely set up by Jews, had to turn into a Jewish communist subculture incompatible with the views of the leadership—a subculture that differed little from the subcultures existing in the other noncommunist youth movements mentioned here. This was partly the case, for example, of Warsaw Murdziel, in which the abovementioned Rotfarb and Greyno operated. The Jewish character of Murdziel could not be eliminated, despite the efforts of the party's central committee. The Łódź Jewish Bureau also contested the central leadership's disciplinary interventions aimed at limiting everyday cooperation with the Bund and Po'alei-Tsiyon-Left.[65] "Jewish Jews" were not accepted into the party's central apparatus. Everyone of Jewish descent was polonized, having renounced anything that smacked of nationalism, including Yiddish. Meanwhile, most of the communist participants in the YIVO competition belonging to the party base did not meet with non-Jews in their work at all. They operated in Yiddish-speaking circles, organized demonstrations only in the Jewish environment, and conducted propaganda work only there. The experience of interethnic integration, which had anything to do with the internationalism of the communist movement, occurred only with entry into the upper leadership levels or imprisonment, where Jewish communists met non-Jewish comrades. Prison was thus a very important stage of communist political socialization.[66] The youngest rank-and-file members of the Communist Party from Warsaw, Łódź, Kielce, Vilna, and Działoszyn mentioned here lived in their own subculture, on the other side of the ethnic wall, the same one that separated them from their Christian peers in elementary school or in the labor market. The phenomenon of a communist Jewish youth subculture does not mean, however, that party membership and its ideology were accepted on the Jewish Street. In general and local elections, the vast majority of Jewish society, including its poorest strata and classes, rejected communism.[67]

The situation was different in the case of acculturated authors, coming from completely different backgrounds. Their Jewish identity was not very well established, and they did not know Yiddish, so they could not "recover" it from the Jewish Street or even from among Jewish communists coming from poor backgrounds. The reasons for and nature of their political activity were different. Their entry into communism resulted mainly from their rejection by the Polish community. Political radicalism in its most extreme form—communism—was particularly attractive to acculturated, wealthy, urban young people, who felt discrimination and antisemitic rejection very strongly. In contrast to the Jewish poor community described above, here the causes of radicalism lay outside the Jewish community. This is evidenced by the few works among the entire collection of autobiographies by female students from metropolitan secondary schools written in Polish. Bronka came from a Polish-speaking home of the rich Warsaw bourgeoisie. I previously quoted an excerpt from her autobiography in which she described how she realized the significance of her Jewish origin only when she encountered the insults of students of the elementary school adjacent to her elite private Jewish secondary school. Describing the atmosphere among its students, Bronka emphasized their politicization and daily discussions and disputes between communists and Zionists. The author found in communism the answer to the "Jewish question."[68] Thanks to Marxist ideology and revolution, Bronka wanted to rid herself of the stigma of her origins, of a culture with which she had little in common. The political initiation of a student at a private secondary school for Jewish girls in Lviv, teaching in Polish, was identical. The author first heard about communist ideas in elementary school, when she learned that her beloved cousin had been arrested. When the girl went to the secondary school, she wrote, "I began to look with contempt at these stupid schoolmistresses, who fluttered around every doctor's or lawyer's daughter as if she were an important person. It was then that for the first time within me arose a revolt that it should not be like this, that this was a terrible screaming injustice. I read a lot of books and newspapers and finally understood that there was one way out of this disgusting, filthy life, without any tomorrow. That way out is socialism."[69]

During junior high and high school, her idol was her cousin, who after leaving prison did not cease his political activity. The author's communist initiation, begun in the safe environment of secondary school, was augmented by participation in the funeral of an unemployed person shot by the police. This funeral most likely turned into a communist demonstration:

> At that time, things were very bad in our city. The unemployed, no longer able to bear hunger and misery, staged a demonstration. During this demonstration, a man named Kozak was killed by a policeman's bullet. A large-scale funeral was arranged for him. . . . During the funeral, there was a clash with the police and, as a consequence, some shooting. I saw everything. I watched this tragedy of people who were not even allowed to honor properly the deceased, and something was taking place in my heart that I could not describe. Oh, how I hated those policemen, those low dogs in the service of fascism! I wanted to run out of the house and rush blindly into this crowd of people, into this mass of unhappy, innocent people who wanted nothing but *freedom*, nothing but a dry crust of bread. I wanted to run out there and fight.[70]

This kind of experience of acculturated female authors, looking for a way to rid themselves of the Jewish stigma among the international proletariat, was not shared by most authors, even the communists. They were not driven to communism by the crisis of the traditional Jewish world and the deep generational conflict taking place within it but by external factors. Anna Landau-Czajka mentions such factors as widely felt antisemitism, anti-Jewish violence, and the general polarization of political moods in Europe as conducive to polonized young people joining the communists.[71] The same reasons can be found in the autobiographies of both the female authors mentioned here.

The entry into politics of some of the highly acculturated authors who became Zionists was different. Interestingly, this was the only group among the participants in the YIVO competition that changed its environment by joining a political organization. As we saw earlier, most of the young people from traditional homes, rejecting everything that their parents' world represented, went mainly where their peers from similar backgrounds went. Boys and girls from Orthodox, elite homes joined the Orthodox parties. Even the Jewish communists who came from poor backgrounds were mainly among their own people in whatever organization they joined. The communist girls quoted above, who spoke Polish on a daily basis, met comrades from Christian homes in their organizations, for whom, as for Bronka or the anonymous girl writing in Lviv, ethnic origin was not that important. It was different in the case of the Zionists who, with a weak knowledge of Jewish languages or culture, having experienced antisemitic rejection, opted for Jewish nationalism. They joined mainly youth movements with a centrist or moderately left-wing orientation, which attracted rather richer young people, or the radical but more polonized Ha-Shomer ha-Tsa'ir or the far-right Betar. In joining them, they most often had to change their peer environment, which was not easy and could pose many problems.

Zyg. Hor., like the other polonized participants in the YIVO competition introduced previously (Ludwik Stöckel, Prowincjał, and Kitka), was active in the Zionist movement. He grew up in Zakopane, spending his childhood not among Jews but among Polish highlanders. Despite his father's attempts to send him to a heder and later hire a private Hebrew teacher for him, he grew up in an atmosphere of Christian culture. He attended secondary school and started college. He had big ambitions. During his school years, he joined the right-wing Zionist youth group Ha-Shomer ha-Tahor.[72] In his autobiography, he emphasized that he had only the experience of antisemitism and Zionism in common with Jewish society. His cultural reference points were determined by national Polish culture.[73] Zyg. Hor. admitted that in "returning" to the bosom of the Jewish people, he was actually entering a completely new environment:

> At that time, because of my brother's insistent promptings, I joined the said organization. My first impressions at the chats and organizational meetings were not very favorable. I noticed that my peers received me with some apprehension, surprise and reluctance. I understood their position, I knew that it was difficult for them to spend time with such an "apikores" and in a national

organization as well, and in one with which I actually had nothing in common. They knew my exploits in the synagogue when, during the kohanim's blessing, I had caused scenes by turning towards those giving the blessing. Moreover, these lads were mostly a type of unspoiled, simple, playful boy, a healthy, courageous, prudent and strong generation of people, while I was dreadfully alien, weak, cowardly. . . . What could connect these pious boys with me, who celebrated Christmas with a decorated tree, who used highland slang rather than Yiddish?[74]

PARENTS' OBJECTIONS

The vast majority of autobiographers' parents did not have specific political sympathies, or at least their children did not write about them. Even if this was the consequence of older generations' "backwardness," which was undoubtedly exaggerated in the competition works, they certainly saw politics in a completely different way. The authors' parents, who voted in the 1920s in parliamentary, municipal, and local elections, were not a generation of mass political movements that called for membership expressed in everyday commitment and in maximalist aspirations for a comprehensive transformation of the surrounding world. The most radical socialist parties certainly created an especially large gap between Jewish, mostly traditional parents and their children. The latter's activities in Jewish revolutionary parties—Po'alei-Tsiyon-Left and the Bund—were, in addition to communism, understandably most often opposed. For most traditional parents, any relationship between a child and any of these parties was a violation of norms, a denial of the values they sought to pass on to their children. Moshe Kligsberg has rightly described the premises of youth parties and organizations: "The place was the opposite of home. Home represented all the problems faced by young people—poverty, social downgrading and economic decline, outdated tradition. . . . The premises moved young people into the sphere of hope, wider horizons, they represented an ideology that proclaimed positive solutions and gave them a real face."[75]

Since the premises of a youth organization or political party were a repudiation of the traditional world, it is not surprising that very often traditional parents tried not to allow their children to go there. One of the previously quoted participants in the YIVO competition described the brutal reaction of a religious father to the news that the author's older brother had joined the Bund at the age of fifteen. He was severely beaten and thrown out of the house. According to his parents, being active in a socialist party disgraced them. Undoubtedly, this kind of apostasy of one of the family's members exposed it to the ostracism of a large part of the inhabitants of the conservative small town in Volhynia. Later, the author described how his classmates from the seventh grade of elementary school abandoned it to go to the kibbutz for Zionist hakhshara. However, all of them had to return as a result of their parents' robust intervention. Their opposition was the most important daily obstacle to the activities of the local He-Halutz Ha-Tsa'ir cell.[76] Despite his parents' opposition, the author, his brother, and two sisters all rejected the value system transmitted at home and turned to radical politics.

Gamalielis's home situation was very typical. His Orthodox father snatched out of his hands and threw away any Po'alei-Tsiyon-Left publications found at home.[77] It was not appropriate for a future rabbi, a student at the local yeshiva, to read them. The same was true for Yud-Giml. Her father did not accept her work in the Bund: "At home I was not allowed to go to the party offices, which was incompatible with our yikhes."[78] Here too a religious parent was unable to influence the attitude of a child who completely rejected his worldview.

The strongest resistance on the part of Jewish parents was provoked by their children's activities in the communist movement. In the face of his refusal to cease activity in Pioneer (the youth wing of the Communist Party), Kola was thrown out of his home.[79] This happened again when, after his arrest, a short stay in custody, and his release, Kola refused to cease communist activity, despite his father's entreaties.[80] Police harassment also terrified a religious merchant, the father of Ajzyk Rozen. The description of his reaction to the arrest of his elder son, a communist, also bears the hallmarks of the "cowardice" and weakness described in chapter 1, attributed by the young to the older generation: "Meanwhile, the police caught my brother and his companions at subversive work and sent them to the Kielce prison. . . . At home things are not amusing. My father, fearing the searches that were made in houses suspected of communism, burns close to the entire library consisting mostly of sociological works and political pamphlets, but legal. My father knows very well that these works can be safely kept, but this psychosis of fear of arrest that gripped all parents so overwhelmed him that he did something stupid."[81]

Resistance to children joining political organizations was exhibited not just by poor, traditional parents. In some wealthier Orthodox families, parents opposed their children's membership even in Orthodox youth organizations. This was the case in Galitsyaner's home, where his father did not want his son to be active in Bnei Akiva, the youth wing of the Zionist-religious Mizrahi party, fearing that, like secular youth organizations, it could corrupt the lad.[82] Galitsyaner's autobiography is further proof that the social institution of a youth organization was for most parents a novelty that they approached with the greatest distrust. Many, even if they were unable to put it into words, probably felt that the zeitgeist of the 1930s was irrevocably condemning their children to live according to completely different social patterns than those they had passed on at home.

At this stage, one is tempted to make a few generalizing statements regarding the patterns and directions of recruitment of young people by individual political movements. Apart from acculturated authors who turned to Jewish nationalism, most young people who described joining a political party as a "life revolution" did not change their social milieu. Rebelling against their parents, they usually entered the same organizations as their older siblings or peers known from the neighborhood or school. So, they usually encountered people with similar status and cultural capital. What united almost all the authors and the various organizations they represented was the shared generational experience shaping their radical habitus. The latter went beyond particular ideological and tactical divisions. Young people's views were rarely conditioned by domestic political traditions. All this, despite the often-similar social profile of many organizations, at the same time led to fairly high randomness in ending up in any particular one. As often as not, a young person's political initiation was determined by which movement was active in their immediate environment or to which one older friends or siblings belonged. Nevertheless, there were some trends that increased the likelihood of people from specific backgrounds joining certain political movements. Young people from cities and towns doing manual labor were most often accepted into the Bund, which especially in the second half of the 1930s was on the political offensive. The reasons for its success among poor youngsters lay undoubtedly in the party's traditional dislike of the rich and in its rejection of much of the Jewish tradition. At the end of the 1930s, the Bund's decisive attitude toward anti-Jewish violence was equally important (more on this later). At the same time, however, the Bund instilled a love for a new, socialist national tradition based on the modern Yiddish language. Po'alei-Tsiyon-Left affected this group of young people very similarly. If youngsters from this milieu were not admitted into these two parties, they were susceptible to the propaganda of communist organizations. As we have seen, being active in them, at least at the initial stage, did not necessarily mean renouncing Jewish identity. As will be shown later, the frequency of the flow of members between the three parties proves their social and cultural proximity. In the authors coming from the poorest backgrounds, the sense of economic deprivation and discrimination that characterized young people in general, unrequited love for Polish culture, the feeling of antisemitic rejection, and the inability to be a Jew and at the same time a Pole appeared together with the resentment felt toward the Jewish upper classes. The aversion toward them on the part of traditional luftmenschen, artisans, and workers found excellent fodder in contemporary political discourse, mixed with the modern rhetoric of class struggle. The most isolated circles of the Jewish poor were for the first time filled with high individual and collective aspirations, and the youngest among them had nothing to lose. Feeling contempt from all sides, they were the most susceptible to revolutionary messaging. Among this social group, communism competed with other socialist radicalisms more prominently displaying nationalist themes, including the Zionist and revolutionary Po'alei-Tsiyon-Left and the Bund, which hesitated between revolution and social democracy. In the autobiographies one can notice a tendency whereby the greater the young people's Jewish cultural capital, the greater the chance that they ended up not in the KPP but in Jewish parties. The decisive factor, however, was geography. While supporters of the Bund and Po'alei-Tsiyon-Left could be found in the central and eastern provinces of the country (much less often in the south), KPP sympathizers among the autobiographers were recruited mainly from large urban centers in central Poland.[83] In the shtetls in the east, Jewish communists were active in the Communist Party of Western Ukraine and the Communist Party of Western Belarus. However, I have not found any of them among the YIVO autobiographies.

Zionism was not an obvious option for the lowest Jewish social classes, whose children, poorly acquainted with Talmudic and biblical culture, did not have the opportunity to learn Hebrew. Until the interwar period, especially in central Poland and Galicia, this political movement was traditionally supported by the financial and social elites. The fact that among the contestants in the YIVO competition there were Zionists from the poorest backgrounds (although relatively fewer than those from the richer classes) is the result of the evolution of the Zionist movement in the interwar period and the change in its character compared to the earlier period. First, in the 1920s, the so-called general Zionists led by Yitshak Grünbaum, Yehoshua Thon, and Leon Reich became the most popular Jewish party in parliamentary elections. Electoral success, especially among the lower middle class, assured a relentless struggle for the economic, civil, and cultural rights of Jews in Poland. A decade later, when hopes of improving the position of Jews in Poland had generally vanished, the Zionist movement focused mainly on emigration. The end of parliamentary democracy and free elections brought about the collapse of centrist Zionism. At the same time, hakhshara, out of the activities of small groups of idealistic enthusiasts operating mainly in the east, became a mass movement, and its kibbutzim moved to the center of the country. In the 1930s, moderately left-wing

Zionism, centered around the officially nonparty organization He-Halutz, which coordinated hakhshara, as well as youth organizations and parties such as Po'alei-Tsiyon-Right, Frayhayt, Gordonia, Ha-Shomer ha-Tsa'ir, and later Dror, found itself at the high point of its heyday.[84] It is no coincidence that, despite the successes achieved in central Poland, it was still most popular in the east, based on the tradition of local Hebraism, sympathy for Zionism among the local Orthodoxy, and a weaker clash between modernity and tradition. Among the authors from central Poland, there was a large number of left-wing Zionists from small towns rather than big cities. Preparations for emigration consisting in working on the land hardly appealed to the imagination of young people living in these cities—hence, inter alia, the movement's relative weakness in metropolitan centers, such as Warsaw, Łódź, Białystok, Vilna, or Lviv. Among the participants in the YIVO competition, big-city Zionists most often came from completely different social groups than those from Volhynia or the Lithuanian or Belarusian provinces. Like those from Galicia, they belonged mainly to acculturated environments. Their Zionism was of a completely different tone. Very often this was mainly a consequence of an inability to enter the Polish world, a reaction to rejection. This Zionism expressed itself in Polish, and its supporters were most strongly characterized by what I have previously called the symbolic dimension of acculturation. For this reason, the radical right-wing, Zionist Betar was more popular in central Poland than in the east. In addition to young people from poor homes, it attracted a relatively large group of people from rich and at the same time polonized homes. Young people from this environment, like all Jews, felt the hostility of Polish nationalist groups. However, their attitude toward them was not so much hostile as characterized by a mixture of hatred and admiration. Like Polish nationalist young people, Jewish youth from Betar wanted to be disciplined, strong, unified, and prepared. Here we can see some of the reasons why many representatives of this group enthusiastically built up the cult of their leader Ze'ev Jabotinsky.[85]

To join an Orthodox youth movement, one had to continue to be a religious person during adolescence. According to the autobiographies, it was very difficult not to give in to the temptation to abandon the religious lifestyle in one's youth. To avoid doing this, one had to receive a very careful, expensive, elite traditional education lasting for many years, providing cultural and social capital to resist secularizing temptations and feel pride in one's own religiosity, which was possible if one came from a wealthy Orthodox home that understood the social processes at work. There were far fewer such homes than traditional families lost in modernity. Such social demands favoring the religiosity of the youngest generation say a great deal about the strength of the secularizing processes taking place among Jews in the last decade of the interwar period. People from Orthodox circles entered elite Orthodox institutions, building the previously described modern wall and defending them against the negative aspects of modern change. Within these well-defined social spaces, young people were recruited into Orthodox youth organizations. The unique and quite rare social features of this group of authors confirm the findings of historians of Jewish Orthodoxy regarding its place in the interwar Jewish world. In the 1930s, it was in retreat and was able only to limit the effects of but not to counteract the youngest generation's secularization and ideological radicalism.

THE SOCIAL ROLE OF POLITICS

Contrary to what the participants in the YIVO competition wrote, the most important motive for joining political organizations was not in any way to "repair" the surrounding world. Much more important were a political party's multiple social roles and the institutions associated with them. Young people's involvement went far beyond the strictly political sphere. Above all, it created for them a new social space, free from intergenerational conflict and from hard and unsatisfying work. For young people, politics meant, among other things, the only way available to spend their free time among their peers. It was in parties, organizations, and related institutions that young people could realize their personal aspirations. It was there that they supplemented their education and improved themselves, confirming the conviction, strongly expressed in their autobiographies, that they were already among the "new people," different from all previous Jewish generations. Politics also provided young and lost people with an important signpost, an indisputable basis for answering their troubling doubts. The only exceptions were the young Orthodox, although they too saw clear differences between themselves and previous generations of religious Jews.

Gitman N. described himself and his friends joining SKIF as people without any direction in life, lost in the surrounding world. After joining the organization, he stated, "From now on, we will no longer be referred to as a group of young people or a group of rascals, as I have often heard; from now on, they will refer to us as a SKIF group, and each of us will be a 'skifist.' The abbreviation SKIF stands for Socialist Children's Union. We shall be united in it, we shall study, read, write, and be aware young workers. From now on we shall be united, one with the other, with all our comrades, men and women, through one word—fraternity."[86] In his opinion, only in SKIF was there a place and time for "natural" friendship between young people; only this organization gave him the opportunity to forget temporarily about the daily hard work of a tailor's assistant.[87]

For Refleg, an unspecified Zionist organization also represented an escape from a lonely, meaningless life. At the time, he was studying at a public vocational school. He was disappointed with the low level of the classes, the lack of contact with friends, and poor future prospects. He wrote, "I enlisted in the ranks of the organization. I devoted myself to this work passionately. Everyone liked me very much. I became an ardent patriot—a Zionist. Work in the organization. The vision, the zeal to work for the good of the nation . . . all this gave me some relief. Organizational life had a certain charm."[88]

The communist Pioneer was the only place where Kola could escape from his home pathology after graduating from school.[89] Drori wrote about the Częstochowa Frayhayt cell as his "second home, in which my entire social life is situated."[90] Margalit wrote, "The influence of organizational life on me was very beneficial. I started to think seriously and got down to work with a will."[91] In her autobiography she described the decision to abandon the all-Zionist youth organization and join the left-wing Ha-Shomer ha-Tsa'ir as the most important of her life, the consequences of which shaped her character and personality:

> Their lives were eventful, carefree, just like their dance—the "crazy hora."
> But because at the same time it had deep content, it soon drew us, standing
> for some time on the sidelines, into its vortices. I don't know about others, but
> for me the life that soon swept me away caused a complete change of concepts
> and attitudes. My old shyness, the tendency to think deeply and hide my
> thoughts, completely disappeared. I began to live a full life and only now did I
> understand what youth was. At home and at school they did not know to what
> to attribute this change, and they were surprised that this could have hap-
> pened to me. It was also here that I met the first people with whom I became
> really close—for the first time I experienced true friendship.[92]

Later, quick promotion in the ranks of Tarnopol Shomer and a prominent position in the regional leadership were the greatest sources of satisfaction to her.[93]

In Yud-Giml's autobiography, the Bund cell that had just been established in her home shtetl was an institution that "only the intelligentsia in our shtetl" could set up. She considered herself and seventy other young people, graduates of a TsYShO school but unable to realize their dreams of studying in a secondary school, as part of this group.[94] For the same reasons, despite her disappointments in the organization, it was very difficult for her to leave. Being outside a political organization in a small shtetl meant for Yud-Giml" putting herself outside her peer environment.[95]

For young people coming from traditional, very conservative homes, youth organizations were also very often places where they could first encounter the opposite sex. The opportunity created by political movements was all the more important because young people most often entered them during the turbulent period of adolescence. The Communist Union of Polish Youth was the place where Abraham Rotfarb first encountered not only sexual education but also knowledge about this area of life in general.[96] The same was true in the case of A. Remez, who discussed "sexual problems" at Tsukunft meetings.[97] Among his women friends from the political organization, he met his first love. When the couple broke up, the author stated, "These hours are more important to me than all the others. In addition to 'spiritual' pleasures, I meet here with my friends of both sexes, I spend time in the company of girls."[98] Likewise, Hanzi, brought up in an Orthodox home according to restrictive moral rules, first paid attention to boys during her junior high school education, when she was a member of Betar.[99]

In the autobiographies, life space for young people, consisting of culture, entertainment, and social groups, very often overlapped with political space. Youth culture, a category alien to the traditional world, developed in the space that most strongly challenged this traditional world and constituted its antithesis. It seems that it was for this very reason that Yud-Giml, so critical of her first party, the Bund (which had steered her toward the communists), after leaving Zdzięcioł and going to work for a few months in Baranowicze, almost immediately joined the Bund's Morgnshtern there.[100] More important to her than ideology was the opportunity to participate in a peer group, and this was provided by the Bund sports organization. Typical too are Binyomin R.'s memories of the subsequent fortunes of his friends and himself after graduating from a heder metukan. One of his friends went with his rich parents to America, another emigrated as a halutz to Palestine, and two others joined a communist organization. The still nonpartisan author—later he was close to Betar and eventually became a supporter of left-wing Zionism—commented, "I am the only one without a home so far."[101] In his view, finding a "home" meant either emigrating or joining one of the political organizations. Of his initial refusal to join a political organization, he wrote, "Today I regret that I did not join Shomer . . ., I would be physically stronger and more spiritually developed and, most importantly, I would not be wandering alone, but with my close comrades."[102] According to Binyomin R., young Jews at that time had no choice but to go to the communists or to He-Halutz, "because they cannot just sit around while the ground is burning under their feet."[103] The entry of young people into adulthood and the need to achieve rapid economic independence were huge problems for youth movements. The demands of everyday life severely limited the ability of older members, who often had to devote all their attention to economic, professional, and family matters, to work on behalf of the movement. As the autobiographies show, although at this stage of life the authors limited their political involvement, also as adults they sought opportunities to participate in party activities and youth movements. Politics was still the primary factor in the organization of their social lives and their free time after work. From the age of thirteen, throughout the entire period of his education in secondary school, Gershon Pipe's life revolved around Ha-Shomer ha-Tsa'ir. The question that crops up so frequently in other autobiographies—"What next?"—also appeared in this author's after he passed the *matura* qualifying examination, when he was faced with the need to find a job. For this purpose, he left Sanok, and, taking advantage of the connections he had developed as a Shomer activist (he received, among other things, letters of recommendation from the author and well-known Zionist activist Yosef Heftman), he looked for work in Łódź. Activists of the local Shomer cell helped him settle in and naturally became his new friends.[104] For young Jews of the 1930s, politics was an indispensable part of life; it was one its most important, natural aspects, requiring no justification.

Young Jews assessed living conditions in the traditional world as unnatural, artificial, and detached from nature and the world. This was another element of their modernist imagination, drawing categories of assessment and description of surrounding reality from the ideas born at the end of the nineteenth century of the degeneration of European civilization and the Jewish nation. As people detached from nature and became physically weak, traditional Jews were defined by the most important Jewish ideologies—Zionism, the nationalism of the diaspora, or socialism. The influence of these ideas was also reflected in the autobiographies. In addition to the negative assessment of Jewish small towns, ambivalence characterized the attitude of young people toward large cities. On the one hand, the city was a space in which a political new life was possible, and in its factories and workshops the desired productivization of the Jewish people was taking place; on the other hand, metropolitan districts of poverty and hard, poorly paid work were pathologies symbolizing the crisis of capitalist civilization. Criticism of it did not come only from the followers of Marxist ideology. This attitude toward big cities was undoubtedly influenced by the literature young people read, as well as the tradition of youth movements, drawing their attachment to nature and dislike of metropolitan civilization from the traditions of various movements, such as the Russian Narodnaya

Volya, Baden-Powell's British scout movement, or the German Wandervogel tradition, and the fin-de-siècle discourse on the Western world's crisis and degeneration.[105] The influence of these ideas can be seen most often in descriptions of Zionist kibbutzim but also of camps, trips, and outdoor activities organized by non-Zionist groups.[106]

Ha-Shomer ha-Tsa'ir camps, at the end of which Yesh joined the organization, appear in her autobiography as a breakthrough moment—a transition from childhood to adolescence: "At that time, the Stanisławów 'nest' arranged the first camp in a beautiful area in the Carpathians.... Life here was extremely pleasant, completely free, away from the hubbub and city dust, with the addition of various shows, games and excursions. Every day had its own work schedule, its surprises, everything was full of happiness and joy. I would like at least once more in my life to spend my time this happy and so carefree."[107]

The first unforgettable vacations in the autobiography of another author were the He-Halutz camps: "We danced, we sang, we played. At first, one felt ashamed. It was especially new for us to be with girls. I did not know that thirteen- and fourteen-year-old young men could already be real gentlemen behaving in such a relaxed manner. Before, I was always a shy person, staying rather on the sidelines. Talking to a girl was like the end of the world for me, just something unimaginable."[108]

It was in He-Halutz that the author was able for the first time to get rid of his superstitions, shyness, and antisocial attitude, brought from his traditional home. As in many other autobiographies, the camps were supposed to bring young people back to nature, dragging them out of the degenerate world of the shtetl, the Jewish districts of large cities, and the norms and values of the traditional family.

Hailing from a wealthy, bourgeois home, Margalit wrote of the camps as "one of the most beautiful chapters" of her life:

> Now I was free.... Our camp was located in a remote village, lying on a narrow, extremely picturesque river lake. Never in my life had I seen such a beautiful and at the same time wild secluded place, as if untouched by man.... The camp began at 6 o'clock in the morning with reveille. We leapt up and washed in the stream. Then there were gymnastics and Hebrew classes until noon. At noon there was an hour of swimming and lying on the beach on the nearby river, or near a waterfall, lunch in the open, and then quiet time when we read or lay on the grass. In the afternoon another talk up to afternoon tea. In the evening, the whole camp rang with songs, and there was dancing until dinner, evening rollcall and trumpets.... The camp lasted 4 weeks, and by the time we left, all of us young people from different cities and previously quite

unknown to one another, had become so close that we said goodbye to each other with sincere regret.[109]

The camps represented a new world. They were a place where young people could stay in each other's company and participate in the new form of culture, which was youth culture. Camp entertainment allowed young people to mingle and to let out all the energy that had been suppressed by the shackles of tradition, by formalized, most often "foreign" school, or by economic scarcity. Contact with nature was an ideological symbol, another testimony to the revolution that political movements were to implement in the lives of young Jews. Trips, camps, spending time outside the city, a "healthy life"—these were successive antitheses to the world of tradition. The camps were the modern well-run world, building relations with nature in a controlled and rational way as well as shaping daily life. Camp life was filled with political education having the status of the most important form of knowledge about the surrounding world. Organizational training was aimed at the values of the world of tradition and at the same time, something that the young people appreciated, had a Jewish character.

For Drori, too, the camps were a key stage of political socialization, from which he returned as a fully ideologically formed member of the organization. He emphasized that they taught him above all about "life in a collective" and convinced him that a socialist, "collective" organization of society and the economy of the future was possible.[110] Abraham Rotfarb's autobiography suggests that communist youth groups' camps played the same role in young people's lives as did those organized by the Zionists or the Bund.[111] Ben-Tikva wrote the same about Bin camps, Bin being the officially apolitical Jewish scouting organization.[112] Calling the camps "collectives" and presenting them as substitutes for the society of the future were indicators of how firmly rooted were the language and symbolism of radical modernism in young people's consciousness.

The role of political movements in educating young people and in general in providing them with access to culture was very important. Political organizations represented an important alternative to formal education, which—at the postprimary level—was inaccessible to most young people. In this form of upbringing, the boundaries between what was still education and what was already political indoctrination were blurred.[113] Even seemingly purely literary or theatrical cultural activities were subordinated to the ideologies of individual movements. Most authors, especially those who had to give up other forms of schooling very early, clearly show that they very quickly became convinced that their new ideological knowledge was the key to reading the whole world around them. The organizations that provided it allowed young people, at least on a symbolic level, to leave traditional society.[114] Most often, this entailed a complete break with religion and its associated lifestyle. In the case of Aguda or Mizrahi youth groups, it meant leaving a traditional community for an Orthodox community, differing significantly from the former.

In terms of an Orthodox community, Damaszek's autobiography is very interesting. Like the antireligious people of his generation, he sought opportunities for a secular education and new possibilities that the world of the shtetl could not provide him:

> In 1925, a famous orator, the young Rabbi Hirschhorn from Lviv, visited our small town, brought in by the Orthodox faction with a view to establishing the "Agudat Israel" organization.... I signed up for this organization and as an active member did intensive work for the Good of the organization and for the Good of the public.... A rich Hebrew-Jewish library was assembled, filled with numerous valuable masterpieces from Orthodox Hebrew-Jewish literature. Tanakh classes were taught ..., papers and lectures were given, with the aim of familiarizing young people with Old Hebrew literature and educating them strictly in a religious spirit. Our organization was well-known in the city, and so it was possible in a relatively short time to recruit members and win them over to the sacred Torah and ancient tradition.... Our organization published from time to time a local Hebrew-Yiddish newspaper called *Ha-Moreh*, or *The Teacher*, from whose platform I spoke on many matters concerning our organization, and I also published and edited a Polish-language supplement.... I held various offices such as treasurer, secretary and librarian of the organization, most recently board member. Generally speaking, I owe this organization my mental and intellectual development and the entire body of my knowledge of Old Hebrew literature, and thanks to it I have remained a hundred-percent religious Jew, unseduced by the evil currents of the time, and for this I shall always be grateful to it and remain in the future a life member of it.[115]

Damaszek was a representative of the new type of young eastern European Orthodox described above, not rejecting all modern changes in advance but using selected elements from them to defend the Jewish religion, thus giving it new, modernist forms. This author's life was given meaning not by a heder, a yeshiva, or a beit midrash but by a political party and related institutions. The aforementioned Esther, a Bais Yaakov teacher, spoke in very similar terms, criticizing traditional parents' limited horizons. The Zionist religious youth organization Bnei Akiva played a similar role in the life of another Orthodox. The most important element of this youth group's work was education. Imparting modern knowledge to members in an appropriate Orthodox form at the same time strengthened their attachment to religion and religious community. Galitsyaner in his autobiography was convinced that it was Bnei Akiva, the Mizrahi party's youth organization, that had allowed him to resist secularizing temptations and remain a religious Jew. It was there that he could learn Hebrew and Jewish history and read Hebrew books.[116] An Orthodox, religious-nationalist organization allowed him to find a compromise between secular interests and religiousness. Orthodox parties and youth movements had modern institutions in the form of libraries and the press, and they tried to soften the elitism of traditional education by organizing courses and lectures. They were modern organizations but at the same time taught respect for Jewish tradition. Here the similarity between the Aguda or Mizrahi institutions and those founded by secular political movements ended, since secular organizations approached education in entirely different ways.

Abraham Rotfarb saw joining the communist Pioneer organization as an opportunity to learn about society around him, which in his case was impossible outside the organization. Pioneer's library enabled him to read books and newspapers and understand socialist ideas, which in his opinion allowed him finally to understand the world around him.[117] For Greyno, too, the most important aspect of the communist trade union was its educational activity:

> I was drawn into a secret underground group whose task was to set up self-improvement circles for young people. . . . This connected me powerfully to the union that I saw as a place providing cultural and educational opportunities to those who, at a very young age, had been torn from their homes and pushed into stinking workshops. . . . My life entered a new stage. I was proud of the knowledge I was acquiring, of becoming the opposite of a Philistine, who is all preoccupied with his personal life and does not know the historical development of the society to which he belongs.[118]

A similar role in Feygeles's life was played by the materialistic ideology of the Bund: "The ethics of socialism. The abolition of poverty, hunger, suffering. Sacrifice for the victims. That is a great goal. Every day I expanded my knowledge. The world suddenly seemed bigger, but at the same time more accessible. Every day I learned and understood new things. . . . I gained a new faith in a beautiful world. I began to see the individual as part of humanity, of a unified human collective. This was made possible by a thorough acquaintance with materialistic philosophy. . . . Everything began to me to seem brighter and more sun-filled."[119]

The more traditional and secularly uneducated was the home environment, and the more the family shtetl lay far from the educational centers, the greater the role played by local political organizations, which often provided the only educational opportunities.[120] The way in which "knowledge" became "politics" for shtetl youngsters is perfectly shown by the autobiography of M. Schwarzklat. When he graduated from elementary school (and a few heders) at the age of fourteen, he "realized his naivety." The public institution had taught him nothing but "Poland's past" and a knowledge of historical (but not contemporary) literature. Schwarzklat described the essence of his ignorance as a lack of knowledge of contemporary "political and social problems."[121] The way in which he broke through this "ignorance" was typical of other participants in the YIVO competition and most of the ambitious people of his generation who undertook self-improvement. When he went to the yeshiva, being one of the outstanding students, he also became interested in politics, which was to "change his whole life."[122] It all began with the elections to the Sejm in 1928, which resonated with yeshiva students, who spent nights arguing about the words, programs, and goals of Jewish parties and their politicians. Thanks to the 1928 elections and his interest in politics, he and several of his yeshiva friends began to read the secular press. As Schwarzklat wrote, "This fact alone was a revolutionary step, because this activity was strictly forbidden. The yeshiva wanted its students to know nothing about the world. Naivety, ignorance were its highest virtues."[123] Here politics was the core of knowledge about the "outside world." Reading the press, as well as secular, Yiddish, and Hebrew books, led him to a "different life" in the form of socialism. After leaving the yeshiva, he worked as a tutor of Hebrew and Judaism, and the evenings he devoted to reading, having a special liking for "books with a revolutionary message."[124]

Educational activity (exerting ideological influence through mass gatherings, meetings, discussions, and political-consciousness-raising talks during *kestl-ovntn*) was the most important activity of Tsukunft in Maków Mazowiecki.[125] Such ideologically instructive evenings were some of the most important points of the daily activity of youth movements. Another important element was reading, discussing, and explaining articles from the party press to less knowledgeable members. This kind of political education was the most important element in the activities of an author from Horodenka in Podlasie, successively in the local communist organization and later in the Bund.[126] This kind of political education also involved children from the Bund children's organization SKIF, where the Bund children's newspaper *Klayne Folkstsaytung* was read aloud to children.[127] An important element of Gershon Pipe's work in Ha-Shomer ha-Tsa'ir in Sanok was writing articles for the movement's local Hebrew news sheet.[128] Margalit did the same (in one of the Zionist youth organizations in Tarnopol), as did Yesh (a Ha-Shomer ha-Tsa'ir activist in Stanisławów).[129] Education also played a large role in right-wing Betar. Here, too, it had an eminently ideological character. In addition to military training and teaching the young about the Jewish Yishuv in Palestine (about the Halutz movement, the Jewish Legion, economic reconstruction, and military conquest of the future Jewish homeland), the habit of reading the revisionist press and carefully selected national literature was drummed into them. The author of an account on this subject wrote that on party premises he read books about the two greatest Jewish apostates of the early modern era, Shabatai Zvi and Jacob Frank. This reading must have been an important element of nationalist education, since the boy wrote about his great hatred for both "national traitors."[130]

Learning Hebrew played a very important role in the Zionist movements. Gershon Pipe studied at a secondary school in Sanok and at the same time worked in Shomer. He could meet the high intellectual and status requirements of his movement—obtaining a secondary education and an excellent knowledge of Polish and Hebrew—because his parents could afford it. Given the abovementioned costs of postprimary education, the following quote confirms Ha-Shomer ha-Tsa'ir's social elitism: "Since 'Hebraization' was one of Shomer's most important tasks, I enrolled in a Hebrew school."[131] The organization recruited mainly secondary school students. The paradox was that this socialist youth movement, because of its elitist ideology and its recruitment of only well-educated young people into its ranks, rejected many potential members of the "new Jewish people" unable to meet these standards. Learning Hebrew, the language of the "new Jew" building a Jewish homeland in Palestine, was one of the basic tasks of the Zionist movement in the diaspora. This task created specific problems for the movement. The elitist Hebraism of the Zionist movement made it difficult to recruit new followers. This aspect of organizations such as Ha-Shomer ha-Tsa'ir and Gordonia is evident in the autobiographies of Margalit, Gershon Pipe, Ludwik Stöckel, Ben-Tikva, and Garner Borysław. Other examples of this kind of elitism are also given by Ido Bassok. He points out that the desire to obtain "the best human material" often led to extreme selectivity in other Zionist organizations as well, such as the moderately left-wing Gordonia and Frayhayt or the religious Akiva. Even right-wing Betar, which generally appealed to the poorest youth, had its elite cell recruiting only secondary school students.[132] Class and social barriers limited the influx of young people even to He-Halutz—by design a mass movement—and to hakhshara run by it. It aspired to take over most young Jewish people, and in the years of increased emigration to Palestine—1931 to 1934—it was indeed close to doing so.

Specific, ideological knowledge was a key prestige element in all the radical youth organizations cited here. To a large extent, it also determined formal positions in the organization. Demonstrating a real interest in study, A. Remez was sent by the leadership of the youth group to Warsaw for a "course for Tsu-kunft group leaders" to prepare him to become the leader of the local cell in his small town. At the course in Warsaw, young participants were greeted by members of the party central committee. The students visited the editorial offices of Bundist magazines and trade union headquarters and participated in marches and demonstrations, as well as those organized jointly with the Polish Socialist Party (PPS) (including one on the anniversary of the death of the first president of the Polish Republic, Gabriel Narutowicz). Young people were shown Alexander Ford's film *Mir kumen on*, which was popular at the time in left-wing Jewish circles.[133] A very important element of the training was making young people thoroughly familiar with the history of the Bund in Tsarist Russia, as well as imparting as much "organizational knowledge" as possible, which they were to use after returning to their home areas.[134] Chaim Berl, a tailor's assistant from Działoszyn, entered politics because of a desire to acquire knowledge and to supplement his education, interrupted at the age of eight. The author identified the development and intellectual activity of shtetl youth in Działoszyn with political activity. Acquiring knowledge and writing in the local newspaper merged in the author's life with politics. Activity in these related fields greatly increased his prestige among his peers: "I became a regular contributor to the newspaper and wrote various articles for it every week. . . . I began to be recognized in the town as an 'author' and an active Zionist, and people began to look at me as a better person."[135]

FORMS OF POLITICAL ACTIVISM

The scale of educational initiatives undertaken by political organizations is striking. Their ideological character and sometimes even the overtly ideologi-cal worldview of the young people under their influence are further examples of the extreme politicization of Jewish youth culture in the 1930s. It had a specific character. Considering the enormous ideologization of the autobiographies, there were relatively few accounts of strictly political actions, such as attempts at influencing the authorities in order to change reality within the current system. Undoubtedly, the decisive factor was that Poland in the 1930s was an authoritarian country in which free parliamentary elections were not held and in which Jews, like other minorities, did not see many opportunities to exert political influence. Moreover, even before the May 1926 coup d'état and in the first years of Sanacja rule, Jewish parliamentary policy failed. Apart from a short episode, which was the so-called *Ugoda* (Agreement) between Stanisław Grabski's government and the Parliamentary Jewish Caucus in 1925—which achieved nothing in the long term—none of the ruling Polish groups decided on parliamentary cooperation with any of the Jewish political parties. They were isolated in the Sejm and had no chance of implementing their demands. They could only use the parliamentary platform to publicize their ideas. This ended in the 1930s. In the 1935 elections controlled by the government, only four Jewish deputies got into the Sejm, representing areas that were conciliatory toward the Sanacja governments. The same was true three years later, during the final elections.[136]

No wonder, then, that young people did not pay much attention to the Polish parliament. Only a few autobiographies from 1934 make brief mentions of the 1928 and 1930 elections. Apart from them, the only political campaigns mentioned by the participants in the competition were the local elections of 1938 and 1939. Of course, references to them were found only in the works submitted to the final competition. If active politics was mentioned at all, it was most often in the form of descriptions of demonstrations, strikes, or, in the case of the Zionists, public speeches on events in Palestine. The dominance of politics as an ideology, education, rhetoric, or illegal activity, treating the state as an oppressive institution, says a great deal about the conditions and forms of young people's political involvement.

Another aspect of youth involvement in politics seems so obvious that its significance has escaped the attention of scholars. For almost all the authors, Polish political parties (except for the National Democrats, mentioned for their antisemitism) simply did not exist. Even the communists participating in the YIVO competition were usually active in the Jewish cells of their party and wrote little about other communists. The PPS was also mentioned sporadically, but only as a potential electoral ally of the Bund, never as a party to which young Jews could belong. If the Sanacja camp and its Non-Party Bloc for Cooperation with the Government were mentioned, it was mainly in the context of the corrupt Jewish deputies of the latter political grouping. Almost no one wrote about the activity of Jewish politicians at the level of local government. This fact is another element testifying to the alienation of Jewish youth from many basic spheres of civic life of the Second Republic. At the level of young Jews, national Jewish policy in the 1930s was played out in strikes, demonstrations, trade unions, and kibbutzim but not in parliamentary or civic space linking up with different ethnic groups.

I begin with an autobiography that in this regard is unique. The author, a Tsukunft activist, emphasized the involvement of young people in the Bund's electoral campaign during the local elections in Warsaw and Łódź toward the end of 1938.[137] She was pleased that the Bund had joined forces with the PPS at the polls:[138] "The Socialists have become the most important force in Warsaw, they were the majority in Łódź. Or, putting it another way 'Łódź stayed red.'"[139] In almost all the other works analyzed here, we look in vain for the hope expressed by this Tsukunft activist for changes in Poland caused by the democratic political process. In the autobiographies, the awaited change was almost always revolutionary.

In terms of current political issues, young Zionists were mainly interested in events in Palestine. Young people from He-Halutz and Po'alei-Tsiyon-Right in Bielsk Podlaski were particularly engrossed in the case of the murder of Chaim Arlosoroff, which was high-profile in the Zionist movement.[140] Widely accused of the murder, the revisionists organized meetings all over Poland, during which they convinced the Jewish public of their innocence. In this matter, as the author of one of the accounts wrote, "The 'duce' himself, Jabotinsky, came to Bielsk." Young left-wing Zionists used the opportunity to organize an antirevisionist demonstration. They were also actively involved in the elections to the World Zionist Congress that took place shortly afterward. Adults among them bought shekels entitling them to vote.[141] As another participant in the YIVO competition wrote, what stirred young Zionists in Tarnopol were the anti-Jewish incidents in Jerusalem in August 1929.[142]

Orthodox elites reacted ambivalently toward modern, mass politics. According to the ideology of the Da'at Tora, active political activity was the domain of the highest rabbinical authorities; the religious masses were not to get involved with it on a daily basis but to carry out the orders of the rabbis when they were called to do so. In Aguda, the ideology of *shtadlanut* (i.e., great rabbis or specially delegated representatives of the Orthodox elite interceding with local or state authorities) was still in force. This type of politics was, according to secular, national political parties, one of the worst features of the traditional or Orthodox community.[143] In fact, however, eastern European Orthodoxy from the last decades of the nineteenth century, conscious of new threats as well as of the need to participate in democratic political processes, had combined shtadlanut with modern rallying of the Jewish masses supporting them.[144] But toward the end of the nineteenth century and in interwar Poland, this rallying was to have a different character than that used by secular groups. Aguda never sought to create a fully developed political ideology that it would try to instill in its supporters. Boys studying in yeshivas were particularly discouraged from getting involved in politics because it distracted them from studying the Talmud. That is why students in elite yeshivas did not join Tsei'rei Agudat and especially Po'ala Aguda (Aguda Workers), which attracted boys who were manual workers, unable to dream of studying in yeshivas. In the interwar period, Agudat Israel founded youth movements mainly to counteract the influence of secular parties among the poorer traditional young.[145] However, as the autobiographies show, forced by circumstances, Aguda sometimes also called on yeshiva students to take a political stand. One of them wrote,

> The 1928 elections to the Sejm and the Senate were approaching. On the "Jewish Street" there was a fierce electoral struggle between the Zionists and Aguda. Among the yeshiva teachers there were active agudists, and pious parents fully supported its electoral list.... I was pleased that my teachers and my father entrusted me with several technical tasks related to electoral work. As part of these activities, I organized a program of discussion with my friends, who were working for our opponents at the time. I got involved in the electoral struggle with all my energy. I was sure of victory.[146]

However, such involvement on the part of yeshiva students and young members of Aguda in parliamentary elections was an exception. The above-quoted autobiographies of members of Orthodox youth organizations clearly indicate that the most important element of their daily activities was religious education, not current political activity.

For understandable reasons, things were completely different in communist circles. Ido Bassok, on the basis of an analysis of the autobiographies of young people involved in the communist movement, emphasizes a strong imperative to undertake "dangerous" (because illegal and possibly leading to prison) political activities, such as scattering leaflets and spreading party proclamations, distributing illegal literature, participating in demonstrations, and protesting against the nationalist policies of the state discriminating against ethnic minorities.[147] Without a doubt, being a communist was the most dangerous of political choices. The political nature of the organizational involvement of young communists differed significantly from that represented by supporters of Jewish parties. In most autobiographies, the state and its most important institutions were described as hostile to the Jews. For reasons of self-censorship and fear of the police, most of these types of youthful judgments were general statements about pervasive class discrimination and antisemitism. However, while most authors emphasized the injustice and even hostility of the political system toward them, only in the case of the communists was the most important feature of their political activity confrontation with state institutions, which took various forms. One of the most important tasks for Kola, entrusted to him by Pioneer, was communist agitation among the people with whom he worked. The boy was arrested by the *defensywa* (the political police) as early as 1932 during a communist demonstration, the first in which he took part.[148] Arrests, very often mentioned in the autobiographies of young people involved in the activities of revolutionary parties, rarely deterred them from continuing their activities. Police harassment most often only strengthened their attachment to the movement. Greyno wrote, "I was gradually becoming a revolutionary. The authorities persecuted us energetically, we lived under the constant threat of arrests. Many senior members were arrested. We were beaten up by the police and legally received heavy sentences spending years in prison. . . . After each arrest, the number of union members fell. The best and most committed were taken, but soon our activity was renewed with great energy."[149]

Greyno's idols were those among his comrades who did not break after repeated arrests and long sentences, who showed an indomitable attitude in court, and who after leaving prison returned to revolutionary activity with redoubled strength.[150] Jaff Schatz confirms that the leading place in the pantheon of KPP activists was held by people who were killed during battles with the police or received death sentences for killing police informants.[151] In the case of Greyno, his participation in an antiwar rally, his and his comrades' beatings by the police, and his arrest, trial, and imprisonment were the most important, final stage of his political baptism.[152] A similar description can be found in the autobiography of Kola, arrested for participating in a march "in defense of peace." He spent the night in a louse-ridden and crowded cell, beaten and insulted by antisemitic policemen.[153] In the autobiographies of revolutionaries, the state was an institution that was doubly hostile: hostile in class terms and hostile toward the Jews.

Descriptions of steadfast behavior during trials and in prison by communist participants in the YIVO competition were primarily reflections of the ideological desires of young revolutionaries. In their competition works, they simply boasted of behavior consistent with a demanding party ethos. This confirms the existence of norms of political activity and appropriate behavior behind prison walls, too, known from other sources and literature, as well as their enormous role in the final molding of young communists.[154] In the case of authors working in Jewish cells of the Communist Party, it was often in prison that they first established closer relations with non-Jewish comrades. Prison was also a very important area of educational activity, often even called "communist college." They improved their knowledge of Polish, and they learned foreign languages. The most important thing was, of course, to become familiar with Marxist ideology, from the perspective of which classes in social history, the history of revolution, or contemporary economics and social relations were conducted. There were also lectures on subjects such as Polish literature, mathematics, and the theory of evolution, prepared using materials in the prison library and some that were illegal and smuggled in. Formal self-study groups were run by senior party intellectuals who were serving sentences.[155]

Kola described his second arrest, in which his comrades turned out to be police agents. Despite the beatings and insults, he did not betray the location where he kept materials for communist propaganda. Later, he did not break during the interrogations either. He was not persuaded to betray his comrades by a brutal beating or by a proposal of financial reward for becoming a police agent. The same heroic attitude characterized many other communist prisoners in Łukiszki in Vilna, "tortured by the *defensywa*." Kola felt great pride that he too "managed to live up to the ideals of the workers' struggle."[156] An important form of maintaining ideological unity was strike actions taken from time to time by communist prisoners. They were mentioned by Greyno, especially the hunger strike, which was a form of protest against the inhumane treatment of prisoners and which was also described by Kola.[157] All the actions by communists in prison that did not bring tangible benefits or results had one goal, which was the ideological raising of spirits and consolidating attachment to the movement on the part of imprisoned young prisoners. Greyno and his prison comrades quickly established contact with other political prisoners, including non-Jews. The "politicals" regularly passed notes to one another, transmitted news in Morse code, and as much as possible worked on their own self-improvement. An attempt was made in prison to commemorate the fourth anniversary of the death of a Kielce comrade, shot during a prison protest.[158] According to Kola's account, the cells of the Łukiszki penitentiary resounded with tapped Morse code, by means of which prisoners communicated not only on everyday matters but also about the situation in Abyssinia, which was fighting fascist Italy.[159] Despite harassment by the guards, the communists quickly managed to organize educational activities in the prison, which in fact was a form of political work. The more politically advanced prisoners taught others and encouraged them to join the revolutionary movement. Kola worked with a Belarusian fellow prisoner and, like other authors, mentioned non-Jewish comrades for the first time only in the context of prison.[160] Participation in the specific subculture of political prisoners meant that young people often came out of prison as more experienced and determined revolutionaries.

Jewish socialists who did not engage in illegal acts also believed the state and its agents to be simply enemies. Having nothing to do with revolutionary activity, an author who was at the time a He-Halutz activist described how he left his hometown at the age of fifteen. At the station, his older brother, a Bund activist, said goodbye to him. He instructed the author on how to behave in the face of threats lurking for him during his journey. Importantly, young Jews traveling by train attracted the attention of the police. Indeed, as the author wrote, while still at the station, they were stopped by a policeman and interrogated about the purpose of their trip.[161] In this as in many other noncommunist autobiographies, the state was alien or even hostile to young Jews.

All the autobiographers express rebellion, which among the communists was most often manifested in action against government institutions. Other autobiographies confirm another dominant form of reaction, which was retreating into one's own party's subcultural environment. Perhaps the most important feature of the political organizations described here was their creation of a substitute alternative social space, in which young people could forget about immutable political reality, at least for a moment. Zionism certainly provided the most direct form of creating a new reality. During the 1930s, the Zionists more or less abandoned their political involvement in Polish affairs and focused on emigration. Its first stage was the ideological and practical preparation that was hakhshara. Between 1932 and 1935, at the height of the Fifth Aliyah—mass emigration to Palestine—it attracted tens of thousands of young people. In 1935, hakhshara under the auspices of the He-Halutz movement and independent youth organizations brought together eighteen thousand participants in Poland alone, training them in 550 kibbutzim. A similar number was waiting for an opportunity to begin hakhshara.[162] He-Halutz alone had twenty-nine thousand members at that time.[163] Hakhshara pursued two basic goals: one was to prepare young people for manual labor in Palestine; the other was their cultural-ideological education in the form of learning Hebrew, the geography of their new homeland, and the history of the Jews interpreted from the Zionist point of view.[164] Actual hakhshara, in the form of a stay in a kibbutz, usually lasted no more than six months. Later, one had to wait up to several years for an exit certificate. In the 1930s, the purpose of hakhshara and the communes organized within it was to extend this period, in order to keep their members in them as long as possible, so that when they returned home, they would not lose their Zionist zeal in the hurly-burly of everyday affairs.

The heyday of He-Halutz, which coordinated hakhshara, coincided with periods in which there were great opportunities for emigrating to the Middle East. He-Halutz was a cross-party organization. As part of it, members of most Zionist youth movements took classes in farming, communal life, Hebrew, and ideology. They all had autonomy within this broad movement, sometimes organizing hakhshara groups consisting only of their own members. In the 1930s, however, the leaders of He-Halutz were people directly associated with the Mapai party in Palestine (its sister party in Poland was Po'alei-Tsiyon-Right). Their primary goal was to transform He-Halutz into a mass movement and to encourage hundreds of thousands of young Jews to get involved in its activities, regardless of their social origin. At the beginning of the 1930s, at the height of the popularity of emigration to Palestine, young people who were not associated with specific Zionist parties or youth organizations, who were called *stam halutz* (simply halutz), entered He-Halutz en masse. It was possible to join hakhshara at the age of nineteen. To attract large numbers of underage, unaffiliated young people, He-Halutz established its youth group in the form of He-Halutz Ha-Tsa'ir. It was most popular where the Halutz movement itself was strong and at the same time other Zionist parties and youth parties were weaker: in Białystok, Vilna, and Nowogródek provinces. Over time, its increasingly strong influence extended southward, toward Volhynia.[165] Against this background, there were often conflicts between the leadership of He-Halutz and its constituent organizations, such as Gordonia or Ha-Shomer ha-Tsa'ir, which tended to be more elitist.[166] They said that it was the board's fault that the "stam halutsim" or He-Halutz Ha-Tsa'ir were shattering the ideology, discipline, and internal cohesion of the Zionist movement.[167] Testimony to the growing mass appeal and thus weakening of the elitist character of Zionism by the He-Halutz movement was the fact that about 90 percent of its members had only a basic or incomplete elementary education.[168]

The beginning of the 1930s was described by one of the autobiographers as the "golden age" of He-Halutz in Volhynia's Odziatycz. On the occasion of the departure of its first member to Palestine, a grand "banquet" was held.[169] Hakhshara was of a different nature than the other undertakings of Zionist organizations. It provided the best chance of obtaining an emigration exit certificate, since undertaking it was tantamount to a declaration of willingness to leave. Of course, young people most often justified their decision ideologically; they wanted to take part in the construction of a new Jewish society in the ancient homeland. However, it emerges from the autobiographies that the main reasons for trying to leave were more prosaic. They were associated with disappointed hopes of achieving their own life goals in Poland. Margalit, coming from a wealthy Zionist home, was educated from early childhood in a way that assured her an appropriate position among the Hebrew national intelligentsia. Her parents invested heavily in her education in Tarbut (primary and secondary) private schools, at the same time sending her to a primary school and then to a state teachers' college. Eventually, after graduating from high school, having lost hope of taking the social position that her parents had achieved, Margalit was forced to learn a craft, and this fact, it seems, influenced her decision to participate in hakhshara. The author wrote, "At the end of March, my friend also entered *hakhshara*. I also wanted to join He-Halutz, because under the organization's influence I had long since given up the teaching profession and decided to leave for Palestine."[170] Although the author was forced to take up hakhshara and realize her dreams of starting a new, better life in Palestine mainly by her financial situation, her decision was undoubtedly also influenced by her upbringing in the Zionist spirit. Among the autobiographies of young people, however, one can find those in which the decision to leave had nothing to do with the author's political views. An anonymous author from Kolno near Łomża, coming from a large luftmensch family, went to work in a tailor's workshop after graduating from elementary school. Seeing no chance of improving the conditions of her existence in Poland, she tied all her hopes to Palestine. Her elder sister had already followed the path of hakhshara, leaving for the Middle East. Following in her footsteps was the only hope for the eighteen-year-old author.[171] The main nonideological factor for Ben-Tikva entering hakhshara was the long-term inability to find permanent employment in a "productive" trade or profession.[172]

Hakhshara for the most part took the form of communes operating on special farms, designed to imitate the living and working conditions in kibbutzim in Palestine. Descriptions of hakhshara from the 1930s refer to this unique stage as the "great journey." The increase in emigration opportunities in the years 1932–1935 was one of the main reasons for the rapidly growing popularity of Zionism (mainly in its center-left edition, because it was this part of the movement that controlled the distribution of exit certificates). To give hakhshara the status of a mass movement, the kibbutzim implementing it were moved from villages in Volhynia and Polesie to the vicinity of or actually into large cities in the center of the country.[173] The idea of living and working together, cementing the collective, and conducting ideological and educational activities in free time required a reorientation of the economic activity of the kibbutz. In the 1930s, they were not always agricultural settlements but groups of young people living together undertaking casual physical work, often in different places, and sharing their earnings among themselves. One of the flagship collectives was Kibbutz He-Halutz in Grochów near Warsaw. Its center was a farm located there. In 1934, it had thirteen branches and 602 members partially located in Warsaw itself. Some of the people belonging to the collective worked not on the land but in craft workshops and factories in the capital.[174]

Usually held in difficult conditions, hakhshara often became a place of confrontation between lofty ideological notions and the practical side of devoting oneself to the idea of building a new Jewish nation. Margalit wrote about her first hakhshara: "The facility was still setting itself up so almost no one knew anyone else. The apartment was very cramped: a room that was a dining room and a boys' bedroom, a kitchen where the girls slept, and an entry hall."[175] Taking part in hakhshara and deciding to live in a kibbutz commune were often huge challenges. The transition from high-flown Zionist readings and dreams to the harsh reality of a kibbutz must have been a shock. Many Zionists, often secondary school students from wealthier merchant homes, were unaccustomed to these types of conditions. Among them was Margalit, as well as Yesh, a secondary school student and the daughter of a wealthy merchant, describing the shock of encountering the reality of a kibbutz:

> I thought about interrupting my schooling and learning a profession. Soon after, I was quite by chance in a kibbutz and it made a very bad impression on me. The people from the kibbutz were working in a sawmill. When I walked into the huge sawmill, I thought I was going to go deaf. I was terrified at the idea that people could work there. So, life on a kibbutz for various reasons was unlikely to appeal to me. And then something within me that had hitherto been sacred stirred. I stopped believing in the beauty of kibbutz life, forgetting that this was not Palestine.[176]

Hakhshara was also run by groups opposed to left-wing Zionism, such as the revisionists and Mizrahi. Mars, a member of Betar, a revisionist youth group, wrote of his experiences in hakhshara as a denial of the ideals of collective life and work. Its participants quarreled and insulted one other. Their work in the fields was physically exhausting.[177] In the autobiographies there are also accounts of the abovementioned "great journey," during which young halutzim sought employment outside agriculture en masse. Hard physical work in workshops and factories must have often been hell, having nothing to do with ideological images of hakhshara—of a happy, idyllic life and work in the bosom of nature. Margalit wrote, for example, about the hard and poorly paid work of her friends from the kibbutz in the surrounding factories and at tree-felling, as well as about her hard work in the kibbutz kitchen. In the harsh economic reality of the 1930s, there was competition for places in specific kibbutzim. Prepared to work for very low wages, halutzim were also often a thorn in the flesh of both Jewish and non-Jewish workers. When Margalit finally took a job in a factory, in addition to the very difficult conditions, overtime, and very low wages, in her autobiography she emphasized the hostility that she and her friends encountered from the female workers already working in the factory.[178]

Such critical statements about hakhshara appeared in only a minority of submissions. The most common attitude among them was that expressed by Ben-Tikva, who after joining He-Halutz was sent to the most famous Polish kibbutz of this movement, the farm in Grochów. During his stay, there were 180 people there. The conditions in the Grochów kibbutz were something completely new for the author. Enormous sadness and pessimism ran through all the pages of Ben-Tikva's autobiography, and only when the author got to Grochów did its tone change dramatically:

> A large agricultural camp where young Jews change their lives, no longer relying on casual work [*luft parnoses*], but putting it on a productive basis. We live together and sleep together. We live in joy and solidarity. Everyone is part of the collective and together with others is building new foundations. In the kibbutz I experienced this for the first time in my life. . . . My life changed. From an urban worker I became a rural worker. In the city it was different than here in the countryside. I had to get acquainted with pigs, get used to the sun shining on my face all the time.[179]

Later, Ben-Tikva enthusiastically described reveille at daybreak, the joy of communal meals, and the perfect division of tasks in the kibbutz, repeatedly emphasizing the novelty of living in "harmony with nature."[180] Behind what may seem like a comical reference to pigs and behind the entire passage quoted, there is a suggestively expressed belief in an agricultural Zionism that was completely changing the face of the Jewish people. This thread is clearly connected with the previously described issue of a profound change of mentality at the social and political level, as well as changes in the sphere of aesthetics. Contact with nonkosher animals and a sunburned face were some of the most vivid symbols of breaking with the ideal of the religious, "beautiful Jew," a man with a pale face symbolizing detachment from a life in contact with nature and dedication to the study of the Talmud. The popularity of hakhshara was also an expression of fundamental disbelief in the possibility of a legal, evolutionary improvement in the living conditions of Jews in Poland. As Rona Yona writes, "The values of the kibbutz were a repudiation of the Jewish shtetl way of life. . . . The pioneer community was a group with revolutionary potential."[181] Although the kibbutz movement and hakhshara were presented as a new, revolutionary lifestyle, in opposition to the variants offered by non-Zionist political movements, in a social sense they differed little from them. Young people went there mainly for economic reasons, agreeing with the general idea of productivization, and very rarely as a result of deep Zionist beliefs and knowledge of ideology.[182] It was also not new in the sense that it has reproduced inequalities between young men and young women as was the case in the traditional society against which Zionist movement was revolting. Hakhshara, like many other progressive Jewish and non-Jewish political movements of the period, reproduced a great many gender inequities.[183]

The success of the kibbutz movement was a function of the traditional Jewish world's anomie and crisis. Similarly, the formative activity of all the Jewish organizations presented here, which created an alternative, closed subculture, had an inbred character. Belief in action aimed at changing the surrounding reality manifested itself only in antiestablishment activities that challenged the legal and political order of the Second Republic using radical measures, such as strikes or demonstrations. Although Zionist emigration was not directly aimed at this order, it was rooted in the same attitude toward reality. Regardless of its internal diversity, the basic feature of Jewish politics that emerges from the autobiographies was a lack of faith in the value of democratic political action that could change the country and improve the situation of its Jewish citizens. This fact revealed another essential feature of the youth parties and organizations presented here: namely, their impotence in implementing their own demands (until the 1930s, the Zionists also actively fought for the rights of the Jewish population in Poland). It also explains why their activities were dominated by rhetoric and ideological education, carried out in the form of lectures and through books and newspapers, and not by practical political activism.

CONCLUSIONS

Political organizations filled the normative and social void in the lives of young Jews. They created an environment in which young Jews could lead social lives, indulge in play with their peers, and establish their initial male-female contacts. Organized by political groups, camps and youth camps provided the much-needed contact with nature that traditional Jewish life supposedly lacked.[184] Although organizations could not restore lost childhood, they compensated for this with the adolescent life, with which they were often identified. Their activities therefore went far beyond politics. On party premises, the authors could listen to lectures on interesting topics, use the library, and borrow books or newspapers. Moreover, it was in political organizations that young people received a clear and simple explanation of all the complex problems they read about or encountered in their daily lives. In most of the autobiographies, ideology was treated as a specific form of knowledge. Joining a youth party or organization often resembled an act of religious awakening; it was a "conversion," the beginning of a "new life." Thus, most of the authors coming from simple, traditional homes, but not those from Orthodox, acculturated ones or those with nationalist sympathies, emphasized the incompatibility of two worlds: the old one from which they came and the new one that politics gave them. The new one required a completely different political consciousness, a completely different view of their surroundings. A characteristic feature of all the movements mentioned here—from Orthodox to revolutionary—was the fact that they sought to organize young people's whole life, "in its totality."[185]

According to many authors, a new way of assessing and analyzing the world around them could be provided by the broadly understood social sciences: sociology, history, and economics. In fact, they were in touch with a substitute for scholarship in the form of one of the many competing modernist political ideologies. Almost all the works submitted to the YIVO competition had a common core—the ability to describe comprehensively and explain the author's biography and living conditions using the language of politics. A very important feature of this type of knowledge was its absolute clarity and consistency. The world described by young people worked according to one simple mechanism. Gaining ideological knowledge and accepting the party faith was tantamount to renouncing all doubts. This knowledge was not merely contemplative. Its most important function was not to explain the world but to determine the directions of its change. Here, too, there was no room for doubt, focusing on the limitations and ambiguities of a given ideology. A very important feature of the autobiographies is that for many authors, "knowing" meant wholeheartedly believing in the ideology of a given movement. This aspect of knowledge meant that it was not only ideological but also at least partly authoritarian. Political parties and youth organizations, which were its most important carriers, were united by an ambitious, meta-ideological vision of an ideal social order. Ido Bassok has called this aspect of the YIVO participants' consciousness "the pursuit of a theory-based society."[186] In my view, this aspiration had further consequences. It revealed an ideological desire for full control over the modern world and over the present and future of the people inhabiting it. The authoritarianism of young people and the political movements sponsoring them was manifested in the conviction that they had an excellent method of analyzing social mechanisms and a coherent and flawless vision of introducing revolutionary social change. It was also manifested in the desire for purity and order, as emphasized in the excerpts of autobiographies describing the chaos, disorder, and sometimes even "dirt" of the primitive environment or the world of work. This kind of desire is one of the themes most often found in the autobiographies, regardless of the political provenance of the authors, even those who were active in Orthodox organizations. Most young people at some point in their lives had decided to join one of the radical political organizations. This meant that they adopted a radical political habitus, which was also an authoritarian habitus. The authoritarianism of young people can be seen in the descriptions not only of tradition, the world of work, and older generations but also of peer relations. It broke through in their attacks on friends from school or the street, who belonged to other political parties and youth organizations and had other political views. It was revealed too in harsh criticism of the attitudes, which deviated from ideological dogmas, of some of their friends from their own political organizations. It can be seen in the criticism of "philistinism," "empty entertainment," specific patterns of reading, political opponents, or those circles of young people who had not chosen such radical political involvement. The authors did not criticize only those of their peers who lived and thought 100 percent according to the precepts of their parties. Michael Steinlauf draws attention to the attacks of the authors of the YIVO autobiographies on the "frivolity" and "lack of ideology" of their peers who had not joined political organizations, which testifies to the strong ideologization of interwar Jewish youth.[187] Young Jews' imagination, norms, values, and lifestyles broke with those of the previous generations, and their intense political involvement helped them assess the world around them.

EIGHT

POLITICAL CONSCIOUSNESS

THE IDEOLOGIZATION OF JEWISH YOUTH CULTURE

Political organizations played such a large part in their lives that young people applied ideological assumptions to virtually every sphere of private life. Below I cite some evocative examples of how partisanship—and the associated state of consciousness and canon of behavior—affected Jewish youth culture of the 1930s. I have already shown how politics influenced the descriptions of the nonpolitical spheres of young people's lives. Here I reference those fragments of the autobiographies that were intentionally devoted to politics.

Drori was a member of Frayhayt and Po'alei-Tsiyon-Right—left-wing Zionist organizations promoting the halutz ideal of working on the land, preparing for life on or already living in a kibbutz in Palestine. In his autobiography he was clearly trying to justify why, as a person with such views, he had enrolled in a bookkeeping course. He worked in an insurance agency, so learning accounting was important in order to improve his professional qualifications. However, he did not use this argument but another one, writing that "one must know the rules of business" in a society in which "paper and money dominate" and therefore one in which abstract principles ruled and, according to Marxist theory, alienated the working masses.[1] Greyno described his first impressions of work in a Jewish trade union in Kielce, dominated, as his description shows, by the communists. They covered educational activities and an approach to the literature read by young trade unionists. Among these young communists, he learned to judge the books he read not from the perspective of the emotional and intellectual pleasure they gave him but from the point of view of their "socialist content."[2] Extremely ideologized young people often did not shrink from harsh criticism of their peers who could not or did not want to devote all their strength to fighting for a better tomorrow. Many autobiographies contained a meta-ideological demand for devoting all spheres of life to politics. Kola wrote, for example, "But not everyone was like me. There were also those who silently did their work, and after its completion they went to the movies or for a walk. Thanks to my activities in the organization, I knew that they did not understand that the time had now come that could decide tomorrow, whether we would overcome hunger, unemployment, Homelessness and enslavement, or whether we would continue to drown in hardship and pain."[3]

Ideological and para-Marxist categories of social analysis were also used by Binyomin R. to describe his surroundings. Interestingly, although he was an atheist and an activist of the Zionist left, he concealed this from his employers, and at the time of writing his autobiography he was working as a private religious teacher. He described one of the parents of the children he taught as a "petty bourgeois" who had betrayed his former youthful Bundist ideals.[4] Elsewhere in his autobiography, Binyomin R. shows that in his personal dictionary, "petty-bourgeois" was the worst possible epithet he could throw at the "idealless," "philistine," apolitical Jewish young people in his shtetl.[5] Kola was a communist, Binyomin R. a supporter of Po'alei-Tsiyon-Right. Similar categories of description and evaluation of their immediate social environment, including peers and friends from the same organization, can also be found in the works of anticommunist revisionists. They wrote of their dislike and even hatred for the "reds." However, with the rest of the Jewish young people involved, the revisionists shared a dislike of the nonideological petty bourgeoisie and a desire to completely change the world around them. Refleg, criticizing a friend who had turned his back on political activity, remarked,

> Today, a year later, he is a typical petty bourgeois; he is going to get married; when he marries, he will buy himself two beds, a mirror wardrobe and a few more pieces of furniture; when he marries, he will be happy with his wife . . ., I feel sorry for a man as capable as J. . . . The fact that this man does not want to create, work or at least think for anything or for anyone speaks and attests to the degeneration of unfortunately a great number of our young people (and in young Jews' current state, of mental degenerates like J.).[6]

The autobiographers who by virtue of their social origin could have been included in the banal life of gilded youth were hostile toward those leading it. In Margalit's notes, for example, it is clearly visible how dedication to the cause, political commitment, and resignation from the "empty" pastimes of life were powerful social norms among young people, which in their autobiographies required them to condemn young people from their own "bourgeois" environment who did not conform to these norms.[7] At the time of writing his autobiography, "M. Sheynberg," a former yeshiva student, was a communist activist criticizing his native milieu's egoism, narrow horizons, and focus on material values. His role models here were steadfast party activists ready to devote their whole lives to the cause of communism.[8]

Marci Shore, at the end of her work on the dramatic fate of Polish left-wing writers and artists in 1918–1968, wrote about the communist imperative of party self-criticism, noting that in Poland too this was not a product of Stalinist times but had been created earlier, in the interwar period. It must be considered a result of the cult of revolution, which is the negation of all that was and is, in the name of what the future will bring. This was the "kingdom of necessity" that would be introduced by virtue of the iron laws of historical development. In this kind of historiosophy, history has been ruled by the masses. Individuals, their decisions, and finally moral and intellectual autonomy did not count.[9] Shore's conclusions can be successfully applied to most of the authors quoted here, for the most part remote from communism. Although writing an autobiography was undoubtedly an individual action indicating above-average self-awareness and self-reflection, the most important social value of young people was not individualism but on the contrary—far-reaching collectivism. It had the character of absolute fidelity to ideological dictates and political decisions taken in individual parties and youth organizations. Although Shore formulated her thesis on the basis of the specific environment of communist-leaning intellectuals, it can also be applied to other interwar radical circles.

Probably the most vivid examples of the level of ideologization of the participants in the YIVO competition are descriptions of the most personal sphere of their lives: love and intimate contacts. Chaim Berl, who described the object of his disappointed love as a "weekend woman," used an essay by the classic of socialism August Bebel to assess her behavior.[10] Studying at the TsYShO school in Vilna, Kola fell in love for the first time with his teacher, with whom he had passionate arguments about the October Revolution.[11] A few years later, he went into hospital. There he had feelings for a nurse who was taking care of him. This short relationship ended when his beloved announced that she was dating someone else. Trying to understand the reasons for her insincere attitude from the beginning, Kola used ideological knowledge, recognizing the woman's deception as the result of her "petty-bourgeois" mentality.[12]

Knowledge of politics was an important determinant of status among young people. Discussions on this subject were considered by many authors to be the most interesting type of conversation and way of spending free time in general.

Proficiency in the world of ideology, at least at the level of autobiographical declarations, also significantly increased attractiveness in the eyes of the opposite
sex. Refleg, the author of a strongly misogynistic work, looking for arguments
in favor of the intellectual superiority of men over women, wrote, "We never
talked about politics with girls, or about any other issues, or actually about
anything at all. . . . Most of these 'Maidens' did not read newspapers at all, and
if so, only about accidents, suicides, silly romances."[13] In his opinion, the value
of young people was determined by their political consciousness. Margalit
met her first love in a youth movement. Let us note the list that she made of the
young man's qualities:

> The district leader was an intelligent, wise, serious, very experienced man
> well-versed in organizational routine. He was characterized by extraordinary
> energy, idealism, a lust for action and great attachment to the organization in
> which he had worked for many years and which he actually ran entirely. . . .
> There was a complete melding of minds between us. Furthermore, he tried
> to eradicate from me all congenital and acquired defects such as vanity, a
> tendency to pretend. . . . After a few months, I became deeply attached to him
> and sincerely fell in love with him. My feelings were reciprocated and to this
> day we are united by an unbreakable and deep friendship.[14]

Binyomin R. gained great popularity among his peers in his hometown of
Bielsk Podlaski by interrupting a local meeting of revisionists and having a
loud argument with their leader, characterized by ideological insight.[15] Politics was one of the two most important topics of conversation among teenage
boys in his milieu: "Julek led our discussions. He talked either about politics
or about beautiful girls. When he talked about girls, he forgot about politics,
when he talked about politics, he forgot about girls."[16] Gershon Pipe met his
first love in a kibbutz during hakhshara. The couple spent time perfecting their
Hebrew, reading Hebrew books, and discussing topics related to the life of their
organization. The author was impressed above all by the girl's devotion to the
movement and its issues.[17] Evidence of young people's collective spirit, functioning within and in the name of their political organization, is the fact that
when his beloved left Gershon for a shomer from another town, she met with a
sharp reaction, including the condemnation and ostracism of her entire home
cell.[18] The organizational collective often controlled its members' intimate relationships. The author's next love also blossomed and flourished in the youth
organization.[19] When, after graduating from high school, Gershon left Sanok
in search of work and went to Łódź, he met a girl there. He described her using
typical categories: "She was very nice, interesting, because she knew a lot about

the problems of economics and social life. As a factory worker, she had given up all dreams of Palestine and joined the ranks of the revolutionary front, she had become 'red.'"[20] For Gershon, too, one of the most important features of his beloved was her political views and party affiliation. Young people, describing in their autobiographies the criteria of attractiveness of the opposite sex, undoubtedly downplayed the importance of their potential and actual partners' physical characteristics and focused on their spiritual qualities, such as intellect or idealism. It is also important that these qualities manifested themselves mainly through political activity.

Additional proof of how much young people were ruled by an extremely ideologized and intensive type of politics is the autobiography of Zhanet. The author described how, together with a group of her friends from Ha-Shomer ha-Tsa'ir, she organized a special, formal meeting at which she "judged" and then had ostracized her own cousin, who had passed on information about the activities of their organization to a teacher from the Tarbut school where everyone was studying.[21] In a later passage, she described the sharp ideological and political disputes taking place in the shtetl library and the nonpartisan sports circle in which she worked.[22] In describing this situation, Zhanet belonged to a very small group of authors who noticed the destructive aspects of the widespread politicization of Jewish young people. This state of affairs was also noted by the young woman Yesh, who eventually resigned from working for Ha-Shomer ha-Tsa'ir because it "cut off its members too much from the wider world, giving something, but demanding in return the whole 'me.'"[23] This is exactly what the right-wing Zionist Refleg pointed out in his autobiography.[24] He, as well as Zhanet, Yesh, and several other authors, critically analyzed their generation's ideological nature and the totalism of the movements and political organizations to which they belonged. This totalism, regardless of the differences between them, characterized to some extent all the political youth movements and parties that competed for the allegiance of Jewish youth. Most young people were critical of their entire environment except for that small part, participation in which gave them new life. This new life required unwavering faith in one of the political ideologies that proclaimed it. The critical voices quoted here, juxtaposed with those illustrating the ideologization of young people, make it possible to understand the central role of radical ideology and politics in Jewish youth culture of the interwar period.

As in the case of patterns of participation in high culture, so too in the case of the extreme ideologization of youth culture, its importance is best seen in those few autobiographies by authors who were critical of it or noticed it at all. Tor was one of them. Before becoming a critical intellectual, he had experienced a political episode, the nature of which did not differ from those emerging from almost all the autobiographies presented here. After abandoning the yeshiva, he found employment as a weaver in one of the Warsaw factories. Like many unskilled workers, he worked seasonally, averaging five months a year without work. During this period, he joined a Zionist organization. He quickly left it because he realized the consequences of replacing knowledge with ideology, how much party politics suppressed independent thinking (including Tor's literary interests), and how far it interfered with private life and with relations between peers. For these reasons, the author decided to leave the organization and stay away from party politics.[25]

Of course, it cannot be assumed that these most intimate spheres of youth life were full of ideology and politics, but the autobiography excerpts quoted above cannot simply be written off as fabrications dictated by a desire to win an award in the YIVO competition. The fact that so many young people coming from such different places and backgrounds emphasized the importance of political topics in conversations between young people in love, as well as the importance of ideology in assessing the attitudes of their peers, testifies to the existence of a strong social norm, which consisted of being interested in and "doing" politics, treating ideological doctrines with deadly seriousness. Following them gave young people seriousness and gave meaning to their hard lives. Politics was an important element of aspiring to adulthood and, importantly, an adulthood different from that of their parents and one that challenged the world of tradition, which young people rejected. The general view and attitude toward the surrounding world and the radical habitus of young people, contrary to what they wrote, did not facilitate the adoption of an individualistic, critical attitude in life. Difficult conditions, a colorless life, and a radical rejection of them required the search for an alternative social space. In the social and cultural environment in which young Jewish people lived, only radical politics could provide this. This explains why so many authors who professed a belief in individualism, nonconformity, and intellectual self-reliance failed to notice the contradiction between these values and the norms and lifestyles of the political movements to which almost all of them belonged.

POLITICAL CONFLICT WITHIN THE JEWISH WORLD

The 1930s were the apogee of the Polish Jewish community's political fragmentation. Individual party organizations became entangled in endless ideological disputes. The reason for this state of affairs was an inability to influence surrounding reality, which was conducive to ideological and organizational particularisms. This feature of Jewish political culture of the interwar period also had a strong influence on young people. Political disputes and divisions often ran within families. Young people were deadly serious about their political ideologies, which often assumed the status of the highest life truths for them. In the conditions of Jewish political fragmentation, this ideologization of the generation I am describing often pitted its representatives against one other.

Yud-Giml emphasized the need to have a political faith that would give her life direction and, above all, meaning. She found it initially in the Bund and later among the communists; at the same time, she was horrified by the scale of the conflict between individual groups on the left. She wrote with dismay that the pages of the newspapers she read were full of party quarrels.[26] Another author described how in his town two Zionist political organizations, Frayhayt and He-Halutz, competed for the same young people. Both fought for support with the socialist Tsukunft. In this sharp political conflict in a small town, young people who knew each other well were more or less automatically involved, acting against each other according to the ideological lines of their own parties.[27] Gershon Pipe angrily recalled a friend from secondary school, an "informer" who reported to the school authorities on the forbidden political activity of his friends in Ha-Shomer ha-Tsa'ir. As a result of this denunciation, several of them were expelled from school. Behind the cynical attitude of Pipe's friend supposedly lay hidden communist views and thus hostility toward Zionist groups.[28]

An internal conflict in the world Zionist movement, mostly in Poland and Palestine, moved to the streets of small Polish towns and later to the autobiographies. In the autumn of 1932, fights broke out in several towns in Palestine between left-wing members of the largest Jewish trade union Histadrut and revisionists trying to break the monopoly of this organization among the Jewish community in Palestine. The leader of the revisionist movement, Ze'ev Jabotinsky, in November 1932 announced in a *Haynt* article titled "Yo, Brekhn" ("Yes, Burn It Down!") the need to fight the Zionist left's "Bolshevism," even in the face of physical violence.[29] The latter, led by David Ben-Gurion, responded with a similar call to fight "Jewish fascists." The fighting between both sides spilled over from Palestine into the diaspora, including Poland. In October 1934, Ben-Gurion and Jabotinsky, each convincing their followers (including thousands of members of movements in Poland) of the "Bolshevism" or "fascism" of the other side, suddenly proclaimed "peace." This caused consternation among many rank-and-file members in Poland and Palestine. Sometimes it resulted in open rebellion. Brought up in the aggressive rhetoric of conflict and the inability to compromise with "mortal enemies," young people could not understand how sudden agreement with the other side was possible.[30]

Mendl Man, a native of Płońsk, the hometown of David Ben-Gurion (who in fact visited it in 1933, on the day of elections to the World Zionist Congress), described how he and other young members of Po'alei-Tsiyon-Left took to the streets, protesting Ben-Gurion's and Jabotinsky's "joint plotting." He expressed his anger at the "left-wing schemers" (Ben Gurion and Po'alei-Tsiyon-Right) first preaching struggle against the revisionists and now colluding with them and preying on the "ignorant" Jewish masses. On November 7, 1934, the writer and his party convened a mass meeting in Płońsk to condemn such actions. Po'alei-Tsiyon-Right was accused of building a common front with Jabotinsky and his "fascists." Mendl rejoiced because it was finally possible to show the false "idealism" of the moderate Zionist left. Now it was his party that was to become the only option for Jewish workers. He concluded his speech at the Po'alei-Tsiyon-Left mass meeting expressing satisfaction at this turn of events.[31] Mendl Man's autobiography and subsequent ones, cited below, are evidence of fundamental features of Jewish (and general) political culture of the 1930s. These were an ideological lack of readiness to compromise, constant conflict, and rhetorical and sometimes also physical aggression. Tactical volte-faces, negotiations, and changes in window-dressing at the top influenced rank-and-file members of political parties and organizations much less than did general extremely ideologized discourse, marked by aggression and conflict.

The autobiography of Binyomin R., who was exceptionally well read compared to other authors and proficient in the ideological twists of Jewish politics, provides testimony to how strongly Jewish young people were involved in internal political conflicts in Bielsk Podlaski in the 1930s.[32] The notes of this autobiographer, a sympathizer of Po'alei-Tsiyon-Right, covered the same political conflict on which the abovementioned Mendl Man took a position. Binyomin R, unlike Man, was a follower of David Ben-Gurion. The writer's short autobiography was accompanied by an extensive diary, recounting his experiences from several spring and summer months of 1934:

> Yesterday there was a revisionist meeting. . . . I'd already heard a few revisionist lectures, but I've never heard such lies, such demagoguery, nothing like it. But what made me most angry was that I didn't dare to interrupt him! It was a small hall, the few halutzim there did not decide to interrupt the speech. I made a decision then. From now on, I would go to revisionist readings and interrupt them! . . . In our town, there is more talk about disruptions than about the lectures themselves. In this way, each lecture became something like a soccer match, and disruptions were goals.[33]

The writer did not hesitate to write about his close friend, the leader of the local Betar cell, as he "who played the role of Goering [sic] in his organization and Goebels [*sic*] in another";[34] he called another revisionist "a Nazi,"[35] and the right-wing Zionist daily *Hazit ha-Am* was supposed to be a carbon copy of the Nazi "*Voelkisher* [*sic*] *Beobachter.*"[36] Binyomin R., as a sympathizer of He-Halutz and Po'alei-Tsiyon-Right with the same commitment as the hated revisionists, also attacked movements located to the left of his political sympathies: the communists or Po'alei-Tsiyon-Left.[37]

The intra-Jewish political struggle on the streets of cities and small towns had a sharp, sometimes brutal and physically violent character. The young people participating in it were often friends from the same backyards, heders, beit midrashes, or elementary schools.[38] Binyomin R. described attacks by young left-wingers on shops belonging to revisionists and fights that took place between them and left-wing halutzim.[39] There was also a brawl in the Bielsk Podlaski synagogue on Yom Kippur, the most important Jewish holiday. It was triggered by the display of a tin in the synagogue in which donations were collected for the revisionist Keren Tel Hai fund, which provoked the rage of both left-wing Zionists and the faithful.[40] A similar mutual hatred held by young Jews who were associated with competing political organizations was described by the Bundist Yudl. In his short sixteen-year life, he had come a long ideological way from the radical right-wing Betar to a left-wing, anti-Zionist socialist party. Writing his autobiography as a Bundist, this "true proletarian" attacked his former youth group without mincing his words: "They talked about nothing but gold buttons and brown uniforms—Hitler's colors. It wasn't for me. I learned how immoral their leaders were. They were nothing more than swindlers, criminals, blackmailers, Jewish Hitlers, Jewish fascists! I left."[41] The heated political disagreements between Jewish students did not bypass the schools either. In the 1930s, sharp internal Jewish political disputes moved to the Jewish Street and were part of the everyday experience of young people growing up at that time.

POLITICAL MOBILITY AND RADICAL HABITUS: WHY DID YOUNG PEOPLE CHANGE THEIR ORGANIZATIONAL AFFILIATION SO OFTEN?

It seems paradoxical that the same young people who were so strongly involved in the sharp conflicts between individual Jewish political organizations very often changed their organizational affiliation. Young people who left one party or youth movement and joined another opted for the one that they had hitherto bitterly opposed almost as often as for an ideologically related one. Certainly, frequent changes in party and organizational affiliation were influenced by the general political situation. Among young Jews in the first half of the 1930s,

Zionism dominated, which was facilitated by the relatively broad possibilities of emigration to the Land of Israel. These began to shrink rapidly after Hitler came to power in Germany in 1933, when priority was given to German Jews to emigrate to Palestine. The change in the economic situation, riots and later the civil war in Palestine, the limits on immigration quotas in 1936, the dissolution of the Polish Communist Party in 1938—all these events were to strengthen the anti-Zionist Bund, which experienced the peak of its popularity at the end of the 1930s. In the years 1936 and 1938–1939, the Bund enjoyed hitherto unprecedented success in elections to the boards of local Jewish communities, as well as to the local governments of the most important Polish cities and many small towns.[42] Faced with the impossibility of leaving the country, many Jews began massively to support the party most loudly opposed to antisemitism and discrimination. Likewise, in the communist movement, increases and decreases in the number of its Jewish members followed each other in waves and depended on the complex political situation. Many Jews joined the movement between 1921 and 1923, along with dissenters coming from Po'alei-Tsiyon-Left, the Bund, and Fareynikte. The next stages of the increase in the popularity of the KPP, KPZU, and KPZB among Jews were the years 1926–1928 and the beginning of the 1930s.[43] Nathan Bistricki, visiting Poland at the turn of the 1920s and 1930s when the British were limiting the possibility of emigration to Palestine, and observing young Jews, emphasized their susceptibility to changes in the political situation and thus their political mobility.[44] Such situations occurred during all the Zionist crises caused by restrictions on emigration to Palestine. During one of them in 1926, it was discovered that the leaders of the then-flagship kibbutz in Poland, in Kłosów in Volhynia, had changed their political sympathies and had begun to work for the Communist Party.[45] For Nachum Sokolov, visiting Poland in 1933, Jewish politics resembled the Talmudic commentary of Rambam with its confusion and sophistry of ideological disputes. The historian Ezra Mendelsohn has confirmed his observation: "It does, in fact, require something of a Talmudic mind to understand the differences between Left Po'alei-Tsiyon and Right Po'alei-Zion in Eastern Galicia, Right Po'alei-Tsiyon in Congress Poland, Zeirei Zion, Hitahdut, and Dror (all these parties belonged to the Zionist Left)."[46]

This kind of circularity of ideological disputes, often incomprehensible to outside observers, concealed significant similarities between the political opponents fighting one another. I would supplement the opportunistic reasons for the Jewish mobility in the 1930s, mentioned here in the professional literature, with one important factor: the state of political consciousness among the youngest generation, which changed party affiliations most often. For an analysis of this political consciousness, the often very subtle ideological differences between individual political movements are of little use. What is crucial, however, is a certain general worldview, an ideological basis, social norms, and lifestyles in force in party organizations, generating a specific type of social and political consciousness. More than half of the autobiographers discussed here changed their political sympathies at least once in their lives, often radically—for example, by starting in the communist Pioneer organization and ending up in the right-wing Betar movement. Evidence of how the migration of members between such distant groups was possible can be found in certain elements of their ideologies, functioning beyond detailed ideological divisions. Here I analyze just a few of the most characteristic examples.

As we have seen, elements of socialist ideology (or, more broadly, modern collectivism) penetrated even into decidedly nonsocialist Jewish political movements, which was expressed by their young members submitting their autobiographies to the YIVO competition. One can add a remark about the phenomenon of Orthodox youth organizations, which in matters of labor relations, the ideal economic system, and the desired Jewish economic structure in the 1930s clashed sharply with their parent parties. Since the early 1920s, youth groups of religious and conservative Mizrahi had often been in more or less open opposition to their parent grouping, pushing for productivization; the situation was similar in He-Halutz. Unlike the parties for adults, bringing together many rabbis and yeshiva graduates, these organizations preached the need for their members to participate in hakhshara. This was organized by the Torah and Labor movement (Tora ve-Avoda) bringing together religious participants in hakhshara preparing to leave for Palestine.[47] Officially, they were renouncing the socialist idea. Members' spiritual training took place as part of the study of the Torah and reading it in a new way, proclaiming the productivization and rebirth of the Jewish people in the Promised Land. However, both this movement and organizations such as Ha-Shomer ha-Dati, Bnei Akiva, and Ceirei Mizrahi proclaimed the ideas of connecting young people with nature and building a physically and spiritually healthy and productive society. Their ideology was deeply egalitarian and collectivist.[48] Founded in 1922 by young Orthodox activists, the Po'alei Aguda organization spoke directly about the need to value physical labor in Orthodox circles and to fight for "social justice" in accordance with the laws of the Torah.[49] The autobiographies of young Aguda members repeatedly proved that they were very firmly detached from the older generation by the experience of growing up in modern, modernist discourse, proclaiming the necessity of "organization," a modern transformation of "anarchism," and adaptation to modern living conditions.[50] The generational chasm between the supporters of Aguda was also pointed out in one of the reports of the interwar Polish Ministry of Internal Affairs, describing the friction between the movement and its workers' and youth organizations, and its genesis was identified as follows: "Orthodox young people . . . were becoming radicalized by striving to assimilate secular and cultural forms in normal social life."[51] The theme of generational difference—that is, the pressure of the modernist worldview on young Orthodox—appeared in their criticism of traditional heders, in a positive attitude toward the reformed ones, and in the condemnation of the older generation's "mercantile mentality." Despite Aguda, members of its youth organizations sympathized with the idea of agricultural productivization in Palestine and, not being Zionists, were certainly not as unequivocally anti-Zionist as most Orthodox rabbis, and they called for the need to cooperate with the movement. In the 1930s, many members of this organization took part in hakhshara, thanks to which they obtained emigration certificates. In 1937, the Polish organizations Tse'irei and Po'alei Aguda forced the World Congress of Aguda in Mariánské Lázně, Czechoslovakia, to recognize their cooperation with the world Zionist movement, aimed at increasing the chances for young Orthodox to emigrate to Palestine.[52] Aguda's youth activists proclaimed that their "Torah socialism" was the opposite of "Marx's socialism." An analysis of their publications shows that the gap between the two socialisms is exceedingly problematic. An article in the Aguda Workers' central mouthpiece, *Yidisher Arbeter Shtime*, referring in April 1937 to the cooperation established by the world organization of Aguda with the Zionist movement, stated, "Young and healthy, full of hope and ready for heavy sacrifice, we shall unite all the authentic youthful forces of the world Aguda movement in the 'League on behalf of a Religious Land of Israel for Workers.' . . . Young Halutz 'agudism' will unite the Aguda camp in the Land of Israel into a single disciplined organization. The young people of Aguda will carry out their sacred task of establishing agricultural kibbutzim and cooperatives."[53]

In addition to the "domination of the Torah in private life and in the life of the collective," the overriding values of the young Orthodox were "the sanctity of labor" and "social justice."[54] Even before the Marienbad conference, the ideology of Palestinism—the Jewish national and religious revival in Palestine—and the idea of changing the Jewish class structure were present in the statements of young Aguda activists. For Hillel Seidman, "building one's own life in the Land of Israel," "in the struggle against enemies and various obstacles," was one of the most important innovations in the lives of Orthodox Jews.[55] Threads of harsh criticism of capitalism, collectivism, and the productivization of Orthodox society, called "Torah socialism," at the same time rejecting

Marxism—although it undoubtedly influenced their way of analyzing social reality—appeared in many other publications by people from the Aguda youth movements.[56] The influence of the socialist idea on Orthodox youth circles was also manifested in the Arkadi Grupe, founded in 1936, an organization bringing together young, religious sympathizers of the socialist Bund.[57]

The influence of certain socialist ideas was present in even the most anticommunist of Jewish political movements, which were undoubtedly revisionism and its youth wing Betar. Ze'ev Jabotinsky wrote in *Ideologia Bejtaru* (The ideology of Betar), published in Polish in 1935, that the class struggle was one of the most important social phenomena governing the world. The task of the Zionists who wanted to save Jews scattered all over the world was simply to temporarily suppress it, especially in Palestine. "National economic arbitrage," slated to start there, would stop intra-Jewish class struggles and allow a new Jewish nation to be built. Jabotinsky adopted the general principles of the Marxist analysis of capitalist reality. He accused contemporary socialists, especially the Jewish ones, of misunderstanding Marxism and exposing the remaining Jewish masses in Europe to physical destruction or "assimilation."[58] Likewise, another important revisionist activist active in Poland, Józef Margolin, used Marxist categories in his analyses of social reality and his criticism of the Jewish socialist movement. He agreed with the Bund and even the communists about the necessity of productivizing the Jewish people. He considered the changes in social structure in the USSR to be very positive. He simply alleged that the productivization carried out in Europe, on a foreign land, would lead the Jewish people to inevitable and complete assimilation. Therefore, the only chance was productivization carried out by one's own efforts and in one's own homeland.[59] The Jewish right and left were united by radical collectivism, visible in all the sources cited here. Another common element was certainly a belief in the collapse of capitalism in its liberal form created in the second half of the nineteenth century and the need to replace it with new forms of sociopolitical organization. This was possible only through a radical transformation of societies. These common elements made up the specific total ideology of the period, here called radical modernism. It stood above the programmatic and local differences between individual political movements. This is clearly seen in the autobiographies, which are full of symbols drawn from the ideologies of political movements, often in sharp disagreement with one other. At the level of young Jews' political consciousness, the general ideology of radical modernism showed itself to be at the disposal of a kind of political attitude—that is, in a radical habitus.

Binyomin R., in addition to taking part in the second YIVO competition in 1934, a year later sent Max Weinreich his "thoughts and remarks" on the subject of *Der veg tsum unzer yugent*—Weinreich's book about Jewish youth. In them, he wrote about Jewish young people who, in their short lives, could pass through the most hostile political organizations. Of the communists, whom he hated, he noted that "they come from all our movements, from the Bund, He-Halutz, Betar and Aguda."[60] Kitka began his career in the centrist youth organization Ha-No'ar ha-Ivri (Hebrew Youth); later, in 1931, answering its leaders' summons, he joined the unifying organization Ha-No'ar ha-Tsiyoni (Zionist Youth). When two years later the separatists of the revisionist organization founded their own youth movement, Brit ha-Kanaim (the Canaanite Association), he joined it at the urging of his older brother. After the dissolution of its local group in 1937, the Drohobycz activists returned to Ha-No'ar ha-Tsiyoni.[61] In this author's case, the change of political affiliation took place within the same milieu and between ideologically close organizations. However, these political odysseys often had a much greater reach, as confirmed by many autobiographers. Ajzyk Rozen's autobiography shows the role played by both political circumstance and the common radical core of political consciousness on the part of the majority of youth, which greatly facilitated their change of political colors. His family environment—his political sympathies and religious but modern lifestyle—predisposed the author to join the Zionist movement. The first organization to which he belonged was Brit Ha-Shomer, in which his older brother was already active. As a person coming from a modern, religious, and partly acculturated home (he wrote his autobiography in Polish), he felt strongly the antisemitism he experienced while attending elementary school. He left it with great resentment, not only toward antisemites but also toward the state, which seemed to favor anti-Jewish activities. Perhaps Ajzyk's fate would have been different had it not been for the political situation, specifically the crisis in the Zionist camp after the 1929 riots in Palestine and the temporary cap on Jewish emigration. During this time, his older brother, for health reasons, could not take advantage of the certificate granted to him by his organization allowing him to go to Palestine. He broke down, left Brit Ha-Shomer, and, as Ajzyk wrote, "under[went] a spiritual evolution and join[ed] a far-left party, becoming an active member."[62] In a short time, Ajzyk's brother transformed himself from a moderate Zionist into a declared communist. Meanwhile, Ajzyk's eldest brother, "who was also a member of a Zionist organization, under some still inexplicable influence, becomes a backward cleric, wears a Jewish cap, a frock coat and becomes a fanatical supporter of Hasidism from Góra Kalwaria . . ., under the influence of some higher power, young people with atheistic views turn back to the religion of their ancestors. Imagine the astonishment of the Hasidim when, after a very short time, all of us, with my brother in the lead, renounce the religious life and put on old spiritual robes?"[63]

These excerpts reveal the already well-known insecurity of young people and the search for radical political solutions to overcome it. Ger Hasidism and its partial party emanation "agudism" turned out to be only a short-lived episode, and it was not able to contain for long secularizing young people coming from religious homes who were looking for holistic solutions to change the world around them:

> Father and my ex-Hasid brother are getting down to intense and positive work in the business. The former Hasid is an excellent trader, he travels to obtain goods and sells them so favorably that father has a lot of use for him; the opposite is the case with my brother who wanted to go to Palestine. When mother died, he felt a release and began to work seriously for a far-left party, becoming its most prominent member. He boldly organizes illegal rallies and organizes Pioneer and is dragging me in. Father's threats that he will throw him out of the house, or that if he goes to prison, he'll show no interest in him, produce nothing; he just cheekily carries on. At first my brother's ideals impress me, they are dangerous and conspiratorial, so I join the party not out of political conviction, but because I am attracted to its secrecy and danger. My political convictions had tendencies that were very close to the idea of the liberation of Palestine, but my brother knew this very well and it is not enough for him that I am a pioneer in a far-left party . . . he takes me on to make me aware and acquaint me with the scientific works of the most famous sociologists, and so together we work through: Karl Marx, Bukharin, Runow and others; I won't say that I understood these works well despite his tireless efforts, that is my brother's beside me, and despite the fact that I read so much. He is systematically becoming an enlightened member of the party. But despite my materialistic understanding of the history and life, I cannot put the idea of the liberation of Palestine fully out of my mind.[64]

In the above excerpt, it is clear that it was not political views but the social proximity of various organizations and certain meta-ideological elements of youth political consciousness and culture that were the main factors determining the involvement of young people in the activities of a given movement. This also explains the ideological syncretism so often present in many autobiographies, in which some of the authors' detailed views conflict with their movements' programs. Ajzyk Rozen, explaining at length the reasons for his "final disillusionment" with Zionism, at the same time constantly expressed admiration for the idea and for the young people devoting themselves to it.[65]

Like many of the authors presented here, not being a high-ranking activist or ideologue who spent his days studying political writings, he did not think according to the standard ideological line of his own movement. His radical habitus allowed him to feel sympathy for all ideologies proclaiming demands for a far-reaching reconstruction of the surrounding world. This type of unorthodoxy can be seen not only in the author's views but also in his attitudes. Being a communist did not prevent him from joining the Zionist sports organization Ha-Koakh (Strength), where members engaged in soccer, athletics, or chess and passionately immersed themselves in political disputes.[66] Ajzyk Rozen, in addition to having sympathies for the Zionist movement despite being a member of the communist Pioneer, also chose not to embrace his organization's atheism, constantly declaring faith in God and disagreeing with the idea that religion is simply "the opium of the masses."[67] In his case, as in the cases of a great many other authors, a kind of ideological intensity in the form of a general radical habitus did not mean full ideological orthodoxy, but it also did not exclude a change of party affiliation.

Similar examples are to be found in many other autobiographies. Ludwik Stöckel was encouraged for the first time to join a Zionist organization, the Marxist Ha-Shomer ha-Tsa'ir, by one of his closest secondary school friends. Sometime later, the same friend was one of the founders of the local cell of far-right Betar.[68] The whole autobiography of Chaim Berl from Działoszyn is also a politico-ideological odyssey. His first organization was the right-wing Zionist Ha-Shomer ha-Le'umi. Soon afterward, a new friend drew him into a discussion about the impossibility of reconciling Zionism with socialism and the chances of the former solving the "Jewish problem." Chaim discovered that "the only way is socialism." He broke with his Zionist friends and was "born again." He wrote, "Yes, I saw a new light above my horizon, I found new paths, paths different from everything else, and I chose my path. . . . The path of socialism, the path of social revolution, the path of Leninism . . . I left the Zionist organization, thanking them for their cooperation."[69] Chaim changed his political affiliation, moving between such ideologically distant movements as the right-wing Zionist scout movement and the Communist Party. Although the author did not admit it, this ease, at least in part, was the result of having a rather superficial knowledge of both movements' ideologies. It could not have been deeper in the case of a self-taught man who had interrupted his formal education at the age of eight and had worked in a tailor's workshop from the age of eleven. What seemed to be the most important for Chaim Berl and many people like him was the radicalism of both movements, their opposition to both the world of traditional parents and the one represented by the sociopolitical system of the Second Republic. After he moved to the communist Pioneer, his new life was focused on underground work and police raids.[70] After he was expelled from the KPP, finding a political organization that was a source of knowledge and hope, a peer environment, and a place to spend his free time was an imperative for him. A former Zionist, then a communist, he joined the Bund despite the ideological chasm and hostility dividing these political camps.

Binyomin R., fragments of whose autobiography, filled with hatred toward revisionists and "reds," are quoted above, was a revisionist before he became a devoted supporter of Po'alei-Tsiyon-Right and He-Halutz. His autobiography, in addition to descriptions of sharp ideological and sometimes even physical confrontation, is full of testimonies of discussions and even friendship between representatives of hostile camps. He was friends with revisionists and communists with whom he had grown up in the same backyard. Binyomin R. attended revisionist meetings (not always trying to disrupt them) and listened to the debates of communists and Trotskyists, some of whom belonged to the circle of his closest acquaintances.[71] He also read the daily press, pamphlets, and books by the anti-Zionist revolutionary left and had ideological disputes with friends belonging to opposing camps.[72] Binyomin R.'s notes show two interesting phenomena. On the one hand, the social, companionable, and cultural proximity of the parties involved in shtetl political conflict made it particularly sharp. On the other hand, the fact that activists of such different political organizations came from the same social space made it very easy for young people to change their political affiliation. A specific political ideology determined this to a much lesser extent than the political situation, social and family connections, which organization was operating in a given city or district, and finally the general radical worldview of young people. It is worth looking in this context at two other excerpts from Binyomin R.'s autobiography:

> During my last month in Bielsk, I came to the Betar offices. How did I get there? The story is as follows: during the holidays Julek Neumark, Yeruham Hering and Schmulke Bulowski came to Bielsk.[73] Julek had been expelled from Ha-Shomer ha-Tsa'ir due to personal conflicts, and in Białystok he had joined Ha-Shomer ha-Le'umi. After spending a short time there, he abandoned it for Betar. Revisionism attracted him more than general Zionism. My neighbor Yeruham Hering had previously studied at the "Tahkemoni" Warsaw seminary. There he became a Tse'irei Mizrahi activist. However, he was cunning and did not want to become a rabbi. Before graduating, he left school and enrolled in a Polish-Jewish secondary school and became a revisionist. The third one, Schmul Bulowski, had already graduated from a Polish secondary school and was already thinking about going to college. The three of them started working and founded Betar.[74]

Young people from different camps were united by political radicalism, which, however, cannot be put in terms of a specific, strictly structured ideology. In this regard, Binyomin R., who was well versed in politics and ideology, was an exception. Especially in small Jewish towns, there was a lack of family and local political traditions among their traditional inhabitants. Few autobiographers wrote something about their parents' political views. For this reason, the political situation was no less important than young people's peer contacts or their general ideological radicalism. Once again, Binyomin R.'s" autobiography provides a perfect example:

> At that time, people from all sides began to storm the ranks of He-Halutz. In the winter of 1933, Tsukunft was disbanded, and its members ran to He-Halutz or to the "reds." One of the "reds" had already become a halutz. It was my old friend Schmulik Bergman. After completing his studies . . . he became a barber and a member of Frayhayt. After spending some time there, he went crazy and joined the Bund. He did not stay in the Bund for long and became a Communist Party activist. He would have stayed in the Communist Party had it not been for his difficult financial situation. He had no other option left but to emigrate, and for this reason he was ready to join even Betar. . . . Eventually, people took pity on him, and he was admitted to He-Halutz.[75]

All the abovementioned threads of the social intimacy of supporters of hostile Jewish political groups, as well as the ideological and nonideological reasons for the relative ease of changing party affiliation, also appear in the autobiography of A. Remez. When he was ten, friends from his poor, traditional, artisanal environment drew him into SKIF—the children's organization of the socialist Bund. A year later, greatly impressed by the military image of right-wing Betar (the organization probably most hated by the Bund and described by its members as "fascist"), he joined that organization. He did this despite sniping from his own left-wing milieu. While in Betar, the boy also had many friends who were members of the communist Pioneer. He spent a great deal of time with them, listening to stories about their activities, including the illegal demonstrations in which they took part. The young Betar member and his communist pals spent hours discussing ways of creating a new, better world. What brought the Jewish representatives of various political camps closer together was not only the general, radical perspective of looking at surrounding reality but also the social intimacy of a small town. Remez described himself as the only boy in the local Betar who was not mad about soccer. There was a "workers' sports club" (probably run unofficially by the communists) in the town, which, as the author wrote, caused many Zionist soccer fans to abandon

Betar and join the left-wing camp out of a passion for sports. As is often the case in the YIVO autobiographies, the author of this competition work presented himself as a unique person in his milieu. He also eventually left Betar and joined the communist Pioneer, but in his case this happened supposedly as a result of thoughtful ideological studies and social observation, the result of a conscious, personal decision. Although the author described his changes of interest and political affiliation in terms of ideological reflection, his work also shows how nonideological factors—namely, socioeconomic circumstances— played an important part in this. When Remez was active in Pioneer in 1933, he complained that it was a time of economic crisis and the Fifth Aliya (1931–1935), when Zionist organizations were relatively easily obtaining certificates from the British mandate authorities to leave for Palestine. As a result of this situation, young people from the non-Zionist left were meant to go over en masse to the Zionists. The author himself, a few pages earlier describing his dreams of taking part in the military conquest of Palestine, now recalled how much he hated the Zionists and what they were doing in the Middle East. Eventually, he ended up in the Bund. At the time of writing his autobiography, while working as a carpenter, he was also chairman of the local branch of Tsukunft in his native Horodenka. He did not describe exactly how he switched from communism to Jewish socialism, so we can only surmise that most likely Pioneer shut down its operation in Horodenka. Remez, together with a group of friends with communist views, worked as part of a self-improvement group, reading revolutionary literature and then discussing it. According to his autobiography, the young people lived to see the moment when Tsukunft began a large recruitment drive in their town, and without any great soul-searching the whole group simply joined the organization. Thus, the twenty-year-old, before writing his autobiography, had managed to be briefly in the Bund children's SKIF, radical right-wing Zionist Betar, the communist Pioneer, and finally, completing a kind of circle, the Bund's Tsukunft, where over time he was promoted to the position of the organization's local leader.[76]

An equally interesting political odyssey was the short biography of M. Schwarzklat. Up to the age of fourteen, he had no interest in politics. After graduating from elementary school, having no permanent occupation, more out of boredom he began to participate in the local Zionist organization, raising funds in a "blue tin." As he noted, this kind of political involvement meant that "his popularity in town increased" very quickly. At that time, however, he did not strongly feel the idea of the Land of Israel, and his Zionist involvement soon ended.[77] Not long after, he began studying in a yeshiva, which he eventually abandoned. Quickly and radically secularizing, seeking the path of a new life for himself, he tried to join the Communist Party, to which he was accepted despite his earlier rejection. He was living at the time in Vilna. After a while, avoiding military conscription and looking for work, he left for a small town. There Schwarzklat met a girl, a committed Zionist, who "did not want to live in Poland, did not want to live amid hatred, only in the Land of Israel, among Jews." At first, he made fun of her; then he became confused, berating himself for falling in love with a Zionist. Soon, however, this short ideological crisis and a change in his personal life brought him to a new way of life and to a new political worldview. As Schwarzklat wrote, analyzing his previous views on life, he dreamed of obtaining the coveted profession of a teacher and returning to Vilna. But what awaited him there? Lodgings, tedious work, and a lonely life. How could he realize his collectivist, socialist ideals in such a life in Vilna? Consequently, he gave up everything and followed his beloved to He-Halutz. After a few months, he did hakhshara on a kibbutz, where he wrote his competition autobiography. The kibbutz also did not turn out to be the coveted idealistic collective of which he dreamed. However, he was sustained by the chance to go to Palestine and start a new life there.[78]

Schwarzklat's worldview, like that of the other young people depicted here, was characterized by a radical habitus. According to Pierre Bourdieu, the habitus is the social structure embodied in the individual and the discourse that surrounds him, the result of his individual history and the wider history of the social groups that he joins and with which he interacts: "Habitus is socialized subjectivity."[79] "Radical habitus" in the case described here was an individual internalization of the collective experience of young Jews growing up in the Second Republic, who did not accept the social order in which it was their lot to live, and who demonstrated their attachment to political visions of radical change. Schwarzklat, Binyomin R., Ajzyk Rozen and his brothers, and others, apart from all the differences, were characterized by common generational elements of biographical trajectory. They also resulted in a common, rarely self-conscious feature of sociopolitical awareness. For most young Jews in the Second Polish Republic, regardless of their political affiliation and actions taken or not taken, this was radical, and it consisted in a lack of acceptance of the sociopolitical reality surrounding them.

A common characteristic of all the political organizations listed here, including Orthodox ones, is their totalism. They produced a specific youth counterculture, on which the beginnings of a new, alternative society were to be based.[80] The latter, of course, at the level of ideas, was to be inclusive, open to all, the first in history from which dogmatism and discrimination would be banished, and in which truly free individuals would live. The announcement of this society in the form of "islands of new life"—that is, youth and political organizations—implemented the model of a closed community, separating itself from the external world and from the influence of disbelieving people and milieux. The paradox of the organizational culture described here is that it defined the everyday life of the first generation brought up in the nation-state, entirely subjected to the influence of acculturation. They moved more or less freely in two national cultures: thanks to education, they had access to Polish elite culture, and as young people they moved best in popular culture. Meanwhile, young people formed in this way, socialized in the conditions of a modern state, were directed to closed organizations by the situation and the lack of alternative paths. Their culture and organizational principles clearly did not harmonize with the requirements of a modern state and society, which required participation in many institutions and interacting with different people and in different social contexts. The politicized youth counterculture of the 1930s favored separation and escapist, antisystem, or revolutionary attitudes. The forms of social organization that created it were based on a specific model of identity. Furthermore, and most important for the issues of this work, these specific organizational forms and their own model of identity created a certain type of political consciousness.

CATASTROPHE, THE NEW WORLD, AND RADICAL MODERNISM

Assessments of political reality and ideological visions of the world were openly expressed by the authors most often on the last pages of their competition submissions. The exceptions were descriptions of experiences from the first years of young people's lives between 1914 and 1921, a time of wars and revolution. In young people's political worldview, two themes were the most important. The first theme was the weakness of the Jewish people and the parents' generation that represented them, who did not understand the violence around them, were passive toward it, and had neither the ability nor the will to oppose it. The second was disappointment, a sense of injustice and rejection by the emerging Polish state. This theme was represented by accounts of accusations against the Jews of national treason and Bolshevism (especially numerous in the years 1918–1921), as well as of requisitioning, violence, and pogroms carried out by the army and by the civilian population.[81] Of course, this kind of political consciousness was not only a direct result of the experiences of the war years but also the result of later experiences, as well as of accounts by their parents, the Jewish discourse of the 1920s and 1930s, and the entire interwar collective biographical trajectory of young Jews. David Roskies has shown how the experiences of World War I influenced then-emerging Jewish literary modernism, in which the problems of world chaos and its imminent violence took center stage.[82] A similar self-awareness of the age was revealed by young Jews' autobiographies. Their sense of impotence and injustice as Jewish people resonated strongly with other themes of political awareness, including the desire for force to put an end to injustice and chaos.

The 1930s in Poland saw the triumph of political radicalism, characterizing especially the youngest generation. In the case of young Jews, too, it was not just a question of left-wing radicalism. The Second Republic was the country where the greatest number of supporters of the revisionist movement and members of its youth wing, Betar, were located. If the classic division into left and right does not accurately describe the ideological, organizational, and social differences between the statist, fascist, and communist movements of the 1930s, all of which focused on the radical transformation of the world, it is all the more difficult to describe these inexperienced young people using the classical categories of left and right. Their outlook was characterized by ideological syncretism. Polish politics and Polish youth organizations also exhibited similar features at that time.[83]

A large number of both Polish and Jewish young people were characterized by a set of views, an aesthetic sensitivity, which I call radical modernism, internalized in the form of a radical habitus—an individual disposition to adopt specific emotional, cognitive, and behavioral attitudes. Among the Jews, such elements as the belief in the necessity of taking a leap into the future, a critique of the past and the present (including contemporary economic and social chaos), values such as modern collectivism, and a belief in the necessity of planned and organized social change were selectively internalized even by young Orthodox, who were not radicals; they were also typical of members of right-wing Betar. At a time when the Zionist right was dominated by a single organization, there were a great many left-wing Zionist groups. Young people's support of them was undoubtedly inflamed by widespread antisemitism as well as by a belief in a discriminatory attitude toward the Jews on the part of the state, with which the revisionists remained in an informal alliance. Inevitably, therefore, among young Jews, the most popular were left-wing groups and the symbols and beliefs they spread. The latter were shared even by those who did not consider themselves leftists or who simply were not. This kind of ephemeral leftism distinguished young Jews from young Poles, who tended to lean toward right-wing organizations. In the case of the former, whether their ideals were to be realized "here" or in

Palestine was, of course, very important, but it was of secondary importance and dependent on the general political situation.

The most glaring example of this aspect of young people's political consciousness is the special place occupied in it by the Soviet Union and the revolutionary symbolism that that country embodied. This does not mean that all the autobiographers were cryptocommunists or uncritical supporters of that country. They were usually radicals quite poorly versed in the twists and turns of politics and ideology, who were attracted by the symbolism of the communist state, in addition to its being the embodiment of power and thus of radicalism, which had a chance of being implemented. This was particularly important for young people who were convinced of their economic weakness, low social prestige, and the collective and mythical weakness of the nation they represented. Also, according to Jaff Schatz, the image of the might of the USSR and the communist movement was attractive to part of the Jewish population that observed the deep fragmentation of the political scene and the impotence of their own parties in implementing their demands for improvement of the situation of citizens of the Jewish faith. The image of the power of the communist movement was particularly attractive to young people.[84] The reasons for the relatively high popularity of the communist idea and the Soviet Union, beyond just members and sympathizers of the KPP, included a modernist vision of the centralist order, which supposedly prevailed in Poland's eastern neighbor. Its economy was supposed to be distinguished by resilience to crises, full employment, and huge industrial projects. It was there that the hitherto most extensive productivization of the Jewish people dreamed of by young people was being implemented. As I have written, young people, regardless of their political origins, more or less obsessively repeated in their autobiographies the themes of chaos and of the disintegration of the world around them. The general vision of social crisis was almost always supplemented by an element of a specific crisis in the Jewish world. Soviet communism, with its image of absolute order, control, and the power to change reality around it, often seemed to be the only answer to double crisis and to double discrimination. The image of communist power spoke to young people convinced of the Jewish people's exceptional weakness and vulnerability, especially those from its poorest strata. Here, it seems, the reasons for the popularity of communism were similar to those of the revisionist movement, the furthest removed from it, appealing to the ideas of Jewish military power and of the new Jewish man as a soldier, which had a chance of becoming a reality in Palestine. Young people who did not belong to the Communist Party, and who were often members of movements declaring hostility to communism, appeared to pay less attention to the knowledge commonly available in the 1930s (also in the Bundist or Zionist press) about the millions of victims of the Soviet authorities' repression of their own citizens. The message about the lack of ethnic discrimination in the Soviet Union and the image of the only European state consistently combating antisemitism appealed strongly to the imagination of many young Jews.

Hanzi was not a supporter of communism. She was brought up by a pious grandmother whose milieu held very strong Zionist views. During her time in secondary school, she joined right-wing Betar. Yet even she, a person seemingly remote from communist influence, describes in her autobiography the impact that the symbolism of the Soviet revolution and the Soviet Union had on her:

> At the time, a striking event made a deep impression on me, one that I shall always remember. It was the end of winter and the start of spring. One Saturday morning I saw a kitten lying outside, dying from cold and hunger. I stole some bread from the cupboard and, in the middle of the street, I tore it into pieces for the cat. A Polish shoemaker approached me from behind. He kissed me on the forehead and said that Poland didn't deserve a girl like me. I didn't understand what he meant. There was much talk about this shoemaker in our town. Everyone was afraid of him, and there were rumors that he had come from Russia in order to organize the workers. They even said that he had once set fire to a house, which then caused an enormous conflagration in the town. I knew nothing about this, but I was very interested in him and listened to every word I heard about him.[85]

The enormous cultural and social distance between Hanzi and the non-Jewish world was overwhelmed in her autobiography only by radical, revolutionary symbolism and mythology. It alone allowed one to imagine its representatives differently than, as the author's autobiography suggests, they were perceived daily—alien, incomprehensible, hostile. The growing influence of leftist and Marxist symbolism caused Hanzi to abandon religion toward the end of her studies at the Vilna Tarbut secondary school, as well as Betar, joining the Zionist-leftist Ha-Shomer ha-Tsa'ir youth organization with Marxist tendencies. The author's religiosity and conservatism did not make the transition easy for her. How Hanzi's internal evolution took place is further evidence of the symbolic and ideological pressure exerted by left-wing political radicalism on young Jews. The author described her time in Betar as follows: "I went to Betar only on days when there were meetings, in order to take care of my organizational responsibilities. I loathed every moment that I spent there. Whenever I returned from a meeting, I experienced an internal struggle. On the one hand, I felt strong national religious feelings; on the other hand, I thought about the workers, the poor, the victims of war."[86]

For a few more years, Hanzi was torn by such dilemmas. In addition to reading Jabotinsky's writings, she more and more often peeked into Marxist literature, such as the works of Karl Kautsky or August Bebel. A great influence on the evolution of her political consciousness was exerted by a teacher from the Tarbut school (which is quite surprising), a Marxist and a supporter of secular Yiddishism. Marxist and communist symbolism also greatly influenced discussions among the students at the Hebrew school that Hanzi attended, educating mainly the bourgeois young and spreading Zionist ideology: "What did we talk about? We discussed the different types of people, the society of the future—in short, everything under the sun. . . . Quite unexpectedly, I experienced an ideological crisis. One the one hand, I felt a sense of national pride, while on the other I felt enormous sympathy for the world proletariat and for Russia and its revolution. I had great respect for those who marched on May Day, holding the red flag of the workers. I wanted to be like them and to add my voice to the song of their uprising."[87]

Eventually, under the influence of a lecture by Nathan Bistricki, Hanzi abandoned Betar and joined Ha-Shomer ha-Tsa'ir.[88] The YIVO autobiographies indicate that revolutionary and workers' symbolism, led by May Day celebrations, was dear to young people in all left-wing Zionist organizations, including those that renounced revolutionary slogans and focused only on emigration to Palestine. Interestingly enough, although the official position of He-Halutz, Gordonia, or Dror said nothing about the involvement of members in the workers' struggle in Poland, Ben-Tikva's autobiography shows that he understood the May Day ideals differently, giving them a revolutionary meaning. For him and his comrades, it was the most important day of the year: "Hundreds of thousands of people stand in a straight line, proud of their happiest day: May First. They are in favor of a better tomorrow. It won't happen today, but it must come." At the end of his autobiography, he expressed his enthusiasm for the coming revolution, in which the Polish and the Jewish proletariat would come together.[89]

The power of communist or simply revolutionary symbolism was by no means limited to young Zionists. It can also be found in the works of supporters of the Bund, often directly on the streets confronting communist militias. Yud-Giml, initially active in the Bund and Tsukunft, was repulsed by communism on the issue of "bloodshed."[90] She heard about frequent cases of attacks by KPP militias on the premises of Jewish socialist groups in the 1930s, and it can be assumed that she also heard about the introduction of the communist system in the Soviet Union that was claiming millions of victims. Despite this, in the Bund she was increasingly disturbed by the lack of action, the idle conversation, the inaction of local leaders, and the nature of the local Bund organization of which she was a member, "saturated with the spirit of the shtetl."[91] Yud-Giml's autobiography is further proof of how important in the lives of young people was a general radical attitude, or rather a predisposition to this type of attitude (radical habitus), less so ideologies having the status of advanced ideological constructs. When the local Bund cell in the author's shtetl collapsed, most of its activists went over to a communist organization.[92] What most attracted Yud-Giml was the image of the power of the communist movement, so important against the background of surrounding political impotence. Some of the young people were tired and horrified by the number of disputes and conflicts between dozens of rival organizations. For some, communism spoke with a seemingly clear, uncompromising message—internationalism and the fact that a world empire was behind it.

This theme is most evident, of course, in the autobiographies of declared communists. Abraham Rotfarb described the appeal of the communist idea as "a consistent, fearless and powerful struggle for justice." Perhaps the most important feature of the movement for him was its "strength."[93] Another communist, Greyno, concluded his autobiography with a fiery declaration:

> I have felt the pain of dozens of people—shabby, half-naked, barefoot men, women and children. I have seen the hunger in their eyes; I have seen it eat away at their still-young bodies—emaciated, bones protruding from singed flesh, covered with dirt and grime. This mass of people, a true sign of our era, cries out in the streets. . . . And above it all, above the desolation and chaos, stands a tall, sturdy watchtower that illuminates the world around it with knowledge, culture, and progress. This is the Soviet Union, the only country in the world that belongs to the workers and peasants. The Soviet Union shows us, teaches us: see how people can and should live, when workers and peasants come to power! And I know that class instinct is awakening and embracing more and more people, people who are clenching their fists to deliver the final blow and who follow the example of that country which occupies one-sixth of the globe.[94]

Especially in the 1930s, in the era of powerful successes achieved in Europe and Poland by fascist and far-right movements, the power of the Soviet Union, as the only force that seemed at the time to oppose them, appealed not only to the communists. In her diary entry dated March 15, 1938, an activist of the Bundist Tsukunft from Maków Mazowiecki wrote, "I have just heard on the radio that Hitler has occupied Czechoslovakia. Hitler is exactly like Napoleon, who occupied all of Europe and was defeated at Moscow. So it will be with

Hitler, he will also occupy the whole of Europe, but when he comes to the Soviet Union, he too will be defeated."[95]

The picture of the world emerging from all these autobiographies quoted above is one of chaos and impending catastrophe. The only salvation here would be a complete change of surroundings: either as a result of leaving for Palestine (or far less often emigrating across the Atlantic) or a revolution that would completely change the surrounding world. One did not have to be a member of Po'alei-Tsiyon-Left to promote both these variants of bringing change to the Jewish people's disastrous situation. Young people very often wrote about themselves as part of a "generation without a future." For the authors who defined their lives as passing in a social void, devoid of any prospects, dreams of Palestine were dreams of changing the surrounding world, and they were fundamentally no different from their other friends' revolutionary desires.

Binyomin R. wrote on the last pages of his autobiography, "For me there is no other way . . ., either Eretz Israel or suicide."[96] Regardless of whether the authors declared their desire to take part in the revolution in Europe or spoke only about their personal emigration plans, they were characterized by a similar assessment of Polish reality. One of the participants in the YIVO competition, a graduate of a Hebrew secondary school, who had no chance of going to college and finding a job that satisfied her aspirations and was forced to learn the trade of a corset maker, wrote, "I learned English and French, gave lessons until late in the evening, so as not to have time to think about my situation. . . . Around me, I felt an emptiness. . . . I really would like to go away somewhere, change my surroundings, because I know that I would change if I met new, different people. I currently intend to go to Palestine as a student."[97]

For precisely the same reasons, a would-be medical student from Lviv, Moses S., dreamed of going to Palestine. In his opinion, only having their own country and working for it would allow young Jews like him to break out of a stagnant life and take a stand against the hopelessness of the world around him.[98]

At the ends of their autobiographies, the young people, following the competition's guidelines, presented their general views on life, their future plans, and their dreams. The works' conclusions often took the form of the authors' political credos and were simply descriptions of the ideologies of the political movements within which they situated their own biographies. Autobiography endings that did not directly evoke ideological slogans also had a political dimension. As was the case at the beginnings of works with their descriptions of early circumstances, authors, when describing the actual moment in which they were living, often ended their autobiographies by presenting their own visions of the social order surrounding them. Yud-Giml at the end of her work wrote about the illness of her older brother. As she wrote, her "heart was filled with hatred" for the whole world, in which her brother was condemned to die slowly. The "degeneration of today's order of things" was to blame for his death.[99] In a letter to YIVO attached to his autobiography, Kola addressed the Vilna institution in typical fashion: "My autobiography—its second part—is not just my autobiography. It is a description of the fate of many thousands of young Jews. It is a cry for help in a dark night: 'Do not let us rot!'"[100] Mendl Man added a poem to his autobiography and several "reports" sent to the YIVO competition entitled "Ikh hob gezeyn" ("I have seen"). The essence of the reality surrounding the poem's narrator was hunger, tears, and the misery of working-class children growing up in basements.[101] Even those authors who were able to look critically at their own political camps and their ideologies could not free themselves from the modernist belief in the necessity of a great breakthrough, which would bring an end to both the misery of their own lives and the suffering of all humanity. This was the case with the Zionist-socialist Drori, among others. On the last pages of his autobiography, he wrote about "young people, men and women, who once thought of the future as a road strewn with roses . . . and in the end all their dreams, all their hopes disappeared like a dream, withered like a flower."[102] According to Drori, this fate of all young people was the product of the specific historical era in which they lived. It was social conditions that determined their future. As the author wrote, "eating bread today they do not know whether they will eat it tomorrow," and they did not know whether another world war would break out soon. Nevertheless, he was also defined by the belief that after the period of the coming wars and revolutions, and the inevitably accompanying violence, a new era would come and bring them to an end.[103]

Behind the basic assessments and interpretations of surrounding reality common to both the Zionists and the revolutionary anti-Zionists lay a very similar vision of the "new man," who would finally put an end to the current time of chaos.[104] The ideal halutz from Palestine and the worker fighting for revolution in Europe had a great deal in common. The leader of the local Ha-Shomer ha-Tsa'ir cell and the secretary of He-Halutz was for Binyomin R. the ideal of the "new man." He was a "spiritually and physically developed" person. Spirituality in this case meant a deep knowledge of political issues.[105] The fact that the author was impressed by halutzim working on the land, who were putting into practice the ideal of the "new Jewish man" in Palestine, is understandable. At the same time, Binyomin R. was also impressed by "artists of nature," which is how he saw engineers and builders.[106] These, we know, were very important elements of the pantheon of socialist and communist heroes. How close the new man "created" by the Zionists was even to some communists is shown in Greyno's autobiography when he describes his cousin: "A cousin of mine on my mother's side came to visit us. She was from a rich family. She had joined the Zionist movement, had gone with her fiancé to Palestine, and had married him there. After six or seven years she came on vacation to visit her parents, who lived in a small town. A beautiful, tall, healthy, normal woman, she awakened boyish feelings of love and respect within me."[107]

This cousin from Palestine, like his older communist comrades, was for the author the antithesis of the human types filling the world of the traditional urban Jewish poor that he rejected. The autobiographies of young people, in contrast to the ideological statements of their leaders and the programs of their movements, very often contained such contradictions.

What united visions of the new man emerging from the autobiographies of people belonging to different and mutually antagonistic political movements was their spiritual and vital strength. Attachment to these visions was combined with the anxiety of "Jewish impotence" that is prominent in the autobiographies. Both autobiographical and other sources confirm that in the case of right-wing Zionist Betar, the most attractive ideological feature of this organization for young people was its militarism. This is how A. Remez, hitherto a left-wing "Skifist," recalled the moment of joining the "Trumpeldor Union" ("Brit Trumpeldor"—an expanded version of the acronym Betar). "I sewed myself a smock for marches organized by revisionist Brit Trumpeldor. I became a 'Britnik.' I couldn't resist the temptation to march like a soldier through the streets of our small town. We marched through the streets in smocks girded with blue and white sashes."[108] One of the most important elements of the ideological education of the young members of Betar was military drill. The new members were fed stories about Ze'ev Jabotinsky's Jewish Legion during World War I, fighting alongside the British against the Turks in Palestine. In the party office hung a large map of the future Jewish homeland. The author, like his friends, dreamed of its military conquests and of his role in this as the commander of one of the detachments. Among the young people, worship of the "chairman" was developing.[109] Here Remez was probably referring to the cult of Jabotinsky. Apart from militarism, this was one of the most important ideological motifs of interwar Betar. Militarism, of course, was associated with the value of discipline. As another of the young revisionists, Refleg, wrote, "Where the nation is united, organized, the state is strong—there is this law of strong discipline (more along the lines of coercion). There, citizen-soldiers were 'taken in hand,' like tethered horses, let's say as if by an orchestra conductor."[110]

This was a diary entry of Chai, a Gordonia activist (and thus a left-wing Zionist woman, hostile to revisionists): "Oct. 28, 1930: . . . in the evening, at seven o'clock, I was present at an *aseyfo* with Gordonia, where my friend K . . . spoke about the present Jewish situation. . . . We shall go out to fight the world as lions, we are a force!"[111]

Some of the autobiographies highlight the role of violence and the cult of physical strength, characteristic of almost all radical political ideologies of the 1930s, and from which Jewish political culture was also not free. Undoubtedly, its role was reinforced by anti-Jewish violence and antisemitism. The dignity of the new Jewish people—or the Jewish proletariat—required a response to these phenomena. The symbolic acculturation of young people was also not without influence. The closer the young people culturally approached their surroundings, the more they were offended by the antisemitic insults and stereotypes that flowed from them. As we know, two of the most important traits attributed to Jews were physical impotence and cowardice. Symbolic acculturation made young Jews particularly sensitive to such opinions, and they wished to undermine them. The admiration in the autobiographies for the new physicality of the halutzim or Jewish workers, for the successes of Jewish athletes (especially in boxing),[112] and for marches and demonstrations, which were manifestations of collective national strength, was specific testimony to the growing role of the symbolism of violence and physical strength in the political consciousness of Jewish youth. Binyomin R. wrote that the fights between Jewish youth on political grounds horrified the older generation in Bielsk Podlaski. Its representatives used to say that "Jewish children are now worse than shaygets,"[113] criticizing behavior completely alien to the canon of traditional Jewish values. This conviction of the values and symbols related to violence and physical strength for Jewish youth culture is also shown in an excerpt from Drori's autobiography in which he describes a trip to the military draft board in Łódź. On the train to the board, he sat in a compartment with five Christians going for the same purpose. He was sure that he would have problems, but to his surprise he got into a lively conversation with them. One of the Christian youths asked Drori if he was not afraid to fight, because after all this kind of fear was a typical Jewish feature. The author launched into a tirade, convincing his interlocutors that Jews never started fights themselves and so were not prepared for them. Therefore, they had no experience "in crazy street violence." This did not mean, however, that he would not be able to fight, because, as he argued, it was widely known that the best boxers in his native Częstochowa were Jews. He also recalled the most recent sports news, reporting the sensational victory in the ring in the US of the Jewish boxer Max Beer, who defeated the Italian favorite, Primo Carnera. Jewish strength and the ability to meet violence with violence were important political values for him.[114]

Many political movements used an image of force, unity, and discipline to attract new members. For example, Betar organized its members along military lines. Some elements of its ideology and internal structure were close to the fascist organizations of the day. Betar preached the organic unity of the Jewish people (sometimes seen in racial terms), total hierarchy, and obedience to the leader, Jabotinsky. Among the most important values spread by the movement were physical strength, military prowess, and self-defense.[115] Toward the end of the 1930s, as part of the alliance of revisionists and later Sanacja governments and their joint efforts to evacuate the Jewish population to Palestine, members of Betar participated in secret training by the Polish army.[116] Many militaristic elements of ideology emphasizing the ideals of the "struggle for the liberation of the nation," "order," and "discipline" were adopted by Betar from the arsenal of Polish nationalist movements.[117] As Ze'ev Jabotinsky wrote in an ideological manifesto widely distributed among young Jews in Poland in the 1930s, his movement's goal was "to create from Betar a truly world organization, which would be able to obey a command from the center, using tens of thousands of hands, the same action in every country and every location.... For this is the most important achievement of masses of free men, when they are able to work all together, all of them with the absolute precision of a machine."[118]

In several of the autobiographies quoted above, we have seen young leftists attack militarism and the cult of violence present in Betar, calling its members "Jewish fascists." However, the same values, although in a different guise, were shared by the most important of the Jewish socialist parties—the Bund. Strength and discipline were the overriding values of all the major political movements popular on the Jewish Street. Perfect examples in this respect are the memoirs of Bernard Goldstein, the head of the Warsaw branch of the Ordener Grupe (the Bund's self-defense organization), and of Lucjan Blit, the leader of the self-defense organization of the Bund youth group, Tsukunft Shturem. Ordener Grupen and Tsukunft Shturem were characterized by paramilitary structures. The latter in particular was modeled on the Republikanischer Schutzbund, the Austrian Social Democrats' militia. In their memoirs, Goldstein and Blit emphasized the idea of unity, discipline, and physical strength. To augment its own image, Tsukunft Shturem introduced uniforms. Important elements of its activity included the defense of the Jewish population against attacks or clashes with communist militias as well as parades and marches. As Blit recalled, "I suppose Tsukunft Shturem's most memorable actions were always the May Day parades. Its members formed an elegant group, marched nicely, and radiated confidence. People probably thought they represented a much greater force than they actually did. This was very important for the morale of not only the youngsters, but also of all Warsaw Jews. That was a very bad time. . . . And here we had a group marching proudly and without fear."[119]

In the same way, creating the myth of the power and strength of the Bund's self-defense, Emanuel Nowogródzki wrote after the war about its Warsaw leader: "The role of the militia in training the Jewish population for organized resistance was of historical significance. The Bund militia was commanded by Bernard Goldstein, a member of the Warsaw city committee of the Bund, admired and respected by all. His incredible courage, inspiring the Jewish masses to self-defense and instilling fear among antisemitic militias even before an armed clash took place, was legendary. . . . In certain groups of Polish workers, especially among Polish socialists, who at that time belonged to the famous PPS militias, he was the most popular Bund figure."[120]

He continued, "There was no Jewish working-class family in Poland that the news of the heroic clashes of the Bund group did not reach, and there was no Jewish district in Polish cities where its legends were not revered. May Day parades and demonstrations . . . became a place of open fighting between antisemitic militias on the one hand and the Bund militia on the other. . . . For the Bund, this was an opportunity to demonstrate its strength in public."[121]

Jewish youth political culture in the 1930s, the widespread worship of physical and military power, physical confrontations between representatives of different Jewish political parties and Jewish communists, and self-defense groups fighting antisemitic violence should be studied together. From the eighteenth century to the interwar period, one of the most important elements of the discourse on the Jews was a conviction of their weakness, cowardice, and resulting reluctance to defend themselves, the inability to oppose physically the harm done to them.[122] This discourse, deeply internalized by Jews, had a great influence on the definitions of national characteristics formulated by the participants in the YIVO competition. "Weakness" was laid by them on all previous generations. It was a complex that could be remedied only by acquiring individual physical and collective strength. The desire for this strength was followed by values such as militarism and admiration for and pride in Jewish self-defense. The sense of impotence and the dream of strength were undoubtedly important components of Jewish youth political culture and the habitus that it was producing in young people. All this constituted the culture's authoritarian nature, which was closely related to such values as sacrifice and discipline described above.

Personal physical or collective strength, dedication, and discipline in the young Jews' autobiographies represented a response to a difficult situation. The fact that the 1930s were perceived as a time of catastrophe is particularly evident in the works written in 1939 for the last YIVO competition. They refer to events that, according to the authors, foreshadowed the inevitable arrival of the apogee of the crisis of world civilization. These events included the civil wars in Palestine and Spain (1936–1939), the Nuremberg Laws and the rise of Nazi Germany, and the war in Ethiopia. However, even in autobiographies of 1934, authors predicted the coming apocalyptic moment of the struggle between good and evil. For young Jews, the latter was chiefly fascism. Almost half of the over sixty-page work of a member of Tsukunft from Maków Mazowiecki was the author's diary attached to her autobiography, kept in 1938 and 1939. It shows perfectly what political events and what interpretations of them dominated the imaginations of young Bund activists at that time. Beginning on December 12, 1938, the diary contains a record of the emotions aroused in its author by information about the Spanish Civil War. She was horrified by the victories of the fascists in Catalonia and the involvement of Mussolini and the German Luftwaffe in the conflict. The defeat of the republican forces in Spain was a sign of an inevitable pan-European confrontation, a life-and-death struggle against fascism.[123] As another author, a communist activist, wrote, "My dark mood was not only due to the nature of my daily life, but also to the political events of the day, especially those taking place in Spain. I hear on the radio: 'General Franco carried out a successful offensive against Madrid. Thousands of communists murdered.' I walk with my head bowed. The road is hard, as if the fallen fighters for Spanish freedom were actually lying along it."[124]

In several autobiographies from 1939, the Spanish Civil War represents the central generational experience for the Jewish Left. It was undoubtedly one of the most important formative experiences influencing the shape of their political consciousness. A. Remez described how in 1937–1939 he closely followed all press reports about the war in Spain and how much time was devoted to it during discussions in Tsukunft. He wrote that the "fascist murders" in Germany and Spain, the eventual occupation of Czechoslovakia in 1939 by the Nazis, and the tragedy of Jewish refugees from Germany filled him with "a sense of hopelessness, hatred and a desire for revenge."[125] Other authors wrote about similar emotions, which were undoubtedly a very important component of the political consciousness of many people from this generation. The 1930s have very often been interpreted as a period of struggle between the camps of progress and "fascist reaction."

Binyomin R. was one of those to describe his times as a "period of fascism."
The author reported how at the end of 1931 in his native Bielsk, the famous Vilna
"Wacławski case" began to have growing repercussions.[126] During school vacation at the turn of 1931/32, the local economic boycott of Jews was supported
by National Democratic students from Vilna. There were fights between them
and the Jews and arrests of representatives of both groups. He commented on
the development of a new Polish radical organization—the National Radical
Camp—and the news about several local communist activists bring sent to
the camp in Bereza Kartuska as manifestations of the country's growing descent into fascism.[127] Writing his autobiography in 1939, Chaim Berl on the last
pages reported on the increasingly frequent antisemitic incidents in his native
Działoszyn. In the evenings young Jews were afraid to walk the streets. The
author and his peers fell into apathy, seeing the hopelessness of their situation.
They lived in hope of revolutionary change.[128]

The only life guidance during this all-encompassing chaos for young Jews
was politics. The specific form of the young people's worldview required searching in one of the political ideologies for a typical, modernist vision of an alternative world. Unlike the real one, it would be well run, governed by clear rules,
and free from all manifestations of social injustice. This kind of utopianism is
a very characteristic feature of the young people's autobiographies. Terms such
as *compromise, political pragmatism*, and *realpolitik* appeared in none of the cited
works, and quite rarely is there in them a shadow of doubt as to the absolute
truth of the ideologies professed by the authors. Ideological doubt appeared
in a minority of the autobiographies, and if it occurred, it was replaced by an
allegiance to the new movement and its ideological message. Most participants
in the YIVO competitions shared an unwavering belief that these ideologies
were able to describe and explain every facet of reality. Of course, to a large
extent this kind of vision was conditioned by the authors' very young age. However, Ezra Mendelsohn characterized Jewish politics of the interwar period
as the politics of powerlessness, unable to significantly improve the situation
of Jewish citizens of the Second Republic. These politics tried to balance this
fundamental weakness by uncompromising ideology, in fact utopianism.[129]
Values such as reformism and liberalism were alien to radical politics and to
the youngest generation. The following quote from Greyno's work is typical of
the autobiographies in general:

> It often happens that a person acts against his own convictions and reason-
> ing, which usually control his behavior, and he falls helplessly under the
> influence of his close contemporaries, if only to avoid being humiliated and
> ridiculed by them. And, despite his own initial, powerful impulse to resist, he

is still overwhelmed by whoever possesses the power and ingenuity to influence others and win them over. . . . He becomes more and more caught up in
the course of events that are repugnant to him, that at first seem to him to be
absurd, even disgusting. And he tries not only to avoid being left behind, but
to outdo the others.[130]

Greyno included the above passage in a description of his childhood years
when any kind of politics was alien to him. Evidently, it was supposed to suggest the author's lack of alternatives. Someone like him was doomed to radicalism. The chaos of the environment had to lead him to radical politics that
gave direction to his life. Describing his political initiation (among Jewish
communists) during a secret meeting in the forest during Yom Kippur, he
wrote, "I thought: 'Oh, there, in the synagogue the old generation cries, and
their hearts' laments travel all the way to the heavy clouds.' I looked around.
We are so many, so many and so young. We are the new generation. We are the
ones who must destroy the old, decadent way of life, filled with suffering and
pain. We must build a new society, full of joy for all, in which the existence of
two separate classes is no longer possible."[131]

Chaim Berl dressed up his decision to leave the Zionist camp and go over
to the communists in lofty words. For him, too, the new political ideology
he adopted had the status of universal, absolute knowledge determining his
direction in life: "Like a child who, after birth, opens its eyes for the first time,
sees the world in bright colors, the sunlight and nature surrounding it, so I too
opened my eyes and began to see the world, a world free, bright and beautiful. . . . Socialism allows for anything. It brings the light of freedom! . . . Socialism! Yes, it speaks of bread, of hunger, of the oppression of one by another, of
all that I work so hard on."[132]

Kola concluded his autobiography, written in the summer of 1939, with the
following words: "Everywhere there is a struggle and from everywhere come
black clouds obscuring the sun. If we, the working masses, do not speak out,
unite the forces of the international proletariat, throw off our bloodsuckers, I
and my generation will be left with only the gray road of even greater hunger
and suffering. We are filled with lofty thoughts. We have dimmed eyes, but
trembling hearts that are ready to ignite at any moment, to become our torch
in the final battle. That is what I think, at the age of twenty-two."[133]

Bon Tikva, a halutz with dreams of going to Palestine, combined the ideology of his movement speaking of the transformation of the Jewish people in
the Land of Israel with faith in the revolution that was to come also in Poland.
This was no longer in line with the political program of his movement. On the
last two pages of his autobiography, he very suggestively described a visit to

Warsaw and the view he saw on the other side of the Vistula, giving it a significant interpretation:

> We drive down a street, where thousands of zlotys are spent on amusement and other such things. We drive down another one, where thousands of unemployed people are lying around. . . . People are thrown out on the streets, where disease awaits them, where there is cold and hunger. All this is a product of today's order. The situation in the Jewish quarter is a little different, but also bad: stalls, barrows, bagel sellers, poverty. This is how the Jewish people live, from trade. Even at night it is not quiet here. People ask, how long will this be the case, how long will they live like this? And they reply: the eternal wandering Jew who travels through country after country. Will we finally be like other nations? No, we will be left with a basket of bagels.[134]

The response to this situation, provided by the movement to which he belonged, He-Halutz, was to build a new Jewish life in the Land of Israel. This did not mean, however, that this particular nationalist response was the only one Ben-Tikva had in mind. The vision of a worldwide revolution also appealed to him. At the end of his autobiography, he wrote, "I was born during a volcanic eruption that has not died down to this day. Today's question is, where can you hide from its lava? The answer is a powerful one: you must fight for another tomorrow. The moment must come for the millions of workers crushed by capital to rise up. Then they will act, spill their hot lava, flood cities and towns with it, and build a new world on earth along socialist lines. Will I live to see it?"[135]

Political radicalism gave young people's lives meaning and direction. It also allowed them to articulate a deep resentment and sometimes hatred for the conditions in which they were living and growing up. Feygeles, in several pages of notes attached to his autobiography, which are like a political creed, wrote about the "deep demoralization of the society around him," about the need for people like him to "cleanse the social organism of various bacteria that are ruining it," and that "a mass movement should turn to the clerics crying Away with you!" Religion, according to this young man, the son of a traditionalist tailor, stood "in the path of the values of life: progress, culture and civilization."[136] This new society would have to eradicate two basic features of the present one: the disorganization and the exploitation of some people by others. The working masses were restrained from activism by the rabbis, the religious establishment, and fatalistic faith. The Jewish religion (as well as others) operated with a false idea of brotherhood, which did not encourage the masses of workers to act. On the way to their goal, other "hostile social forces" would also have to be defeated, above all the "petty bourgeois."[137] Binyomin R. wrote, "As long as there are such educational 'institutions' as heders and yeshivas among us, the Jewish people will not be healthy, either physically or spiritually." The author did not believe in the possibility of modernizing these institutions or of reforming "Jewish clerical parties." The "winds of history" were meant to sweep away "the spiritual oppression of these parties and the culture they represent."[138]

Some of the views of the Bundist and left-wing Zionist quoted above can equally be attributed to both communists and supporters of the radical right. A certain radical habitus, consisting in the complete rejection of the surrounding world in the name of something completely new and consent to the use of radical means to realize it, united the vast majority of autobiographers and, I would argue, dominated among Jewish young people in general in the 1930s.

Young Jews were also pushed toward political radicalism by the modernist culture of the time and its futuristic symbolism, as well as having its roots in the fin-de-siècle diagnosis of the crisis of values, chaos, and the collapse of the contemporary world. To feel the impact of this culture, it was not necessary to read much; fragments of specific literary works, party manifestos, speeches, slogans, and images from the party press, banners, and posters were enough. This belief in the end of the world did not have to be a fully recognized philosophical concept at all; it was enough that it was part of a radical habitus. Marci Shore has written about the cultural atmosphere that pushed Polish futurists of the interwar period toward communism: "The catastrophism of the 1920s arose from this sense of a void, and abyss of nothingness, the degeneration of civilization; the simultaneous utopianism and catastrophism of 1930s arose from a sense of impending horror, the rise of fascism and of Stalinism."[139] Not being fully aware of the origins of the categories of their own thinking, young Jews describing the family home, everyday life, school, and work followed in the footsteps of sophisticated futurists. The essence of the radical habitus uniting young Jews, members or sympathizers of such programmatically different political movements, was to ascribe their own life situation and the fate of the Jewish people to a general diagnosis of a world buffeted by crisis. Gamalielis concluded his autobiography as follows:

> I haven't done anything significant these last two years. These two years
> have been monotonous, every day has looked the same, and it is on this basis
> that I have the courage to say that these two years have taught me more
> than yeshiva and school combined. Both my political consciousness and my
> character have been strengthened. Two years ago, if someone had asked me
> to lead an illegal self-study circle, I would have replied that I was afraid of a
> police baton. Today this is not a problem for me, because I have become a
> radical. I burn with a proletarian love for work. I feel it with my whole body,

I am connected to work and the struggle for bread. I know that one step away from my home I shall find myself in a working-class environment that impresses me with its simple working life. I have become a great enemy of those creatures that "will not dip their hand in cold water." ... I see around me bitter young people who would like to toil and develop their muscles, but have nowhere to do it. I have become a staunch opponent of the modern world, death no longer frightens me, I am ready for anything and when I see and think about all this, I ask myself, where am I going? Where?[140]

CONCLUSION

INTERWAR RABBI AND POLITICIAN YEHOSHUA Thon referred to youth during his time as the "steel crucible generation," forged in the fervor of world war and deep social and national conflicts. The older generation had returned from the front convinced of the effectiveness of brutal solutions in social life and politics and no longer prepared for calm reflection. The younger generation learned from the older generation and drew its own conclusions. Although his piece published in *Haynt* in 1932 entitled "Yugent un mir" ("Young People and Us") refers to Polish and European youth in general, he was pointing to young Jews in particular. Thon's grumbling might easily be dismissed as typical of an older generation that did not understand its descendants. However, his assessments reflect the essence of the socialization experience and political consciousness of young people in the 1930s.

Thon, a nineteenth-century liberal Zionist rabbi with a doctorate in philosophy, complained that young people were not interested in art or high culture and were drawn instead to popular culture, cheap sensationalism, and "brutal egoism that is their sport." He lamented that this new generation "grew up without the Torah and without wisdom." In this new era, life was treated without due seriousness, like a game where participants did not subject the directions or effects of their actions to deeper reflection. Thon considered antisemitism, Nazism, and communism to be this kind of "sport," symptoms of the era's sickness. These movements did not propose solutions to important social problems, but their supporters did not want a solution; they wanted a thoughtless game, some "sport and fun." The same role was played in Poland by anti-Jewish speeches at universities, economic boycotts, and physical attacks on the Jewish community. Thon thought that young "Bolsheviks" admiring the Soviet

Union's five-year plan engaged in the same "sport and fun," action for action's sake, bringing no improvement. According to the Zionist liberal, the native communists behaved in the same way, "stirring up strikes," "arranging mass meetings," "playing cat and mouse with the police," and understanding neither the goals nor the effects of their actions. Young people, Jewish and non-Jewish, knew nothing of the canon of European cultural heritage. The youth replaced the Western canon with radical politics and modernist literature.[1] Thon's complaints show his disgust with twentieth-century mass society and the culture it generated, and at the same time his helplessness in the face of these phenomena. The older liberal elites were unable to cope with the effects of this new society: the increasing popularity of fascism and communism, radical modernism, and the brutal behavior and the authoritarian tendencies they encouraged.

Jehuda Kelner in the *Memorial Book for Szczebrzeszyn* included an excerpt from his memoirs, which is a perfect summary of what young people wrote about themselves for the YIVO competition. According to Kelner, "fresh winds" came to his town with the outbreak of World War I:

> Seeing the changes in town, young people abandoned the bet ha midrash and shtibl, threw off the long coats and Jewish caps, dressed in suits and put on hats. . . . I recall that on every Shabbat, during walks, Bundists walked in one group and sang their anthem *Di Shvue* (The Oath), the other group were the Zionists, singing Zionist songs. When the two groups came across one other, they quickly separated like two hostile armies. . . . This is what young people's life was like. And the older generation was unable to understand the spirit of the times and it cut itself off from the new currents.[2]

Though Jews were hardest hit by the negative consequences of radical modernism, this does not mean that they themselves were free from its influence. The last generation of Jewish youth before the Holocaust succumbed to its charms, not differing in this from their non-Jewish peers. The above quotation, aligning perfectly with the YIVO autobiographies, reflects the totalism of 1930s Jewish political movements and the fact that they came to dominate most, if not all, dimensions of youth culture. It also confirms the thesis advanced in this book about the high levels of authoritarianism of these movements and of the young people under their influence. The memoirs of Yehuda Kelner, like dozens of autobiographical examples, emphasize the pervasiveness of this culture and the fact that it was produced by mutually antagonistic movements such as Zionism (of all ideological shades), Bundism, communism, and, to some extent, even Orthodox youth movements. Despite their mutual hostility, these movements were similar in their desire to control their members' lives (though to varying degrees), their radical visions for changing society (except Orthodox and liberal or right-wing Zionists), their organizational forms, and their emphasis on education and young people's ideological development.

The general ideology of radical modernism was the most important factor in the development of the sociopolitical consciousness of the last generation of Polish Jews before the Holocaust. It played a key role in the way most YIVO participants reconstructed their own biographies. However, the construction of the young people's comments does not mean that they did not reflect the real social processes to which an entire generation was subjected. Traditional Jewish culture was disintegrating with its most important premodern institutions, such as the heder, and the dominant thrust of economic activity in the form of petty trade. Secularization was progressing. As a result, most young Jews abandoned religion, and those who retained it cultivated it in its modern forms—that is, Orthodox, not traditional (reformed heders and religious schools for boys and girls, modern yeshivas, increased secular and non-Jewish education, and religious youth organizations and political parties). The economic structure of Jewish society was changing dynamically. Young people strove to obtain as much secular and, most importantly, formal education as possible. At the same time, most young people, after finishing their education, sought work not in commerce but as skilled laborers and in industry. Progressive processes of urbanization caused the migration of people, especially young people, from small towns to large cities.

An important and unique experience was—for most—their education in public schools and, for all young Jews, growing up in the nationalistic Polish state. It was at school—but not only there—that young people from traditional, most often Yiddish-speaking homes learned Polish and internalized the symbolic universe of Polish culture. Thanks to school, they felt more connected with the country in which they lived than their parents and grandparents. But they also had much higher expectations of the country and of their futures in it. In modern social spaces, young Jews from traditional homes encountered their peers brought up in acculturated families. All of them, sharing the experience of their own particular Polishness, felt antisemitism as more than hatred and discrimination; this ideology was literally depriving them of their rightful place in the Polish community. For acculturated Jews, whose parents often considered themselves to be Poles of Jewish faith or religiously indifferent people of Jewish origin, or simply Poles or Europeans, continuing with this type of identity was becoming increasingly difficult. Those who took part in the YIVO competition made a fundamental ideological switch, joining one of the national Jewish organizations or the communist movement, thus challenging the world of their parents' values.

Young people joined political organizations while unhappy with their jobs, education, and life prospects. The parties and their youth groups, as well as the associated cultural sphere in the form of libraries, self-study groups, sports clubs, excursions, and so on, were the most important space for spending free time. Such broad social functions were also performed by Orthodox organizations. Undoubtedly, many young people who started families before the outbreak of World War II limited their party involvement, but this did not mean a change in political sympathies. These, as we know, in the 1930s revolved mainly around radical parties, striving in various ways for far-reaching change in the surrounding world. The exceptions were the Orthodox political organizations, but, as we have seen, the young people involved with them also succumbed to the influence of radical modernism. Apolitical individualism or political liberalism seemed to be finally buried in the 1930s. Of course, in the Jewish space of the Second Republic there were also movements of a different kind, as well as social activists promoting slow and gradual change rather than radical transformation. However, with few exceptions, they are not present in the autobiographies submitted to the YIVO competition. When asked to describe their lives, young people presented them mainly through the prism of radical political ideologies and felt that participation in these organizations provided them a promising lifestyle, an opportunity, or simply a substitute for their disappointed ambitions; this fact is perhaps the strongest proof that the struggle for the control of this generation's soul was won by national ideals or universal revolution, not by reform. The political consciousness of most young Jews of the interwar period was close to the "politics in a new key" born at the turn of the nineteenth and twentieth centuries. Among its features were, as Carl Schorske argued, "the response to the social and spiritual needs of its supporters in the form of ideological collages formed from fragments of modernity, flashes of futurism, resurrected remnants of a half-forgotten past," as well as totalism— that is, "a concept of life and a model of action going beyond the sphere of pure politics and part of a wider cultural revolution that was bringing in the twentieth century."[3] Political modernism reached its radical apogee in the 1930s, and young Polish Jews ended up at the center of its storm.

At the same time, this does not mean that radical modernism was a form of all-encompassing total ideology to which there was no alternative. In a groundbreaking book, Kenneth Moss draws attention to the development in 1930s Polish Jewish society of an alternative to radical modernism. It was a belief that Jews had no future in eastern Europe. This conviction had been growing since the end of the nineteenth century and particularly gained popularity in the last decade before the Holocaust, combined with doubts as to whether the dramatic situation of Jews in that part of the continent could be remedied by Zionism, communism, Bundism, or any other dominant collectivist political ideology. In view of the impossibility of organizing a mass departure of Jews from Poland, many saw individual emigration as the only solution. That was also the context for the development of so-called Eretz Israelism, a belief that Palestine was, in the 1930s, the most realistic direction of escape from eastern Europe. Faith in this idea was not the same as Zionism. In the 1930s, as some of the autobiographies quoted above also show, one could even be an anti-Zionist and also think about escaping to Palestine. Moss's innovative ideas do not contradict but dovetail with the findings of this book.[4] As we have seen, in the sincere, authentic comments of young people, faith in radical ideologies and devotion to and personal involvement in the lives of the youth parties and organizations proclaiming them often appeared alongside emotions such as despair, doubt, and deep pessimism about the future of their personal and collective future as Jews in Poland. Young people often doubted elements of the ideology of the movements to which they belonged or with which they sympathized, but even when they thought about an individual departure from eastern Europe, about a future elsewhere outside the framework of the movements to which they belonged, they were still under the enormous influence of radical modernism.

Radical elements of youth political culture came from outside. Jewish parties and organizations modeled themselves on the modern and mass political movements that had been emerging in Europe since the second half of the nineteenth century. The interwar period was the final moment when traditional Jewish forms of social organization could be replaced. At the same time, however, the speed and effectiveness of this substitution were based on the fact that all the organizations referred to here harkened back to an old ethnic bond with premodern roots. The Jewish case exemplifies the view that nations are a modern phenomenon but are based on premodern ethnic bonds. The 1930s were therefore not only a high point in the development of Jewish political radicalism in eastern Europe but also the final decade of the development of the Jews as a modern nation, headed by its vanguard in the form of the generation described here. The ethnicity or Jewishness of those movements explains the widespread voluntary nature, commitment, and enthusiasm around them. Jewish premodern ethnicity manifested itself in the traditional version of the Yiddish language, in Hebrew symbolism and legends of Zion, in Hasidic courts (created in the nineteenth century and in themselves an expression of "defensive modernization"), and in their marriage with party politics.[5] Young people's conviction of the unique situation of the Jewish people had similar roots. Indeed, it drew much from the nineteenth- and twentieth-century concepts of the "Jewish question," but at the same time the traditional category *am sgula*, a people different from all others, resounded again and again in the autobiographies of recently secularized authors, who studied in heders and prayed with their fathers in the synagogue, and in their opinions about the uniqueness of the Jewish situation. The success of a specific type of Jewish politics in winning over hundreds of thousands of followers was to reconcile completely new forms of political organization and social radicalism with ethnonationalism. Jewish political involvement was not supported by state institutions but was created within the minority itself. As such, it was not coercive but entirely voluntary. Only in this sense can modern organizational forms, led by youth parties and movements, be considered a continuation of traditional forms in the shape of a shtetl, a chevra kadisha, or local self-government.

The autobiographies, as well as many nonautobiographical sources used here, tended to minimize the importance of the influence exerted by the state and by Polish elite and mass culture on Jewish youth. A specific type of influence explicitly emphasized by the sources was antisemitism. As I have tried to demonstrate through a critical analysis of these sources, the symbolic acculturation often hidden by the participants in the YIVO competitions was no less important. The latter manifested itself at the level of the everyday language of young people, their reading material, and their ideas about themselves and their non-Jewish environment. Young people were part of the Jewish imaginary community, but the elements of symbolism that form the basis of these images came from Polish schools or books. Increasing Polish acculturation, patriotism, and attachment to the Polish nation and its historical narratives only increased bitterness due to antisemitic rejection. The mixture of these two influences fueled young Jews' political radicalism and caused masses of young people to join youth parties and organizations. The main determinants of the popularity of modern, nationalist Jewish politics in interwar Poland were therefore acculturation and simultaneous rejection. At the same time, the phenomenon of young people's acculturation was an indicator of the failure of some of the most important goals of national Jewish politics in east-central Europe. It failed to achieve either Jewish autonomy or integration with the surrounding society. Autonomy was impossible mainly because of antisemitism and the refusal of dominant nations to grant any formal autonomy to the Jewish minority. Integration was a failure because of both antisemitism and internal inconsistencies within Jewish national politics. Parties proclaimed the need for Jews to put down roots in the new reality and to have the same rights and duties toward the country, a knowledge of its culture, and a positive attitude toward it, as well as Polish patriotism. Meanwhile, Jewish national institutions failed to develop guidelines to help young people understand when integration turned into a total loss of identity—assimilation, labeled as unequivocally negative. The result was a situation in which Jewish institutions, especially political organizations, coming out against multifaceted acculturation processes that they were unable to counteract, proposed a model of Jewish social and cultural autarky, separatism, everyday life in a closed Jewish circle, and a single national culture. Consequently, Jewish politics proposed only one coherent model of individual identity: Jewish and only Jewish, which did not fit into the reality of a multinational state. Its popular definitions did not contain parameters on how to reconcile Jewish national identity with the need for social and cultural integration with the Polish majority and other national groups living in the Second Republic.

The Jewish minority was not only a victim and an object but also a subject of politics. Jews adopted an active approach toward social issues concerning themselves. This community's problems, including anomie, were not merely produced by the non-Jewish majority. The formation of a specific character of Jewish political culture in the 1930s and its popularity among young people were influenced by the decades-long internal crisis, or rather, the conviction of the weakness and pathology of the traditional forms of Jewish life. Successive generations of Jewish reformers demanded ever-more-radical solutions to the crisis, not only adopting external ideological solutions but also demonstrating innovation in this field. This kind of radicalism peaked in the 1930s. The external impact in the form of a kind of spirit of the decade, peculiar to the whole of Europe at that time, was very important here. But in addition to external causes, there were also no less important internal Jewish factors that shaped the radicalism of the youngest generation. The specific counterculture of the political organizations presented here, with its emphasis on the ideologization of all spheres of life, was coresponsible for the separation of young people from the non-Jewish environment and for their sociopolitical exclusion.

This does not mean, however, that the broader sociopolitical context did not have a significant impact on Jewish political culture. It was a minority culture, and the influence of the majority was one of the most important factors determining its character. According to the experience of young Jews growing up in the reality of the Second Republic, the separatist character of their organizations was partly an unintended consequence of the policy of the Polish state. Alienation was undoubtedly reinforced by ubiquitous antisemitism in its many guises, including attacks on the Jewish community and its culture, norms, values, lifestyles, and dominant forms of economic activity. A perfect example of this was the experience of Jewish students in Polish schools. Public institutions, even if they did not themselves engage in openly anti-Jewish practices, permitted antisemitism. Not only hatred of Jews influenced Jewish alienation but also the lack of a civic definition of the nation, analogous to the situation on the Jewish side, the absence of an imagined community encompassing all people in the Second Republic to transcend national divisions. Jewish children encountered Polish ethnic patriotism in schools; some of them did not want to become part of this nation, and the rest simply could not. This is most evident in the experience of acculturated Jews, who were not allowed to become Poles. The paradox was that the more young Jews became polonized, the more they felt that, regardless of their attitudes and declarations, the country in which they grew up and that they had learned to love was not their own. The experience of young Jews thus marks the failure of integral nationalism (both Polish and Jewish) as a model of individual identity and group organization in the reality of a multinational, modern state. This reality required the creation of a possibility to be both a Pole and a Jew, not defining all everyday attitudes and choices in national terms. Thus, young people operated between two exclusivist national definitions—Polish and Jewish. Given the scale of interwar antisemitism and strong ethnic bonds, the majority of them unequivocally opted for the latter. And it was precisely in this situation that radical organizations, the function of which went far beyond politics, were able to attract young people and tend to their needs. This was most evident in the case of informal education, so important in the lives of Jewish youth parties and organizations. The high level of ideologization, or often even indoctrination, took place under conditions where the vast majority of citizens of the Second Republic (Jews and non-Jews) did not have access to fee-paying secondary and higher education, and where systemic discrimination aimed specifically at Jews—numerus clausus rules, antisemitism, and violence at universities, as well as secondary and elementary schools—was rampant.[6]

The influence of the Polish state on Jewish youth, led by universal education, affected life beyond the political sphere. The nationally oriented state significantly accelerated acculturation processes among the Jewish population and the development of Polish Jewish culture. Hitherto only a segment of the richer elites living in the largest cities in Poland and in Galicia had embraced the culture of Polish Jews expressed in Polish. Now this culture was dramatically increasing its social and geographical reach. In the 1930s, children from traditional Yiddish-speaking families entered this culture en masse. One of the paradoxes of the interwar era was that this widespread social process had virtually no politically significant patron. On the Polish side, discrimination, antisemitism, and calls for limiting the presence of Jews in Polish social life, the economy, and culture were too strong. On the Jewish side, guided by the ethnonationalist definition of a unified national culture, free from external influences, the fear of losing one's national identity was too strong. As the statements of important Jewish politicians and cultural activists attest, in their opinion Polish Jewish culture was clearly part of this loss of national identity. Young people's attitude of ambivalence toward the Polish language and culture did not only result from the fact that they were writing their works for the competition for YIVO, a national and Yiddishist institution. The institute was only one of many national Jewish institutions that rejected Polish Jewish culture. This rejection was the dominant approach, but not the only one. In the 1930s, groups focusing on the Warsaw Institute of Judaic Studies, Braude's utraquist schools, and Yiddish literary circles began to realize not only the sterility of the dispute between Hebraism and Yiddishism, the struggle for the only language of true Jewish national culture, but also the inevitability of the processes of polonization. Polish reality was leaving a growing imprint on the culture of Polish Jews. Although they did not use the word fashionable today, they realized that it would develop as a "hybrid" minority culture. Jewish culture in the Second Republic was becoming Polish Jewish culture. Inhabitants of this in-between space appealed to the Polish majority to accept them as a valid part of Polish culture, respecting Jewish diversity as well as literature in Yiddish and Hebrew functioning alongside Polish literature. On the Polish side, it was very difficult to find supporters of acceptance. As the young people's autobiographies attest, these voices were not heard by the Jewish masses either.[7]

The generational pattern of thinking and political action, formed in the specific conditions of the interwar period, played an important role during World War II. The simultaneous deep acculturation and resentment toward the Polish state, resulting from the antisemitic rejection of the polonized generation, and the total submission to the political culture of radical modernism explain the attitudes of many young Jews toward the political situation in the east of the country in 1939–1941 and the large numbers of people from this generation who decided to cooperate with the Soviet authorities.[8] At the same time, the younger generation's hostility toward the adult world and their patterns of accommodation and cooperation with external authority are certainly factors explaining the attitudes of many well-known figures of this generation toward the Judenrat and their own resistance activities.[9] These factors may also go some way to explaining the often generational character of various patterns of Jewish responses to Nazi extermination policy.[10] Interwar Jewish youth and political organizations shaped the attitudes and the methods of self-organization, action, and thinking about the world of members of Jewish resistance movements during the Holocaust in Poland.[11] At the same time, models of modern ethnonational separation established in the Second Republic and the distance between Jews and Christians had tragic consequences in this context. During the Holocaust, many Christians treated their Jewish neighbors, people who had lived with them and next to them for many generations as strangers, as not part of the Polish community or even with hostility. Recent research shows that interwar ethnonationalism played a key role in the participation of some citizens of the prewar Polish state in the Holocaust.[12]

I do not believe that it makes much sense to speculate as to how the lives of 3.5 million Polish Jews would have turned out had it not been for World War II. Would Poland, following the example of other countries in that part of Europe (Hungary and Romania), have continued to move toward authoritarianism, discrimination, and the exclusion of Jewish citizens? Or would a democratic or social-democratic revolution have occurred under the pressure of all the deep social crises of the interwar period? What influence could these two and other possible scenarios have had on the phenomena described in this work: radical Jewish political culture, the formation of modern Polish Orthodoxy, the further evolution of modern Yiddish culture, the Zionism of Polish Jews, Polish Jewish culture, and Polish patriotism? These questions cannot be answered, if only because hypothetical answers to them also depend on other alternative scenarios in the course of history throughout Europe, the Middle East, and the United States, which also had a huge impact on the fate of the Polish Jewish community.

The fact is that the modern culture and civilization of Polish Jews, established in the nineteenth century and reaching its peak in the interwar period, was largely destroyed during the Holocaust. This does not mean, however, that there were no elements of its continuation after 1945. Postwar Zionist sympathies, the desire to emigrate to Palestine/the Land of Israel or the United States should be analyzed not only in the context of the trauma of the Holocaust but, as Kenneth Moss points out, also in the context of the interwar crisis and further back. Since the 1880s commentators developed the concept of *yetsiyes Eyrope* (leaving Europe), and among politicians, creators of culture, and an increasing number of the Jewish masses of east-central Europe, there was a growing conviction that the center of Jewish world was moving or should move to the south, to the Land of Israel, or to the west, to the United States.[13] At the same time, elements of continuation of interwar Polish Jewish culture can also be seen in the opposite phenomenon—in the attempts made after the Holocaust, especially in 1945–1948, to rebuild the Polish Jewish community in various manifestations, such as the patterns of raising children orphaned

by the Holocaust living in Jewish orphanages; in the everyday postwar political culture of Zionist organizations operating in the country at that time; in
the Bund; and finally in the faith of many survivors in building a new, better
communist Poland.[14] For many, it was not the Kielce pogrom of the summer of
1946 but the most severe period of communist dictatorship between 1948 and
1956, the outbreak of grassroots, popular antisemitism in 1956–1957, and the
state-led antisemitic campaign of 1968 that put an end to these hopes. Today,
those elements of the pre-Holocaust civilization of Polish Jews that survived
the Holocaust are evolving, are continued, and are being creatively developed
outside Poland among its descendants who live in the United States, Israel,
South America, Canada, Australia, or western Europe. However, elements of
this civilization are also available to a few Polish Jews and Poles in the form of
a rich, largely unrecognized, difficult but at the same time fascinating heritage,
the study of which provides important lessons for the future.

NOTES

INTRODUCTION

1. Wiktor Alter, *Człowiek w społeczeństwie* (Światło, 1938), 5–6.

2. Stanley G. Payne, *Civil War in Europe, 1905–1949* (Cambridge University Press, 2011), 15–18.

3. Payne, *Civil War in Europe*, 67–70.

4. *Sanacja* was the popular name used to refer to the postcoup regime; the Polish word is derived from the Latin word *sanatio* and means "healing" or "cleansing." This was in reference to a perceived need to "cleanse" the government of corruption, waste, and all that was holding the country back from achieving its full potential.

5. In this introduction, which deals with the main problem of this book (i.e., the socialization and political consciousness of Jewish young people), there is no space for anything other than a very general and cursory presentation of the history of the Second Polish Republic. Those aspects of it that are relevant to the problems discussed in this work are discussed in more detail in the following chapters. For readers interested more deeply in various other aspects of the political and social history of Polish in the interwar period, I refer primarily to Brian Porter-Szűcs, *Poland in the Modern World: Beyond Martyrdom* (Wiley Blackwell 2014), 65–143; Antony Polonsky, *Politics in Independent Poland, 1921–1939: The Crisis of Constitutional Government* (Oxford University Press, 1972); Eva Plach, *The Clash of Moral Nations: Cultural Politics in Piłsudski's Poland, 1926–1935* (Ohio University Press, 2006); Włodzimierz Mędrzecki, *Odzyskany śmietnik: Jak radziliśmy sobie z niepodległością w II Rzeczypospolitej* (Wydawnictwo Literackie, 2022).

6. Joanna Michlic, *Poland's Threatening Other. The Image of the Jew from 1880 to the Present* (University of Nebraska Press, 2006), 24–130; Paul Brykczyński,

Primed for Violence: Murder, Antisemitism, and Democratic Politics in Interwar Poland (University of Wisconsin Press, 2016); Grzegorz Krzywiec, "The Balance of Polish Political Antisemitism: Between 'National Revolution,' Economic Crisis, and the Transformation of the Polish Public Sphere in the 1930s," in *Right-Wing Politics and the Rise of Antisemitism in Europe, 1935–1941*, ed. Frank Bajohr and Dieter Pohl (Wallstein Verlag, 2019), 61–80; Paul Hanebrink, *A Specter Haunting Europe: The Myth of Judeo-Bolshevism* (Harvard University Press, 2018); Zofia Trębacz, *Nie tylko Palestyna: Polskie plany emigracyjne wobec Żydów, 1935–1939* (ŻIH, 2018).

7. The best introduction to all the most important problems of Jewish political, social, and cultural life in interwar Poland is still the classic text by Ezra Mendelsohn, *The Jews of East Central Europe between the World Wars* (Indiana University Press, 1987), 10–83.

8. See, e.g., Ezra Mendelsohn, *On Modern Jewish Politics* (Oxford University Press, 1993), 120–121; Joseph Marcus, *Social and Political History of the Jews in Poland, 1919–1939* (Mouton, 1983), 261–262.

9. Kenneth B. Moss, *An Unchosen People: Jewish Political Reckoning in Interwar Poland* (Harvard University Press, 2021).

10. This book attempts to fulfill the demands of "Jewish social history standing over and above nationalist aims, extending beyond the historiography of the elites and their ideas." On this subject, see Lloyd P. Gartner, "Paths to Jewish Social History," *Studies in Contemporary Jewry* 3 (1987): 204–212; Todd M. Endelman, "In Defense of Jewish Social History," *Jewish Social Studies* 7, no. 3 (2001): 52–67.

11. Roman Wapiński, *Pokolenia Drugiej Rzeczypospolitej* (Ossolineum, 1991), 248–249.

12. Emanuel Melzer, *No Way Out: The Politics of Polish Jewry, 1935–1939* (Hebrew Union College Press, 1997); Alina Cała, *Żyd—wróg odwieczny? Antysemityzm w Polsce i jego źródła* (Nisza, 2012), 325–418; Paweł Korzec, "Antisemitism in Poland as an Intellectual, Social and Political Movement," in *Studies on Polish Jewry, 1919–1939: The Interplay of Social, Economic and Political Factors in the Struggle of a Minority for Its Existence*, ed. Joshua A. Fishman (YIVO, 1974), 12–104.

13. For a classic definition of antisemitism as a cultural code, see Shulamit Volkov, "Antisemitism as a Cultural Code: Reflections on the History and Historiography of Antisemitism in Imperial Germany," *Leo Baeck Institute Year Book* 23 (1978): 25–46. For its application to the case of Poland, see Grzegorz Krzywiec, "Żydzi, 'kwestia żydowska' i antysemityzm na ziemiach polskich w kontekście środkowoeuropejskim na przełomie XIX i XX wieku: Antysemicki habitus—kod antysemicki-ideologia antysemicka," in *Drogi odrębne, drogi wspólne: Problem specyfiki rozwoju historycznego Europy Środkowo-Wschodniej w XIX–XX wieku*, ed. Maciej Janowski (Instytut Historii PAN, 2014), 281–300.

14. Włodzimierz Mędrzecki, "Polskie uniwersum symboliczne w Drugiej Rzeczypospolitej," in *Kultura i społeczeństwo w II Rzeczypospolitej: Metamorfozy społeczne*, ed. Włodzimierz Mędrzecki and Agata Zawiszewska (Instytut Historii PAN, 2012), 25.

15. Gershon Hundert, *Jews in Poland-Lithuania in the Eighteenth Century: A Genealogy of Modernity* (University of California Press, 2004); Moshe Rosman, "Innovative Tradition: Jewish Culture in the Polish-Lithuanian Commonwealth," in *Cultures of the Jews: A New History*, ed. David Biale (Schocken, 2002), 519–570.

16. Rebbeca Kobrin, *Jewish Bialystok and Its Diaspora* (University of Indiana Press 2010); Jonathan Dekel-Chen, "Transnational Intervention and Its Limits: The Case of Interwar Poland," *Journal of Modern Jewish Studies* 17 (2018): 265–286; Rona Yona, *Nehiye kulanu halutzim: Ha-tnuat ha-avoda ve-ha-aliya mi-Polin 1923–1936* (Magnes, 2021).

17. Moshe Rosman, *How Jewish Is Jewish History?* (Littman, 2008), 94.

18. Rosman, *How Jewish*, 95–104.

19. For this kind of understanding of the category of a particular generation of interwar Poland, see Wapiński, *Pokolenia*, 10–11; Marci Shore, *Caviar and Ashes: A Warsaw Generation's Life and Death in Marxism, 1918–1968* (Yale University Press, 2006); Jaff Schatz, *The Generation: The Rise and Fall of the Jewish Communists of Poland* (University of California Press, 1991).

20. Karl Mannheim, *Ideology and Utopia* (Routledge, 2003).

21. Yaacov Shavit, *Jabotinsky and the Revisionist Movement, 1925–1948* (Frank Cass, 1988), 6–7.

22. Clifford Geertz, "Ideology as Cultural System," in *Ideology and Discontent*, ed. David Apter (Collier Macmillan, 1964), 53, 56.

23. Geertz, "Ideology as Cultural System," 64.

24. Mary S. Mander, "Bourdieu, the Sociology of Culture and Cultural Studies: A Critique," *European Journal of Communication* 2 (1987): 432.

25. Itamar Even-Zohar, *Papers in Culture Research* (Porter Chair of Semiotics, Tel-Aviv University, 2005), 50–67.

26. Even-Zohar, *Papers in Culture Research*, 21.

27. Pierre Bourdieu and Loïc J. D. Wacquant, *An Invitation to Reflexive Sociology* (Polity, 1992), 120–122.

28. Pierre Bourdieu and Jean-Claude Passeron, *Reproduction in Education, Society and Culture* (Sage, 1990), 5.

29. Mander, "Bourdieu," 428.

30. Thirty-one of them, also used here, have been published in two books: Jeffrey Shandler, ed., *Awakening Lives: Autobiographies of Jewish Youth in Poland before the Holocaust* (Yale University Press, 2002); Alina Cała, ed., *Ostatnie pokolenie: autobiografie polskiej młodzieży żydowskiej okresu międzywojennego: ze zbioru YIVO Institute for Jewish Research w Nowym Jorku* (Wydawnictwo Sic!,

2003). A few years later, a Hebrew collection of YIVO autobiographies appeared, in which there were also several new ones, never before published anywhere, in addition to some of the same autobiographies published in Cała's and Shandler's collections: Ido Bassok and Avraham Novershtern, eds., *Alilot ne'arim: Autobiografiot shel bnei no'ar yehudim mi-Polin bein shtei milhamot ha-olam* (Institute for the History of Polish Jewry, 2011). Thanks to Ido Bassok's generosity, originals of some of these previously unpublished ones have been used in this work.

31.   For more on the competition's principles, its general social and political contexts, and their effect on the autobiographies of young Jewish people, see Kamil Kijek, "Max Weinreich, Assimilation and the Social Politics of Jewish Nation Building," *East European Jewish Affairs* 41, nos. 1–2 (2011): 25–55; Leila Zenderland, "Social Science as a 'Weapon of the Weak': Max Weinreich, the Yiddish Scientific Institute, and the Study of Culture, Personality, and Prejudice," *Isis* 104, no. 4 (2013): 742–772; Katherine Lebow, "The Conscience of the Skin: Interwar Polish Autobiography and Social Rights," *Humanity* 3, no. 3 (2012): 297–319. On the history of YIVO between the wars, see Cecile E. Kuznitz, *YIVO and the Making of Modern Jewish Culture: Scholarship for the Yiddish Nation* (Cambridge University Press, 2014).

32.   In this regard, leaflets on the competition were modeled on similar announcements by Polish sociologists collecting autobiographies of the younger generation of workers and peasants. See, e.g., YIVO Archives, RG 4, 3880 *Berikht far Merts-May 1939*, 5–6.

33.   *Yedies fun YIVO* nos. 1–3 (vols. 42–44), (1934), 5. See, too, the almost similar content of the 1932 competition leaflet. YIVO Archives, RG 584, 346. During the second, and at the same time first national, competition in 1934 (in 1932 it was limited to Vilnius and the surrounding area), a sentence on intrafamilial relations was added to the one on the family, as was one on the issue of relations with friends to the question on friends. See Max Weinreich, *Der veg tsu undzer yugnt: Yesodes, medotn, problemn fun yidisher yugnt forshung* (YIVO Institut, 1935), 129, n. 87.

34.   *Yedies fun YIVO* nos. 1–3 (vols. 42–44), (1934), 5–6; *Yedies fun YIVO* nos. 4–5 (45–46), (1934), 2; YIVO Archives, RG 584, 346, competition leaflet in Yiddish.

35.   What is striking is the lack of guidance as to which language should be used for writing the autobiographies. This could suggest to young people that YIVO, as a Yiddish-supporting institution, would regard work written in Yiddish more highly. Indeed, in the collection of autobiographies there are works written in Yiddish, which the writers spoke fluently but did not necessarily know how to write.

36.   *Yedies fun YIVO* nos. 1–3 (vols. 42–44), (1934), 5–6. See too *Yedies fun YIVO* nos. 4–5 (vols. 45–46), (1934), 2; as well as YIVO Archival Inventory to RG 584, 346, 1932 competition leaflet in Yiddish. What is striking here is the consistent use of the same guidelines for writers in the succeeding competitions.

37. The overwhelming majority of participants in the prewar competition tried to maintain their anonymity. In many of the autobiographies, the writers did not even give the names of the places from which they came. This emphatically distinguished them from young Americans, who were writing their autobiographies for a competition organized by Weinreich and Kligsberg in 1942. Jewish immigrants into the United States for the most part ignored the guidelines on sending in their personal details in sealed envelopes and signed their own autobiographies. This is direct proof of a strong generational conflict within the Jewish community between the wars, about which more later. See Moshe Kligsberg, "Socio-Psychological Problems Reflected in the YIVO Autobiography Contest," *YIVO Annual of Jewish Social Science* 1 (1946): 244.

38. See, for example, Weinreich's similar thoughts in *Der veg tsu undzer yugnt*, 186–189.

39. *Oysforshung vegn der antviklung fun der yidisher yugnt (Yugfor)*, YIVO Archives, RG 4, 3881, doc. no. 150752, 1; Max Weinreich, "Yidishe yugnt-forshung," *YIVO Bleter* 7, nos. 1–2 (1934): 4, 18–19; YIVO Archives, RG 584, 64—*Culture and Personality Studies Among the Eastern European Jews and Their Relation to the General Problems of Social Science*, 5–6; Weinreich, *Der veg tsu undzer yugnt*, 26, 203–207.

40. Weinreich, *Der veg tsu undzer yugnt*, 9–10.

41. YIVO Archives, RG 4, 3887, two-page competition leaflet, reverse side.

42. In fact, YIVO was frequently roiled by internal conflicts as to the limits of its own political involvement. For more on these political conflicts, see Kuznitz, *YIVO*, 99–109, 148; Samuel D. Kassow, *Who Will Write Our History? Rediscovering a Hidden Archive from the Warsaw Ghetto* (Indiana University Press, 2007), 40–41. These conflicts were about whether the institute was to work closely with revolutionary parties like the Bund or Po'alei-Tsiyon-Left, or to keep its distance in order to avoid a crackdown by the authorities. Its actual assessment of the sociopolitical reality placed the institute unambiguously on the side of the left.

43. For more on this subject, see Kamil Kijek, "Między uniwersalną nauką a narodową polityką: Charakter projektu badań nad młodzieżą Żydowskiego Instytutu Naukowego (JIWO) w Polsce międzywojennej," *Kwartalnik Historii Żydów* 2 (2010): 177–183.

44. For more on this, see Katherine Lebow, "Autobiography as Complaint: Polish Social Memoir Between the World Wars," *Laboratorium* 6, no. 3 (2014): 13–26.

45. *Oysforshung vegn der antviklung*, YIVO Archives, RG 4, 3881, doc. no. 150752, 4; YIVO Archives, RG 584, 148, lack of pagination, and an extract from *Forverts*, a letter to the editor from Jacob Lestchinsky, dated August 30, 1934; see also Barbara Kirshenblatt-Gimblett's introduction to Shandler, *Awakening Lives*, xxv; Barbara Kirshenblatt-Gimblett, "Coming of Age in the 1930s: Max Weinreich, Edward Sapir and Jewish Social Science," *YIVO Annual* 23 (1996): 91.

46. On Weinreich's negative and even hostile attitude toward interwar Orthodoxy, see, e.g., Weinreich, *Der veg tsu undzer yugnt*, 295–298 (where in his selection of quotations taken from autobiographies submitted to YIVO in 1932 and 1934, he chose only those sharply criticizing Orthodoxy); Kirshenblatt-Gimblett, "Coming of Age," 70–74.

47. For more on this subject, see Kamil Kijek, "Świadomość i socjalizacja polityczna ostatniego pokolenia Żydów Polskich w II Rzeczypospolitej" (doctoral thesis, Instytut Historii PAN, 2013), 27–35.

48. Kijek, "Świadomość i socjalizacja polityczna," 186–193.

49. The first competition, open only to young people from Vilnius and the surrounding area, attracted thirty-four autobiographies. Three of them received awards: 150 zloty for first place, 50 for second, and 25 for third; an additional six competitors received a YIVO publication. In the second competition, in which almost three hundred authors took part, seven of them received money prizes. *Yedies fun YIVO* 1 (51), I (1935), 8; *Yedies fun YIVO* 3 (38), V (1932), n.p.; *Yedies fun YIVO* 2 (41), III (1933), 7; YIVO Archives, RG 584, 346, a competition leaflet in Yiddish.

50. On different motivations for taking part in the competition, see, for example, YIVO Archives, RG 4, Autobiography 3507, in Yiddish, 1934 (letter to YIVO attached to the autobiography); YIVO Archives, RG 584, 368, "Beniamin R.," *Bamerkung un ubertrakhtn tsum bukh fun dr. M. Weinreich* "Der veg tsum undzer yugnt," YIVO Archives, RG 719, 375; Moshe Kligsberg, *Persenlekhe tsiln un gezelshaftlekhe idealn bay der yidisher yugnt in Poyln*, 25.03.1940, YIVO Archives, RG 719, 375, 1–5; YIVO Archives, RG 4, 486, typescript *Oysforshung vegn der antviklung*, 1; Ido Bassok, "Le-she'elat erkan ha-histori shel otobiografiyot bnei no'ar mi-osef YIVO," *Madei Yahadut* 44 (2007): 145–147; YIVO Archives, RG 4, Autobiography 3819, 1, 37; YIVO Archives, RG 4, Autobiography 3645 (letter to YIVO), n.p.; YIVO Archives, RG 4, Autobiography 3701, 43–44; YIVO Archives, RG 4, Autobiography 3629, n.p.; Autobiography 3507 (report attached to the autobiography), 11; YIVO Archives, RG 4, Autobiography 3666, n.p.

51. This was what Mendl Man did, indicating that his autobiography was separate from the literary remarks on his hometown, which accompanied it. See YIVO Archives, RG 4, Autobiography 3802, additional materials sent in together with autobiography, 15–16. Mendl Man was one of a few participants in the YIVO competition who survived World War II. In 1948 he emigrated from Łódź to Palestine, where he became a painter, writer, and important activist on behalf of the development of Yiddish culture in Israel, one of the collaborators on the famous Yiddish publication *Di Goldene Keyt*. In 1961 he emigrated to Paris, and he died in France in 1975.

52. Kijek, "Między uniwersalną nauką," 161–162.

53. YIVO Archival Inventory to RG 4, *Autobiographies of Jewish Youth in Poland: Collection 1932–1939*, ed. Rivka Schiller, 2006. We should bear in mind

that some of the autobiographies contain parts in two languages (for the most part Yiddish and Polish) and sometimes even in three. The introduction to the list gives the incorrect number of 375 (instead of 384) autobiographies that are available to scholars. Some publications inaccurately give the number of 900 autobiographies that the institute supposedly collected. In fact, there were over 900 documents in all, including some that were not autobiographical memoirs. Being at the time in Vilnius and working on the competition material, Kligsberg gave a number of 620 autobiographies that were in the possession of the institute in 1940, of which he personally managed to obtain 410 after the war. Moshe Kligsberg, *Child and Adolescent Behavior Under Stress: An Analytical Topical Guide to a Collection of Autobiographies of Jewish Young Men and Women in Poland (1932–1939)* (YIVO, 1965), 3–4.

54. Kligsberg, *Child and Adolescent behavior,* 10.

1. TRADITION: YOUNG PEOPLE IN THE WORLD OF THEIR PARENTS, RELIGION, THE SHTETL, AND THE JEWISH NEIGHBORHOOD

1. A shoykhet (Yiddish) or shohet (Hebrew) is a person responsible for the ritual slaughter of animals.

2. YIVO Archives, RG 4, Autobiography 3508, 1.

3. *Balebatim* are owners or proprietors of shops or enterprises who run their own business.

4. Autobiography 3508, 1–2.

5. Autobiography 3508, 6.

6. This was probably a coeducational heder (*heder irbuvia*), which girls could attend together with boys, and which began to appear in the area of Litvak Judaism toward the end of the nineteenth century. See Yaffa Eliach, *There Once Was a World: A 900-Year Chronicle of the Shtetl Eishyshok* (Little, Brown, 1998), 168–171.

7. Schools for Jewish girls, run on the women's side of synagogues, began to appear in the future northeastern part of the Second Republic when this area was still in Tsarist Russia. See Chaim Shloyme Kazhdan, *Fun kheyder un 'shkoles' biz TSYSHO* (Shloyme Mendelsohn Fond, 1956), 202–207. On the general characteristics of the modernization of traditional Jewish education, including girls', see Rachel Elboim Dror, "Maslulei modernizatsya ba-hinukh me-ha-heder le beit ha-sefer," in *Ha-heder: Mekorim, te'udot, prakei sifrut ve-zikhronot,* eds. Dawid Assaf and Emanuel Etkes (Beit Shalom Aleichem, 2010), 57–76.

8. Autobiography 3508, 9–12.

9. Autobiography 3508, 2.

10. A *psak* or *psuk* is a halakhic decision by rabbinical authority resolving a dispute on a matter of ritual. It is found most frequently in rabbinical responses.

11. YIVO Archives, RG 4, Autobiography 3718, 2.

12. Autobiography 3718, 2–3.

13. YIVO Archives, RG 4, Autobiography 3581 (not 3587, as Alina Cała states in her collection of autobiographies), cited in Cała, *Ostatnie pokolenie*, 21. It is worth pointing out that the profession of melamed also had no prestige in traditional society. See, e.g., Eliach, *There Once Was a World*, 149–150.

14. YIVO Archives, RG 4, Autobiography 3666, 1.

15. YIVO Archives, RG 4, Autobiography 3802, 1.

16. Autobiography 3802, 2.

17. This type of Haskalah criticism of gender roles in traditional Jewish society probably arrived most frequently by way of later, classical Yiddish literature from the end of the nineteenth century. See Iris Parush, *Reading Jewish Women: Marginality and Modernization in Nineteenth-Century Eastern European Jewish Society* (Brandeis University Press, 2004), 42–46.

18. See, e.g., parents' prohibitions on going to dances that were the domain of Hukei ha-Goy (laws for goyim). YIVO Archives, RG 4, Autobiography 3832 ("Mars"), as cited in Cała, *Ostatnie pokolenie*, 309, 310.

19. Autobiography 3832, 312.

20. YIVO Archives, RG 4, Autobiography 3504, 1.

21. Autobiography 3504, 1.

22. YIVO Archives, RG 4, Autobiography 3591, 8–12.

23. Talmud Torah was the name given to the traditional religious educational establishment for the very youngest children run by Jewish local communities and usually intended for their poorest members.

24. Autobiography 3591, 22–25.

25. YIVO Archives, RG 4, Autobiography 3732, 2.

26. Autobiography 3732, 3–10.

27. Autobiography 3732, 26–27, 30–31.

28. The nature of the sources and the aim of this work do not allow me to speculate about any other reasons than those mentioned above for such great pessimism in the young people's autobiographies. It is possible that certain traditional cultural models played a part in this. Doubtless a sense of being lost, uncertainty as to the future, and finally a critical attitude toward everything symbolizing the "adult world" characterize each younger, not only Jewish generation, and not only between the wars. What distinguished the writers of the YIVO autobiographies was the specific political significance that they gave to their own individual experiences.

29. Marcus Moseley, "Life, Literature: Autobiographies of Jewish Youth in Interwar Poland," *Jewish Social Studies* 7, no. 1 (2003): 1.

30. Moseley is a proponent of this notion—"Life, Literature," 12.

31. Marcus Moseley, "Autobiography and Memoir," *The YIVO Encyclopedia of Jews in Eastern Europe*, accessed July 7, 2025, https://encyclopedia.yivo.org /article/142.

32. Marcus Moseley, *Being for Myself Alone: Origins of Jewish Autobiography* (Stanford University Press, 2006), 50–66; Assaf and Etkes, *Ha-heder*, 349–484; David Assaf, ed., *Journey to a Nineteenth-Century Shtetl: The Memoirs of Yekhezkel Kotik* (Wayne State University Press, 2002); Kazhdan, *Fun kheyder*, 139–154; Yekhiel Shtern, *Kheyder un Beys-Medresh* (YIVO, 1950), 28–32.

33. See, e.g., Salomon Mendelson, ed., *Nowa Szkoła Żydowska, czem jest i do czego dąży* (Biblioteka "Szkolnictwo Żydowskie," 1926), 15–16; Hertz Kowarski, "Dos yidishe kind un di yidishe shul," in *Far undzer shul: Ayntolike oysgabe fun Tsentraln Bildungs-Komitet (TseBeKa) in Vilne*, ed. Shloyme Bastomski (TzeBeKa, 1933), 7–9; *Wychowanie dziecka żydowskiego dawniej a dziś/Di ertsiyung funem yidishn kind amol un Haynt* (Hebrajska Szkoła "Tarbut," 1936), 1–17 (extract in Polish); *Chinuchenu: Nasze wychowanie* (Dyrekcja Kursów "Tarbutu," 1932), 3.

34. YIVO's attitude toward basic traditional Jewish education is perhaps most emphatically exemplified by the competition for memories of heders, organized by the institute in 1927 and 1928 and repeated in 1932. The aim of the study was to provide a reasonably complete picture of the reality of education in a heder, and sixteen of its seventy-nine questions dealt with violence toward children in it. See Diane K. Roskies, "Der kheyder proyekt bay der psikhologish-pedagogisher sektsye fun YIVO," *YIVO Bleter* 46 (1980): 269–281. Similar criticism can be found in the memoirs of Ben-Zion Gold, a future Orthodox rabbi in the United States, who grew up in interwar Radom. Ben-Zion Gold, "Religious Education in Poland: A Personal Perspective," in *The Jews of Poland Between Two World Wars*, ed. Yisrael Gutman et al. (University Press of New England, 1989), 273–274.

35. Autobiography 3591, 1–3.

36. YIVO Archives, RG 4, Autobiography 3726, 17.

37. YIVO Archives, RG 4, Autobiography 3571, 2.

38. Autobiography 3571, 3.

39. Autobiography 3591, 1–2.

40. YIVO Archives, RG 4, Autobiography 3770, 1.

41. Autobiography 3770, 14.

42. YIVO Archives, RG 4, Autobiography 3561, 10.

43. I deal later with the modernized heders, similar to schools, which were seen positively by Z.G. and other writers (associated with centers of modern Orthodoxy while writing their autobiographies).

44. YIVO Archives, RG 4, Autobiography 3507, 2–3.

45. YIVO Archives, RG 4, Autobiography 3663, 2.

46. YIVO Archives, RG 4, Autobiography 3861, 5–8.

47. Autobiography 3861, 9–14, 26–30. On heders and social distance in the YIVO autobiographers' world, see Ido Bassok, "Ma'amadot ve-tfisa ma'amdit etsel yeladim ve-bnei no'ar yehudi be-polin bein ha-milhamot," *Gal-Ed* 18 (2002): 233–234.

48. YIVO Archives, RG 4, Autobiography 3632, 1.

49. YIVO Archives, RG 4, Autobiography 3519, 1.

50. Autobiography 3519, 4.

51. Autobiography 3519, 5–7.

52. A beit midrash (Hebrew) or *beys-midrash* (Yiddish), "house of learning," differed from a synagogue or a house of prayer in that alongside prayers the Torah was also studied there. This term is sometimes used interchangeably with *synagogue*. A similar word is the Yiddish *shul*, "school." In traditional Jewish space, the prayer hall and the school hall were most often next to one another in the same building. A *kloyz* is a house of prayer established by a professional group (e.g., the shoemakers' *kloyz*, the tailors' *kloyz*, etc.) or by a religious group (e.g., the *kloyz* of the Hasidim from Sadagóra).

53. *Kine* (Hebrew) literally means lamentation recalling the destruction of the Temple in Jerusalem or other Jewish disasters; *shnae* (Hebrew) means "hatred."

54. *Chevra Kadisha* (Hebrew) means "a sacred confraternity, association"— a term designating a traditional funeral confraternity. Both men and women belonged to it. Its duty was to assure burial in line with halakhic principles.

55. Linat ha-Tsedek (pronounced "lines ha-tsedek" by the Ashkenazi) (Hebrew) is a religious charitable organization established in the 1930s, closely associated with Agudat Israel.

56. YIVO Archives, RG 4, Autobiography 3548, 1–2. See too other memories of Briańsk, conveying a similar temperature of political and intergenerational disputes—Eva Hoffman, *Shtetl: The Life and Death of a Small Town and the World of the Polish Jews* (Public Affairs, 2007), 180–181.

57. Autobiography 3548, 7–10.

58. YIVO Archives, RG 4, Autobiography 3590, as cited in Shandler, *Awakening Lives*, 54.

59. Autobiography 3590, 53, 55.

60. Autobiography 3590, 59–63.

61. Autobiography 3590, 53.

62. Autobiography 3590, 54–55.

63. On other sources confirming the strength of the processes of secularization among the Jewish population in the Second Republic, see, e.g., Ezra Mendelsohn, "Reflections on East European Jewish Politics in the Twentieth Century," *YIVO Annual* 20 (1991): 29–30; Gold, "Religious Education," 277–278; Joshua M. Karlip, *The Tragedy of a Generation: The Rise and Fall of Jewish Nationalism in Eastern Europe* (Harvard University Press, 2013), 184, 193, 207; Hillel Seidman, *Szlakiem nauki talmudycznej* (Księgarnia F. Hoesicka, 1934) 8–9, 61.

64. Samuel D. Kassow, "Communal and Social Change in the Polish Shtetl, 1900–1939," in *Jewish Settlement and Community in the Modern Western World,* ed. Ronald Dotterer, Deborah Dash Moore, and Steven M. Cohen (Susquehanna University Press, 1991), 56–57, 59–60. See also Jacob Lestchinsky, "The

Jews in the Cities of the Republic of Poland," *YIVO Annual of Jewish Social Science* 1 (1946): 156–157; Szyja Bronsztejn, *Ludność żydowska w Polsce w okresie międzywojennym: Studium statystyczne* (Ossolineum, 1963), 129; Antony Polonsky, "The Shtetl: Myth and Reality," *Polin* 17 (2004): 3–23; Ben-Cion Pinchuk, "Jewish Discourse and the 'Shtetl,'" *Jewish History* 15, no. 2 (2002): 169–179; Dan Miron, "The Literary Image of the Shtetl," *Jewish Social Studies* 1, no. 3 (1995): 1–43; Naomi Seidman, "Gender and the Disintegration of the Shtetl in Modern Hebrew and Yiddish Literature," in *The Shtetl: New Evaluations*, ed. Steven T. Katz (New York University Press, 2007), 193–210.

65. See, e.g., Dan Miron, *The Image of the Shtetl and Other Studies of Modern Jewish Literary Imagination* (Syracuse University Press, 2000), x, 6–10, 43–45; David G. Roskies, *Against the Apocalypse: Responses to Catastrophe in Modern Jewish Culture* (Harvard University Press, 1984), 109–122.

66. The first group's high social status often allowed, if only through marriage, the attainment of financial positions characterizing the second group. More on this later. For more on the Jewish system of social class in interwar Poland, see Moshe Kligsberg, "Di yidishe yugnt-bavegung in Poyln tsvishn beyde velt-milkhomes," in *Studies on Polish Jewry: The Interplay of Social, Economic and Political Factors in the Struggle of a Minority for Its Existence*, ed. Joshua A. Fishman (YIVO, 1974), 144–145; Kassow, "Communal and Social Change," 58.

67. Kassow, "Communal and Social Change," 57–58.

68. The network of Gemilas Chesed branches (a fund providing interest free loans) was established by the largest Jewish charitable organization, the American Joint Distribution Committee, in 1926. In 1937 it had over one thousand branches in Jewish communities throughout Poland. Gemilas Chesed was one of the most spectacular successes of Jewish social activities between the wars. See Kassow, "Communal and Social Change," 67–68.

69. In addition to the article by Samuel Kassow mentioned above, there is an interesting description of changes to the interwar shtetl in Ewa Hoffman's work on Brańsk Podlaski, where the previously mentioned Gamalielis lived. See Hoffman, *Shtetl*, 173–188.

70. In one hundred autobiographies I analyzed, Gemilas Chesed was mentioned just once. See YIVO Archives, RG 4, Autobiography 3819 alef, 25–26.

71. Moseley, "Life, Literature," 1–51. The writer suggests that the basic path of escape for young people from the world of tradition was literature, both works that they read and their own literary efforts. A far more important way was politics, which I try to show in this and subsequent chapters of this work.

72. The sharpness of the criticism of their parents' world quoted here can be attributed to the age of the competition's participants. In the future, had things gone differently, many of them would have stepped into their own parents' shoes and would have looked differently at the "business mentality" or religious traditions

lacking real-life content. This single-minded criticism of their parents was also influenced by the character of an institution like YIVO, and more specifically its competition communications, which deployed a vision of a "misunderstood," "abandoned" generation, picked up so willingly by the young people. However, this does not explain everything. It does not explain why this kind of YIVO communication was so enthusiastically picked up by young people, including Zionists and Orthodox. Nor does it explain the specific character of the language in which the young people, irrespective of their social background, decided to express their natural opposition to the norms and values of the older generation.

2. YOUNG PEOPLE'S PERSONAL AMBITIONS AND WORLD OF WORK

1. I describe this school system in the next chapter.

2. *Szabasówka* was the popular name for public elementary school for Jewish children, in which the Shabbat laws were respected, and which did not operate on Saturdays. The curriculum in these schools was no different from that of other elementary schools. More on this type of school later. In interwar Poland children went to school six days a week.

3. Bnos Aguda is Banot Aguda (Daughters of Aguda) in Sephardic and modern Hebrew.

4. YIVO Archives, RG 4, Autobiography 3764, as cited in Shandler, *Awakening Lives*, 322–324. "Esther" is no less critical of the prohibition on going to the theater in force in Bnos Aguda (Autobiography 3764, 328).

5. Autobiography 3764, 329. Orthodox Esther, just like other similar writers, was far from radically criticizing her own parents. However, even she was critical of a number of their precepts and emphasized the generational difference between her and her father, leading to his lack of understanding of her. Autobiography 3764, 333.

6. Most of these schools were part of two separate school systems: Yavne, directed by religious Zionists, and Bais Yakov, supervised by Agudat Israel. More on both systems below.

7. Esther's personal heroine, Sarah Schenirer, the founder and *spiritus movens* of the Bais Yaakov network, represents the ambivalence of attitudes and lifestyles of women, who were fully religious yet were distinguished by individualism and a desire to operate autonomously. On her life and public activities, see Agnieszka Oleszak, "The Beys Yaakov School in Kraków as a Symbolic Encounter Between East and West," *Polin* 23 (2011): 282–286; Caroline Scharfer, "Sarah Schenirer, Founder of the Bais Yaakov Movement: Her Vision and Her Legacy," *Polin* 23 (2011): 269–275. The life ambitions expressed in Esther's autobiography are very reminiscent of her idol's.

8. The yeshiva in Raduń had been established by Chofetz Chaim (in Hebrew "he who seeks life"), Yisra'el Me'ir ha-Kohen Kagan (1838–1933), in 1869. Its founder was an important figure in the history of Litvak (misnagdim) Judaism. On the history of the yeshiva, its Orthodox evolution between the wars, and the activities of its founder, see David Zariz, "Yeshivvas Radin," in *Mosadot Tora be-Europa ve-binyanam u-ve-hurbanam* [Jewish institutions of higher learning in Europe: Their development and destruction], ed. Samuel K. Mirsky (Ogen, 1956), 189–216; Eliach, *There Once Was a World*, 180–191.

9. YIVO Archives, RG 4, Autobiography 3582 (Henekh), as cited in Shandler, *Awakening Lives*, 114.

10. Autobiography 3582, 114–115.

11. Autobiography 3582, as cited in Shandler, *Awakening Lives*, 115–116.

12. Autobiography 3582, 117.

13. Autobiography 3582, 117. See too other examples of social control by spying used against Hasidic students in the yeshiva in Zamość. YIVO Archives, RG 4, Autobiography 3668, 22, 42.

14. Autobiography 3582, as cited in Shandler, *Awakening Lives*, 118–119.

15. Alongside *Der Moment, Haynt* was the most popular Yiddish daily in interwar Poland, published in Warsaw. See Joanna Nalewajko-Kulikov, "Hajnt," in *Studia z dziejów trójjęzycznej prasy żydowskiej na ziemiach polskich*, ed. Joanna Nalewajko-Kulikov (Neriton, 2012), 61–74.

16. *Sefer ha-brit* was published for the first time in 1797 in Brno (in today's Czech Republic). It saw many reprintings. For more on it, see David Ruderman, *A Best-Selling Hebrew Book of the Modern Era: The Book of the Covenant of Pinhas Hurwitz and Its Remarkable Legacy* (University of Washington Press, 2014).

17. I should the emphasize the continuing ideological impact of a movement that had in practice not existed for several decades. The writer describes like-minded friends trying secretly to acquire secular education (just as in the nineteenth century) as believers in Haskalah.

18. *Maskil* (Hebrew for "enlightened person") was used to describe adherents of the Haskalah.

19. Autobiography 3582, quote from Shandler, *Awakening Lives*, 120–122. At the end of his autobiography, he described his romance and marriage with the daughter of a rabbi, his rapid abandonment of his wife, taking his diploma as an external student, and beginning his studies in the Faculty of Law at the University of Warsaw. It would be very difficult to verify this somewhat sensational and highly unlikely part of his life. Henekh was not necessarily writing the "truth" here; however, he was definitely describing his views at the time of writing the autobiography.

20. On this kind of traditional Orthodox community distinctive to the northeastern borderlands of the Second Republic, see Mendelsohn, *On Modern Jewish*

Politics, 44; Ezra Mendelsohn, *Zionism in Poland: The Formative Years, 1915–1926* (Yale University Press, 1981), 34.

21. YIVO Archives, RG 4, Autobiography 3845, quoted from Shandler, *Awakening Lives*, 5.

22. Peretz Smolenskin (1842–1885) was a writer, a representative of the last generation of the Russian Haskalah, at the same time one of the first Russian Jewish protonationalists, and at the end of his life a fervent Zionist. Mikhah Yosef Berdichevsky (1865–1921) was a writer born in Międzybóż (Mezhbizh) in Podolia, the son of a Hasidic rabbi. He was one of the most radical representatives of antitraditional modernism in new Hebrew literature.

23. The "Ohel Tora" yeshiva in Baranowicze was one of the most important Litvak yeshivas in interwar Poland and was associated inter alia with the previously mentioned yeshiva in Raduń. For more on this, see A. Ben Mordechai, "Mesivta 'Ohel Tora' be-Baranowits," in Mirsky, *Mosadot Tora be-Europa*, 327–334.

24. Autobiography 3845, as cited in Shandler, *Awakening Lives*, 13.

25. Autobiography 3845, 14–16.

26. Sopot (German: Zoppot) was a major vacation resort town on the Baltic Sea. At the time it was part of the Free City of Danzig (Polish: Gdańsk); today it is in Poland.

27. Autobiography 3845, 17–18.

28. Autobiography 3845, 18.

29. YIVO Archives, RG 4, Autobiography 3561, 1.

30. Autobiography 3561, 4–13.

31. *Masmid* (Hebrew) is a traditional term for an exceptionally bright student of the Talmud, foretelling a rabbinical career for him.

32. Autobiography 3561, 14–15.

33. Autobiography 3561, 15–16.

34. Autobiography 3561, 16–28. His mother supported the family with a soda fountain. In his free time, when he was not studying, he helped her at work.

35. Mesivte yeshiva was a so-called small yeshiva (*yeshiva ktana*), an institution for talented graduates of heders, preparing them for serious study at a Talmudic institution of higher learning. The writer probably has in mind the establishment in Warsaw run by Rabbi Yeshayale Prager. It had been established in 1919, and in terms of its curriculum, it had a "Litvak character," distinguishing it in a Warsaw that was dominated by the Hasidim. Unusually, it taught secular subjects. See Abraham Zemba, "'Mesivta' be Varshe," in Mirsky, *Mosadot Tora be-Europa*, 363–380; Gershon C. Bacon, "To Enlist the Enthusiasm of the Young: Orthodox Jewish Non-Political Response to the Challenges of Interwar Poland," *Polin* 33 (2021): 297.

36. The Torat Chaim yeshiva was one of several Litvak yeshivas in Warsaw that, in addition to the standard curriculum, focused on studying the Musar. The

yeshiva's name commemorated its founder, Chaim Brisker. During the interwar years, the founder's son-in-law ran it. M. W. probably had him in mind when writing about the rabbi from Brisk (Brest).

37. Autobiography 3561, 28–33.

38. Autobiography 3561, 33.

39. Autobiography 3561, 34.

40. The writer does not say this directly but suggests it by writing, for instance, that his sick father went to Vienna for treatment. YIVO Archives, RG 4, Autobiography 3819, 1–2.

41. Autobiography 3819, 2.

42. Autobiography 3819, 7.

43. Rabbi Tzvi Hirschhorn was one of the most active members of Agudat Israel in Poland between the wars. In the 1930s he was the rabbi of Jaworzno. He distinguished himself by, among other things, conducting a great many missions, which consisted of visiting small, traditional Jewish communities and encouraging them to establish local branches of Agudat. On the subject of a very similar visit by Hirschhorn to the Galician town of Jasło and the establishment of an Agudat branch there, see the Jasło memory book: Moshe Natan Even-Hayim, ed., *Toldot Yehudei Jaslo me-reshit hityashvutam be-okh ha-ir ad yamei ha-hurban al yadei ha-natsim* (Irgun Yaslo be Israel, 1953), 68.

44. Autobiography 3819, 8–10, quotation on 10.

45. Autobiography 3819, 13 15.

46. See Autobiography 3668, title page, note by YIVO employee dated December 8, 1959.

47. A great Hasidic dynasty, founded by Rabbi Sholom Rokeach (Sad Sholom), from 1817 the rabbi in Belz. The Belz Hasidim were one of the most conservative Orthodox communities. They came out very strongly against the Agudat Israel party, recognizing it as making too far-reaching a compromise in the face of the threat of modernity. According to them, among such bad compromises were yeshivas trying to imitate universities, schools for girls, the introduction of secular subjects into the heders, and agreements with representatives of the Zionist movement.

48. Sholom Rokeah (Sar Shalom) was the founder of the Belz Hasidic dynasty.

49. Autobiography 3668, 20–21.

50. Autobiography 3668, 29–30. This was probably the Yesodei ha-Torah ("Basics of the Torah") school, which was a modernized heder considered to be a modern religious school in which secular subjects were also taught. More on this in chapter 3.

51. Autobiography 3668, 34–35.

52. He meant the Kochav Mi-Yaakov (Star of Jacob) yeshiva, which attracted students from all over Poland and was run by Rabbi Dov Berish Weidenfeld

(1881–1965), who was famous in the Orthodox world. Indeed, this yeshiva was famous for bringing back to the faith young people who had previously abandoned it. This kind of activity by a yeshiva was very rare in the interwar period. https://www.yadvashem.org/yv/en/exhibitions/communities/trzebinia/rabbi-weidenfeld.asp (accessed July 6, 2025).

53. Autobiography 3668, 36–40.

54. Autobiography 3668, 42–44. He wrote that he intervened about this with the yeshiva principal, who eventually changed the draconian rules imposed by fanatical Belz Hasidim. This supposedly exposed the writer to their endless intrigues.

55. Autobiography 3668, 51–56.

56. The young Orthodox quoted here, reading the works of the maskilim in the original, knew these ideas only too well, and such ideas also clashed with the widespread stereotype of the day of the Haskalah as a secularizing movement. The classical Haskalah was a movement aimed not at abolishing but at supporting and modernizing Judaism. See, e.g., Shmuel Feiner, "The Pseudo-Enlightenment and the Question of Jewish Modernization," *Jewish Social Studies* 3, no. 1 (1996): 62–88; Shmuel Feiner, *The Jewish Enlightenment* (University of Pennsylvania Press, 2004).

57. Shaul Stampfer, *Families, Rabbis, Education: Traditional Jewish Society in Nineteenth-Century Europe* (Littman, 2010), 211–228, 252–276; Ben Zion Klibansky, *Kitsur ha-lamish: Tor ha-zahav shel ha-yeshivot ha-litayot be-Mizrach Europa* (Merkaz Zalman Shazar, 2014); Gold, "Religious Education," 272–282; Eliach, *There Once Was a World*, 194–196.

58. For Mizrahi and its relations with Agudat Israel in interwar Poland, see especially Daniel Mahla, *Orthodox Judaism and the Politics of Religion: From Prewar Europe to the State of Israel* (Cambridge University Press, 2020), 75–103; Asaf Kaniel, *Yomra u-me'as: Ha-Mizrachi be-Polin bein shtei milhamot ha-olam* (Bar Ilan University Press, 2011).

59. David E. Fishman, "Musar and Modernity: The Case of Novaredok," *Modern Judaism* 8, no. 1 (1988): 41–64; David E. Fishman, "The Musar Movement in Interwar Poland," in *The Jews of Poland Between Two World Wars*, ed. Yisrael Gutman et al. (University Press of New England, 1989), 247–271.

60. See chapter 3 for more on this subject.

61. Shaul Stampfer is even apt to attribute to interwar yeshivas features of Goffman's "total institutions," taking care to separate their "boarders" from the world outside the institution, strictly ordering and controlling their contacts with the outside world. See Stampfer, *Families, Rabbis, Education*, 224–225.

62. Gershon C. Bacon, *The Politics of Tradition: Agudat Yisrael in Poland, 1916–1939* (Magnes, 1996), 47–63.

63. Bacon, "To Enlist the Enthusiasm," 293–295.

64. In addition to the words mentioned above, see Glenn Dynner, "Replenishing the 'Fountain of Judaism': Traditionalist Jewish Education in Interwar Poland," *Jewish History* 31 (2018): 229–261; Wojciech Tworek, "Mystic, Teacher, Troublemaker: Shimon Engel Horovits of Żelechów and the Challenges of Hasidic Education in Interwar Poland," *Jewish Quarterly Review* 110, no. 2 (2020): 313–342; Naomi Seidman, *Sarah Schenirer and the Bais Yaakov Movement* (Littman, 2019), 144–204.

65. For an exception to this rule, see Asaf Kaniel, "Bein hilonim, masorta'im ve-ortodoksim: Shmirat mitsvot be-rai hitmodedut 'gezirat ha-kashrut,' 1937–1939," *Gal-Ed* 23 (2013): 75–106.

66. Testimony to the fact that before the Holocaust a new type of Jewish Orthodoxy was developing, based on a high level of formal secular education, can be seen too in the biographies of the principal representatives of the younger Agudat Israel generation, Hillel Seidman and Aleksander Zysha Frydman. On Hillel Seidman, see https://congressforjewishculture.org/people/4364/Zaydman-Hilel (accessed July 6, 2025); on Aleksander Zysza Frydman, see Gershon Bacon, "Frydman, Aleksander Zysha," *YIVO Encyclopedia of Jews in Eastern Europe*, accessed January 28, 2012, http://www.yivoencyclopedia.org/article.aspx/Frydman_Aleksander_Zysha. See, too, Bacon, *Politics of Tradition*, 79–80, 119–120, 140–141, 146, 158. Most of Majer Balaban's rabbinical students at the Institute of Judaic Studies at the University of Warsaw had studied previously in yeshivas, and many had an Orthodox semikhah. As university students they all had to have earned their diplomas as external students. Natalia Aleksiun, "Historionim yehudim ve-ha-hatson shel rabanut mi-sug hadash: Beit midrash le-rabanim Tahkemoni le-madaei ha-yahadut be-Varsha bein milhamot ha-olam," in *From Breslau to Jerusalem: Rabbinical Seminaries Past, Present and Future*, ed. Guy Miron (Machon Schechter, 2009), 197; Natalia Aleksiun, "Training a New Generation of Jewish Historians: Majer Bałaban's Seminar of the History of Polish Jews," in *Zwischen Graetz und Dubnow: Jüdische Historiographie in Ostmitteleuropa im 19 und 20. Jahrhundert*, ed. François Guesnet (Akademische Verlagsanstalt, 2009), 157–158.

67. Stampfer, *Families, Rabbis, Education*, 272.

68. YIVO Archives, RG 4, Autobiography 3525, 1–3.

69. Autobiography 3525, 9–11, 16–18.

70. For a short time, the writer belonged to the "Gordonia" youth organization, in which he was marginalized on account of his generally low cultural capital and very poor knowledge of Hebrew. Autobiography 3525, 20–21.

71. Autobiography 3525, 13–14. See too another autobiography of a person coming from the similar absolute social depths (a homeless person) and with a similar desire to acquire any kind of formally accredited education.

72. YIVO Archives, RG 4, Autobiography 3521.

73. The organizers of the competition also used this very emotionally charged phrase. The writer, politically engaged and dabbling in local journalism, could have read Max Weinreich's *Der veg tsum unzer yugent* (*The Path to Our Youth*). The likelihood of this is increased by the fact that he submitted his autobiography to the 1939 competition, when the book had already achieved publishing success, a second edition was being prepared, and the competition for Jewish autobiographies had gained him fame throughout the whole country.

74. YIVO Archives, RG 4, Autobiography 3565, letter dated June 28, 1939, 1–2.

75. Autobiography 3565, 2.

76. Autobiography 3565, 4–9.

77. Autobiography 3565, 9–16.

78. Autobiography 3565, 20–21. Young people who had already succeeded in obtaining employment in a workshop earned between four and ten zloty a week. Their workday lasted between twelve and sixteen hours. The pay quoted by the author is appallingly low. It illustrates the economic gulf dividing provincial workers even from the working poor in major cities. Significant here too is the fact that these studies of earnings were conducted mainly in larger towns. By comparison, in the financial circumstances of 1927 a qualified tailor in Warsaw, working in a first-category establishment, earned between 133 and 141 zloty a week; a rank-and-file worker in a second-category bakery, 50 zloty. Women, who were traditionally paid less (22% to 50% of the salary of an adult male), working in the poorly paid food industry earned around 30 zloty a week. Even rank-and-file workers in a laundry, the worst-paid Jewish "proletariat," earned 15–20 zloty a week. See Bina Garncarska-Kadary, *Żydowska ludność pracująca w Polsce 1918–1939* (ŻIH, 2001), 125, 127–128, 136; Autobiography 3565, 20–21.

79. Autobiography 3565, 24–25.

80. Autobiography 3565, report, 2.

81. On the Jewish economic structure in interwar Poland and changes to it brought about by economic processes, discriminatory national policies, and in the 1930s also antisemitic attacks see, e.g., Garncarska-Kadary, *Żydowska ludność*; Georges Castellan, "Remarks on the Social Structure of the Jewish Community in Poland between the Two World Wars," in *Jews and Non-Jews in Eastern Europe, 1918–1945*, ed. Bella Vago and George L. Mosse (Wiley, 1974), 187–201; Jerzy Tomaszewski, "Between the Social and the National: The Economic Situation of Polish Jewry, 1918–1939," *Simon Dubnow Institute Yearbook* 1 (2002): 55–70; Melzer, *No Way Out*, 39–71.

82. Autobiography 3565, 2–5.

83. YIVO Archives, RG 4, Autobiography 3516 (Polish-language diary attached to the autobiography), 12–13, 15–16, 28.

84. Autobiography 3516, 31.

85. YIVO Archives, RG 4, Autobiography 3701, 1–6.

86. Autobiography 3701, 8.

87. Autobiography 3701, 8–9.

88. Autobiography 3701, 9.

89. Autobiography 3701, 11.

90. Autobiography 3701, 30.

91. Autobiography 3701, 31.

92. Autobiography 3701, 31–32.

93. YIVO Archives, RG 4, Autobiography 3720, 13.

94. Autobiography 3720, 13.

95. Autobiography 3720, 14.

96. Autobiography 3720, 15.

97. YIVO Archives, RG 4, Autobiography 3510, 3.

98. Autobiography 3510, 19.

99. Autobiography 3510, 21–22.

100. Autobiography 3510, 26.

101. Autobiography 3510, 30.

102. Bassok, "Ma'amadot," 229–231.

103. Ido Bassok, "Ne'arim ve-arkhei ne'arim ba-tnuat ha-no'ar ha-polani she-bein ha-milhamot," in *Kiyum ve Shavar: Yehudei Polin le-doroteikhem: Hevra, Tarbut, Le'umiyut,* ed. Yisrael Bartal and Yisrael Gutman (Merkaz Zalman Shazar, 2001), 573–600.

104. The Litvak Orthodox religious movement Musar, as well as some Hasidic groups, also referred to youth themes of contestation and far-reaching reform of the surrounding world. Bassok, "Ne'arim," 578, 586–588.

3. PUBLIC SCHOOLS

1. In category I and category II schools, it sometimes took two or even three years to complete a single grade. The reason for this was that in a one-room school, the teacher taught children from different grades at the same time, which meant that it took each grade longer to cover the syllabus.

2. Karol Sanojca, *Obraz sąsiadów w szkolnictwie powszechnym Drugiej Rzeczypospolitej* (Wydawnictwo Uniwersytetu Wrocławskiego, 2003), 15–18.

3. Dorota L. Wojtas, "Learning to Become Polish: Education, National Identity and Citizenship in Interwar Poland, 1918–1939" (doctoral thesis, Brandeis University, 2003), 46.

4. Stanisław Mauersberg, "Reformy szkolne w Drugiej Rzeczypospolitej (1918–1939)," *Kwartalnik Pedagogiczny* 4 (1995): 19 29.

5. Marian Falski, *Środowisko społeczne młodzieży a jej wykształcenie* (Nasza Księgarnia, 1937), 11–13, 15.

6. Klemens Trzebiatowski, *Szkolnictwo powszechne w Polsce w latach 1918–1932* (Ossolineum, 1970), 84; Mauersberg, "Reformy," 26.

7. Mauersberg, "Reformy,", 11–13, 15, 23; Stanisław Mauersberg, *Komu służyła szkoła w Drugiej Rzeczypospolitej? Społeczne uwarunkowania dostępu do oświaty* (Ossolineum, 1988), 38–39.

8. The average cost of a public or private gimnazjum in 1934 is taken from Mauersberg, *Komu służyła*, 49; the average wages of a qualified worker or a tailor at the same time are taken from Garncarska-Kadary, *Żydowska ludność*, 136.

9. In 1936 the percentage of workers' children in the initial grades of general secondary schools, relative to sixth graders from the same group, was barely 2.3 percent. The percentage for agricultural workers was 0.4 percent. The same percentage for children of professionals was 109.4 percent (in elementary school, some of them were educated at home); for white-collar workers employed in public institutions, it was 80.5 percent. During the same school year, only 17.3 percent of agricultural smallholders' children, studying for the most part in four-grade village schools, were able to boast of completing sixth grade in elementary school. See Falski, *Środowisko*, 31; Mauersberg, *Komu służyła*, 40.

10. Janusz Żarnowski, "Społeczeństwo polskie wobec szkoły w XX wieku," *Kwartalnik Pedagogiczny* 4 (1995), 8–18.

11. *Sprawy Narodowościowe* 2 (1929): 298, as cited in Garncarska-Kadary, *Żydowska ludność*, 189.

12. See Stanisław Mauersberg, *Szkolnictwo powszechne dla mniejszości narodowych w Polsce w latach 1918–1939* (Ossolineum, 1968), 163–164; Samuel Chmielewski, "Stan szkolnictwa wśród Żydów w Polsce," *Sprawy Narodowościowe* 9 (1937): 13.

13. Gershon Bacon, "National Revival, Ongoing Acculturation: Jewish Education In Interwar Poland," *Jahrbuch des Simon-Dubnow-Instituts* 1 (2002): 73.

14. Kassow, "Communal and Social Change," 87.

15. Shimon Frost, *Schooling as a Socio-Political Expression: Jewish Education in Interwar Poland* (Magnes, 1998), 30, 32; Mauersberg, *Szkolnictwo*, 160–163; Celia Heller, *On the Edge of Destruction: Jews of Poland Between Two World Wars* (Schocken Books, 1980), 221.

16. Anna Landau-Czajka, *Syn będzie Lech . . . Asymilacja Żydów w Polsce międzywojennej* (Neriton, 2006), 347–348.

17. Hillel Seidman, *Żydowskie szkolnictwo religijne w ramach ustawodawstwa polskiego/Yudishe religyeze shul-vezen in di ramen fun der poylisher gezetsgebung* (Chorev, 1937), 49–51; Aleksiun, "Historionim," 200; Sean Martin, "Between Church and State: Jewish Religious Instruction in the Public Schools in the Second Polish Republic," *Polin* 30 (2018): 275–276.

18. Parush, *Reading Jewish Women*, 57–70.

19. Yitshak Grünbaum, "Sprawa żydowska," *Natio* 1–2 (1927): 36.

20. Mauersberg, *Szkolnictwo*, 164–165.

21. C. Heller, *On the Edge*, 229.

22. Chone Shmeruk, "Hebrew-Yiddish-Polish: A Trilingual Jewish Culture," in *The Jews of Poland Between Two World Wars*, ed. Yisrael Gutman et al. (University Press of New England, 1989), 294–295. See, too, other statistics of Jewish secondary education: Miriam Eisenstein, *Jewish Schools in Poland, 1919–1939: Their Philosophy and Development* (Columbia University Press, 1950), 63; Frost, *Schooling*, 49–50; *Mały rocznik statystyczny* (GUS, 1939), 319.

23. Mauersberg, *Komu służyła*, 48.

24. On introducing bilingualism into Jewish secondary schooling (that is to say, the growing transformation of schools teaching primarily in Jewish languages into ones teaching at least half the curriculum in Polish), see Frost, *Schooling*, 39, 48–50.

25. Michael C. Steinlauf, "Jewish Politics and Youth Culture in Interwar Poland," in *The Emergence of Modern Jewish Politics: Bundism and Zionism in Eastern Europe*, ed. Zvi Y. Gitelman (University of Pittsburgh Press, 2003), 98.

26. YIVO Archives, RG 4, Autobiography 3713, as cited in Shandler, *Awakening Lives*, 309.

27. YIVO Archives, RG 4, Autobiography 3720, 1.

28. YIVO Archives, RG 4, Autobiography 3519, 20–21.

29. YIVO Archives, RG 4, Autobiography 3792, as cited in Cała, *Ostatnie pokolenie*, 209.

30. The other, no less important factor was the secular Jewish political movements and the majority of cultural institutions associated with them. However, young Jewish people came into contact with them later, when they were already students or had completed elementary school.

31. By and large the children of this last group were the least likely to be enrolled in public schools, since this group could afford an expensive educational route by way of further heders (including modernized ones recognized by school districts as the equivalent of elementary schools), small yeshivas, or true Talmudic establishments of higher education.

32. YIVO Archives, RG 4, Autobiography 3501, 7–11.

33. YIVO Archives, RG 4, Autobiography 3861, 18.

34. Autobiography 3861, 19, 24.

35. Autobiography 3861, 31–33.

36. See H. Seidman, *Żydowskie szkolnictwo*, 14–15. The directive ordering heders to introduce sections of the elementary school curriculum went into force in 1923. In practice it was not always followed to the letter. I have not found in the autobiographies any information on classes in mathematics, biology, or history being given in traditional, unreformed heders. For the most part, the ministerial demands were limited to Polish lessons.

37. The Kultur-Lige (Culture League) was established in Ukraine in 1918, during the short-lived Ukrainian People's Republic, and was one of the bases of the cultural and national autonomy that the Jews were granted there. It was closed down shortly after the Soviet Union absorbed Ukraine. The Kultur-Lige continued its activities in interwar Poland, where it came under the powerful influence of the Bund. The organization ran very wide-ranging activities on behalf of modern Yiddish culture. Among the most important of these was the establishment by the league of its own publishing house, as well as producing the most important Jewish literary magazine in Poland, *Literarishe Bleter*. See Hillel Kazovsky, "Kultur-lige," trans. I. Michael Aronson, *YIVO Encyclopedia of Jews in Eastern Europe*, accessed February 12, 2012, http://www.yivoencyclopedia.org /article.aspx/Kultur-lige; David E. Fishman, *The Rise of Modern Yiddish Culture* (University of Pittsburgh Press, 2005), 87.

38. YIVO Archives, RG 4, Autobiography 3666, 16–17.

39. YIVO Archives, RG 4, Autobiography 3716, 4.

40. YIVO Archives, RG 4, Autobiography 3548, 38–39.

41. Autobiography 3548, 41–42.

42. YIVO Archives, RG 4, Autobiography 3782, as cited in Cała, *Ostatnie pokolenie*, 187–188.

43. See, e.g., YIVO Archives, RG 4, Autobiography 3504, 2; Autobiography 3645, 19; Autobiography 3701, 4–5.

44. If a local heder was not accredited by the educational authorities, its students during the day had to attend a public school or another secular Jewish school accredited by the state. See H. Seidman, *Żydowskie szkolnictwo*, 17–18.

45. In addition to the autobiographies quoted above, see Autobiography 3542 in Yiddish, the author of which was an elite private tutor. In addition to the Talmud and the Chumash, he also taught children from wealthy homes mathematics, Polish, Hebrew, and Yiddish. The writer's traditional employers particularly wanted their children to learn Polish. It was precisely because of his knowledge of these subjects that the author had been able to succeed his predecessor. Autobiography 3542, 5, 14–15. On the teaching of these subjects by tutors in wealthier Jewish families, see too Autobiography 3548, 11–12, 16; Autobiography 3713, 1939, as cited in Shandler, *Awakening Lives*, 306–307.

46. YIVO Archives, RG 4, Autobiography 3510, 8.

47. Autobiography 3510, 8–9.

48. YIVO Archives, RG 4, Autobiography 3514, as cited in Shandler, *Awakening Lives*, 392.

49. Autobiography 3782, as cited in Cała, *Ostatnie pokolenie*, 188.

50. Frost, *Schooling*, 42.

51. Autobiography 3666, 1934, 9.

52. Autobiography 3666, 1934, 11–12. On traditional parents' fears about educating their children in "areligious" TsYShO schools, greater in the case of boys than that of girls, see also Autobiography 3571, 6, 9–10; Autobiography 3726, 5, 31, 33, 35, 79.

53. Autobiography 3861, 16–17.

54. Autobiography 3861, 20.

55. Autobiography 3861, 21.

56. On these types of issues arising even in very polonized families, see Landau-Czajka, *Syn będzie Lech*, 345.

57. YIVO Archives, RG 4, Autobiography 3718, 3–4.

58. YIVO Archives, RG 4, Autobiography 3801, as cited in Cała, *Ostatnie pokolenie*, 152.

59. YIVO Archives, RG 4 Autobiography 3770, 13.

60. See, e.g., YIVO Archives, RG 4, Autobiography 3816, as cited in Cała, *Ostatnie pokolenie*, 382; Autobiography 3764, as cited in Cała, *Ostatnie pokolenie*, 400; Autobiography 3819, 13; Autobiography 3732, 10.

61. YIVO Archives, RG 4, Autobiography 3580, as cited in Cała, *Ostatnie pokolenie*, 144.

62. Autobiography 3580, 360–361.

63. For this see C. Heller, *On the Edge*, 222–223; Monika Adamczyk-Garbowska, Adam Kopciowski, and Andrzej Trzciński, eds., *Tam był kiedyś mój dom: Księgi pamięci gmin żydowskich* (Wydawnictwo UMCS, 2009), 145.

64. Jakub Zineman, ed., *Almanach szkolnictwa żydowskiego w Polsce*, vol. 3 (Renesans, 1938), 275.

65. Arie Tartakower, "Problem szkolnictwa żydowskiego w Polsce," in *Almanach szkolnictwa żydowskiego w Polsce*, vol. 1, ed. Jakub Zineman (Renesans, 1936), 7–8.

66. See, e.g., Adamczyk-Garbowska et al., *Tam był kiedyś*, 141.

4. JEWISH PRIVATE EDUCATION

1. On the growth of Jewish secular education during World War I, see Frost, *Schooling*, 27–30; Chaim Shloyme Kazhdan, *Di geshikhte fun yidishn shulvezen in umophengikn Poyln* (Gezelshaft "Kultur" un "Hilf," 1947), 17–68; Mendelsohn, *Zionism in Poland: The Formative Years, 1918–1926* (Yale University Press, 1981), 47–48, 77–78.

2. Frost, *Schooling*, 29–30; Trzebiatowski, *Szkolnictwo*, 147.

3. Dynner, "Replenishing the 'Fountain,'" 240.

4. See, e.g., Gold, "Religious Education," 272.

5. *Memorandum funem Ortodoksishe Lerer Seminar "Mosad le-Mechanekhim Datiim"* (Chorev, 1937), 2–3, 5.

6. On the system of education for Orthodox boys run by Aguda, see Bacon, *Politics of Tradition*, 145–164.

7. On Bais Yaakov, see N. Seidman, *Sarah Schenirer*; Oleszak, "Beys Yaakov"; Bacon, *Politics of Tradition*, 164–177; Eisenstein, *Jewish Schools*, 82–88.

8. There were also Bais Yaakov establishments, which just taught religious subjects. Thus, they did not meet the requirement of offering a curriculum equivalent to the public schools' one, and their students had also to attend elementary schools. See David Shtokfish, ed., *Sefer Przytyk* (Irgun Yotzei Przytyk be Israel, 1973), 195.

9. Shtokfish, *Sefer Przytyk*, 162.

10. Gershon Bacon points out that many students in the Horev network attended its schools only in the afternoons, since in the morning they attended elementary school. The statistics published by the Horev system also covered Jewish boys (less often girls) between the ages of three and seven who were already attending heders. These facts should be taken into account when comparing the number of students in the Orthodox system with other secular systems or the public schools. Bacon, *Politics of Tradition*, 162–163; Eisenstein, *Jewish Schools*, 81.

11. Eisenstein, *Jewish Schools*, 84, 96.

12. Marcus, *Social and Political History*, 154.

13. Circular issued by the MWRiOP to local school district authorities, September 13, 1923. See H. Seidman, *Żydowskie szkolnictwo*, 14.

14. See Bacon, *Politics of Tradition*, 147–154. For more on the place of Polish and Polish culture in traditional Jewish educational establishments, see below.

15. H. Seidman, *Żydowskie szkolnictwo*, 15–17.

16. What typified them, in addition to the features mentioned, was the fact that they more often admitted girls. It was no accident that precisely in Lithuania these institutions were preceded by (mixed) irbuvia heders. On metukan and irbuvia heders, see Kazhdan, *Fun kheider*, 306–323; Yossi Goldstein, "'He-heder metukan be-Rusia ka-basis le-ma'arekhet ha-hinukh ha-tsiyoni," *Inyanim ba-khinuch* 45 (1986): 147–157; Eliach, *There Once Was a World*, 168–173, 459–462.

17. As early as 1691, *Pinkas Ziemi Litewskiej* remarked on this unusual educational establishment's work. In the nineteenth and twentieth centuries, such great figures in Jewish culture and science as Lev Levanda, Matityahu Strashun, and Rabbis Simcha Katsenelenbogen and Chaim Ozer Grodzieński worked for it. See Morits Grosman, "Di Vilner shtatishem Talmud Tora," in *Yidishe Vilne in vort un bild*, ed. Morits Grosman (Hirsch Matz, 1925), 58.

18. Matitjahu Senicki, "Di Vilner shtatishe Talmud Tora," in *Vilner Almanakh*, ed. A. I. Grodzenski (Ovent Kurier, 1939), 338–339.

19. Shimon Frost states that while the teaching language in Yavne schools was Hebrew, in the eastern provinces in Galicia and central Poland they were fully bilingual. Frost, *Schooling*, 46.

20. See A. I. Lewin, "Beit Sefer le-Banot am shem ha-Rebetsin Ester Rubinstein," in Grodzenski, *Vilner Almanakh*, 343–344; Morits Grosman, "Beit Sefer
le-Banot oyfn nomen fun rabanit Ester Rubinstein," in Grosman, *Yidishe Vilne*, 63.

21. Eisenstein, *Jewish Schools*, 92.

22. Eisenstein, *Jewish Schools*, 90.

23. Eisenstein, *Jewish Schools*, 93, 96. Frost gives different figures. According
to him, in the 1937/38 school year there were supposedly 23,567 students. Frost,
Schooling, 47.

24. YIVO Archives, RG 4, Autobiography 3718, 9.

25. YIVO Archives, RG 4, Autobiography 3559, as cited in Shandler, *Awakening Lives*, 321–322.

26. Autobiography 3559.

27. Here Esther was referring to the szabasówka, which was the popular name
for public school for Jewish children (for characteristics of this type of school,
see above).

28. A 5 was the highest grade in schools in Poland at the time.

29. Autobiography 3559, 322–323.

30. YIVO Archives, RG 4, Autobiography 3707, as cited in Shandler, *Awakening Lives*, 233.

31. *Hakhshara* means work and study on a collective farm in preparation for
leaving for Palestine. More on this later.

32. On this establishment, see A. I. Lewin, "Shmipishkei Talmud Tora (Beit-
Yehuda ha-Merkaz Va'ad Meyuhad 'Tahkemoni')," in Grodzenski, *Vilner Almanakh*, 343–344; Morits Grosman, "Beit Yehuda," in Grosman, *Yidishe Vilne*, 61.

33. YIVO Archives, RG 4, Autobiography 3623, 19–22, as cited on p. 19.

34. YIVO Archives, RG 4, Autobiography 3542, 28–29.

35. Teaching students to read Hebrew using modern textbooks was something new in the heder. In a traditional institution of this type, dominant both in
central Poland and in the east of the country (although now to a lesser extent),
teaching was based on the study of religious texts. See Stampfer, *Families, Rabbis,
Education*, 150–157; Gold, "Religious Education," 272.

36. YIVO Archives, RG 4, Autobiography 3845, as cited in Shandler, *Awakening Lives*, 4. *Hatikvah* (Hebrew) means "hope." This was the basic song of the
Zionist movement developing at the end of the nineteenth century.

37. YIVO Archives, RG 4, Autobiography 3561, 16–28.

38. See, e.g., Mendelsohn, *On Modern Jewish Politics*, 72–73.

39. YIVO Archives, RG 4, Autobiography 3591, 31.

40. Grünbaum, "Sprawa żydowska," 28.

41. See *Tokhnit ha-limudim shel gimnasia bat 8 mahlakot im mekhina "Hertsliya"
ba Vilna* (Drukarnia F. Wajnsztejna, 1927), 3–27; Zineman, *Almanach szkolnictwa*,
3:414–417.

42. See, e.g., Eliach, *There Once Was a World*, 471–474.

43. Nathan Bistricki, *Erets Israel be-hinuch ha-Yehudi be-Polin* (Sefer, 1929), 131; Frost, *Schooling*, 62–63.

44. Kazhdan, *Di geshikhte*, 421–422.

45. *Tokhnit ha-limudim*, 23–24.

46. Eisenstein, *Jewish Schools*, 57–58.

47. Frost, *Schooling*, 35.

48. Mendelsohn, *Jews of East Central Europe*, 65–66. Eisenstein, *Jewish Schools*, 57, provides another number for the same year—44,780.

49. At that time Tarbut had its own secondary schools: Vilnius, 474 students; Łódź, 122; Białystok, 511; Równe, 211; Kowel, 255; Pińsk, 404; Grodno, 261; Lidza, 122; and Krzemieniec, 87. See Eisenstein, *Jewish Schools*, 54.

50. The literature has different numbers for fully accredited Hebrew schools. For instance, Shimon Frost writes that in the mid-1930s only two establishments, those in Pińsk and Białystok, were accredited. Frost, *Schooling*, 36.

51. Morits Grosman, "Der Bildungs Gezelshaft 'Tarbut' in Vilne," in Grosman, *Yidishe Vilne*, 57.

52. Kazhdan, *Di geshikhte*, 441.

53. Zineman, *Almanach szkolnictwa*, 3:232.

54. YIVO Archives, RG 4, Autobiography 3735, 4–5.

55. Autobiography 3735, 26–28.

56. Herzliya was a group of schools including elementary as well as secondary schools. The secondary school in Pińsk was one of the largest and best secondary schools in the Tarbut system. It was fully accredited by the state, allowing its graduates to enter Polish universities. See Eisenstein, *Jewish Schools*, 47, 54; Shmuel Spector, "Pińsk," in *Pinkas ha Kehillot: Poland; Volhynia and Polesie*, ed. Shmuel Spector, vol. 5 (Yad Vashem, 1989); Kazhdan, *Di geshikhte*, 427.

57. YIVO Archives, RG 4, Autobiography 3796, 5.

58. "Binyomin R.," *Bamerkung*, 13–15.

59. Autobiography 3542, 52–53.

60. Autobiography 3796, 5–6.

61. YIVO Archives, RG 4, Autobiography 3869, as cited in Mendelsohn, *On Modern Jewish Politics*, 104.

62. YIVO Archives, RG 4, Autobiography 3519, 10–11.

63. Autobiography 3735, 14–15.

64. Autobiography 3519, 15–17. Despite a generally positive assessment of the school and most of its teachers, Zhanet also described a case in which one of the teachers brutally beat a child and the whole class's protest in solidarity against this.

65. Interestingly enough, when visiting the establishment in 1929, Nathan Bistricki, one of the best-known promoters of Zionist education in the Jewish world,

considered it the best in Poland and in the world, providing a better grounding in Hebrew subjects than even a great many secondary schools in the Land of Israel. See Bistricki, *Erets*, 10.

66. Autobiography 3542, 15, 19.

67. YIVO Archives, RG 4, Autobiography 3669, 7.

68. Autobiography 3796, 5.

69. YIVO Archives, RG 4, Autobiography 3812, 3–4.

70. Autobiography 3812, 7.

71. Autobiography 3812, 17–18.

72. Autobiography 3519, 13.

73. Autobiography 3519, 18.

74. Autobiography 3735, 29.

75. On social-class distance in other, non-Tarbut, schools, see, e.g., YIVO Archives, RG 4, Autobiography 3749, 13–19; Autobiography 3819 alef, 14–20; Autobiography 3618, as cited in Shandler, *Awakening Lives*, 200–201, 208–209.

76. They were treated with much greater suspicion than the nascent Hebrew secular schools or traditional schooling. See Fishman, *Rise*, 31.

77. Frost, *Schooling*, 37.

78. Kazhdan, *Di geshihhte*, 144–155; Eisenstein, *Jewish Schools*, 20–22, 24–25; Yuu Nishimura, "On the Cultural Front: The Bund and the Yiddish Secular School Movement in Interwar Poland," *Eastern European Jewish Affairs* 43, no. 3 (2013): 265–281.

79. Fishman, *Rise*, 91, 104; Shloyme Bastomski, "Der yidish-veltlekher shul-vezen in Vilne," in Grodzenski, *Vilner Almanakh*, 197; Jordana de Bloeme, "Creating a New Jewish Nation: The Vilna Educational Society and Secular Yiddish Education in Interwar Vilna," *Polin*, 30 (2018): 224–226.

80. Frost, *Schooling*, 101.

81. Eisenstein, *Jewish Schools*, 96.

82. Bastomski, "Der yidish-veltlekher," 198–201.

83. Kazhdan, *Di geshikhte*, 185.

84. Eisenstein, *Jewish Schools*, 24.

85. Morits Grosman, "Der Tsentrale Bildungs Komitet (TseBeKa) in Vilne," in Grosman, *Yidishe Vilne*, 52.

86. Mauersberg, "Reformy," 32–33; Eisenstein, *Jewish Schools*, 48–49.

87. The state authorities carried out the first large operation closing down TsYShO establishments as early as 1923. It affected twenty-five schools and over two thousand children attending them—see Nishimura, "On the Cultural Front," 271–272.

88. Kazhdan, *Di geshikhte*, 173–182; Frost, *Schooling*, 38, 72; Eisenstein, *Jewish Schools*, 38–39; Fishman, *Rise*, 92.

89. The gimnazjum, which was not fully accredited until the 1933/34 school year, was an exceptional establishment by any measure. In addition to offering the full state curriculum, it taught Yiddish and Hebrew, modern literature being written in these languages, the Tanakh, and the history and demography of the Jewish nation. The school also had laboratories for subjects such as physics, chemistry, and biology, workshops for teaching carpentry, locksmithing, and sewing, and a library with ten thousand books. See Bastomski, "Der yidish-veltlekher," 203–205; Kazhdan, *Di geshikhte*, 198–203; Frost, *Schooling*, 39, 134–135.

90. Chmielewski, "Stan szkolnictwa," 40.

91. Kazhdan, *Di geshikhte*, 204–205.

92. Frost, *Schooling*, 38. According to Kazhdan, the head of the TsYShO network, the pretext for closing the ceremony was a lecture on Birobidzhan, given by Gina Medem at the invitation of the student council. After the lecture twenty-seven pupils were arrested, and Medem was accused of spreading communist ideology. Faced with the school authorities' refusal to expel the arrested students, the authorities gave the order to close the school. See Kazhdan, *Di geshikhte*, 215–216. On autobiographical accounts of the college's closing, which apparently made an enormous impression on its students, see YIVO Archives, RG 4, Autobiography 3726, 85.

93. Eisenstein, *Jewish Schools*, 60.

94. A. I. Grodzenski, "Shul Kult in Vilne," in Grodzenski, *Vilner Almanakh*, 215–218.

95. Chmielewski, "Stan szkolnictwa," 43.

96. Eisenstein, *Jewish Schools*, 70, 96.

97. Grodzenski, "Shul Kult in Vilne," 218.

98. YIVO Archives, RG 4, Autobiography 3666, 22.

99. YIVO Archives, RG 4, Autobiography 3629, 71–72.

100. Autobiography 3623, 19–22.

101. Adva Selzer, "'Vos vayter?' Graduating from Elementary School in Interwar Poland: From Personal Crisis to Cultural Turning Point," *Polin* 30 (2018): 285–289.

102. Autobiography 3629, 73.

103. Autobiography 3718, 11.

104. Autobiography 3718, 1.

105. Autobiography 3718, 10.

106. Autobiography 3666, 38.

107. Fishman, *Rise*, 57; Frost, *Schooling*, 27. On the Kuperstein School, called Frug-Kuperstein after amalgamating with another establishment in 1934, see Bastomski, "Der yidish-veltlekher," 205–206.

108. YIVO Archives, RG 4, Autobiography 3598, as cited in Shandler, *Awakening Lives*, 357–362.

109. Kazhdan, *Di geshikhte*, 419.

110. Bassok, "Ma'amadot," 230–231, 234–236.

5. PATTERNS OF PARTICIPATION IN CULTURE

1. Shmeruk, "Hebrew-Yiddish-English," 285–311.

2. See the following articles: Kligsberg, "Di yidishe yugent-bavegung"; Moseley, "Life, Literature"; Steinlauf, "Jewish Politics," 95–104; Ido Bassok, "Reading Secular Literature as a New Marker of Ethnic Identity Among Jewish Youth in Interwar Poland," *Jahrbuch des Simon-Dubnow-Instituts* 9 (2010): 15–36; David Shavit, *Hunger for the Printed Word: Books and Libraries in the Jewish Ghettos of Nazi Occupied Europe* (McFarland, 1997), 3–35.

3. Moseley, "Life, Literature."

4. YIVO Archives, RG 4, Autobiography 3542, 47.

5. YIVO Archives, RG 4, Autobiography 3770, 100–101.

6. YIVO Archives, RG 4, Autobiography 3618, as cited in Shandler, *Awakening Lives*, 206.

7. YIVO Archives, RG 4, Autobiography 3673, 25–27, 30–31.

8. YIVO Archives, RG 4, Autobiography 3763, as cited in Cała, *Ostatnie pokolenie*, 37.

9. YIVO Archives, RG 4, Autobiography 3582, as cited in Shandler, *Awakening Lives*, 115

10. YIVO Archives, RG 4, Autobiography 3845, as cited in Shandler, *Awakening Lives*, 4–5, 8.

11. Autobiography 3845, 10–11.

12. YIVO Archives, RG 4, Autobiography 3507, 6–8.

13. Autobiography 3507, 15, 17–18 (additional material, without page numbers).

14. YIVO Archives, RG 4, Autobiography 3548, 21–22.

15. YIVO Archives, RG 4, Autobiography 3510, 13.

16. See Joanna Lisek, *Jung Wilne—żydowska grupa artystyczna* (Wydawnictwo Uniwersytetu Wrocławskiego, 2005).

17. YIVO Archives, RG 4, Autobiography 3718, 13.

18. Autobiography 3718, 20–21.

19. Autobiography 3542, 42.

20. Autobiography 3510, 5–6.

21. Autobiography 3510, 11.

22. Autobiography 3510, 16.

23. YIVO Archives, RG 4, Autobiography 3666, 25–26.

24. YIVO Archives, RG 4, Autobiography 3508, 12.

25. Autobiography 3508, 13.

26. YIVO Archives, RG 4, Autobiography 3690, as cited in Shandler, *Awakening Lives*, 69.

27. YIVO Archives, RG 4, Autobiography 3802, 20, 22–23.

28. Autobiography 3548, 19. This novel deals with the story "Karahod di blondzhenishn fun Avrom Itshze der Kirzhner," published in Vilnius by the Kletskin publishing house in 1928. I would like to thank Karolina Szymaniak and Joanna Lisek for their help in identifying the writer and title of the story.

29. YIVO Archives, RG 4, Autobiography 3782, as cited in Cała, *Ostatnie pokolenie*, 190. *Shtrayml* was one of the most hard-hitting anti-Hasidic satires by Yitskhok Leybush Peretz.

30. See *Tokhnit ha-limudim*.

31. Fishman, *Rise*, 88.

32. Autobiography 3690, as cited in Shandler, *Awakening Lives*, 112.

33. Autobiography 3690, 71, 74.

34. YIVO Archives, RG 4, Autobiography 3571, 10.

35. YIVO Archives, RG 4, Autobiography 3816, as cited in Cała, *Ostatnie pokolenie*, 380.

36. YIVO Archives, RG 4, Autobiography 3573, as cited in Cała, *Ostatnie pokolenie*, 39.

37. YIVO Archives, RG 4, Autobiography 3675, as cited in Shandler, *Awakening Lives*, 161.

38. YIVO Archives, RG 4, Autobiography 3669, 24–25.

39. Otto Weininger was a Viennese philosopher and psychologist of Jewish descent. Recognized by his contemporaries as an outstanding scholar, he became famous for his work *Sex and Character*, published for the first time in 1903, which combined extreme misogyny with radical, racial antisemitism. The book gained notoriety after its writer committed suicide shortly after its publication.

40. He is referring to the 1929 Yiddish edition: Otto Weininger, *Geshlekht un kharakter: Printsipiele ophandlung* (n.p., 1929).

41. YIVO Archives, RG 4, Autobiography 3752, 18.

42. Bronka's autobiography is not now in the YIVO Archives. Alina Cała received a copy of it from the writer, who submitted an autobiography to the second competition in 1934—see Cała, *Ostatnie pokolenie*, 54–57.

43. See Autobiography 3666, 25; Autobiography 3690, as cited in Shandler, *Awakening Lives*, 53.

44. Fishman, *Rise*, 52–53, 61.

45. Moseley, "Life, Literature," 26. Moseley wrongly claims that the main motive that brought young people to party premises was the possibility of reading for free there.

46. The Kultur-Lige, closely associated with the Bund, ran the Grosser and "Ha-Zomir" libraries from the second half of the 1920s. Its youth movement,

Tsukunft, also supervised the network of Bejnisz Michalewicz libraries. The Borochow libraries were run by activists of the Po'alei-Tsiyon-Left and the communists. The former's youth movement also took care of the Y. L. Peretz network of libraries. The communists organized libraries associated with the Dos Lebn network—see Garncarska-Kadary, *Żydowska ludność*, 219.

47. YIVO Archives, RG 4, Autobiography 3735, 23–24.

48. YIVO Archives, RG 4, Autobiography 3505, 52–53, 62–63, 69.

49. Autobiography 3542, 5, 15.

50. Autobiography 3542, 14, 17, 84.

51. Autobiography 3542, 61.

52. Autobiography 3690, as cited in Shandler, *Awakening Lives*, 83.

53. YIVO Archives, RG 4, Autobiography 3749, 41.

54. Autobiography 3802, 2.

55. YIVO Archives, RG 4, Autobiography 3629, 78.

56. Autobiography 3571, 19–20, 22. Japanese Mishka was a Jewish gangster from early twentieth-century Odessa who became the prototype of Benya Krik, the famous protagonist of Isaac Babel's *Odessa Stories*.] Moisey Winnicki (the real name of Mishka the Japanese) was an important figure in the Jewish criminal world in Odessa. In 1917 he fought in the civil war on the side of the Bolsheviks. After deserting from his unit at the front, he was killed by a special detachment of the Cheka.

57. Nathan Cohen, "The Yiddish Press and Yiddish Literature: A Fertile but Complex Relationship," *Modern Judaism* 28, no. 2 (2008): 149–172.

58. Bassok, "Reading Secular Literature," 16, 34–36.

59. Bassok, "Reading Secular Literature," 27–29.

60. See Moseley, "Life, Literature," 22; Bassok, "Reading Secular Literature," 19, 25.

61. Interestingly, at the beginning of his autobiography, Tor expressly pointed out that his work was in theory the dullest description of his own fortunes and had nothing in common with his literary attempts. Thus, this writer, exceptional because he really did "live on literature," confirmed that when writing his competition entry, he did not think of it as a work of literature—see Autobiography 3752, 1.

62. The library was located at 5 Nowolipki Street. It was one of the few institutions of this type, unassociated with any political organization and used by representatives of all groups of the Jewish community. It lent out both Jewish and Polish books (in Yiddish translation).

63. Autobiography 3752, 10–12.

64. Autobiography 3752, 13.

65. Autobiography 3752, 14. This refers to the hero of the series of novels by Zalman Shneour, Shklover Yidn (The Jews of Szkłów), published for the first

time in 1929 and appearing in installments in the Warsaw *Moment*. Tor undoubtedly read it this way. On the biography of Zalman Shneour, see Dan Miron, "Shneour, Zalman," *The YIVO Encyclopedia of Jews in Eastern Europe*, accessed September 16, 2012, http://www.yivoencyclopedia.org/article.aspx /Shneour_Zalman.

66. Kligsberg, "Di yidishe yugent-bavegung," 168. The autobiographer was an activist in the Bund's Tsukunft. *Yugend Veker* was the magazine of Tsukunft, the Bund's youth organization.

67. Autobiography 3749, 8.

68. Autobiography 3571, 34.

69. Autobiography 3666, 62–63.

70. Kligsberg, "Di yidishe yugent-bavegung," 169; Moseley, "Life, Literature," 7; Steinlauf, "Jewish Politics," 98; D. Shavit, *Hunger*, 31.

71. See e.g. Autobiography 3666, 62; Autobiography 3519, 33–34; Autobiography 3690, as cited in Shandler, *Awakening Lives*, 82–83.

72. Autobiography 3763, as cited in Cała, *Ostatnie pokolenie*, 37, 39, 49.

73. Autobiography 3749, 5, 9.

74. Autobiography 3571, 15.

75. YIVO Archives, RG 4, Autobiography 3559, as cited in Shandler, *Awakening Lives*, 325.

76. Autobiography 3752, 18.

77. Garncarska-Kadary, *Żydowska ludność*, 217, 270–271. The percentage of Hebrew books probably refers mainly to prayer books and religious tracts and not to secular literature.

78. Fishman, *Rise*, 86.

79. Shayne Kulkes, "Di Kinder Bibliotek baym Tsentral Bildungs Komitet," in Grodzenski, *Vilner Almanakh*, 213–214. On the TseBeKa Library, see also Grosman, "Der Tsentrale," 52.

80. Cohen, "Decline of Yiddish," 6.

81. On this kind of dislike on the part of Jewish nationalist circles and on the general poor opinion of the sensationalist press and of the popular novel (both Jewish and Polish) and the resultant pressure exerted on people writing autobiographies, see Cohen, "Yiddish Press," 155–156; Bassok, "Reading Secular Literature," 32.

82. Autobiography 3802, 20, 22–23.

83. Autobiography 3749, 62.

84. Autobiography 3749, 35–36, 44.

85. This is confirmed by other nonautobiographical sources. In memoirs published after the war in Poland, writers emphasized that even if they spoke Yiddish at home, the language of the outside world and of their reading matter was chiefly Polish. See Landau-Czajka, *Syn będzie Lech*, 216.

86. See e.g. Autobiography 3542, 2, 19–21; Autobiography 3770, 19–21, 99–101; Autobiography 3519, 8, 19; Autobiography 3543, 21, 28; Autobiography 3749, 1–2; Autobiography 3591, 1, 4, 12–14.

87. Alter Druyanov, "Ha-Tsiyonut be-Polin," *Moznayim* 9, no. 159 (1932): 8, as cited in Cohen, "Decline of Yiddish," 2.

88. Bacon has pointed out the need for research into the educational practice of Jewish schools, daily compromises between practical requirements (such as the demands of the MWRiOP and parents, the progressive polonization of Jewish young people, and preparation for adult life in the Second Republic), and the anti-assimilationist and nationalist ideologies guiding individual schools. See Bacon, "National Revival." Hitherto, attention has focused more on schools' ideological curricular assumptions, all of them emphasizing Jewish distinctiveness in different ways.

89. See Frost, *Schooling*, 40–41; Trzebiatowski, *Szkolnictwo*, 171; Bacon, *Politics of Tradition*, 147–148.

90. Sabina Levin, "Observations on the State as a Factor in the History of Private Jewish Elementary Schooling in the Second Polish Republic," *Gal-Ed* 18 (2002): 65–66.

91. H. Seidman, *Żydowskie szkolnictwo*, 21–22; Gold, "Religious Education," 274.

92. Frost, *Schooling*, 87; Eisenstein, *Jewish Schools*, 78.

93. Grosman, "Beit Sefer," 63.

94. Senicki, "Di Vilner," 338.

95. Morits Grosman, "Tora Emes: Beis Ulpana ve-hawaha le-ne'arim aniim be-Vilne," in Grosman, *Yidishe Vilne*, 60.

96. Eisenstein, *Jewish Schools*, 89.

97. Aleksiun, "Historionim," 189.

98. Landau-Czajka, *Syn będzie Lech*, 368–369.

99. *Tokhnit ha-limudim*, 4.

100. *Tokhnit ha-limudim*, 4–19, 22–23.

101. *Tarbut—Histadrut ivrit le-hinukh ve-le-tarbut be-Polania. Ha-va'ad ha-merkazi. Programa le-limudei ha-yahadut. Ivrit. Tanakh. Historia* (Merkaz Tarbut, 1934), 27.

102. For more on this, see Kamil Kijek, "Was It Possible to Avoid 'Hebrew Assimilation'? Hebraism, Polonization, and the Zionist 'Tarbut' School System in the Last Decade of Interwar Poland," *Jewish Social Studies* 21, no. 2 (2016): 105–141.

103. Fishman, *Rise*, 91.

104. Frost, *Schooling*, 126.

105. Eisenstein *Jewish Schools*, 31–33; Kazhdan, *Di geshihhte*, 217; Bastomski, "Der yidish-veltlecher," 205–209.

106. Frost, *Schooling*, 134–135. On the great importance of national accreditation by the first TsYShO secondary school, see Kazhdan, *Di geshikhte*, 198–201.

107. A. I. Grodzenski, "Szul Kult in Vilne," in Grodzenski, *Vilner Almanakh*, 215–216.

108. Zineman, *Almanach szkolnictwa*, 1:11–13; Frost, *Schooling*, 138–139

109. Autobiography 3542, 46–47; Autobiography 3796, 5; Autobiography 3812, 12.

110. YIVO Archives, RG 4, Autobiography 3598, as cited in Shandler, *Awakening Lives*, 354; Autobiography 3707, as cited in Shandler, *Awakening Lives*, 233; Autobiography 3542, 25; Autobiography 3726, 30; Autobiography 3548, 11; Autobiography 3568, 30, 44–48.

111. C. Heller, *On the Edge*, 188.

112. *Statystyka Polski. Seria C. Zeszyt 62. Drugi Powszechny Spis Ludności z dnia 9.XII.1931. Mieszkania i gospodarstwa domowe. Ludność. Stosunki Zawodowe (Dane skrócone)* (GUS, 1937), 31.

113. For more on this, see Mendelsohn, *Jews of East Central Europe*, 29–30.

114. Shmeruk, "Hebrew-Yiddish-Polish," 295.

115. Kazhdan, *Di geshikhte*, 427–428.

116. Fishman, *Rise*, 84–85.

117. Shmeruk, "Hebrew-Yiddish-Polish," 285–311.

118. Todd M. Endelman, "Assimilation," *The YIVO Encyclopedia of Jews in Eastern Europe*, accessed July 6, 2025, https://encyclopedia.yivo.org/article/2008.

119. See, e.g., Alexander Herz, *The Jews in Polish Culture* (Northwestern University Press, 1988); Landau-Czajka, *Syn będzie Lech*.

120. Mendelsohn, *On Modern Jewish Politics*, 16; Marcin Wodziński, "Good Maskilim and Bad Assimilationist: Toward a New Historiography of the Haskalah in Poland," *Jewish Social Studies* 10, no. 3 (2003/2004): 87–122; Agnieszka Jagodzińska, "Asymilacja, czyli bezradność historyka: O krytyce terminu i pojęcia," in *Wokół akulturacji i asymilacji Żydów na ziemiach polskich*, ed. Konrad Zieliński (Wydawnictwo UMCS, 2010), 15–32.

121. I use the term *symbolic violence* in the sense proposed by Pierre Bourdieu— see in particular Bourdieu and Passeron, *Reproduction*.

122. Autobiography 3770, 1.

123. Autobiography 3770, 38–40.

124. Autobiography 3571, 4, 9, 12, 13, 15.

125. YIVO Archives, RG 4, Autobiography 3516, 16–17. After graduating from elementary school, the writer, thanks to help from friends of her mother, managed to get into Hebrew secondary school. Polish culture also played an important role in school life there. Autobiography 3516, 26–27.

126. Autobiography 3559, as cited in Shandler, *Awakening Lives*, 326.

127. YIVO Archives, RG 4, Autobiography 3823, 4.

128. Autobiography 3598, as cited in Shandler, *Awakening Lives*, 361.

129. Autobiography 3823, 9–10.

130. Autobiography 3735, 35–36.

131. Autobiography 3516, 55.

132. Autobiography 3770, 58.

133. Autobiography 3812, 15–16.

134. Autobiography 3749, 45.

135. YIVO Archives, RG 4, Autobiography 3832, as cited in Cała, *Ostatnie pokolenie*, 329–330.

136. Autobiography 3505, 63–64, 66–67. Yaacov Shavit points out that references to the same poem by Mickiewicz were used by Ze'ev Jabotinsky in published letters to representatives of Polish Betar. See Y. Shavit, *Jabotinsky*, 23.

137. YIVO Archives, RG 4, Autobiography 3681, 43–46.

138. Autobiography 3816, as cited in Cała, *Ostatnie pokolenie*, 377.

139. Autobiography 3816, 381.

140. YIVO Archives, RG 4, Autobiography 3654, as cited in Cała, *Ostatnie pokolenie*, 497.

141. Katrin Steffen, *Jüdische Polonität: Ethnizität und Nation im Spiegel der polnischsprachigen jüdischen Presse 1918–1939* (Vandenhoeck und Ruprecht, 2004).

6. SYMBOLIC EXCLUSION AND ANTISEMITISM

1. On the various forms of antisemitic ideology and rhetoric, see, e.g., Michlic, *Poland's Threatening Other*, 69–130; Małgorzata Domagalska, "Anti-Semitic Discourse in Polish Nationalist Weeklies Between 1918 and 1939," *East European Jewish Affairs* 36, no. 2 (2006): 191–197; Yisrael Gutman, "Polish Antisemitism Between the Wars: An Overview," in *The Jews of Poland Between Two World Wars*, ed. Yisrael Gutman et al. (University Press of New England, 1989), 97–109; Cała, *Żyd—wróg*, 325–418; Ronald Modras, *The Catholic Church and Antisemitism in Poland, 1933–1939* (Harwood Academic, 1994).

2. Melzer, *No Way Out*, 15–94; Andrzej Chojnowski, *Koncepcje polityki narodowościowej rządów polskich w latach 1921–1939* (Ossolineum, 1979), 219–226.

3. Żarnowski, "Społeczeństwo," 7; Mauersberg, *Komu służyła*, 6–7; Anna Landau-Czajka, *Co Alicja odkrywa po własnej stronie lustra: Życie codzienne, społeczeństwo, władza w podręcznikach dla dzieci najmłodszych 1785–2000* (Neriton, 2002), 247–248.

4. Mędrzecki, "Polskie uniwersum," 30.

5. Wojtas, "Learning to Become Polish," 37–38; Trzebiatowski, *Szkolnictwo*, 177–178.

6. Wojtas, "Learning to Become Polish," 43; Trzebiatowski, *Szkolnictwo*, 287; Mauersberg, "Reformy," 31–32.

7. Wojtas, "Learning to Become Polish," 61–63, 68.

8. Anna Landau-Czajka, "Obraz mniejszości żydowskiej w podręcznikach szkolnych okresu międzywojennego," *Biuletyn Żydowskiego Instytutu* 3–4 (1997): 3.

9. Landau-Czajka, "Obraz mniejszości," 3–7.

10. Joanna Sadowska, "Ustawodawstwo jędrzejewiczowskie wobec szkolnictwa mniejszości narodowych w II Rzeczypospolitej," in *Edukacja—państwo—naród w Europie Środkowo-Wschodniej XIX i XX w.*, eds. Aleksandra Bilewicz, Ryszard Gładkiewicz, and Stefania Walasek (Centrum Badań Śląskoznawczych i Bohemistycznych, 2002), 301.

11. Leopold Infeld, *Kordian, fizyka i ja. Wspomnienia* (PIW, 1968), 153, as cited in Landau-Czajka, *Syn będzie Lech*, 144.

12. See, e.g., a textbook repeatedly republished throughout the period of the Second Republic: Cecylia Niewiadomska, *Legendy, podania i obrazki historyczne* (Gebethner i Wolff, 1918).

13. Ks. Dr. M. Białowąs, *Pan Jezus wśród ludzi: Podręcznik do nauki religii rzymskokatolickiej dla VI klasy szkół powszechnych trzeciego stopnia* (J. Jakubowski and Ska, 1939), 43, as cited in Landau-Czajka, "Obraz mniejszości," 9.

14. Landau-Czajka, "Obraz mniejszości," 3–4.

15. Landau-Czajka, "Obraz mniejszości," 7.

16. Landau-Czajka, "Obraz mniejszości," 8–9.

17. Trzebiatowski, *Szkolnictwo*, 287–291.

18. Natalia Aleksiun, "Żydowskie uniwersum symboliczne w Drugiej Rzeczypospolitej," in *Kultura i społeczeństwo w II Rzeczypospolitej: Metamorfozy społeczne*, ed. Włodzimierz Mędrzecki and Agata Zawiszewska (Instytut Historii PAN, 2012), 86–89; Yitshak Grünbaum, ed., *Materiały w sprawie żydowskiej w Polsce: Żydzi jako mniejszość narodowa* (Biuro Prasowe Organizacji Syjonistycznej w Polsce, 1919), 29; Yitshak Grünbaum, ed., *Materiały w sprawie żydowskiej w Polsce: Żółta Łata (Sprawa ograniczeń prawnych)* (Biuro Prasowe Organizacji Syjonistycznej w Polsce, 1922), i–viii, 97–105.

19. Ignacy Schiper, Arie Tartakower, and Alexander Hafftka, eds., *Żydzi w Polsce odrodzonej: Działalność społeczna, gospodarcza, oświatowa i kulturalna* (Warszawskie Zakłady Graficzne, 1932), 1:7–8.

20. Bacon, *Politics of Tradition*, 245; Szymon Rudnicki, *Żydzi w parlamencie II Rzeczypospolitej* (Wydawnictwo Sejmowe, 2004), 73.

21. C. Heller, *On the Edge*, 221.

22. Grünbaum, "Sprawa żydowska," 32.

23. Grünbaum, "Sprawa żydowska," 34–36, 38.

24. *Chinuchenu*, 3. See also quoted a "typical" dialogue between the author and a mother who, driven by ambition, sends her child to a Polish school (the child from the age of four also attends a traditional heder) but who, to her great regret, due to the antisemitism of the teachers, is forced to withdraw him and reluctantly transfer him to a Tarbut school. *Chinuchenu*, 5.

25. *Wychowanie dziecka żydowskiego*, 10.

26. Bacon, *Politics of Tradition*, 175–176.

27. Frost, *Schooling*, 90.

28. Joanna Lisek, "'Dos loszn fun jidiszkajt'—ortodoksyjny jidyszyzm na łamach 'Bejs Jakow' w kontekście religijnego feminizmu żydowskiego w Polsce," in *Studia z dziejów trójjęzycznej prasy żydowskiej na ziemiach polskich (XIX–XX w.)*, edited by Joanna Nalewajko-Kulikov (Neriton, 2012), 349, 351, 357, 363.

29. Zalman Rajzen, "Der kamf far der yidisher shul iz der kamf far undzere rekht," in Bastomski, *Far undzer shul*, 13–14.

30. Centralne Archiwum Syjonistyczne, A127/750-2, 1–3.

31. Eisenstein, *Jewish Schools*, 30.

32. Kazhdan, *Di geshikhte*, 173.

33. Kazhdan, *Di geshikhte*, 425, 436.

34. For more on this dispute, see Kijek, "Was It Possible," 105–141.

35. Arie Tartakower, *Zarys socjologii żydostwa* (Tsofim, 1938), 145.

36. YIVO Archive, RG 4, Autobiography 3598, as cited in Shandler, *Awakening Lives*, 344–345.

37. Autobiography 3598, 96.

38. YIVO Archive, RG 4, Autobiography 3802, 11.

39. YIVO Archive, RG 4, Autobiography 3702, 8. The distance from the goyim exhibited by traditional Jewish social classes manifested itself in different ways, depending on the group of the Christian population, and it was most strongly expressed in relation to the peasants.

40. YIVO Archive, RG 4, Autobiography 3770, 6, 41.

41. YIVO Archive, RG 4, Autobiography 3740, 50.

42. See, e.g., YIVO Archive, RG 4, Autobiography 3505, 41–43; Autobiography 3675, as cited in Shandler, *Awakening Lives*, 154–155.

43. On the subject of interethnic and stratifying distances between acculturated contestants in the YIVO competition writing in Polish and their Christian peers, see also Alina Cała, "The Social Consciousness of Young Jews in Interwar Poland," *Polin* 8 (1994): 44–50.

44. YIVO Archive, RG 4, Autobiography 3812, 19.

45. Autobiography 3675, as cited in Cała, *Ostatnie pokolenie*, 154–155.

46. YIVO Archive, RG 4, Autobiography 3837, as cited in Cała, *Ostatnie pokolenie*, 466.

47. YIVO Archive, RG 4, Autobiography 3673, 23.

48. Autobiography 3812, 20.

49. Autobiography 3812, 21. A *narnik* was a member of the National Radical Camp, a far-right, fascist organization founded in 1934 and involved in physical violence against Jews since its inception.

50. YIVO Archive, RG 4, Autobiography 3669, 8–9.

51. Only two of the hundreds of autobiographies I have read draw attention to the short-term improvement in the situation of Jewish students in public schools related to the replacement of teachers sympathetic to National Democracy with others associated with Józef Piłsudski's Sanacja camp then in power. See YIVO Archive, RG 4, Autobiography 3732, 19; Autobiography 3669, 32–33.

52. Landau-Czajka also writes on this subject in *Syn będzie Lech*, 362–363.

53. An Endek was a supporter of National Democracy, the largest Polish right-wing party, with a decidedly antisemitic ideology.

54. This refers to the ideology of right-wing students beating up Jewish students at the university in Lviv at that time.

55. Autobiography 3675, as cited in Shandler, *Awakening Lives*, 182–183.

56. On the unique Galician conditions of adolescence and a longer and deeper tradition than elsewhere of combining Polish acculturation with Jewish nationalist views by the region's elites, see Kassow, *Who Will Write*, 19–24.

57. Autobiography 3675, as cited in Shandler, *Awakening Lives*, 172–173.

58. Autobiography 3740, 21–22. See also p. 18.

59. Bronka's autobiography, as cited in Cała, *Ostatnie pokolenie*, 58–59.

60. YIVO Archive, RG 4 3739, as cited in Shandler, *Awakening Lives*, 267.

61. Rafael Mahler, *Yehudei Polin bein shtei milhamot olam: Historya kalkalit-socialit le-or ha-statistika* (Dvir, 1968), 172.

62. Szymon Rudnicki, "From 'Numerus Clausus' to 'Numerus Nullus,'" *Polin* 2 (1987): 246–268; Monika Natkowska, *Numerus clausus, getto ławkowe, numerus nullus, "paragraf aryjski": Antysemityzm na Uniwersytecie Warszawskim 1931–1939* (ŻIH, 1999); Melzer, *No Way Out*, 71–80; Cała, *Żyd—wróg*, 380–381.

63. Wapiński, *Pokolenia*, 249–250.

64. See, e.g., a report of the Ministry of Internal Affairs for 1936, "Stan bezpieczeństwa ogólnego w państwie," Archiwum Akt Nowych, Zespół 9: Ministerstwo Spraw Wewnętrznych 1918–1939, 770, 514.

65. See Mahler, *Yehudei Polin*, 172–174; Bronsztejn, *Ludność żydowska*, 192–193.

66. Natalia Aleksiun, "Together but Apart: University Experience of Jewish Students in the Second Polish Republic," *Acta Poloniae Historica* 109 (2014): 109–137.

67. Autobiography 3770, 41.

68. Autobiography 3675, as cited in Shandler, *Awakening Lives*, 188.

69. Autobiography 3675, 188.

70. Autobiography 3675, 195–196.

71. YIVO Archive, RG 4, Autobiography 3543, 21.

72. *Fachalczyk* is an incorrect transcription from Yiddish into English of the surname *Pacholczyk*. In reality, Władysław Pacholczyk was at the time a teacher at a primary school in Opoczno and the local leader of the so-called Młodzi, a radical faction of the nationalist movement. Between 1931 and 1936, he was

directly responsible for an escalation of anti-Jewish violence in Kielce province, which was one of the main direct causes of anti-Jewish incidents in Odrzywół, Przytyk, and other towns in the province. See Archiwum Państwowe w Kielcach (APK), Urząd Wojewódzki Kielecki (UWK) I, 20494, 84–86, 454; APK, UWK I, 20495, 353, 369, 371; APK, UWK I, 20496, 8; AAN, 1378 UWK, 1537/14 vols. 13–267/II vols. 13, 219, 221, 430–431, 663.

73. YIVO Archive, RG 4, Autobiography 3707, as cited in Shandler, *Awakening Lives*, 236.

74. Autobiography 3732, 6–7.

75. Autobiography 3732, 8–9.

76. Autobiography 3669, 11–12.

77. Autobiography 3669, 29.

78. Autobiography 3802, 17–18.

79. YIVO Archive, RG 4, Autobiography 3519, 22–23.

80. Its principal did not want to exempt the religious girl on Saturday from the obligation of writing in class.

81. YIVO Archive, RG 4, Autobiography 3559, as cited in Shandler, *Awakening Lives*, 329–330.

82. Autobiography 3598, as cited in Shandler, *Awakening Lives*, 375–376.

83. See Shulamit Volkov, *Germans, Jews, and Antisemites: Trials in Emancipation* (Cambridge University Press, 2006), 20–32.

7. POLITICAL ACTIVITY

1. Excellent examples of this issue among the younger generation of peasants are the diaries of rural young people—see, for example, Włodzimierz Mędrzecki, *Młodzież wiejska na ziemiach Polski centralnej, 1864–1939* (Neriton, 2002), 169–170, 187–192.

2. YIVO Archive, RG 4, Autobiography 3819 alef, 34–35.

3. Autobiography 3819 alef, 21–22.

4. YIVO Archive, RG 4, Autobiography 3735, 16.

5. On Ha-Shomer ha-Tsa'ir, its ideology, and the social composition of its members, see, e.g., Elkana Margalit, "Social and Intellectual Origins of the Hashomer Hatzair Youth Movement, 1913–1920," in *Essential Papers on Zionism*, ed. Jehuda Reinharz and Anita Shapira (New York University Press, 1996), 454–472; Gideon Shimoni, *The Zionist Ideology* (Brandeis University Press, 1995), 223–226.

6. Yona, *Nehiye kulanu halutzim*, 183–195, 209–215, 273–276.

7. YIVO Archive, RG 4, Autobiography 3548, 13–14.

8. Autobiography 3548, 33.

9. Autobiography 3548, 44, 46–47.

10. Bacon, *Politics of Tradition*, 101–105, 118–119, 122–124, 127–128.

11. YIVO Archive, RG 4, Autobiography 3669, 15–16.

12. YIVO Archive, RG 4, Autobiography 3568, 50–51.

13. *Mashgiach* is Hebrew for "supervisor." As the traditional social religious supervisor of kashrut, the mashgiach worked at the behest and under the auspices of the local rabbi, or the latter carried out his duties. In the twentieth century, the position of mashgiach was introduced to yeshivas. His task was to supervise the behavior of its students. As such, the position of the yeshiva mashgiach was an important modern innovation.

14. *Teg* (Yiddish) means "day." This was how the custom of yeshiva students eating at the homes of local families was described.

15. Autobiography 3568, 100. *Goles* (Yiddish) or *galut* (Hebrew) means "exile." Symptomatic was his use of the word here in the Zionist sense.

16. Autobiography 3568, 114.

17. Autobiography 3568, 122.

18. Autobiography 3568, 124.

19. Orient-Vostok joining the Mizrahi party is also interesting from the point of view of the new model of Jewish Orthodoxy arising in the 1930s. The writer came from the Lubavitch Hasidim and joined a Zionist party, and this movement, also in its religious version, was fiercely opposed by his home milieu. Additionally, Mizrahi attracted mainly non-Hasidim. This autobiography is evidence of a gradual dying out in the Second Republic of the power of the traditional intra-Jewish divisions and the formation of a "Polish Orthodoxy," as well as a new individualistic model for nurturing it.

20. For such exceptions, see, e.g., YIVO Archive, RG 4, Autobiography 3749; Autobiography 3534, as cited in Cała, *Ostatnie pokolenie*, 227–236.

21. Second place in terms of importance was held by numerous Jewish trade unions associated with the party. See Bassok, "Ne'arim," 577. There will be more later on the role of trade unions as factors in political initiation.

22. SKIF (Sotsyalistishe Kinder Farband, the Socialist Children's Union) was the children's organization of the Bund.

23. YIVO Archive, RG 4, Autobiography 3718, 21; emphasis in original.

24. Autobiography 3718, 21–22. On the role of TsYShO schools in the recruitment of children and young people to Bund organizations, see Gertrude Pickhan, *"Gegen den Strom": Der Allgemeine Jüdische Arbeiterbund "Bund" in Polen 1918–1939* (Deutsche Verlag-Anstalt, 2001), 236–248; Jack Jacobs, *Bundist Counterculture in Interwar Poland* (Syracuse University Press, 2009), 16–17, 38–39.

25. YIVO Archive, RG 4, Autobiography 3504, 6.

26. YIVO Archive, RG 4, Autobiography 3623, 22.

27. Autobiography 3623, 22.

28. Betar was a right-wing movement in radical opposition to all left-wing Zionist youth organizations. It mostly brought together young people from traditional homes, at the same time having in its ranks a clearly separate group of people coming from polonized homes, who were strongly influenced by Polish radical nationalism. The youth group was founded in 1926 as a scout organization of the Brit ha-Zohar movement, led by Ze'ev Jabotinsky's opposition within the World Zionist Organization, preaching a "revision" of the latter's conciliatory policies (hence the name *revisionists*). Jabotinsky's group, which opposed the policies of World Zionist Organization Chairman Chaim Weizman, opted for greater activism, militarism, and decisive Zionist action in Palestine, against both the British authorities and the Arab population's growing opposition to Jewish immigration. Betar's official ideology was national monism, rejecting the class struggle within the Jewish people as an obstacle to building their own state in Palestine. In the 1930s, Betar, like other youth and military revisionist organizations, underwent further radicalization, also involving inspiration drawn from fascist movements, which was not necessarily consistent with Jabotinsky's ideas. See Daniel K. Heller, *Jabotinsky's Children: Polish Jews and the Rise of Right-Wing Zionism* (Princeton University Press, 2017); Y. Shavit, *Jabotinsky*, 20–42, 51–57, 99–127, 181–229.

29. Tel Hai was one of the northernmost Jewish settlements in Palestine. In 1920, during the battles between Arab insurgents and the French colonial authorities in Syria, a watchtower was attacked by a detachment of Arab insurgents, most likely the result of a misunderstanding. In the fight with them, Józef Trumpeldor—a distinguished activist of the Zionist movement, one of the founders of He-Halutz, and a veteran of the Russo-Japanese War of 1904–1905, awarded a medal for valor by Tsar Nicholas II—was killed. His death was quickly turned into a legend. Despite his left-wing beliefs, Trumpeldor fell carrying a weapon, and he became a symbol of right-wing Betar, preaching militarism and armed struggle for the independence of Palestine.

30. YIVO Archive, RG 4, Autobiography 3618, as cited in Shandler, *Awakening Lives*, 213.

31. *Kvutsa* (Hebrew) means "group." This refers to a Zionist agricultural commune.

32. YIVO Archive, RG 4, Autobiography 3834, 29–30.

33. YIVO Archive, RG 4, Autobiography 3681, 48–50.

34. In the first decades of its existence, the Bund was an unequivocally revolutionary party. After its final break with the communists in the early 1920s, more because of the latter's aggressive attitude than for any significant ideological differences, in the 1930s it had difficulty reconciling the contradiction arising from the need to be a legitimate social democratic party conducting extensive trade union, cultural, and social activity, and the ideological imperative of being

a revolutionary organization. On this subject, see Pickhan, *Gegen den Strom*, 70–110, 373–400; Abraham Brumberg, "The Bund and the Polish Socialist Party in the Late 1930s," in *The Jews of Poland Between Two World Wars*, ed. Yisrael Gutman et al. (University Press of New England, 1989), 75–79.

35. YIVO Archive, RG 4, Autobiography 3802, 24–27.

36. YIVO Archive, RG 4, Autobiography 3543, 31–32.

37. Autobiography 3543, 33.

38. Autobiography 3543, 34–35. Tsukunft and SKIF (the youth and children's organizations of the Bund, respectively), unlike some Zionist youth groups, were completely under the control of their parent party. See Bassok, "Ne'arim," 583, 589.

39. These social characteristics of young Jews who converted to communism seem to be something new, characteristic of the generation growing up in the Second Republic. Well-known Jewish-born representatives of revolutionary internationalism, who began their political activity before World War I, such as Rosa Luxemburg, Adolf Warski (Warszawski), and Leon Jogiches (pseudonym Jan Tyszka), grew up in richer acculturated environments. See Robert Wistrich, *Revolutionary Jews from Marx to Trotsky* (Harrap, 1976), 76–78, 91.

40. YIVO Archive, RG 4, Autobiography 3598, as cited in Shandler, *Awakening Lives*, 345–347.

41. Autobiography 3598, 347–379.

42. Autobiography 3598, 365.

43. Marcus, *Social and Political History*, 124–127.

44. YIVO Archive, RG 4, Autobiography 3702, 10–27.

45. Autobiography 3702, 27–31.

46. On Yom Kippur, the feast of redemption and repentance for sins committed, there is total fasting. Eating in public, especially of nonkosher meat, during this holiday was a radical display of rejecting Jewish tradition.

47. YIVO Archive, RG 4, Autobiography 3690, as cited in Shandler, *Awakening Lives*, 81.

48. YIVO Archive, RG 4, Autobiography 3581, as cited in Cała, *Ostatnie pokolenie*, 71–86; Autobiography 3701; Autobiography 3708.

49. YIVO Archive, RG 4, Autobiography 3629, 98–99. To be in line with his own communist views, Kola hastily pointed out that he "was no nationalist." However, this does not contradict the fact that he understood his political activity as carried out mainly on behalf of the Jewish masses.

50. See Piotr Wróbel, "Failed Integration: Jews and the Beginning of the Communist Movement in Poland," *Polin* 24 (2012): 205, 214.

51. *Murdziel* is what the communist cell operating in Muranów, a Warsaw neighborhood inhabited mostly by poor Jews, was commonly called.

52. Autobiography 3598, as cited in Shandler, *Awakening Lives*, 366–370.

53. Autobiography 3690, as cited in Shandler, *Awakening Lives*, 107.

54. Autobiography 3629, 69.

55. Landau-Czajka, *Syn będzie Lech*, 394, 396; Julian Stryjkowski and Piotr Szewc, eds., *Ocalony na Wschodzie* (Noir sur Blanc, 1991), 11–48. See also Bassok, "Ne'arim," 576.

56. Autobiography 3702, 28.

57. Autobiography 3702, 29–30.

58. See Kligsberg, "Di yidishe yugent-bavegung," 199–204.

59. Although Po'alei-Tsiyon-Left was by definition a Zionist party, for most of the interwar period the ideologically closest party to it was the KPP. The party rejected cooperation with other Zionists within the framework of the World Zionist Organization, which was at the "service of the bourgeoisie." Jewish emigration to Palestine was supposed to be a stichic process that was caused by objective socioeconomic contradictions. The Jewish proletariat in Palestine, after the country saw the emergence of a real capitalist society, was meant to struggle against the Jewish and Arab bourgeoisie, alongside the Arab proletariat. The Jewish proletariat in Europe was meant to become involved in the European revolutionary movement. Only in 1938, under pressure from the Great Terror in the USSR and its own young people wanting to increase their chance of emigrating to Palestine, did the party return to the World Zionist Organization, and its youth group Yugend entered He-Halutz. This did not, however, mean that Yugend members did not often have communist views. Through them in the late 1930s these views began to appear even in the anticommunist He-Halutz. See Bassok, "Ne'arim," 583. On Po'alei-Tsiyon-Left history and ideology in the interwar period, see Samuel D. Kassow, "The Left Poale Zion in Interwar Poland," in *The Emergence of Modern Jewish Politics: Bundism and Zionism in Eastern Europe*, ed. Zvi Gitelman (University of Pittsburgh Press, 2003), 71–84.

60. Schatz, *Generation*, 54.

61. Joanna Nalewajko-Kulikov, *Obywatel Jidyszlandu: Rzecz o żydowskich komunistach w Polsce* (Neriton, 2009), 38–52.

62. On the statistics of belonging and the identity-cultural divisions among people of Jewish origin involved in the communist movement, see Jeff Schatz, "Jews and the Communist Movement in Interwar Poland," *Studies in Contemporary Jewry* 20 (2004): 19, 24–31; Wróbel, "Failed Integration," 187–190; Moshe Mishkinsky, "The Communist Party of Poland and the Jews," in Gutman et al., *Jews of Poland*, 63–64.

63. See, e.g., David Kutner, *Kartuz Bereze: Der poylisher kontsentratsyon lager* (Royter Hilf, 1936). Depending on the instructions of the Comintern, the temporary tactical alliances of the communists with the Bund or Po'alei-Tsiyon-Left, such as the one in 1933 calling for the creation of a united front to fight fascism, did not prevent them from calling the latter party a "Zionist branch in

the ranks of the proletariat" or an "agent of the bourgeoisie." In fact, these "alliances" were actions directed against the ideologically closest Jewish parties, aimed at winning over their members. See Schatz, "Jews and the Communist Movement," 23, 25.

64. Wróbel, "Failed Integration," 189, 201–222; Mishkinsky, "Communist Party," 60–61, 70.

65. Wróbel, "Failed Integration," 204, 218, 220.

66. Like Greyno (quoted above), Stefan Bergman, who was also active in the Vilnius KPP cell, moved only in a Jewish milieu. He encountered non-Jewish comrades only at a higher level of political initiation, which was imprisonment. See Karen Auerbach, *The House at Ujazdowskie 16: Jewish Families in Warsaw After the Holocaust* (Indiana University Press, 2013), 25–26.

67. See Jeffrey S. Kopstein and Jason Wittenberg, "Between State Loyalty and National Identity: Electoral Behaviour in Inter-War Poland," *Polin* 24 (2012): 171–185; Schatz, "Jews and the Communist Movement," 21.

68. Bronka's autobiography, as cited in Cała, *Ostatnie pokolenie*, 63–65.

69. YIVO Archive, RG 4, Autobiography 3740, 30–31.

70. Autobiography 3740, 38–40; emphasis in original.

71. Landau-Czajka, *Syn będzie Lech*, 397–398. See also Auerbach, *House at Ujazdowskie 16*, 37.

72. Ha-Shomer Ha-Tahor (the True Watchman) was established in south-eastern Poland (in today's Ukraine) in 1926, and Ha-Shomer ha-Le'umi (the National Watchman) a year later in the former Congress Kingdom. These organizations were founded by former members of Ha-Shomer ha-Tsa'ir, which was then turning toward Marxism. They preached retaining old Ha-Shomer ideals now contaminated with Marxism. Combining themselves with other smaller youth organizations throughout the whole country, most of the members of these youth groups formed No'ar Tsiyoni (Zionist Youth) in 1932. This group was close to the idea of the kibbutz and of physical work on the land, but not to other elements of socialist ideology, let alone Marxism. For a time, this organization tried to run its own Halutz movement. See Israel Oppenheim, *The Struggle of Jewish Youth for Productivization: The Zionist Youth Movement in Poland* (Columbia University Press, 1989), 92–101; Bassok, "Ne'arim," 583–584.

73. YIVO Archive, RG 4, Autobiography 3654, as cited in Cała, *Ostatnie pokolenie*, 497.

74. Autobiography 3654, 490.

75. Kligsberg, "Di yidishe yugent-bavegung," 173–174.

76. Autobiography 3543, 9–10.

77. Autobiography 3548, 33.

78. YIVO Archive, RG 4, Autobiography 3666, 48.

79. Autobiography 3629, 77.

80. Autobiography 3629, 90.

81. Autobiography 3669, 21.

82. YIVO Archive, RG 4, Autobiography 3510, 13–14. Bnei Akiva was initially an independent, religious Zionist youth organization formed in Galicia in 1927. It was founded by secessionists from Ha-Shomer ha-Tsa'ir, which was then turning radically left. In 1931 Bnei Akiva merged with one of the Mizrahi youth organizations—Ha-Shomer ha-Da'ti. See Bassok, "Ne'arim," 586–587.

83. This trend is also confirmed by other sources—see Wróbel, "Failed Integration," 203, 214. While in the 1930s the number of Jews in KPP structures usually did not exceed 30 percent, in Warsaw it grew at the same time to 44 percent, and in 1937 it was 65 percent. See Schatz, "Jews and the Communist Movement," 20.

84. Yona, *Nehiye kulanu halutzim*, 255–271; Oppenheim, *Struggle*, 63–71.

85. The Jabotinsky cult, resulting from the ideology of the right-wing nationalist movement Betar, sometimes distorted the ideas of the leader himself and, contrary to his intentions, brought some circles of the revisionist movement closer to the ideology of fascist movements; on this subject, see Yaacov Shavit, "Fire and Water: Ze'ev Jabotinsky and the Revisionist Movement," in Reinharz and Shapira, *Essential Papers*, 544–547, 553–554, 559–562.

86. Autobiography 3543, 34.

87. Autobiography 3543, 37, 62.

88. YIVO Archive, RG 4, Autobiography 3505, 26–27.

89. Autobiography 3629, 74.

90. Autobiography 3681, 58.

91. YIVO Archive, RG 4, Autobiography 3673, 30.

92. Autobiography 3673, 36–37.

93. Autobiography 3673, 38–39, 42.

94. Autobiography 3666. 44.

95. Autobiography 3666, 55–56.

96. Autobiography 3598, as cited in Shandler, *Awakening Lives*, 366.

97. On Tsukunft's sex education, see Jacobs, *Bundist Counterculture*, 21–26.

98. YIVO Archive, RG 4, Autobiography 3571, 27–28, 37–38.

99. Autobiography 3618, as cited in Shandler, *Awakening Lives*, 213.

100. Autobiography 3618, 62.

101. YIVO Archive, RG 4, Autobiography 3542, 28.

102. Autobiography 3542, 36.

103. Autobiography 3542, 56.

104. YIVO Archive, RG 4, Autobiography 3770, 83–89.

105. Bassok, "Ne'arim," 573–575. On the degeneration of European civilization at the end of the nineteenth century, ideas of which decisively influenced the elements of young Jews' sociopolitical awareness described here, see Jerzy Jedlicki, *Świat zwyrodniały: Lęki i wyroki krytyków nowoczesności* (Sic!, 2000), 37–46, 83–112.

106. See Kligsberg, "Di yidishe yugent-bavegung," 176–177.
107. Autobiography 3735, 16–17.
108. Autobiography 3504, 6.
109. Autobiography 3673, 44–47.
110. Autobiography 3681, 54.
111. Autobiography 3598, as cited in Shandler, *Awakening Lives*, 368–370.
112. Autobiography 3623, 23.
113. They were also blurred for some scholars uncritically analyzing young people's autobiographies. Kligsberg correctly writes that the most important role of youth organizations was to provide young people with alternative forms of education. He does not notice, however, how very close they were to one of the political ideologies—see Kligsberg, "Di yidishe yugent-bavegung," 160–161.
114. On this subject, see also Bassok, "Ne'arim," 591–592. I disagree with Bassok that this kind of "social revolution" was more a form of redefinition than an abandonment of traditional Jewish values and ways of perceiving the world. See Bassok, "Ne'arim," 592–596.
115. Autobiography 3819, 7–10.
116. Autobiography 3510, 13.
117. Autobiography 3598, as cited in Shandler, *Awakening Lives*, 365–366.
118. Autobiography 3690, as cited in Shandler, *Awakening Lives*, 83–84; see also 85–88, 93–100.
119. Autobiography 3718, 22.
120. A great example here is Litvak Ejszyszki (Eyshishok), where Zionist organizations made up for restricted access to education. See Eliach, *There Once Was a World*, 468.
121. YIVO Archive, RG 4, Autobiography 3726, 36–37.
122. Autobiography 3726, 48.
123. Autobiography 3726, 50.
124. Autobiography 3726, 51, 58, 77.
125. Autobiography 3726, 58–59. *Kestl-ovntn* (Yiddish) means "box evenings." This is how a form of discussion, popular in youth movements, was described. Members of the organization dropped into prepared boxes cards with questions or with descriptions of issues that they wanted to raise, which were then discussed by the group during the meeting.
126. Autobiography 3726, 20, 22–23.
127. Autobiography 3543, Yiddish, 1934, 38–40; Autobiography 3718, 21.
128. Autobiography 3770, 101.
129. Autobiography 3673, 31; Autobiography 3735, 23–24.
130. Autobiography 3571, 14–15.
131. Autobiography 3770, 30. From the autobiography, it can be concluded that most of the members of the local branch of Ha-Shomer ha-Tsa'ir were children from wealthier merchant families. See, e.g., Autobiography 3770, 61.

132. Bassok, "Ma'amadot," 239–243; Bassok, "Ne'arim," 580; see also Kligsberg, "Di yidishe yugent-bavegung," 205–209.

133. *Mir kumen on* (The way of the young), produced in 1936, was a film directed by Alexander Ford about a Jewish tuberculosis sanatorium run by the Bund in Międzeszyn and well known throughout the country. The film showed how Jewish children were raised in a Bund establishment, transforming them from traditional egoists and slovenly, primitive, and antisocial people into young socialist idealists. *Mir kumen on* did not obtain a permit for general release in Poland. It was shown in France at private meetings of Bund youth organizations. *Mir kumen on* is more proof of the phenomenon described here of the top-down construction of an alternative Jewish youth counterculture based on total negation and a sharp and stereotypical treatment of the world of tradition. The film can be viewed at https://www.youtube.com/watch?v=vozD_XbGHGA (accessed July 6, 2025).

134. Autobiography 3571, 29–31.

135. YIVO Archive, RG 4, Autobiography 3565, 31.

136. Rudnicki, *Żydzi w parlamencie*, 363–366, 399.

137. Autobiography 3749, 39. On the involvement of Bund youth in the activities of the adult party, see also Jacobs, *Bundist Counterculture*, 19; Kligsberg, "Di yidishe yugent-bavegung," 196.

138. On cooperation in these elections and the generally complicated relationship between the Bund and the PPS, see Brumberg, "Bund," 75–94.

139. Brumberg, "Bund," 38–39.

140. Chaim Arlosoroff was one of the leaders of Mapai, the strongest Jewish party in Palestine. As one of the most important politicians of the Jewish Yishuv, representing moderate-left Zionism, he supported a peaceful accommodation with the Arab population, which was increasingly opposed to Jewish immigration. Against this background there was a growingly sharp conflict between Arlosoroff and Jabotinsky's revisionists, who wanted forceful measures. He also played a key role in the conclusion of an agreement between the Jewish Agency, which he led and which organized immigration to Palestine, and the German Nazi government. Arlosoroff was killed two days after returning from Germany while walking on the beach in Tel Aviv. Senior revisionists, including their leading ideologue in Palestine, Abba Ahimeir, were accused of his murder. To this day the murder has not been solved. In 1933, owing to Arlosoroff's murder, the Jewish community in Palestine was on the verge of civil war, and the emotions and hatred between left-wing Zionists and revisionists also moved to diaspora countries, including Poland.

141. Autobiography 3542, 72–73.

142. Autobiography 3673, 26–27.

143. On the politics of shtadlanut and criticism of it by secular Jewish national circles, see Scott Ury, "The 'Shtadlan' of the Polish-Lithuanian Commonwealth: Noble Advocate or Unbridled Opportunist?," *Polin* 15 (2002): 267–299.

144. See, e.g., Elie Lederhandler, "Orthodox Jewish Opinion in Turn-of-the-Century Russia and Poland: A Documentary Study in Culture and Politics," in *Jewish Responses to Modernity: New Voices in America and Eastern Europe* (New York University Press, 1994), 67–103.

145. See Bacon, *Politics of Tradition*, 119–121.

146. Autobiography 3548, 23–24.

147. Bassok, "Ne'arim," 577.

148. Autobiography 3629, 69, 80.

149. Autobiography 3690, as cited in Shandler, *Awakening Lives*, 86.

150. Autobiography 3690, 89–90, 94, 99.

151. Schatz, "Jews and the Communist Movement," 28.

152. Autobiography 3690, as cited in Shandler, *Awakening Lives*, 100–102.

153. Autobiography 3629, 69–70.

154. See, for example, Bassok, "Ne'arim," 577.

155. Schatz, *Generation*, 128–145; Schatz, "Jews and the Communist Movement," 28–30. See also a description of Stefan Bergman's experiences in Auerbach, *House at Ujazdowskie 16*, 27.

156. Autobiography 3629, 80–81, 83.

157. Autobiography 3629, 85.

158. Autobiography 3690, as cited in Shandler, *Awakening Lives*, 107–108.

159. Autobiography 3629, 82.

160. Autobiography 3629, 84, 86.

161. Autobiography 3504, 15.

162. Rona Yona, "A Kibbutz in Diaspora: The Pioneer Movement and the Klosova Kibbutz," *Journal of Israeli History* 31, no. 1 (2012): 9, 30.

163. Oppenheim, *Struggle*, 64.

164. See, e.g., the report of the vice president of He-Halutz in Poland, M. Preker, presented on November 19, 1936, to the Institute of Minority Affairs and the Emigration Committee of the Commission for the Study of the Economic Needs of the Jewish Population in Poland, AAN, Zespół 322: Ministerstwo Spraw Zagranicznych 1918–1939, 2296/B18499, 179–180.

165. Bassok, "Ne'arim," 582.

166. Gordonia lay to the right of Ha-Shomer ha-Tsa'ir, advocated "constructivist socialism," and rejected Shomer Marxism. Elitism connected them, as well as a focus on issues of Palestine and a rejection of political involvement in diaspora issues, except those concerning emigration to the Land of Israel. Its patron in Palestine was the Ha-Po'el Ha-Tsa'ir (Young Worker) party, which joined Mapai in 1929. Despite the patronage of the strongest Jewish party in Palestine, Gordonia enjoyed great autonomy. This organization was one of several youth movements operating within He-Halutz. Bassok, "Ne'arim," 581–582.

167. On the conflicts within He-Halutz during the period discussed here, see Oppenheim, *Struggle*, 72–89.

168. Yona, "Kibbutz in Diaspora," 21.

169. Autobiography 3504, 11.

170. Autobiography 3673, 43–44.

171. Autobiography 3819 alef, 34–37.

172. Autobiography 3623, 22–25. Yona draws attention to this motive as the main factor attracting young people to hakhshara in "Kibbutz in Diaspora," 13.

173. Oppenheim, *Struggle*, 63–65.

174. Yona, "Kibbutz in Diaspora," 11–12; Oppenheim, *Struggle*, 66.

175. Autobiography 3673, 48.

176. Autobiography 3735, 30–31.

177. YIVO Archive, RG 4, Autobiography 3832, as cited in Cała, *Ostatnie pokolenie*, 328–329.

178. Autobiography 3673, 49–50, 52.

179. Autobiography 3623, 26–27.

180. Autobiography 3623, 26–27. Identical collective rules for daily life prevailed in another flagship kibbutz, in Kłosów; see Yona, "Kibbutz in Diaspora," 26.

181. Yona, "Kibbutz in Diaspora," 13.

182. On the descriptions of hakhshara in the autobiographies, see also Kligsberg, "Di yidishe yugent-bavegung," 210–216.

183. See, e.g., Asaf Kaniel, "Gender, Zionism and Orthodoxy: The Women of the Mizrachi Movement in Poland, 1916–1939," *Polin* 22 (2009): 357–360. On interwar Polish Zionist women's ideas of femininity, body, and their place in the nationalist movement, see Jolanta Mickute, "Making of the Zionist Woman: Zionist Discourse on the Jewish Woman's Body and Selfhood in Interwar Poland," *Eastern European Politics, Societies and Cultures* 28, no. 1 (2014): 137–162.

184. It was not only the camps organized by left-wing Zionists that were like that. An identical ideology ruled the Bund's summer camps—see Jacobs, *Bundist Counterculture*, 44.

185. On this subject, see also Bassok, "Ne'arim," 573.

186. Bassok, "Ne'arim," 597.

187. Steinlauf, "Jewish Politics," 99.

8. POLITICAL CONSCIOUSNESS

1. YIVO Archive, RG 4, Autobiography 3681, 55.

2. YIVO Archive, RG 4, Autobiography 3690, as cited in Shandler, *Awakening Lives*, 82. Further on in Greyno's autobiography, there is an excerpt showing how the writer "extracted" Marxist content from the hardly Marxist novel by Romain Rolland, *Jean-Christophe*. Autobiography 3690, 96.

3. YIVO Archive, RG 4, Autobiography 3629, 79.

4. Autobiography 3629, 13.

5. Autobiography 3629, 69.

6. YIVO Archive, RG 4, Autobiography 3505, 68–69.

7. YIVO Archive, RG 4, Autobiography 3673, 33–36.

8. YIVO Archive, RG 4, Autobiography 3702, 30–31.

9. Shore, *Caviar and Ashes*, 370–371.

10. YIVO Archive, RG 4, Autobiography 3565, 40.

11. Autobiography 3629, 23.

12. Autobiography 3629, 96.

13. Autobiography 3505, 30. See also 31–32.

14. Autobiography 3673, 39–40.

15. YIVO Archive, RG 4, Autobiography 3542, 11.

16. Autobiography 3542, 60.

17. YIVO Archive, RG 4, Autobiography 3770, 54–57.

18. Autobiography 3770, 65.

19. Autobiography 3770, 71–77.

20. Autobiography 3770, 90.

21. YIVO Archive, RG 4, Autobiography 3519, 15–16.

22. Autobiography 3519, 35–37.

23. YIVO Archive, RG 4, Autobiography 3735, 33.

24. Autobiography 3505, 27.

25. YIVO Archive, RG 4, Autobiography 3752, 12. At the end of his autobiography, Tor revealed that a year later he joined the Jewish People's Rescue Committee, an organization founded by the well-known writer Hillel Zeitlin. What had attracted the autobiographer to the committee was the struggle against "party antagonisms" that were supposedly destroying the Jewish people. Autobiography 3752, 20–22. For exceptional biographies of Hillel Zeitlin and his views, see Shraga Bar-Sella, "On the Brink of Disaster: Hillel Zeitlin's Struggle for Jewish Survival in Poland," *Polin* 11 (1998): 77–93; Arthur Green and A. E. Mayse, "'The Great Call of the Hour': Hillel Zeitlin's Yiddish Writings on Yavneh," *In Geveb: A Journal of Yiddish Studies*, March 8, 2016, http://ingeveb.org/articles/the-great-call-of-the-hour-hillel-zeitlins-yiddish-writings-on-yavneh.

26. YIVO Archive, RG 4, Autobiography 3666, 57.

27. YIVO Archive, RG 4, Autobiography 3749, 30–31.

28. Autobiography 3770, 45.

29. See Ze'ev Jabotinsky, "Yo, Brekhn," *Haynt*, November 4, 1932, 9. This piece was later reprinted in the revisionist Hebrew press and the most important European magazine of this movement, the Russian-language *Rassvet*.

30. For example, in Kielce in April 1935, two hundred members of the local branch of the League for Working Palestine (an organization led by Ben-Gurion)

conducted a trial of the agreement between its leader and Jabotinsky, condemning the agreement with the revisionists. See AAN, 1378: Urząd Wojewódzki Kielecki, 267/II vol. 13: 1935, 715.

31. YIVO Archive, RG 4, Autobiography 3802 (additional materials), 10.

32. On how closely the author followed intra-Zionist debates concerning, for example, the class struggle, the Jewish-Arab conflict, and the resulting contradictions for socialist Zionism, see Autobiography 3802, 7–8.

33. Autobiography 3542, 5.

34. Autobiography 3542, 7.

35. Autobiography 3542, 17.

36. Autobiography 3542, 74.

37. Autobiography 3542, 9, 11, 16, 19, 71, 78–79.

38. On physical violence, see also Kligsberg, "Di yidishe yugent-bavegung," 202–204.

39. Autobiography 3542, 17, 19.

40. Autobiography 3542, 48.

41. YIVO Archive, RG 4, Autobiography 3514, as cited in Shandler, *Awakening Lives*, 401.

42. See, for example, Daniel Blatman, "The Bund in Poland, 1935–1939," *Polin* 9 (1996): 58–82; Robert Moses Shapiro, "The Polish Kehillah Elections of 1936: A Revolution Re-Examined," *Polin* 8 (1994): 206–226.

43. Schatz, "Jews and the Communist Movement," 20.

44. Bistritzky, *Erets*, 16.

45. Yona, "Kibbutz in Diaspora," 14–15.

46. Ezra Mendelsohn, "Jewish Politics in Interwar Poland: An Overview," in *The Jews of Poland Between Two World Wars*, ed. Yisrael Gutman et al. (University Press of New England, 1989), 10–13, quotation on 13.

47. Oppenheim *Struggle*, 101–110.

48. Bassok, "Ne'arim," 238. This was the case in situations where the Orthodox yeshiva system and other social institutions from this milieu continued to uphold traditional class-stratified distances, propagating elitism and individualism as central values in the lives of prominent Talmud scholars. The Aguda elite and the yeshiva authorities clearly wanted to separate future prominent rabbis from the mass of less-educated religious young people. Against this background, there were many conflicts between party and rabbinical elites and Orthodox youth organizations.

49. Bacon, *Politics of Tradition*, 102.

50. On the nonautobiographical evidence of such beliefs, see Bacon, *Politics of Tradition*, 124, 132–133, 139–140.

51. *Sprawozdanie z życia mniejszości narodowych: Za I kwartał 1935 r.*, 79, AAN, Zespół 9: Ministerstwo Spraw Wewnętrznych 1918–1939, IV/98.

52. Oppenheim, *Struggle*, 110–113.

53. "Der yunger halutsisher agudizm marshirt mit fareynikte koykhes," *Yidisher Arbeter Shtime*, April 16, 1937, 6.

54. "Der yunger halutsisher agudizm," 6.

55. H. Seidman, *Szlakiem nauki talmudycznej*, 9, 38, 48–49.

56. See, for example, L. From, "Der ershter May!," *Yidisher Arbeter Shtime*, April 30, 1937, 1; M. H. Berg, "Yahades un sotsyalism," *Yidisher Arbeter Shtime*, December 12, 1937, 4. On the ideology of "Torah socialism" among Aguda workers, see also Bacon, *Politics of Tradition*, 115–116.

57. On this subject, see Jacobs, *Bundist Counterculture*, 15; Pickhan, *Gegen den Strom*, 272.

58. Włodzimierz Żabotyński, *Ideologia Bejtaru* (Komenda Okręgowa Bejtaru dla Małopolski Wschodniej, 1935), 12–17, 39–43. On Jabotinsky's attitude toward Marxism, see Michael Stanislawski, *Zionism and the Fin de Siècle* (University of California Press, 2001), 210–216; Y. Shavit, "Fire and Water," 556–559.

59. Józef Margolin, *Idea syjonizmu* (Atid, 1937), 64, also 63–89, 110–130.

60. "Binyomin R.," *Bamerkung*, 1–2.

61. YIVO Archive, RG 4, Autobiography 3837, as cited in Cała, *Ostatnie pokolenie*, 470–472, 479.

62. YIVO Archive, RG 4, Autobiography 3669, 14–15.

63. Autobiography 3669, 15–16.

64. Autobiography 3669, 18–19.

65. Autobiography 3669, 36–37.

66. Autobiography 3669, 38.

67. Autobiography 3669, 19–20.

68. YIVO Archive, RG 4, Autobiography 3675, as cited in Shandler, *Awakening Lives*, 157, 167.

69. Autobiography 3565, 27–34, quotation on 35–36.

70. During one police search, the words "You won't become a rabbi now" came from his mother's lips, comical in this part of the autobiography. Autobiography 3565, 37.

71. Autobiography 3542, 16, 59–60, 66–67, 76.

72. Autobiography 3542, 55, 66.

73. The names of these people have been changed by a YIVO contestant hiding his or her identity. On the real personalities of these people and the writer of the autobiography, see Kamil Kijek, ed., *"Płonęli gniewem": Autobiografia młodego Żyda*, trans. Anna Kałużna and Anna Szyba (PWN, 2021), x–xviii.

74. Autobiography 3542, 41–42.

75. Autobiography 3542, 68. On this subject, see also the commentary on Max Weinreich's book attached to the competition entry: "Binyomin R.," *Bamerkung*, 12.

76. YIVO Archive, RG 4, Autobiography 3571, 11, 13–14, 16–20, 23, 33.

77. YIVO Archive, RG 4, Autobiography 3726, 37.

78. Autobiography 3726, 58, 74, 78, 80–81, 88, 92–97.

79. Bourdieu and Wacquant, *Invitation to Reflexive Sociology*, 126–140, quotation on 126.

80. Jack Jacobs attributes the creation of this kind of counterculture in the interwar period only to the Bund and sees in it (in his view, moreover, significantly exaggerated and not taking into account the political situation of the late 1930s) the reason for the party's electoral successes in 1936 to 1939—see Jacobs, *Bundist Counterculture*. As I have tried to show in this work, all those features that the writer attributes to the Bund (i.e., the creation around the party of youth movements, children's movements, women's organizations, trade unions, and cultural institutions) also characterized all of the Bund's most important political opponents.

81. For more on this topic, see Kamil Kijek, "'Naród słabych i skrzywdzonych': Wojny i rewolucja lat 1914–1921, w pamięci młodzieży żydowskiej okresu międzywojennego," *Studia Judaica* 18, no. 2 (2014): 81–104.

82. D. G. Roskies, *Against the Apocalypse*, 97–98.

83. Jacek Majchrowski, *Silni—zwarci—gotowi: Myśl polityczna Obozu Zjednoczenia Narodowego* (PIW, 1985); Wapiński, *Pokolenia*, 283–313.

84. Schatz, "Jews and the Communist Movement," 16–17, 20–21, 23.

85. YIVO Archive, RG 4, Autobiography 3618, as cited in Shandler, *Awakening Lives*, 206.

86. Autobiography 3618, 213.

87. Autobiography 3618, 219.

88. Autobiography 3618, 222–225.

89. YIVO Archive, RG 4, Autobiography 3623, 26, 30–31.

90. Autobiography 3666, 47.

91. Autobiography 3666, 49–51.

92. Autobiography 3666, 53–54.

93. YIVO Archive, RG 4, Autobiography 3598, as cited in Shandler, *Awakening Lives*, 365.

94. Autobiography 3690, as cited in Shandler, *Awakening Lives*, 111.

95. YIVO Archive, RG 4, Autobiography 3749, 54–55.

96. Autobiography 3542, 83.

97. Autobiography 3735, 38.

98. YIVO Archive, RG 4, Autobiography 3732, 34–36.

99. Autobiography 3666, 65–70.

100. Autobiography 3629, autobiographer's letter to YIVO.

101. Autobiography 3802, 14.

102. Autobiography 3681, 62.

103. Autobiography 3681, 63–65.

104. On the subject of the "new man" in its Bundist version, see, for example, Jacobs, *Bundist Counterculture*, 20–21; on his Zionist versions, see, for example, Yael Zerubavel, *Recovered Roots: Collective Memory and the Making of Israeli National Tradition* (University of Chicago Press, 1995), 20–31; Anita Shapira, *Land and Power: The Zionist Resort to Force, 1881–1948* (Oxford University Press, 1992), 22–30, 72–75, 100–104, 142–143, 267–276.

105. Autobiography 3542, 64.

106. Autobiography 3542, 26–27.

107. Autobiography 3690 as cited in Shandler, *Awakening Lives*, 78.

108. Autobiography 3571, 13–14.

109. Autobiography 3571, p. 14.

110. Autobiography 3505, 63.

111. YIVO Archive, RG 4, Autobiography 3516, diary attached to the autobiography, 13–14.

112. On the importance of boxing in the ideology of Po'alei-Tsiyon-Left and the Bund and the activities of their sports organizations, see Jacobs, *Bundist Counterculture*, 53–54. On sport and the importance of "brawn and muscle" in the young people's autobiographies, see Kligsberg, "Di yidishe yugent-bavegung," 177–178, 195. On Jewish sport in general in the interwar period, see Diethelm Blecking, "Marxism versus Muscular Judaism: Jewish Sport in Poland," in *Sport and Physical Education in Jewish History*, ed. George Eisen, Haim Kaufman, and Manfred Lammer (Wingate Institute, 2003), 48–55.

113. Autobiography 3542. 49.

114. Autobiography 3681, 59–61. Sources other than YIVO autobiographies also provide evidence of the popularity of boxing among young Jews during the interwar period. See, for example, Adamczyk-Garbowska et al., *Tam był kiedyś*, 179. Identical emotions and reasons for pride were supposedly supplied by Jewish boxers for American Jews, who were also suffering from a complex of alleged cowardice and weakness. See Elliot Horowitz, "'They Fought Because They Were Fighters and They Fought Because They Were Jews': Violence and Construction of Modern Jewish Identity," *Studies in Contemporary Jewry* 18 (2002): 25–26, 32–34; Elliot Horowitz, *Reckless Rites: Purim and the Legacy of Jewish Violence* (Princeton University Press, 2006), 203–205.

115. D. Heller, *Jabotinsky's Children*.

116. On the cooperation of the revisionist movement and late Sanacja Polish governments, see Laurence Weinbaum, *The New Zionist Organization and the Polish Government, 1936–1939* (Boulder, 1993).

117. D. Heller, *Jabotinsky's Children*, 134–135, 142–166; Yaacov Shavit, "Politics and Messianism: The Zionist Revisionist Movement and Polish Political Culture," *Studies in Zionism* 6, no. 2 (1985): 229–246.

118. Żabotyński, *Ideologia Bejtaru*, 21–22. On Jabotinsky's fascinating strategy of mobilizing Jewish right-wing young people in Poland in the 1930s, see also

Daniel K. Heller, "Obedient Children and Reckless Rebels: Jabotinsky's Youth Politics and the Case for Authoritarian Leadership, 1931–1933," *Journal of Israeli History* 34, no. 1 (2015): 45–68.

119. Leonard Rowe, "Jewish Self-Defense: A Response to Violence," in *Studies on Polish Jewry, 1919–1939: The Interplay of Social, Economic and Political Factors in the Struggle of a Minority for Its Existence*, ed. Joshua A. Fishman (YIVO, 1974), 147. Rowe, in an uncritical and apologetic article from which the above quotation comes, claimed that on the basis of these memories he recreated the most important aspects of the history of the Ordener Grupe in Warsaw. The noisy declarations of the leaders of the Bund should be treated not as factual descriptions of specific events but as testimony to the ideology and ideological desires of Jewish socialists, dreaming of universal support from the Jewish Street and of their own strength. See Rowe, "Jewish Self-Defense," 105–149.

120. Emanuel Nowogródzki, *Żydowska Partia Robotnicza Bund w Polsce w latach 1915–1939* (ŻIH, 2005), 242.

121. Nowogródzki, *Żydowska Partia Robotnicza Bund*, 244.

122. See, for example, Horowitz, "They Fought," 23–25.

123. Autobiography 3749, 33, 36, 40, 63.

124. Autobiography 3629, 92.

125. Autobiography 3571, 33, 35. On the expulsion of Jews who were Polish citizens from Germany and their tragedy in the camp in Zbąszyń, see Bonnie Mae Harris, "From German Jews to Polish Refugees: Germany's Polenaktion and the Zbąszyń Deportations of October 1938," *Kwartalnik Historii Żydów* 230 (2009): 175–205; Jerzy Tomaszewski, "The Polish Right-Wing Press, the Expulsion of Polish Jews from Germany, and the Deportees in Zbąszyń, 1938–1939," *Gal-Ed* 18 (2002), 89–100.

126. Stanisław Wacławski was a student activist in the Polish nationalist movement who was killed during anti-Jewish riots at Wilno University on November 9–12, 1931. The commemoration of the anniversary of his death organized by the Polish radical right was often a pretext for attacks on the Jewish population. See, for example, AAN, Zespół 9: MSW 1918–1939, 866, k. 88.

127. Autobiography 3542, 62.

128. Autobiography 3565, x–xi.

129. Mendelsohn *On Modern Jewish Politics*, 21–22, 63–78, 120–125.

130. Autobiography 3690, as cited in Shandler, *Awakening Lives*, 65. Meetings in the forests after the Shabbat by young people breaking away from the influence of traditional revolutionary parents already had a long tradition. See, for example, Adamczyk-Garbowska et al., *Tam był kiedyś*, 116.

131. Autobiography 3690, 82.

132. Autobiography 3565, 33, 35.

133. Autobiography 3565, 100.

134. Autobiography 3623, 30.

135. Autobiography 3623, 31.

136. YIVO Archive, RG 4, Autobiography 3718, supplement to the autobiography, iii.

137. Autobiography 3718, supplement to the autobiography, i–vii.

138. Autobiography 3542, 26.

139. Shore, *Caviar and Ashes*, 368.

140. YIVO Archive, RG 4, Autobiography 3548, 47–48.

CONCLUSION

1. Yehosua Thon, "Di Yugend un mir . . .," *Haynt* 1, no. 1 (1932): 5. I would like to thank Joanna Nalewajko-Kulikov for pointing me toward this piece.

2. Adamczyk-Garbowska et al., *Tam był kiedyś*, 262.

3. Carl E. Schorske, "Politics in a New Key: An Austrian Trio," in *Fin-de-Siècle Vienna: Politics and Culture* (Alfred A. Knopf, 1980), 120.

4. Moss, *Unchosen People*.

5. Moshe Rosman, "Hasidism as a Modern Phenomenon: The Paradox of Modernization Without Secularization," *Simon Dubnow Institute Yearbook* 6 (2007): 215–224.

6. Carl Schorske, characterizing "politics in a new key," emphasizes that alienated groups were the most susceptible to its influence. The protest movements that were taking over these groups sought to develop their members' social space and life as widely as possible, establishing their own sports clubs or schools. Schorske, "Politics," 143.

7. Karolina Szymaniak, "Speaking Back: On Some Aspects of the Reception of Polish Literature in Yiddish Literary Criticism," *Polin* 28 (2016): 153–172.

8. Antony Polonsky, *The Jews of Poland and Russia*, vol. 3, *1914–2008* (Littman, 2012), 384–396.

9. Polonsky, *Jews of Poland and Russia*, 477–479, 482, 500–525.

10. Steinlauf, "Jewish Politics," 102–103; Kligsberg, "Di yidishe yugent-bavegung," 137–138.

11. See, for example, Zivia Lubetkin, *In the Days of Destruction and Revolt* (Am Oved, 1981); Yitzhak Zukerman and Barbara Harshav, *A Surplus of Memory: Chronicle of the Warsaw Ghetto Uprising* (University of California Press, 1993).

12. See, for example, Barbara Engelking-Boni and Jan Grabowski, eds., *Dalej jest noc: Losy Żydów w wybranych powiatach okupowanej Polski*, vols. 1–2 (Stowarzyszenie Centrum Badań nad Zagładą Żydów, 2018); Jan Grabowski, *Hunt for the Jews: Betrayal and Murder in German-Occupied Poland* (Indiana University Press, 2013).

13. Moss, *Unchosen People*.

14. See, for example, Tara Zahra, *Reconstructing Europe's Families After World War II* (Harvard University Press, 2015), 62, 82–87, 99, 103–109, 120, 122, 133–134; Kamil Kijek, "A New Life? The Pre-Holocaust Past and Post-Holocaust Present in the Life of the Jewish Community of Dzierżoniów, Lower Silesia, 1945–50," in *Jewish Lives Under Communism*, ed. Katerina Capkova and Kamil Kijek (Rutgers University Press, 2022), 15–34; Kamil Kijek, "Only Ashes? Western Jewish Visitors to the New Poland in 1946 and the Future of Polish Jewry," *Journal of Modern European History* 20, no. 1 (2022): 111–126.

BIBLIOGRAPHY

PRIMARY SOURCES

Archives

Archiwum Akt Nowych (Archives of New Acts), Warsaw: RG 9, RG 322, RG 1378.

Archiwum Państwowe w Kielcach (State Archives in Kielce): RG UWK I.

Archiwum Żydowskiego Instytutu Historycznego (Jewish Historical Institute Archives), Warsaw: RG 124.

Centralne Archiwum Syjonistyczne (Central Zionist Archives), Jerusalem: RG A127.

YIVO Archives, New York: RG 4, RG 584, RG 719.

Source Materials

Bassok, Ido, and Avraham Novershtern, eds. *Alilot ne'arim: Autobiografiot shel bnei no'ar yehudim mi-Polin bein shtei milchamot ha-olam.* Institute for the History of Polish Jewry, 2011.

Cała, Alina, ed. *Ostatnie pokolenie: Autobiografie polskiej młodzieży żydowskiej okresu międzywojennego—ze zbioru YIVO Institute for Jewish Research w Nowym Jorku.* Sic!, 2003.

Kijek, Kamil, ed. *"Płonęli gniewem": Autobiografia młodego Żyda.* Translated by Anna Kałużna and Anna Szyba. PWN, 2021.

Shandler, Jeffrey, ed. *Awakening Lives: Autobiographies of Jewish Youth in Poland Before the Holocaust.* Yale University Press, 2002.

Printed Sources

Alter, Wiktor. *Człowiek w społeczeństwie*. Światło, 1938.

Bastomski, Shloyme, ed. *Far undzer shul: Ayntolike oysgabe fun Tsentraler Bildungs-Komitet (TseBeKa) in Vilne*. TzeBeKa, 1933.

Bistricki, Nathan. *Erets Israel be-Hinukh ha-Yehudi be-Polin*. Sefer, 1929.

Chinuchenu: Nasze wychowanie. Dyrekcja Kursów "Tarbutu," 1932.

Chmielewski, Samuel. "Stan szkolnictwa wśród Żydów w Polsce." *Sprawy Narodowościowe* 9 (1937): 32–74.

Falski, Marian. *Środowisko społeczne młodzieży a jej wykształcenie*. Nasza Księgarnia, 1937.

Grodzenski, A. I., ed. *Vilner Almanakh*. Ovent Kurier, 1939.

Grosman, Morits, ed. *Yidishe Vilne in vort un bild*. Hirsch Matz, 1925.

Grünbaum, Yitshak, ed. *Materiały w sprawie żydowskiej w Polsce: Żółta Łata (sprawa ograniczeń prawnych)*. Biuro Prasowe Organizacji Syjonistycznej w Polsce, 1922.

Grünbaum, Yitshak, ed. *Materiały w sprawie żydowskiej w Polsce: Żydzi jako mniejszość narodowa*. Biuro Prasowe Organizacji Syjonistycznej w Polsce, 1919.

Grünbaum, Yitshak. "Sprawa żydowska." *Natio* 1–2 (1927): 26–38.

Kutner, David. *Kartuz Bereze: Der poylisher kontsentratsyon lager*. Royter Hilf, 1936.

Mały rocznik statystyczny. GUS, 1939.

Margolin, Józef. *Idea syjonizmu*. Atid, 1937.

Memorandum funem Ortodoksishe Lerer Seminar "Mosad le-mechanechim Datiim." Chorev, 1937.

Mendelson, Salomon, ed. *Nowa Szkoła Żydowska, czem jest i do czego dąży*. Biblioteka "Szkolnictwo Żydowskie," 1926.

Niewiadomska, Cecylia, *Legendy, podania i obrazki historyczne*. Gebethner i Wolff, 1918.

Schiper, Ignacy, Arie Tartakower, and Aleksander Hafftka, eds. *Żydzi w Polsce odrodzonej: Działalność społeczna, gospodarcza, oświatowa i kulturalna*. Vol. 1. Warszawskie Zakłady Graficzne, 1932.

Seidman, Hillel. *Szlakiem nauki talmudycznej*. Księgarnia F. Hoesicka, 1934.

Seidman, Hillel. *Żydowskie szkolnictwo religijne w ramach ustawodawstwa polskiego/ Yudishe religieze shun-vezen in di ramen fun der poylisher gezetsgebung*. Chorev, 1937.

Shtokfish, David, ed. *Sefer Przytyk*. Irgun Yotzei Przytyk be Israel, 1973.

Statystyka Polski. Seria C. Zeszyt 62. Drugi Powszechny Spis Ludności z dnia 9.XII.1931. Mieszkania i gospodarstwa domowe. Ludność. Stosunki Zawodowe (Dane skrócone). GUS, 1937.

Tarbut—Histadrut ivrit le-hinukh ve-le-tarbut be-Polania. Ha-va'ad ha-merkazi. Programa le-imudei ha-yahadut. Ivrit. Tanakh. Historia. Merkaz Tarbut, 1934.

Tartakower, Arie. *Zarys socjologii żydostwa*. Cofim, 1938.

Tokhnit ha-limudim shel gimnasia bat 8 mahlakot im mekhina "Hertsliya" ba Vilna. Drukarnia F. Wajnsztejna, 1927.

Weininger, Otto. *Geshlekht un kharakter: Printsipiele ophandlung.* n.p., 1929.

Weinreich, Max. *Der veg tsu undzer yugnt: Yesodes, metodn, problemen fun yidisher yugnt forshung.* YIVO Institut, 1935.

Weinreich, Max. "Yidishe yugnt-forshung." *YIVO Bleter* 7, no. 1–2 (1934).

Wychowanie dziecka żydowskiego dawniej a dziś/Di ertsiyung funem yidishn kind amol un Haynt. Tarbut, 1936.

Żabotyński, Włodzimierz. *Ideologia Bejtaru.* Komenda Okręgowa Bejtaru dla Małopolski Wschodniej, 1935.

Zineman, Jakub, ed. *Almanach szkolnictwa żydowskiego w Polsce.* Vol. 1. Renesans, 1936.

Zineman, Jakub, ed. *Almanach szkolnictwa żydowskiego w Polsce.* Vol. 3. Renesans, 1938.

Periodicals

Haynt (Warsaw), 1932.

Natio (Warsaw), 1927.

Ofakim (Warsaw), 1933.

Sprawy Narodowościowe (Warsaw), 1929.

Yedies fun YIVO (Vilna), 1932–1935.

Yidisher Arbeter Shtime (Łódź), 1937.

YIVO Bleter (Vilnius), 1934.

Memoirs

Adamczyk-Garbowska, Monika, Adam Kopciowski, and Andrzej Trzciński, eds. *Tam był kiedyś mój dom: Księgi pamięci gmin żydowskich.* Wydawnictwo UMCS, 2009.

Even-Hayim, Mosze Natan, ed. *Toldot Yehudei Jaslo me-reshit hityashvutam be-okh ha-ir ad yamei ha-hurban al yadei ha-natsim.* Irgun Yaslo be Israel, 1953.

Gold, Ben-Zion. "Religious Education in Poland: A Personal Perspective." In *The Jews of Poland Between Two World Wars,* edited by Yisrael Gutman et al. University Press of New England, 1989.

Shtern, Yekhiel, *Kheyder un Beys-Medresh.* YIVO, 1950.

Spector, Shmuel, ed. *Pinkas ha Kehillot: Poland; Volhynia and Polesie.* Yad Vashem, 1989.

Stryjkowski, Julian, and Piotr Szewc, eds. *Ocalony na Wschodzie.* Noir sur Blanc, 1991.

SECONDARY SOURCES

Aleksiun, Natalia. "Historionim yehudim we-hatson shel rabanut misug hadash: Beyt ha-midrash le-rabanim Tahkemoni ve-ha-makhon lemadei ha-yahadut be-Varsza bein milhamot ha-olam." In *From Breslau to Jerusalem: Rabbinical Seminaries Past, Present and Future,* edited by Guy Miron. Machon Schechter, 2009.

Aleksiun, Natalia. "Together but Apart: University Experience of Jewish Students in the Second Polish Republic." *Acta Poloniae Historica* 109 (2014): 109–137.

Aleksiun, Natalia. "Training a New Generation of Jewish Historians: Majer Balaban's Seminar of the History of Polish Jews." In *Zwischen Graetz und Dubnow: Jüdische Historiographie in Ostmitteleuropa im 19. und 20. Jahrhundert*, edited by François Guesnet. Akademische Verlagsanstalt, 2009.

Aleksiun, Natalia. "Żydowskie uniwersum symboliczne w Drugiej Rzeczypospolitej." In *Kultura i społeczeństwo w II Rzeczypospolitej. Metamorfozy społeczne 4*, edited by Włodzimierz Mędrzecki and Agata Zawiszewska. Instytut Historii PAN, 2012.

Assaf, David, ed. *Journey to a Nineteenth-Century Shtetl: The Memoirs of Yekhezkel Kotik*. Wayne State University Press, 2002.

Assaf, David, and Emanuel Etkes. *Ha Heder: Makorim, teudot, prakei sifrut we zichronot*. Beit Shalom Aleichem, 2010.

Auerbach, Karen. *The House at Ujazdowskie 16: Jewish Families in Warsaw After the Holocaust*. Indiana University Press, 2013.

Bacon, Gershon C. "National Revival, Ongoing Acculturation: Jewish Education in Interwar Poland." *Jahrbuch des Simon-Dubnow-Instituts* 1 (2002): 71–92.

Bacon, Gershon C. *The Politics of Tradition: Agudat Yisrael in Poland, 1916–1939*. Magnes, 1996.

Bacon, Gershon C. "To Enlist the Enthusiasm of the Young: Orthodox Jewish Non-Political Response to the Challenges of Interwar Poland." *Polin* 33 (2021): 285–308.

Bar-Sella, Shraga. "On the Brink of Disaster: Hillel Zeitlin's Struggle for Jewish Survival in Poland." *Polin* 11 (1998): 77–93.

Bassok, Ido. "Le-she'elat erkan ha-histori shel otobyografiyot bnei no'ar mi-osef YIVO." *Madei Yahadut* 44 (2007): 137–164.

Bassok, Ido. "Ma'amadot ve-tfisa ma'amadit etsel yeladim ve-bnei no'ar yehudi be-Polin bein ha-milhamot." *Gal-Ed* 18 (2002): 225–244.

Bassok, Ido. "Ne'arim we arkhei ne'arim ba-tnuat ha-no'ar ha-Polani she-bein ha-milhamot." In *Kiyum ve-shavar: Yehudei Polin le-doroteikhem: Hevra, tarbut, le'umiyut*, edited by Yisrael Bartal and Yisrael Gutman. Merkaz Zalman Shazar, 2001.

Bassok, Ido. "Reading Secular Literature as a New Marker of Ethnic Identity Among Jewish Youth in Interwar Poland." *Jahrbuch des Simon-Dubnow-Instituts* 9 (2010): 15–36.

Blatman, Daniel. "The Bund in Poland, 1935–1939." *Polin* 9 (1996): 58–82.

Blecking, Diethelm. "Marxism versus Muscular Judaism: Jewish Sport in Poland." In *Sport and Physical Education in Jewish History*, edited by George Eisen, Haim Kaufman, and Manfred Lammer. Wingate Institute, 2003.

Bourdieu, Pierre, and Jean-Claude Passeron. *Reproduction in Education, Society and Culture*. Sage, 1990.

Bourdieu, Pierre, and Loïc J. D. Wacquant. *An Invitation to Reflexive Sociology*. Polity, 1992.

Bronsztejn, Szyja. *Ludność żydowska w Polsce w okresie międzywojennym: Studium statystyczne*. Ossolineum, 1963.

Brumberg, Abraham. "The Bund and the Polish Socialist Party in the late 1930s." In *The Jews of Poland Between Two World Wars*, edited by Yisrael Gutman et al. University Press of New England, 1989.

Brykczyński, Paul. *Primed for Violence: Murder, Antisemitism, and Democratic Politics in Interwar Poland*. University of Wisconsin Press, 2016.

Cała, Alina. "The Social Consciousness of Young Jews in Interwar Poland." *Polin* 8 (1994): 42–65.

Cała, Alina. *Żyd—wróg odwieczny? Antysemityzm w Polsce i jego źródła*. Nisza, 2012.

Castellan, Georges. "Remarks on the Social Structure of the Jewish Community in Poland between the Two World Wars." In *Jews and Non-Jews in Eastern Europe, 1918–1945*, edited by Bella Vago and George L. Mosse. Wiley, 1974.

Chojnowski, Andrzej. *Koncepcje polityki narodowościowej rządów polskich w latach 1921–1939*. Ossolineum, 1979.

Cohen, Nathan. "The Yiddish Press and Yiddish Literature: A Fertile but Complex Relationship." *Modern Judaism* 28, no. 2 (2008): 149–172.

De Bloeme, Jordana. "Creating a New Jewish Nation: The Vilna Educational Society and Secular Yiddish Education in Interwar Vilna." *Polin* 30 (2018): 221–236.

Dekel-Chen, Jonathan. "Transnational Intervention and Its Limits: The Case of Interwar Poland." *Journal of Modern Jewish Studies* 17 (2018): 265–286.

Domagalska, Małgorzata. "Anti-Semitic Discourse in Polish Nationalist Weeklies Between 1918 and 1939." *East European Jewish Affairs* 36, no. 2 (2006): 191–197.

Dynner, Glenn. "Replenishing the 'Fountain of Judaism': Traditionalist Jewish Education in Interwar Poland." *Jewish History* 31 (2018): 229–261.

Eisenstein, Miriam. *Jewish Schools in Poland, 1919–1939: Their Philosophy and Development*. Columbia University Press, 1950.

Eliach, Yaffa. *There Once Was a World: A 900-Year Chronicle of the Shtetl Eishyshok*. Little, Brown, 1998.

Endelman, Todd M. "In Defense of Jewish Social History." *Jewish Social Studies* 7, no. 3 (2001): 52–67.

Engelking-Boni, Barbara, and Jan Grabowski, eds. *Dalej jest noc: Losy Żydów w wybranych powiatach okupowanej Polski*. Vols. 1–2. Stowarzyszenie Centrum Badań nad Zagładą Żydów, 2018.

Even-Zohar, Itamar. *Papers in Culture Research*. Porter Chair of Semiotics, Tel-Aviv University, 2005.

Feiner, Shmuel. *The Jewish Enlightenment*. University of Pennsylvania Press, 2004.

Feiner, Shmuel. "The Pseudo-Enlightenment and the Question of Jewish Modernization." *Jewish Social Studies* 3, no. 1 (1996): 62–88.

Fishman, David E. "Musar and Modernity: The Case of Novarodek." *Modern Judaism* 8, no. 1 (1988): 41–64.

Fishman, David E. "The Musar Movement in Interwar Poland." In *The Jews of Poland Between Two World Wars*, edited by Yisrael Gutman et al. University Press of New England, 1989.

Fishman, David E. *The Rise of Modern Yiddish Culture*. Pittsburgh University Press, 2005.

Frost, Shimon. *Schooling as a Socio-Political Expression: Jewish Education in Interwar Poland*. Magnes, 1998.

Garncarska-Kadary, Bina. *Żydowska ludność pracująca w Polsce 1918–1939*. ŻIH, 2001.

Gartner, Lloyd P. "Paths to Jewish Social History." *Studies in Contemporary Jewry* 3 (1987): 204–212.

Geertz, Clifford. "Ideology as Cultural System." In *Ideology and Discontent*, edited by David Apter. Collier Macmillan, 1964.

Goldstein, Yossi. "'Ha-heder metukan' be-Rusia ka-basis le-ma'arekhet ha-hinukh ha-Tsiyoni." *Inianim ba-hinukh* 45 (1986): 47–157.

Grabowski, Jan. *Hunt for the Jews: Betrayal and Murder in German-Occupied Poland*. Indiana University Press, 2013.

Green, Arthur, and A. E. Mayse. "'The Great Call of the Hour': Hillel Zeitlin's Yiddish Writings on *Yavneh*." *In Geveb: A Journal of Yiddish Studies*, March 8, 2016. http://ingeveb.org/articles/the-great-call-of-the-hour-hillel-zeitlins-yiddish-writings-on-yavneh.

Gutman, Yisrael. "Polish Antisemitism Between the Wars: An Overview." In *The Jews of Poland Between Two World Wars*, edited by Yisrael Gutman et al. University Press of New England, 1989.

Hanebrink, Paul. *A Specter Haunting Europe: The Myth of Judeo-Bolshevism*. Harvard University Press, 2018.

Harris, Bonnie Mae. "From German Jews to Polish Refugees: Germany's Polenaktion and the Zbąszyń Deportations of October 1938." *Kwartalnik Historii Żydów* 230 (2009): 175–205.

Heller, Celia. *On the Edge of Destruction: Jews of Poland Between Two World Wars*. Schocken, 1980.

Heller, Daniel K. *Jabotinsky's Children: Polish Jews and the Rise of Right-Wing Zionism*. Princeton University Press, 2017.

Heller, Daniel K. "Obedient Children and Reckless Rebels: Jabotinsky's Youth Politics and the Case for Authoritarian Leadership, 1931–1933." *Journal of Israeli History* 34, no. 1 (2015): 45–68.

Herz, Alexander. *The Jews in Polish Culture*. Northwestern University Press, 1988.

Hoffman, Eva. *Shtetl: The Life and Death of a Small Town and the World of the Polish Jews*. Public Affairs, 2007.

Horowitz, Elliot. *Reckless Rites: Purim and the Legacy of Jewish Violence*. Princeton University Press, 2006.

Horowitz, Elliot. "'They Fought Because They Were Fighters and They Fought Because They Were Jews': Violence and Construction of Modern Jewish Identity." *Studies in Contemporary Jewry* 18 (2002): 23–42.

Hundert, Gershon. *Jews in Poland-Lithuania in the Eighteenth Century: A Genealogy of Modernity*. University of California Press, 2004.

Hundert, Gershon, ed. *The YIVO Encyclopedia of Jews in Eastern Europe*. Yale University Press, 2008.

Jacobs, Jack. *Bundist Counterculture in Interwar Poland*. Syracuse University Press, 2009.

Jagodzińska, Agnieszka. "Asymilacja, czyli bezradność historyka: O krytyce terminu i pojęcia." In *Wokół akulturacji i asymilacji Żydów na ziemiach polskich*, edited by Konrad Zieliński. Wydawnictwo UMCS, 2010.

Jedlicki, Jerzy. *Świat zwyrodniały: Lęki i wyroki krytyków nowoczesności*. Sic!, 2000.

Judt, Tony, and Timothy Snyder. *Thinking the Twentieth Century*. Penguin Books, 2012.

Kaniel, Asaf. "Bein hilonim, masortaim ve ortodoksim: Shmirat mitzvot b'rai hitmodedut 'gezirat ha kashrut,' 1937–1939." *Gal-Ed* 23 (2013): 75–106.

Kaniel, Asaf. "Gender, Zionism and Orthodoxy: The Women of the Mizrachi Movement in Poland, 1916–1939." *Polin* 22 (2009): 346–367.

Kaniel, Asaf. *Yomra u-me'as: Ha-mizrahi be-Polin bein shtei milchamot ha-olam*. Bar Ilan University Press, 2011.

Karlip, Joshua M. *The Tragedy of a Generation: The Rise and Fall of Jewish Nationalism in Eastern Europe*. Harvard University Press, 2013.

Kassow, Samuel D. "Communal and Social Change in the Polish Shtetl, 1900–1939." In *Jewish Settlement and Community in the Modern Western World*, edited by Ronald Dotterer, Deborah Dash Moore, and Steven M. Cohen. Susquehanna University Press, 1991.

Kassow, Samuel D. "The Left Poale Zion in Interwar Poland." In *The Emergence of Modern Jewish Politics: Bundism and Zionism in Eastern Europe*, edited by Zvi Gitelman. University of Pittsburgh Press, 2003.

Kassow, Samuel D. *Who Will Write Our History? Rediscovering a Hidden Archive from the Warsaw Ghetto*. Indiana University Press, 2007.

Kazhdan, Chaim Shloyme. *Di geshikhte fun yidishn shulvezen in umophengikn Poyln*. Gezelshaft "Kultur" un "Hilf," 1947.

Kazhdan, Chaim Shloyme. *Fun kheider un 'shkoles' biz TsYShO*. Shloyme Mendelsohn Fond, 1956.

Kijek, Kamil. "Max Weinreich, Assimilation and the Social Politics of Jewish Nation Building." *East European Jewish Affairs* 41, no. 1–2 (2011): 25–55.

Kijek, Kamil. "Między uniwersalną nauką a narodową polityką: Charakter projektu badań nad młodzieżą Żydowskiego Instytutu Naukowego (JIWO) w Polsce międzywojennej." *Kwartalnik Historii Żydów* 2 (2010): 157–193.

Kijek, Kamil. "'Naród słabych i skrzywdzonych': Wojny i rewolucja lat 1914–1921 w pamięci młodzieży żydowskiej okresu międzywojennego." *Studia Judaica* 18, no. 2 (2014): 81–104.

Kijek, Kamil. "A New Life? The Pre-Holocaust Past and Post-Holocaust Present in the Life of the Jewish Community of Dzierżoniów, Lower Silesia, 1945–50." In *Jewish Lives Under Communism*, edited by Katerina Capkova and Kamil Kijek. Rutgers University Press, 2022.

Kijek, Kamil. "Only Ashes? Western Jewish Visitors to the New Poland in 1946 and the Future of Polish Jewry." *Journal of Modern European History* 20, no. 1 (2022): 111–126.

Kijek, Kamil. "Świadomość i socjalizacja polityczna ostatniego pokolenia Żydów Polskich w II Rzeczypospolitej." Doctoral thesis, Instytut Historii PAN, 2013.

Kijek, Kamil. "Was It Possible to Avoid 'Hebrew Assimilation'? Hebraism, Polonization, and the Zionist 'Tarbut' School System in the Last Decade of Interwar Poland." *Jewish Social Studies* 21, no. 2 (2016): 105–141.

Kirshenblatt-Gimblett, Barbara. "Coming of Age in the 1930s: Max Weinreich, Edward Sapir and Jewish Social Science." *YIVO Annual* 23 (1996): 1–103.

Klibansky, Ben Zion. *Kitsur halamish: Tor ha-zahav shel ha-yeshivot ha-litayot be-Mizrach Europa*. Merkaz Zalman Shazar, 2014.

Kligsberg, Moshe. *Child and Adolescent Behavior Under Stress: An Analytical Topical Guide to a Collection of Autobiographies of Jewish Young Men and Women in Poland (1932–1939)*. YIVO, 1965.

Kligsberg, Moshe. "Di yidishe yugent-bavegung in Poyln tsvishn beyde velt milk-homes." In *Studies on Polish Jewry, 1919–1939: The Interplay of Social, Economic and Political Factors in the Struggle of a Minority for Its Existence*, edited by Joshua A. Fishman. YIVO, 1974.

Kligsberg, Moshe. "Socio-Psychological Problems Reflected in the YIVO Autobiography Contest." *YIVO Annual of Jewish Social Science* 1 (1946): 241–249.

Kobrin, Rebecca. *Jewish Bialystok and Its Diaspora*. Indiana University Press, 2010.

Kopstein, Jeffrey S., and Jason Wittenberg. "Between State Loyalty and National Identity: Electoral Behaviour in Inter-War Poland." *Polin* 24 (2012): 171–185.

Korzec, Paweł. "Anti-Semitism in Poland as an Intellectual, Social, and Political Movement." In *Studies on Polish Jewry, 1919–1939: The Interplay of Social, Economic and Political Factors in the Struggle of a Minority for Its Existence*, edited by Joshua A. Fishman. YIVO, 1974.

Krzywiec, Grzegorz. "The Balance of Polish Political Antisemitism: Between 'National Revolution,' Economic Crisis, and the Transformation of the Polish Public Sphere in the 1930s." In *Right-Wing Politics and the Rise of Antisemitism in Europe, 1935–1941*, edited by Frank Bajohr and Dieter Pohl. Wallstein Verlag, 2019.

Krzywiec, Grzegorz. "Żydzi, 'kwestia żydowska' i antysemityzm na ziemiach polskich w kontekście środkowoeuropejskim na przełomie XIX i XX wieku: Antysemicki habitus—kod antysemicki-ideologia antysemicka." In *Drogi odrębne, drogi wspólne: Problem specyfiki rozwoju historycznego Europy Środkowo-Wschodniej w XIX–XX wieku*, edited by Maciej Janowski. Instytut Historii PAN, 2014.

Kuznitz, Cecile E. *YIVO and the Making of Modern Jewish Culture: Scholarship for the Yiddish Nation*. Cambridge University Press, 2014.

Landau-Czajka, Anna. *Co Alicja odkrywa po własnej stronie lustra: Życie codzienne, społeczeństwo, władza w podręcznikach dla dzieci najmłodszych 1785–2000*. Neriton, 2002.

Landau-Czajka, Anna. "Obraz mniejszości żydowskiej w podręcznikach szkolnych okresu międzywojennego." *Biuletyn Żydowskiego Instytutu Historycznego* 3–4 (1997): 3–12.

Landau-Czajka, Anna. *Syn będzie Lech . . . Asymilacja Żydów w Polsce międzywojennej*. Neriton, 2006.

Lebow, Katherine "Autobiography as Complaint: Polish Social Memoir Between the World Wars." *Laboratorium* 6, no. 3 (2014): 13–26.

Lebow, Katherine. "The Conscience of the Skin: Interwar Polish Autobiography and Social Rights." *Humanity* 3, no. 3 (2012): 297–319.

Lederhandler, Elie. *Jewish Responses to Modernity: New Voices in America and Eastern Europe*. New York University Press, 1994.

Lestchinsky, Jacob. "The Jews in the Cities of the Republic of Poland." *YIVO Annual of Jewish Social Science* 1 (1946): 156–177.

Levin, Sabina. "Observations on the State as a Factor in the History of Private Jewish Elementary Schooling in the Second Polish Republic." *Gal-Ed* 18 (2002): 59–71.

Lisek, Joanna. "'Dos loszn fun jidiszkajt'—ortodoksyjny jidyszyzm na łamach 'Bejs Jakow' w kontekście religijnego feminizmu żydowskiego w Polsce." In *Studia z dziejów trójjęzycznej prasy żydowskiej na ziemiach polskich (XIX–XX w.)*, edited by Joanna Nalewajko-Kulikov. Neriton, 2012.

Lisek, Joanna. *Jung Wilne—żydowska grupa artystyczna*. Wydawnictwo Uniwersytetu Wrocławskiego, 2005.

Lubetkin, Zivia. *In the Days of Destruction and Revolt*. Am Oved, 1981.

Mahla, Daniel. *Orthodox Judaism and the Politics of Religion: From Prewar Europe to the State of Israel*. Cambridge University Press, 2020.

Mahler, Rafael. *Yehudei Polin bein shtei milhamot olam: Historia kalkalit-socialit le-or ha-statistika*. Dvir, 1968.

Majchrowski, Jacek. *Silni—zwarci—gotowi: Myśl polityczna Obozu Zjednoczenia Narodowego*. PIW, 1985.

Mander, Mary S. "Bourdieu, the Sociology of Culture and Cultural Studies: A Critique." *European Journal of Communication* 2 (1987): 427–453.

Mannheim, Karl. *Ideology and Utopia*. Routledge, 2003.

Marcus, Joseph. *Social and Political History of the Jews in Poland, 1919–1939*. Mouton, 1983.

Margalit, Elkana. "Social and Intellectual Origins of the Hashomer Hatzair Youth Movement, 1913–1920." In *Essential Papers on Zionism*, edited by Jehuda Reinharz and Anita Shapira. New York University Press, 1996.

Martin, Sean. "Between Church and State: Jewish Religious Instruction in the Public Schools in the Second Polish Republic." *Polin* 30 (2018): 265–282.

Mauersberg, Stanisław. *Komu służyła szkoła w Drugiej Rzeczypospolitej? Społeczne uwarunkowania dostępu do oświaty*. Ossolineum, 1988.

Mauersberg, Stanisław. "Reformy szkolne w Drugiej Rzeczypospolitej (1918–1939)." *Kwartalnik Pedagogiczny* 4 (1995): 19–29.

Mauersberg, Stanisław. *Szkolnictwo powszechne dla mniejszości narodowych w Polsce w latach 1918–1939*. Ossolineum, 1968.

Mędrzecki, Włodzimierz. *Młodzież wiejska na ziemiach Polski centralnej, 1864–1939*. Neriton, 2002.

Mędrzecki, Włodzimierz. *Odzyskany śmietnik: Jak radziliśmy sobie z niepodległością w II Rzeczypospolitej*. Wydawnictwo Literackie, 2022.

Mędrzecki, Włodzimierz. "Polskie uniwersum symboliczne w Drugiej Rzeczypospolitej." In *Kultura i społeczeństwo w II Rzeczypospolitej: Metamorfozy społeczne 4*, edited by Włodzimierz Mędrzecki and Agata Zawiszewska. Instytut Historii PAN, 2012.

Melzer, Emanuel. *No Way Out: The Politics of Polish Jewry, 1935–1939*. Hebrew Union College Press, 1997.

Mendelsohn, Ezra. "Jewish Politics in Interwar Poland: An Overview." In *The Jews of Poland Between Two World Wars*, edited by Yisrael Gutman et al. University Press of New England, 1989.

Mendelsohn, Ezra. *The Jews of East Central Europe Between the World Wars*. Indiana University Press, 1987.

Mendelsohn, Ezra. *On Modern Jewish Politics*. Oxford University Press, 1993.

Mendelsohn, Ezra. "Reflections on East European Jewish Politics in the Twentieth Century." *YIVO Annual* 20 (1991): 23–37.

Mendelsohn, Ezra. *Zionism in Poland: The Formative Years, 1915–1926*. Yale University Press, 1981.

Michlic, Joanna. *Poland's Threatening Other. The Image of the Jew from 1880 to the Present*. University of Nebraska Press, 2006.

Mickute, Jolanta. "Making of the Zionist Woman: Zionist Discourse on the Jewish Woman's Body and Selfhood in Interwar Poland." *Eastern European Politics, Societies and Cultures* 28, no. 1 (2014): 137–162.

Miron, Dan. *The Image of the Shtetl and Other Studies of Modern Jewish Literary Imagination*. Syracuse University Press, 2000.

Miron, Dan. "The Literary Image of the Shtetl." *Jewish Social Studies* 1, no. 3 (1995): 1–43.

Mishkinsky, Moshe. "The Communist Party of Poland and the Jews." In *The Jews of Poland Between Two World Wars*, edited by Yisrael Gutman et al. University Press of New England, 1989.

Modras, Ronald. *The Catholic Church and Antisemitism in Poland, 1933–1939*. Harwood Academic, 1994.

Mordechai, A. Ben. "Mesivta 'Ohel Tora' be-Baranowits." In *Mosadot Tora be-Europa ve-binyanam u-ve-hurbanam* [Jewish institutions of higher learning in Europe: Their development and destruction], edited by Samuel K. Mirsky. Ogen, 1956.

Moseley, Marcus. *Being for Myself Alone: Origins of Jewish Autobiography*. Stanford University Press, 2006.

Moseley, Marcus. "Life, Literature: Autobiographies of Jewish Youth in Interwar Poland." *Jewish Social Studies* 7, no. 1 (2003): 1–51.

Moss, Kenneth B. *An Unchosen People: Jewish Political Reckoning in Interwar Poland*. Harvard University Press, 2021.

Nalewajko-Kulikov, Joanna. "Hajnt." In *Studia z dziejów trójjęzycznej prasy żydowskiej na ziemiach polskich*, edited by Joanna Nalewajko-Kulikov. Neriton, 2012.

Nalewajko-Kulikov, Joanna. *Obywatel Jidyszlandu: Rzecz o żydowskich komunistach w Polsce*. Neriton, 2009.

Natkowska, Monika. *Numerus clausus, getto ławkowe, numerus nullus, "paragraf aryjski": Antysemityzm na Uniwersytecie Warszawskim 1931–1939*. ŻIH, 1999.

Nishimura, Yuu. "On the Cultural Front: The Bund and the Yiddish Secular School Movement in Interwar Poland." *Eastern European Jewish Affairs* 43, no. 3 (2013): 265–281.

Nowogródzki, Emanuel. *Żydowska Partia Robotnicza Bund w Polsce w latach 1915–1939*. ŻIH, 2005.

Oleszak, Agnieszka. "The Beys Yaakov School in Kraków as a Symbolic Encounter Between East and West." *Polin* 23 (2011): 277–290.

Oppenheim, Israel. *The Struggle of Jewish Youth for Productivization: The Zionist Youth Movement in Poland*. Columbia University Press, 1989.

Parush, Iris. *Reading Jewish Women: Marginality and Modernization in Nineteenth-Century Eastern European Jewish Society*. Brandeis University Press, 2004.

Payne, Stanley G. *Civil War in Europe, 1905–1949*. Cambridge University Press, 2011.

Pickhan, Gertrude. *"Gegen den Strom": Der Allgemeine Jüdische Arbeiterbund "Bund" in Polen 1918–1939*. Deutsche Verlag-Anstalt, 2001.

Pinchuk, Ben-Cion. "Jewish Discourse and the 'Shtetl.'" *Jewish History* 15, no. 2 (2002): 169–179.

Plach, Eva. *The Clash of Moral Nations: Cultural Politics in Piłsudski's Poland, 1926–1935.* Ohio University Press, 2006.

Polonsky, Antony. *The Jews of Poland and Russia.* Vol. 3, *1914–2008.* Littman, 2012.

Polonsky, Antony. *Politics in Independent Poland, 1921–1939: The Crisis of Constitutional Government.* Oxford University Press, 1972.

Polonsky, Antony. "The Shtetl: Myth and Reality." *Polin* 17 (2004): 3–23.

Porter-Szűcs, Brian. *Poland in the Modern World: Beyond Martyrdom.* Wiley Blackwell 2014.

Roskies, David G., *Against the Apocalypse: Responses to Catastrophe in Modern Jewish Culture.* Harvard University Press, 1984.

Roskies, Diane K. "Der kheyder proyekt bay der psikhologish-pedagogisher sektsye fun YIVO." *YIVO Bleter* 46 (1980): 269–281.

Rosman, Moshe. "Hasidism as a Modern Phenomenon: The Paradox of Modernization Without Secularization." *Simon Dubnow Institute Yearbook* 6 (2007): 215–224.

Rosman, Moshe. *How Jewish Is Jewish History?* Littman, 2008.

Rosman, Moshe. "Innovative Tradition: Jewish Culture in the Polish-Lithuanian Commonwealth." In *Cultures of the Jews: A New History,* edited by David Biale. Schocken, 2002.

Rowe, Leonard. "Jewish Self-Defense: A Response to Violence." In *Studies on Polish Jewry, 1919–1939: The Interplay of Social, Economic and Political Factors in the Struggle of a Minority for Its Existence,* edited by Joshua A. Fishman. YIVO, 1974.

Ruderman, David. *A Best-Selling Hebrew Book of the Modern Era: The Book of the Covenant of Pinhas Hurwitz and Its Remarkable Legacy.* University of Washington Press, 2014.

Rudnicki, Szymon. "From 'Numerus Clausus' to 'Numerus Nullus.'" *Polin* 2 (1987): 246–268.

Rudnicki, Szymon. *Żydzi w parlamencie II Rzeczypospolitej.* Wydawnictwo Sejmowe, 2004.

Sadowska, Joanna. "Ustawodawstwo jędrzejewiczowskie wobec szkolnictwa mniejszości narodowych w II Rzeczypospolitej." In *Edukacja—państwo—naród w Europie Środkowo-Wschodniej XIX i XX w.,* edited by Aleksandra Bilewicz, Ryszard Gładkiewicz, and Stefania Walasek. Centrum Badań Śląskoznawczych i Bohemistycznych, 2002.

Sanojca, Karol. *Obraz sąsiadów w szkolnictwie powszechnym Drugiej Rzeczypospolitej.* Wydawnictwo Uniwersytetu Wrocławskiego, 2003.

Scharfer, Caroline. "Sarah Schenirer, Founder of the Beit Ya'akov Movement: Her Vision and Her Legacy." *Polin* 23 (2011): 269–275.

Schatz, Jaff. *The Generation: The Rise and Fall of the Jewish Communists of Poland.* University of California Press, 1991.

Schatz, Jaff. "Jews and the Communist Movement in Interwar Poland." *Studies in Contemporary Jewry* 20 (2004): 13–37.

Schorske, Carl E. *Fin-de-Siècle Vienna: Politics and Culture.* Alfred A. Knopf, 1980.

Seidman, Naomi. "Gender and the Disintegration of the Shtetl in Modern Hebrew and Yiddish Literature." In *The Shtetl: New Evaluations,* edited by Steven T. Katz. New York University Press, 2007.

Seidman, Naomi. *Sarah Schenirer and the Bais Yaakov Movement.* Littman, 2019.

Selzer, Adva. "'Vos vayter?' Graduating from Elementary School in Interwar Poland: From Personal Crisis to Cultural Turning Point." *Polin* 30 (2018): 283–297.

Shapira, Anita. *Land and Power: The Zionist Resort to Force, 1881–1948.* Oxford University Press, 1992.

Shapiro, Robert Moses. "The Polish Kehillah Elections of 1936: A Revolution Re-Examined." *Polin* 8 (1994): 206–226.

Shavit, David. *Hunger for the Printed Word: Books and Libraries in the Jewish Ghettos of Nazi-Occupied Europe.* McFarland, 1997.

Shavit, Yaacov. "Fire and Water: Ze'ev Jabotinsky and the Revisionist Movement." In *Essential Papers on Zionism,* edited by Jehuda Reinharz and Anita Shapira. New York University Press, 1995.

Shavit, Yaacov. *Jabotinsky and the Revisionist Movement, 1925–1948.* Frank Cass, 1988.

Shavit, Yaacov. "Politics and Messianism: The Zionist Revisionist Movement and Polish Political Culture." *Studies in Zionism* 6, no. 2 (1985): 229–246.

Shimoni, Gideon. *The Zionist Ideology.* Brandeis University Press, 1995.

Shmeruk, Chone. "Hebrew-Yiddish-Polish: A Trilingual Jewish Culture." In *The Jews of Poland Between Two World Wars,* edited by Yisrael Gutman et al. University Press of New England, 1989.

Shore, Marci. *Caviar and Ashes: A Warsaw Generation's Life and Death in Marxism, 1918–1968.* Yale University Press, 2006.

Stampfer, Shaul. *Families, Rabbis, Education: Traditional Jewish Society in Nineteenth-Century Europe.* Littman, 2010.

Stanislawski, Michael. *Zionism and the Fin de Siècle.* University of California Press, 2001.

Steffen, Katrin. *Jüdische Polonität: Ethnizität und Nation im Spiegel der polnischsprachigen jüdischen Presse 1918–1939.* Vandenhoeck und Ruprecht, 2004.

Steinlauf, Michael C. "Jewish Politics and Youth Culture in Interwar Poland: Preliminary Evidence from the YIVO Autobiographies." In *The Emergence of Modern Jewish Politics: Bundism and Zionism in Eastern Europe,* edited by Zvi Gitelman. Pittsburgh University Press, 2003.

Szymaniak, Karolina. "Speaking Back: On Some Aspects of the Reception of Polish Literature in Yiddish Literary Criticism." *Polin* 28 (2016): 153–172.

Tomaszewski, Jerzy. "Between the Social and the National: The Economic Situation of Polish Jewry, 1918–1939." *Simon Dubnow Institute Yearbook* 1 (2002): 55–70.

Tomaszewski, Jerzy. "The Polish Right-Wing Press, the Expulsion of Polish Jews from Germany, and the Deportees in Zbąszyń, 1938–1939." *Gal-Ed* 18 (2002): 89–100.

Trębacz, Zofia. *Nie tylko Palestyna: Polskie plany emigracyjne wobec Żydów, 1935–1939.* ŻIH, 2018.

Trzebiatowski, Klemens. *Szkolnictwo powszechne w Polsce w latach 1918–1932.* Ossolineum, 1970.

Tworek, Wojciech. "Mystic, Teacher, Troublemaker: Shimon Engel Horovits of Żelechów and the Challenges of Hasidic Education in Interwar Poland." *Jewish Quarterly Review* 110, no. 2 (2020): 313–342.

Ury, Scott. "The 'Shtadlan' of the Polish-Lithuanian Commonwealth: Noble Advocate or Unbridled Opportunist?" *Polin* 15 (2002): 267–299.

Volkov, Shulamit. "Antisemitism as a Cultural Code: Reflections on the History and Historiography of Antisemitism in Imperial Germany." *Leo Baeck Institute Yearbook* 23 (1978): 25–46.

Volkov, Shulamit. *Germans, Jews, and Antisemites: Trials in Emancipation.* Cambridge University Press, 2006.

Wapiński, Roman. *Pokolenia Drugiej Rzeczypospolitej.* Ossolineum, 1991.

Weinbaum, Laurence. *The New Zionist Organization and the Polish Government, 1936–1939.* Boulder, 1993.

Wistrich, Robert. *Revolutionary Jews from Marx to Trotsky.* Harrap, 1976.

Wodziński, Marcin. "Good Maskilim and Bad Assimilationist: Toward a New Historiography of the Haskalah in Poland." *Jewish Social Studies* 10, no. 3 (2003/2004): 87–122.

Wojtas, Dorota L. "Learning to Become Polish: Education, National Identity and Citizenship in Interwar Poland, 1918–1939." Doctoral thesis, Brandeis University, 2003.

Wróbel, Piotr. "Failed Integration: Jews and the Beginning of the Communist Movement in Poland." *Polin* 24 (2012): 187–222.

Yona, Rona. "A Kibbutz in Diaspora: The Pioneer Movement and the Klosova Kibbutz." *Journal of Israeli History* 31, no. 1 (2012): 9–43.

Yona, Rona. *Nehiye kulanu halutzim: Ha-tnuat ha-avoda ve-ha-aliya mi-Polin 1923–1936.* Magnes, 2021.

Zahra, Tara. *Reconstructing Europe's Families After World War II.* Harvard University Press, 2015.

Zariz, David. "Yeshivvas Radin." In *Mosadot Tora be-Europa ve-binyanam u-ve-hurbanam* [Jewish institutions of higher learning in Europe: Their development and destruction], edited by Samuel K. Mirsky. Ogen, 1956.

Żarnowski, Janusz. "Społeczeństwo polskie wobec szkoły w XX wieku." *Kwartalnik Pedagogiczny* 4 (1995): 3–19.

Zemba, Abraham. "'Mesivta' be Varshe." In *Mosadot Tora be-Europa ve-binyanam u-ve-hurbanam* [Jewish institutions of higher learning in Europe: Their development and destruction], edited by Samuel K. Mirsky. Ogen, 1956.

Zenderland, Leila. "Social Science as a 'Weapon of the Weak': Max Weinreich, the Yiddish Scientific Institute, and the Study of Culture, Personality, and Prejudice." *Isis* 104, no. 4 (2013): 742–772.

Zerubavel, Yael. *Recovered Roots: Collective Memory and the Making of Israeli National Tradition.* University of Chicago Press, 1995.

Zukerman, Yitzhak, and Barbara Harshav. *A Surplus of Memory: Chronicle of the Warsaw Ghetto Uprising.* University of California Press, 1993.

INDEX

KAMIL KIJEK is Assistant Professor of Jewish Studies at the University of Wrocław. He is author of many articles and book chapters in Polish and English.

For Indiana University Press

Tony Brewer, Artist and Book Designer

Anna Francis, Assistant Acquisitions Editor

Anna Garnai, Production Coordinator

Samantha Heffner, Marketing and Publicity Manager

Katie Huggins, Production Manager

Alyssa Nicole Lucas, Marketing and Publicity Manager

Annie L. Martin, Editorial Director

David Miller, Lead Project Manager/Editor

Dan Pyle, Online Publishing Manager

Jennifer Wilder, Senior Artist and Book Designer